Also by Alvin J. Ziontz

A LAWYER IN INDIAN COUNTRY

Alvin

STORY OF A LIFE

For Judy

Al Ziontz

THE AUTOBIOGRAPHY OF

Alvin J. Ziontz

ISBN-13: 978-1532928352
ISBN-10: 1532928351

To my beloved wife, Lennie,
who has sustained me and loved me for over sixty years.

CONTENTS

PREFACE

The book you are about to begin is a lengthy history of my life. The book began as nightly ruminations on age and decrepitude, morphed into a journal of my wife's cancer and then expanded into a collection of stories. Indeed the chapter called "Living In The Red Zone" originally began as a journal, a journal of my physical decline and then a journal of Lennie's battle with cancer. It was transformed into an autobiography at the urging of three people; my wife and two dear friends, Linda Chan and her partner, Evan Upchurch. I met Linda and Evan as a result of a serendipitous encounter in our local mall. For the past five years we have met there regularly and I have entertained them with many of the stories in this book. It was Linda who insisted that they be included in the book. She has played a large role in the completed product because she has training in art and computer programs and took on the task of selecting and scanning photographs to be included in the text.

The result is an overlong, self-edited tale of the growth and old age of a lucky man. Lucky because in retrospect my life decisions have resulted in many happy and successful years of life for me and others whose lives I have affected.

The book begins with my parent's life in Russia, their early years in America and then it takes up my experiences in Chicago, growing up as a Jewish boy in a Gentile world. It follows my path to law school and my entry into the law of American Indian rights. My story encompasses the time I spent with the movie star, Marlon Brando, and my short but intense debate with the woman who would later become a Supreme Court Justice, Ruth Bader Ginsburg.

My law career began at rock bottom and grew to the establishment of a law firm, a "boutique" firm, which has established itself as one of the nation's leading firms defending Indian rights. Now, some fifty years after its founding, the firm continues, deeply committed to the defense of the Indian people.

During my life, I have experienced America in the interwar years; 1930 to 1942, the period of the Second World War, the Cold War years and the explosion of technology that followed. I have become a husband , a father and a grandfather. I have been blessed with the love of my devoted wife, Lennie, and had the experience of arguing a case in the United States Supreme Court, piloting a private plane through the skies and writing a book published by a university press. For over twenty years, both during and after my career as a lawyer, I immersed myself in the world of fine art photography and enjoyed the pleasure of creating a body of work that still gives me pleasure.

If I am going to be remembered outside my family, it will be for my accomplishments as an advocate for the rights of the Indian people. I have followed the development of Indian life in America and have felt pride in the growth of Indian tribal government. I was privileged to enter into the world of Indian affairs in the 60's, a time when the modern revival of tribal governments as members of the family of American governments was just beginning. And now I have seen the respect that tribal governments command reach levels not dreamed of in those early days. There is more to come and though I won't be alive to see it, I am happy to have had a part in the establishment of the new Indian nation.

So, now at age eighty-seven, with the shadow of death never far from my thoughts, I have tried to capture the totality of my years in this autobiography. I recognize that it is a very imperfect work, but I hope its readers will get to know, "Alvin".

CHAPTER ONE

BEGINNINGS

Alvin is me ~ now age eighty-seven. In these eighty-seven years my life has encompassed a middle class life in the America of the thirties, the forties, the fifties and on to the improbable year of 2016. During that life I have experienced the warmth of the Jewish community of Chicago, the subtle anti-Semitism of America in the years before the growing knowledge of the Holocaust, and the life of the working class. I have been a lawyer representing Indian tribes and have founded a law firm dedicated to this work ~ a law firm that continues the work I began fifty years ago. This lifespan has taken me from the era of steam engines to jets, from chalk boards to computers and beyond. As a lawyer I have come to know many Indian people, I have argued cases in many courts, even the Supreme Court of the United States, as well as to ordinary juries of ordinary people.

Even though I attended what is regarded as one of America's best law schools, I learned little. I was an indifferent student, finding the study of law tedious and disappointing. It seeming to focus intensely on a narrow world of court opinions, emphasizing values far removed from the idealism of my college years. After completing law school, one year of graduate studies and two years in the Army my legal education was a thing of the past, leaving me with only vague recollections of the doctrines and rules that so dominated law school education. I was not sure I wanted to be a practicing lawyer, but having a wife and two children, left me with no alternative.

Starting my career in Seattle as a young associate of a manic-depressive older lawyer who absented himself from his office for most of the seven years I worked for him, meant I was left to learn law on my own. Somehow, I developed into a competent, even, on occasion, an accomplished lawyer. During my years as a lawyer in Seattle I immersed myself in cases, many in fields familiar to general practitioners, and many that were off the beaten path of conventional law practice. When I began representing Indian tribes in the courts, I joined a tiny minority of lawyers in America doing this work. I was a strong advocate for treaty rights, tribal government, the preservation of tribal natural resources and the reconstruction of Indian culture. My work has made me a familiar name in the tribal world and the legal community. Much of the work is recounted in my book, "A Lawyer in Indian Country" published in 2009, and I will try to avoid repeating it at any length here.

In searching my past I must dredge my memory, but some facts are well known. I emerged from my mother's womb at Mt. Zion hospital in Chicago on August 8, 1928. My mother's name was Rose and my father's Harry. From my parents' citizenship papers which gave their ages, I calculated that my mother was 28 and my father 31 when I came into the world.

They were Jews who had emigrated from Russia in the great wave of outflow from a country where they were barely tolerated and often put in fear for their lives by the semi-official attacks, called "pogroms". That they had the courage to make the difficult journey to America is something for which I became ever more grateful as I came to know more about the "old country" and the "new country" to which they came. Chicago, the city of my birth, was separated from their birthplaces by thousands of miles and by an enormous cultural distance.

Each had spent their earliest years in separate villages located in what was known as "The Ukraine". Their villages were thickly peopled by Jews, all speaking Yiddish and leading a closed existence. The Russian government provided no schools for children, so education was a matter for the people of the villages; a school for boys five to twelve years old, called a "Cheder", typically taught by a young man, called a "melamed", supported by the contributions of the community, often paltry but supplemented by dining at the homes of the villagers whose contributions supported the school.

In the "Cheder" the boys learned basic reading and writing in Yiddish ~ the language of the Ashkenazic or Eastern Jews. They also learned the basics of Judaism: reading the Old Testament, called the "Chumesh" in Hebrew. For the Jews, the "Chumesh" was the basic text of Judaism. It was the Holy Book containing the narrative of the Jewish people. In English it is the Pentateuch, the Five Books of Moses. The study was primarily by memorization. The Hebrew language was not a conversational language during the years preceding the creation of the State of Israel. It was voiced only during the oral reading from the Bible and the prayers. These boys were also taught the practice of Judaism; the meaning of the holidays and the prayers. The only concession to the secular world was basic arithmetic ~ that was needed for commerce. There was no science, no history and no geography. For them there was no "enlightenment". They might as well have been living in the 14th century.

There were no girls in the class; girls were taught at home by the melamed; reading, writing, the prayers and the rituals and some simple arithmetic. Their education rarely extended beyond three or four years since they were destined for marriage and child rearing. Girls proficient in sewing might apprentice to a "seamstress" and hope to earn a bare living for their efforts.

The longer period of schooling for boys was mandated by religion ~ not occupation. The boys had to be prepared for their "bal-mitzvah", as it is pronounced in traditional Yiddish, but now called "bar-mitzvah" in America. This important ritual required them to mount the "bima" or pulpit and lead the congregation in prayer followed by a solo performance; chanting from the torah, using ancient musical signs. Then the nervous acolyte was expected to deliver a speech ~ usually an exegesis on the portion of the torah he had read.

In the "old country", in the small towns and villages, called "shtetls" in Yiddish, medicine was primitive, doctors were a rare luxury, streets were unpaved and sanitation, that is, the disposal of human waste was in an outdoor pit over which was built an "outhouse". The inhabitants of such an unenlightened place could hardly be blamed for their faith in folk remedies and superstition.

4

In Russia and the Ukraine of the late 19th century these villages were populated by two separate peoples; the Jews and the Gentiles, whom the Jews called the "Goyim". They had an uneasy relationship even though they knew each other well. The Gentiles looked upon the Jews as a strange pariah people. This hostility was accepted and even fostered by the Ukrainian Orthodox Church and by the Russian government. Jews knew they could expect no support from the police or the local government. Bribes, or blood money, were the only way to ameliorate hostility and violence.

Terrible falsehoods were told about the Jews. The Orthodox Christian Church was often the source of the libels and the Jews regarded it as the seat of Jew hatred and the cross the very symbol of this hatred. Anti-Semitism was often a deliberate policy of the Russian government and attacks were carried out by militias, called Cossacks. The purpose was apparently to keep the Jews submissive and to provide an outlet for social unrest. These attacks, called "pogroms", were carried out by armed bands and often resulted in injury or death of the Jewish targets, and always included looting. The Jews did not dare to fight back and for the most part hid in their cellars or in nearby forests. When the Cossacks left they returned to their homes, often to find them in shambles and valuables gone. Sometimes they were warned of an impending Cossack attack by the local Chief of Police who expected and received bribe money from the wealthier Jews of the village and, in return might try to restrain the brigands from excessive violence. The authority for the Pogroms came from Moscow, usually from the Czar's Secret Police. Indeed it was this organ which was responsible for the writing and distribution of the poisonous document known as, "The Protocols of the Elders Of Zion", a wholly specious writing claiming to be the authentic plans of the Jews to undermine governments, control a nation's wealth and promulgate wars for their own gain. The document is still in circulation and is exploited by anti-Semites to perpetuate hatred of the Jews.

How did the Jews of these "shtetls" earn a livelihood? Entry into the professions was barred and ownership of land also barred. So, many were tradesmen, buying and selling lumber, liquor and anything else they could deal in. Some were tailors, cobblers, locksmiths ~ anything a man with skills could do. Most girls learned how to sew and the more proficient became dressmakers, as my mother did.

Till the early part of the twentieth century, autos were seldom seen in these villages. Transport was by horse and wagon. Movies and radios were unknown. But America was known. Many had relatives who had immigrated to America and had written about this extraordinary country. There Jews could make a decent living ~ even become wealthy. Most important they could live without fear of "pogroms". In Yiddish, America was called "die goldene Medina", the Golden Eden.

From 1890 to 1914 over 2.5 million Jews left their villages in Russia, often leaving behind family members, to make the difficult trek to America. They headed for cities where they had relatives and "lantsleit", ~ fellow townspeople. Most ended up in New York, Philadelphia, Chicago and Detroit.

My mother and father were part of this mass migration. My mother, Rose (maiden name, Bolasny) left behind three brothers and four sisters in the village of Chodorkov. She had gone to the nearby city of Kiev as a teenager to become an apprentice dressmaker. She too was attracted to the idea of bettering her life in America and wrote to an aunt who lived in Chicago. The aunt sent her a steamship ticket. By that time she had developed her skills so that she was a full-fledged dressmaker. In other words, she was able to make a dress copying a photograph or using her own designs and adjusting it to satisfy the customer.

Rose was a very attractive girl and had many suitors. In leaving for America she was audacious but far sighted, since she was only seventeen. She faced the painful task of telling her family that she would be leaving to cross the ocean. The news was greeted by anger and recrimination. "We'll never see you again," they charged. She tried to reassure them that she would send them all tickets as soon as she

My mother's family, Bolasnys in Russia, approx. 1912
My mother (back row center)

had saved enough money, but it didn't resolve their qualms. They remained opposed, and she left behind a sad and angry family.

Whatever her desire may have been, she could not foresee World War I and the Russian Revolution, both of which made it impossible for her family to leave Russia. It turned out they were right; they never saw her again. Even twenty years later their bitterness had not entirely dissipated.

My father, Harry had a more difficult path. He was born in the village of Rizhin, also in the Ukraine, but some distance from Chodorkov. His father's name was Eli and his mother's name was Shayndle. She was devout and wore a Keitel ~ a wig. Like all Jewish women, she kept a kosher house and honored the Sabbath ~ Shabbes in Yiddish. He was her first child and she named him Aaron, which means, hold on; a superstitious wish that there would not be a miscarriage and he would be a full term, healthy baby. Tragically, his father died when he was three, leaving Shayndle a widow with no means of support, with no means of income. She was reduced to selling needles, thread and buttons door to door. It soon became evident that she was unable to support herself and her infant, Aaron. But her deceased husband, Eli, had a brother living in a nearby village who was married and had no children. He ran a business and had a good income. Desperate, she made a painful decision. She would bring Aaron to her brother in law and ask if they would be willing to take Aaron into their home and raise him as their own. The brother-in-law and his wife had seen Aaron several times and seemed fond of him, so she had reason to believe they would treat him kindly. People make such hard decisions when life offers few alternatives. It is difficult

"Bobi" (Grandma) Shayndle, my father's mother, in Detroit

for affluent Americans to appreciate the dire conditions of a penniless widow with an infant living in a Russian shtetl.

So Shayndle gave her son to these relatives, hoping he would have a better life than she could provide. But her brother-in-law was a strict man ~ a devout believer, or in Yiddish, "a frumer eyd", a humorless iron disciplinarian ~ quite unsuited to be a father, even a surrogate father. He enforced his authority with his belt ~ a practice that so traumatized the child that I believe that was the reason my father never laid a hand on me more than thirty years later.

Like all Jewish boys Aaron attended Cheder, but he had a miserable childhood, never forgetting his mother, and often crying out for her. He was so unhappy that when he was eight he ran away, walking miles to his mother's village of Rizhin. She hugged and kissed him but returned him to his uncle. But within a short time she remarried; a man named Cohen, by whom she had two children; a boy named Samuel and a girl named Minnie. Cohen earned enough to support her and the children and Shayndle couldn't bring herself to send Aaron back to his cruel uncle and brought him home to live with his new family; a half-brother Samuel and a half-sister named Minnie.

The family lived on in Rizhin until another cataclysmic event; Cohen died. The family could no longer count on his support. By this time Jews were leaving for America and Minnie had relatives in Detroit. She wrote them, describing her plight and asking for help. They responded with four Steamship tickets to America. Aaron (Whose name was Americanized to Harry after they had settled in America) had kept his father's last name: Ziontz, and he and the Cohens departed

Russia, never to see it again. Harry was 14, Sam was 12 and Minnie 10. They docked in Philadelphia and boarded a train for Detroit.

In Detroit they took whatever jobs they could find. Sam went to work for a "Shechet", killing chickens for sale. The "Shechet" would slaughter the chicken in the kosher manner; slitting the throat and then cutting off the wings, thighs and breasts so the butcher could market them to Jewish housewives. It was common for a horseradish vendor to station himself at the entrance to the chicken store on a stool or box behind a large spinning stone wheel, operated by a foot pedal. When a customer wanted, "chrain" or horseradish, he would hold the radish against the wheel and the grindings would fall into a box to be wrapped in paper and handed to the customer for fifteen cents.

Harry, who was small for his age, managed to get a job on the Michigan Central Railroad, hawking sandwiches, milk, chewing gum and candy to passengers traveling to Chicago. His English was poor and the other boys working on the train harassed him because he was a Jew. More than once he was robbed of his earnings. So at the age of 14, of short stature, he was forced to learn how to fight. Here he was, a 14 year old little Jew, spending long days walking up and down the aisles of trains, calling out, "Sendviches, meelk, kendy" and struggling to understand English, much less speak it, hoping to earn a few dollars to help his family to survive. After all, this was the Golden Land. He was learning that making money in the Golden Land took an enterprising spirit and courage.

For a boy less than five feet tall, he had to rely on his strength and determination. He learned early on that he could rely on himself alone and that he was living in a Gentile world that, at best, merely tolerated his people, but felt free to ridicule them. This was the Golden Land in 1910.

After months of struggle to make a few dollars on the trains of the Michigan Central, he gave up and found work in Detroit. It was a poor paying job in the fruit and vegetable jobber's market, heaving sacks of produce onto the horse drawn wagons of Jewish peddlers. The work was back breaking and the pay pathetically small. He was gaining nothing but muscle, but he was keeping an eye out for better paying work.

Somewhere he heard that the Schlitz beer brewery in Milwaukee was looking for workers in their bottle washing department. So, off to Milwaukee he went. He was thrilled to be hired. At last, a regular paycheck. Working in the bottle washing shop, he had to plunge his hands in near boiling water, immerse four fingers of each hand and seize eight bottles by the neck and put them on a conveyor belt. This process had to be repeated endlessly over a ten hour day. Over time his hands and fingers grew strong and he was able to withstand the physical demands of the job. What he could not withstand was the endless bullying, insults and beatings from the other workers in this predominantly German work force. Finally, he had enough and quit.

He then heard that one could make money collecting scrap iron and found a Jewish scrap metal dealer in Detroit who had several horses and wagons he would rent out to scrap collectors. They received a few dollars based on the weight of their load less, of course, the charge for the rental of the horse and wagon. The job required him to go out to the farms and small towns of south central Michigan finding farmers or town dwellers and asking whether they had any old metal implements they wanted to be rid of. Harry was provided with a small sum to buy the scrap at nominal prices, every penny of which had to be accounted for with signed receipts, though Harry could barely read.

It was daunting. He didn't know how to harness a horse to a wagon; he didn't know the dirt roads of rural Michigan and his English was barely adequate to bargain with farmers or farmer's wives. But by sheer will, he succeeded. He was discovering a new America, a rural America. His experience up to that time, both in Russia and Detroit, had conditioned him to expect hostility, or at best, tolerance. Instead, he was surprised and warmed by the kindness and decency of the farmers he encountered. But the life was hard; he had to be out in all kinds of weather; often the only place to sleep was beneath his wagon. When the winter months arrived, and the roads were impassible, he knew that his career as a scrap metal buyer was at an end till spring. It was time to find another way to make a dollar. His work on the trains had given him some acquaintance with Chicago. He knew it was a big bustling city with lots of businesses. Surely a Jew could find work there. The year was 1914 and he was almost nineteen years old. He decided to strike out on his own.

The women of that time were wearing elaborate hats with raised crowns, supported by internal wire frames. There were sixty or seventy millinery shops, and hat makers earned a living wage. Harry got a job at a hat manufacturer shop as an apprentice. He soon mastered the art of shaping the wire frames using long-nosed pliers. With a job and the prospect of regular pay, he rented a room in a rooming house on Archer Avenue, on the southwest side of the city. He was beginning to live the American Dream. The life of the "Shtetl" was far behind him.

Meanwhile, the woman he would marry, my mother, Rose, was also living in Chicago, working as a dressmaker and living in a rooming house in the heart of Chicago's Jewish ghetto, Twelfth Street. She was skilled in fashioning dresses to suit the tastes of the most elegant and was earning a good salary.

Harry continued working as a milliner till fashions changed and crowned hats were no longer in style. It was 1920 and he was once again looking for a job. He could hardly anticipate that an amendment to the American constitution would open the way for him to earn a handsome income. The Amendment called for Prohibition of the production and sale of whiskey, beer and wine. It was a new era in American History, the era of Prohibition.

Harry found that there was money to be had in bringing whiskey into the U.S. from Canada. He got an old car and was soon smuggling the prohibited liquor across the border from Canada to America. He had more money than he had ever earned in his life. Soon he could afford to buy a new car. He was living the good life.

He developed a list of customers who preferred Canadian whiskey to the "hooch" produced by bootleggers in backyard distilleries in Chicago. In time he grew weary of the lengthy and risky drives to and from Canada and considered setting up his own distillery, called a "still". That way the profits stayed in his pocket and not the Canadian middleman's. The risk was low, considering the endemic corruption of the Chicago police. All he needed to do was find a garage to rent in a safe neighborhood and buy the equipment. He had the cash and soon set up a still. He would have to hire a man to run the "still", but that was no problem. There were plenty of men looking for work.

Meanwhile, his half-sister, Minnie had married a ne'er-do-well in Detroit, named Willie Marcus. Willie never held any job for long and Minnie was living in poverty. She called Harry. Could he help? Harry said he would hire Willie to run his "still" but the family would have to move to Chicago. Running a still was not that complicated and Harry could teach him the essentials. So Minnie and Willie together with her three daughters, Esther, Mollie and Annie moved to Chicago and Willie went to work at Harry's still.

But Willie proved to be a problem. He was unreliable, often late, sometimes not showing up at all, and careless in mixing the ingredients. After several months of putting up with his indifferent attitude, Harry had to make the painful decision to fire him. Willie had relatives in New York, so he and the entire family moved there. They settled in a tenement in Brooklyn, in a neighborhood called Brownsville. Their apartment was on the fourth floor of a fifty year old tenement at 202 Amboy Street. The neighborhood was entirely Jewish. The building had no elevator and their apartment consisted of two bedrooms, a living room and a kitchen. Two girls shared a bed and one slept on the couch. Outside their living room window was a fire escape landing which, like many tenement dwellers, they sometimes used as an outdoor bedroom on hot summer nights.

Willie got a job driving a limo in the summer months, hauling vacationers to resorts in the Catskills. Sadly, one day he went off the road on a curve and was killed. Minnie was again a widow ~ with three daughters. Minnie found work in a sweatshop making socks. Each of the girls finished high school and went to work: Esther and Molly in a garment factory and Annie as a bookkeeper for a small company.

My mother, Rose Block (left)
and her cousin, Fannie Nabedrick (right) in Chicago, 1920

Meanwhile, Harry found a worker to replace Willie and his bootlegging business was thriving. But he had not forgotten his sister and her family; he regularly sent them money. It was hard for Minnie, supporting the three girls when they were still in school. All of them spent hours on the subway traveling to work and back again and then there was the housework; cooking, cleaning and washing.

My mother, Rose, (whose family name Bolasny was later Americanized to Block) having become a skilled dressmaker, was self-supporting. Her skill and taste in creating fashionable women's clothes provided a good income and she was able to live a happy and independent life. She was very popular and could sing and play the mandolin. Judging from the snapshots I have of picnics and social gatherings she attended before she met my father, she had a vibrant social life. Unlike most young women of the time, she enjoyed her independence and was in no hurry to find a husband. When Harry, who was three years older than her, met her he quickly decided this was the woman he wanted to marry.

Their courtship lasted only a year before they married. Harry was an attractive young man. He dressed in good suits; indeed, he could be described as "dapper". Not only was he good looking and well dressed, he also had a good livelihood ~ liquor. There was no stigma attached to the business. Though illegal, it was winked at and many respectable people were engaged in it.

My parents settled in Chicago because Chicago was the home of many businesses, shops and industries and a magnet for immigrants. Not only Russian Jews, but Poles, Lithuanians, Germans and Italians made it their home. Indeed, there was a very large Polish population

~ larger than Warsaw. There was also a substantial "Bohemian" population, actually Austro-Hungarians, whose homeland after World War I was called Czechoslovakia. Chicagoans called them "Bohunks".

There were also a sizable number of Italians, Irish, Greeks and Chinese who had found their way to Chicago. Most settled in neighborhoods predominantly populated by their own kind ~ often anchored by churches culturally oriented toward their ethnicity. All had found work in the steel mills, stores and shops of Chicago. There was another immigrant group that had little in common with these people: American blacks, most of whom had come from the former Southern slave states, seeking a place of refuge from the humiliation, oppression and even the danger they lived under in the South. They too found work in Chicago; hard labor, menial jobs, but not equality. They too lived in segregated neighborhoods, and while they did not suffer the subjugation and brutality of the South, in many ways they learned that they could not expect equal protection under local government.

This was the Chicago where Harry Ziontz and Rose Block made their home, married and raised their only child ~ Alvin. The city's identity is evoked by the names of its streets: Kedzie Avenue, Crawford Avenue (later renamed Pulaski Road), Damon Avenue, Douglas Boulevard, Arthington Street, Keeler, Karlov, Western Avenue, Lake Street, Elston Avenue, State Street, Wabash Avenue, Dearborn, Michigan Boulevard, Randolph, Division, Grand Avenue, Clark Street. These and hundreds of others will resonate in the minds of millions of Chicagoans. The streets, the buildings, the bridges, became part of the consciousness of all who had lived there.

My parents, Rose and Harry Ziontz, at their wedding in 1926

Copy of my parents' wedding certificate requested from the Chicago County Clerk

CHAPTER TWO

CHILDHOOD

My birth was difficult; I weighed over nine pounds, and my parents decided to have no more children. Growing up an only child of doting parents shaped my personality. My early years were plagued by illness; diphtheria, asthma and eczema, which drove my parents frantic. Our family doctor, Isaac Singer, was a frequent visitor to our house, called in by my parents to treat me when I was sick.

During the early years of my life; 1928-1933, we lived in the mainly Jewish West side of Chicago; first at 905 S. Karlov for a year or two and then at 4037 W. Gladys Avenue, both apartments within a mile of the heart of Jewish Chicago ~ 12th street. During that time my father was in the bootlegging business, profitable enough to allow us to lead a comfortable life.

The apartment on Gladys Avenue had five rooms; a living room, dining room, kitchen and two bedrooms. The living room had a false fireplace with glass coals lit by a red light. We also had a maid and over time there were a succession of maids who stayed for a while

My parents and I (age 3) in Chicago

My tricycle and I (age 3½) at front entrance of Karlov Avenue apartment building in Chicago

and then left, or were "let go". The building had a large courtyard in front and in the rear a typical Chicago wooden porch which extended across the back side of the building and also served the apartment next door. We lived on the second floor and a wooden staircase led up to the third-floor and down to the yard ~ what we called the backyard. That was my home till I was five years old. We stayed there three or four years and during this time we were relatively affluent.

The period of affluence must have been while my father was either selling contraband liquor or running a still and later a speakeasy. How did I know we were affluent? Well, we lived in a rather nice apartment and had a maid. My father hired a professional photographer to photograph my fourth birthday and the next year again, my fifth birthday. I still have both these pictures and the fifth birthday party picture is revealing; it shows a little boy with a somber unsmiling visage. That was typical for me. I'm not sure why, but I was frequently ill at ease in the company of other children.

My memories of the first five years are fragmented into physical objects like our large green alarm clock; in Yiddish called a "zager". I also remember one toy: my big red fire truck. The fire truck was made of heavy-duty steel painted a bright red and its front wheels turned. It carried two ladders, one on each side. They hung on hooks and were removable. I recall with shame taking one of these off and hitting our maid in the leg with it. This brought a sharp rebuke from her and she pulled it out of my little hands. I think I was about four years old at the time. I have no idea what led me to do such a cruel thing.

The toy that left the deepest impression on me was an electric train my father bought for me. It consisted of a large, realistic model

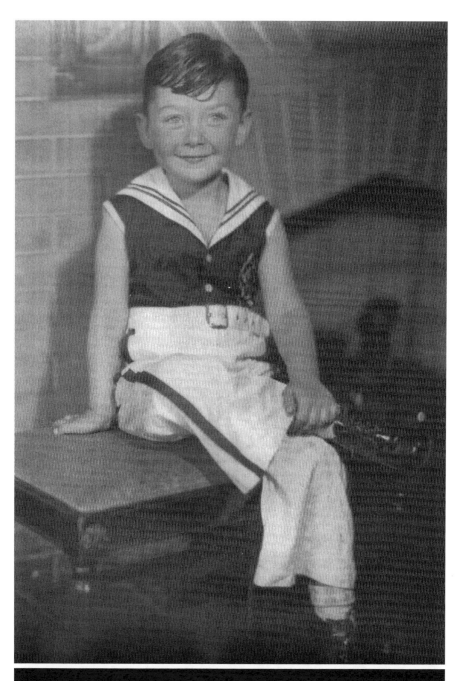

At age 4 in Gladys Avenue apartment in Chicago

electric locomotive with headlights that turned on when the power was connected. The locomotive had its cab in the center of the engine; a large engine compartment in the back and an identical one in the front. There were no rods connecting the driving wheels and thus no exciting motions to observe. It ran around a loop pulling a train of four passenger cars, each lit by interior lights.

I have sometimes wondered whether my boyhood passion for steam locomotives originated in that toy electric train. But I have, on reflection, concluded that the origin was more mundane. My mother used to walk to the store pushing me in my stroller. Along the way we would pass beneath a railroad viaduct. When I asked my mother what a viaduct was she told me it was a bridge for trains. The viaduct itself fascinated me, no doubt because the sidewalk went downhill beneath the viaduct and uphill on the other side. The viaduct cut off the light and it was dark beneath it. For these reasons alone a trip under the viaduct was exciting. But one day, as we were approaching the viaduct, a steam locomotive crossed overhead emitting loud chuffing sounds, together with clouds of smoke. Although it passed out of sight in a minute, my four-year-old eyes were struck by the complex movement of its rods. It was a powerful sight to behold; this elongated black machine blowing powerful clouds of smoke as a strange collection of circling rods drove it along. I never forgot that sight and afterwards watched for other locomotives each time we went under that viaduct in Chicago. It seems strange to me now that this left such a lasting impression.

There were other objects that form part of my memory of these first five years. There was the huge wooden cabinet containing the RCA radio in our living room, my mother's iron kettle and the yellow mesh curtains that hung in front of the dining room windows. But the most important part of my memory is not the physical objects, but the language. My mother and father spoke Yiddish to each other around the household and Yiddish was the common language spoken by all my relatives. My mother and father spoke to me in English and I spoke it naturally without any accent. But both my mother and father spoke with strong accents; for example, their W's came out as 'V's ~ so wife was pronounced "vife" and wagon was pronounced "vagon". I never spoke Yiddish, but understood household Yiddish and can even speak it today.

My father read the Chicago Herald Examiner (a Hearst publication) as well as the Yiddish daily "Forvitz" (Forward). Somehow, without formal education he had taught himself to read. My mother read little besides the Yiddish newspaper, but it was my mother who was my daily companion. She took me along on her daily trips to the grocery (Plotnick's), the meat market (where the floor was covered with sawdust), the fish market and Woolworth's five and ten cents store.

When I was about four or five, there was a shocking incident which I have never forgotten. My father came home one night, his face swollen and bloodstained and his suit torn. We were horrified. He told us that he had been attacked in downtown Chicago that night by a group of drunken American Legionnaires, in Chicago for a national convention. He was returning to his parked car, he said, when a group of Legionnaires approached him and began taunting him. He tried to joke his way out of the confrontation but they were not to be dissuaded and began to push him violently against his car. Then he became angry and warned them off. That resulted in his being attacked physically as he tried to punch his way free, but he was badly outnumbered. When he tried to escape they grabbed him by his suit and in the pulling tore it. Finally they tired of their fun and walked off, leaving him bloody and dazed. I have never stopped thinking of the American Legion as a group of bigots, like the Nazi brown shirts. They may have draped themselves in the American flag, but I saw them as low and violent men parading as patriots.

As I grew older, my relatives came to occupy a larger place in my life. The majority were my mother's relatives. The dominant person was Aunt Gertie, my mother's aunt. She was a fierce dominatrix who had a daughter named Adele. Adele was three or four years older than me and shared many of her mother's traits. She was brazen and aggressive. Gertie's husband was a tall handsome man with white hair and a white mustache. He was the opposite of Gertie, mild-mannered, pleasant and congenial. His name was Harry Sapoznick and he worked as a presser in a downtown men's clothing store ~ a menial and low paying job that required him to be on his feet for eight or ten hours. His English was heavily accented and limited.

During my early years I didn't see them often because they lived in a neighborhood far to the north of us called Albany Park. To go there required a streetcar ride of about forty five minutes. But Gertie was a Bolasny, like my mother and the Bolasnys, like my mother, changed their name to Block. There were a number of them and they formed a club called the Block Family Circle. Whenever they had a meeting we would go, usually without my father. I would bring a book and find a place to sit and read while the grownups met and afterwards played cards.

The most distinctive member of this group was Ben Bolasny, a dentist. He was much wealthier than the rest of the family members, and because he had been born in Canada, he spoke clear and confident English. He was the most respected member of the family, because of his confident air and his wealth. Gertie had a rival for the domination of the Block family, Rose Bolasny (not to be confused with my mother Rose). Rose had a son, Sydney and a daughter, Ruth. Sydney was drafted into the Army during the Second World War and tragically, killed. Another strong Bolasny was Tillie, a woman of elegant manners, who had two daughters, Thelma and Doris, slightly older than me. These people formed the backdrop of my young life.

My 5th birthday party in Chicago. I am third from the left at the table. My parents, Harry and Rose standing behind me surrounded by friends, neighbors and relatives.

In Chicago there were also a few relatives on my father's side, the Cohens. The wife, Shirley, was short and tubby. She was also brassy and flamboyant. Shirley tried her hand in the retail millinery business. It ultimately failed. Her husband, Sam, was quiet and mild-mannered. He worked as a clerk in a cigar store. They had a daughter who was two or three years older than me, Deanna. My cousin Deanna was a sweet, well-behaved little girl who wore her hair in long curls. Very different than my Aunt Gertie's daughter, my cousin Adele, who was loud and aggressive.

We lived a rather isolated social life and saw little of our relatives, I suppose because of the geographical distance between us. Yet, they formed my world ~ a Jewish world. Early on I knew that we, the Jews, were different than the people who were the majority of society; they were "the goyim", the Gentiles. Our relationship with them was uneasy and I never felt completely comfortable around Gentiles. Jewish people seemed warm, affectionate and tender hearted and the Gentiles by comparison seemed less sensitive, colder and harder. As I grew older I was exposed to language which revealed their attitude toward us; a reviled race. "Jewing him down" was a common expression.

My Dad was a charismatic figure; and though only five feet two inches tall, he projected self-confidence and wisdom. He was the master of the house, but a kind and loving master. There was never any corporal punishment ~ a firm directive was all that was needed for me to obey. Both he and my Mom were open and demonstrative in their love for me and I knew that as an only child I was prized. Too much so, for in time I developed into a brat; willful, teasing and given to playing tricks on others. While I would not dream of disobeying my Dad, my mother was so indulgent that I almost always got my way.

Both called me "Alvin" but my Dad sometimes called me "sonny" affectionately.

There were only four books in our house: the 1924 and 1925 Annual Reports of the U.S. Department of Agriculture, illustrated and bound in blue hard cover. I have no idea how they came into my parent's possession. There was also a history of the First World War with photographs, some in color, on almost every page, and on the cover, a portrait of the U.S. general who was the commander in chief of Allied Forces, John J. Pershing. Our fourth book was a tattered and worn English Dictionary bound in a red leather cover. I never saw my parents look at any of these books or read anything other than the Forvitz (the Jewish newspaper) or one of the Chicago dailies. And I don't recall either of them telling me any stories and certainly not fairy tales. And yet I grew into an avid reader and lover of books. This seems to contradict current theories of childhood education.

I didn't learn to read till I was in the first grade but somehow I developed a love of books, a vivid imagination and an appreciation of pictures. But I had other traits that were not desirable; I didn't enjoy the company of other children and I was highly sensitive. One incident is telling. We were at a picnic when I was about six, and a foot race was organized by the parents, for our entertainment, I suppose. I had never competed in a race and this was a new experience for me. Some twenty or thirty kids of all ages and sizes were lined up behind a rope stretched to make a starting line. I had no idea of how fast I could run, but I soon found out.

At the starter's whistle the rope holders let it fall to the ground and the race was on. All the kids began running. I remember reacting to the drop of the rope with uncertainty. When I realized all the kids were running I started after them. They were far ahead of me and though I ran as fast as my little legs would go, it soon became obvious I would never catch up to them. Within fifteen or twenty yards or so, I gave up, quit running and began crying. I remember not wanting to be alone on the field, a loser, and ran off into a grove of shrubbery to my left, to be out of sight, crying bitterly. Reflecting on my emotional outburst, it seems to me that feeling inferior to others was intolerable. Those feelings remained with me into adulthood.

CHAPTER THREE

THE TILTON YEARS

When Prohibition ended, my father had to find another way to make a living. With only a fourth grade education and no skills other than making wire frames for lady's hats that had gone out of style twenty five years before, the only business he knew was the liquor business. With limited capital, his choice was limited; he would open a tavern ~ a bar.

After some scouting around he found a store for rent in a very desirable location; the corner of Crawford Avenue, a major streetcar line, and Lake Street, above which ran the elevated train, the "El". The corner was even more choice because the El station was at that intersection and stairs led down to the street practically at the front door of the store.

He rented the store, bought a bar and tavern equipment, and opened what he called, "The Economy Club", a name which he hoped would attract customers looking for low prices. To my knowledge, no one ever called it "The Economy Club"; to the public it was "Harry's". There he would spend the next twenty years of his life and it would become an important part of my life experience.

My mother and I (age 7) in New York for a wedding

To be closer to his place of business we moved to an apartment at 4050 West End Avenue, a distinctly non-Jewish neighborhood. When we began our life in that apartment my mother and I entered the Gentile world. I was six and even to my young sensibilities, the differences were apparent. The people of the neighborhood looked different than us, they talked differently and they were members of a social class that I somehow, felt was hostile to us. The differences became more meaningful to me when I enrolled in the local elementary school, Tilton Elementary School.

I quickly adjusted to Gentile kids and Gentile teachers. The teachers were all women, many Roman Catholic. I recall the name of my first grade teacher: Mrs. Jackman. It was the custom for the students to give the teachers Christmas gifts. I told my parents and my father solved the problem. He gave me a fifth of whiskey, "Four Roses", in a Christmas box to present to my teacher. When I handed her the box, she smiled and thanked me, saying nothing about the unusual offering. I would bet she is the only teacher in the Chicago Public School system who received a bottle of whiskey as a Christmas gift.

My dad was at his tavern from eleven in the morning till two in the morning when he closed. There he worked behind the bar, usually with a hired bartender, but often alone. I would frequently bring him his dinner in a shopping bag. I spent a lot of time in that tavern. Sometimes I would draw a beer from the tap and serve it. To the customers I was "Harry's kid". The customers were working men, employed at the factories on Lake Street or at the nearby Chicago and Northwestern Railroad yards, a huge facility covering acres of land between Lake Street and Chicago Avenue, a mile to the North

My father, Harry Ziontz (second from left) behind the bar of his tavern around 1935

and from Pulaski Road on the east to one mile west. Although my father had only the equivalent of a fourth grade education, he was an intellectually curious man.

Early on, he recognized that I was far better informed in many ways than he was. One day he asked me, "Sonny, they say the world is round. How do they know its round?" I recited the example of earliest voyagers who had circumnavigated the globe. He seemed unconvinced, preferring to trust his own eyes that showed the earth to be flat.

Lake Street was defined by the "El" which ran on elevated tracks above it and it made the street below dark and dingy. Harry's customers came from both the residential areas abutting Lake Street. To the South were middle and lower class residential areas, including the apartment building where we lived, and to the North, the Chicago and Northwestern railroad yards. The tavern catered to a working class clientele, entirely non-Jewish.

He hired a carpenter to build a partition separating the tavern into two halves, the front half for the bar and the rear for booths. In practice, these booths were for women patrons who, by custom, did not sit at the bar, and for couples. I spent a lot of time in that tavern. In the tavern I would sit at one of the tables in the rear and read or draw, and often I would go behind the bar. I got to know the names of the major whiskey brands he carried: Four Roses, Jim Beam, Johnnie Walker, and Fleischman's

My dad easily struck up a warm relation to people and all of his customers called him Harry. Some were drunks and he often had to firmly tell them, "You've had enough. Time to go home." He was sufficiently respected that he rarely had any back talk when he said this. Usually, it was "Okay, Mr. Harry." Sometimes there were violent arguments in the tavern. One day, while I was there, two big guys got into a loud altercation. Suddenly they were on their feet punching each other. My father quickly ran out from behind the bar and interposed himself between them, saying, "All right, boys. That's enough!" I was fearful that he would get hurt, a five foot two little man holding apart two behemoths. But the two stepped back and said, "Okay Harry." Then they left.

None of the customers at the tavern were black. Almost all the blacks of Chicago lived on what was called, "the South Side". This encompassed a large area of South Chicago. I had never been there and saw black people only as laborers or as railroad porters. In film, blacks were portrayed as simple, ignorant people ~ uneducated, acting as menials; maids and field hands. In fact, real life for blacks in Chicago was quite different. Many were employed in factories, on the railroads, as postmen ~ all jobs with solid middle class status. As a child I had seen black people occasionally but as distant and somewhat strange. My father always had a feeling of empathy toward, black people. His expression was "Give 'em a break."

During the war, some black men found jobs in the factories nearby and occasionally would stop in his tavern for a beer or a shot of whiskey. A black man named Henry came in often and he and my father were on a first name basis. One day he was sitting at the bar after work drinking his beer when he got up and walked over to the dice table where two men were playing, "Twenty six". I don't remember the details of the game but men would play for a beer. Henry said, "Mind if I join the game?" This was met with an ugly racial epithet by one of the men who told him "I don't play with N- - -s." Henry said something in reply, but my dad, sensing trouble, came over and said, "Henry, just forget it and go home." "Okay, Mr. Harry," said Henry and he left.

But instead he went to the factory where he worked and got a pistol out of his locker. Fifteen minutes later he returned and confronted the man who had insulted him. I wasn't there, but my dad said another ugly shouting argument ensued and Henry shot the man. It all happened very quickly and Henry ran out of the tavern. The man was seriously wounded and the police were called. They quickly found Henry and arrested him. When the shooting victim died, Henry was charged with murder. It ended with Henry receiving a long sentence and being sent to the state penitentiary in Joliet Illinois.

My father was pained by Henry's fate. The shooting had occurred in his tavern and he regarded Henry as a friend. He decided to drive to Joliet and visit Henry. Henry was glad to see him. During the visit Henry told him that the prison shoes were hurting his feet and my dad said, "Tell me your size and I'll get you a new pair." That is what he did. He drove down to Joliet again, bringing with him the pair of shoes he had bought for Henry. My father's empathy for black people must have become a part of my values too.

Having a job as a public school teacher was a good occupation at a time when few jobs were open to women, outside of offices and hospitals. I recall noticing their speech; their diction was crisper and they used words I never used, and my parents never used. With rare exceptions, they were earnest and hard-working. Classroom discipline was often a challenge, but in the era when authority was unquestioned, it rarely led to serious consequences. A few sharp words from the teacher usually put an end to the misbehavior. Of course, as the kids got older and bolder, harsher methods were employed; standing in the corner, being sent out of the room to stand in the hall, and in extreme cases, being sent to the Principal's office.

When I was about seven or eight, my mother and I went to the movies at the Paradise Theater to see, "Elizabeth, Queen of Scotland". It was evening as we walked the four blocks back to our apartment. My mother unlocked and opened the front door. I entered first and immediately saw a man emptying the contents of our closet into a pillowcase and hastily running to the back of our apartment. Burglars! I ran into the apartment and saw the men running to the kitchen and out the back door. I followed and saw them making their exit down the rear stairs. My mother was nearly hysterical. We immediately called my father who called the police. Afterward my mother was so nervous that she insisted we move out immediately. My father rented a two room apartment in an apartment hotel on Washington Boulevard ~ two blocks away.

My graduation photo from Tilton Elementary School (age 13)

My mother and I (age 14) in front of the Karlington Apartments on Washington Boulevard in Chicago

This was a rented and furnished hotel apartment. Since my parents expected to be there only a few months till they rented another apartment, they put all their furniture in storage. The apartment hotel was called "The Karlington" and our quarters were not nearly as roomy as our apartment. The largest room was the living room, but was taken up at night by an in-a-door bed, which, when lowered took up most of the space in the room. There was a tiny kitchen, and what would be called a dinette, into which my parents placed a narrow bed. Logically I should have been assigned the dining room cot, but because they felt I was such a precious child, they opted to squeeze onto the narrow bed while I slept on the two person in-a-door bed in the living room, sacrificing their own comfort for me.

We stayed in the Karlington for five years, though we had moved there only as a temporary rental. There was no back yard, garbage was thrown down a chute in a small room at the end of our corridor, and to add to the novelty, there was an elevator; with push buttons, which I enjoyed riding till eventually the novelty wore off.

Meanwhile my life at Tilton went on. Fights between boys in the schoolyard were infrequent, but reputations were made by winning such contests. (Girls had a separate schoolyard.) Early on I realized I was no match for these fighters, nor could I run as fast as they did. Besides, I was terrified of being punched in the face. Perhaps that is why I allied myself with a gang whose toughness was unquestioned.

The gang was led by a devil-may-care boy named Steve Bodnar. He was quiet and undramatic, but he was openly indifferent to the teachers and the requirements of schoolwork. More importantly he was an adventurer. Several times he ran away from home, rode freight cars to remote places and slept who knows where. He was the Huck Finn of Tilton School. I was drawn to him and followed him and his little band of urchins. With them I perched on the tailgates of trucks and explored remote industrial districts of Chicago.

Why did they accept me? I was certainly no fighter, but about this time I began to draw and showing some talent I was soon the leading artist of Tilton School. And even though I could speak with the same obscenity-laden speech as my gang mates, they knew I was not a "tough guy". In fact, I was no match for any of the boys in this little group in strength, speed or agility.

The most glaring contrast was between us was my attitude toward learning and reading. In school I performed near the top of my class and read books voraciously. Theirs was a different world. For them, distinction came with physical fearlessness and hostility to authority. They broke the rules with impunity. As I accompanied them on their urban adventures with my heart pounding, we stole items from the local dime store, snuck into movie theaters without paying, and rode around the city on the backs of trucks, facing the uncertainties of getting back to our own neighborhood on other trucks. One day, I followed them up a railroad embankment and, heart pounding, crouched into a tiny space below the tracks on a bridge approach and squeezed my eyes shut as a freight train rumbled overhead.

They introduced me to their game of "flipping trucks" ~ surreptitiously climbing onto the tail gate of a truck stopped for a traffic light, and riding a series of trucks to a distant industrial neighborhood. Once we climbed up a railroad embankment in a distant industrial neighborhood as a steam locomotive approached. Three of us sat on the railroad ties dangerously close to the tracks to show our fearlessness. But we were outsmarted by the engine crew who saw our perilous position; toying with death. When the steel monster neared to within fifty yards, the engineer opened the cylinder cocks (valves used to discharge accumulated water from the cylinders) releasing bursts of steam spewing 20 or 30 feet to the side of the engine. To avoid being scalded, we all leaped down the embankment to the ground below and laid there as clouds of steam spurted harmlessly above us.

"Flipping trucks" could be hazardous. The technique was simple; two or three of us would lurk on the sidewalk near an intersection with a traffic light and wait for a stopped truck with a tailgate lowered, or some decking on which we could sit. When the truck stopped, we would quickly run out to it and hop aboard, being careful not to make any noise or give away our presence to the driver. A few times the driver became aware of his unintended passengers and stormed to the rear of the truck, shouting, "Hey, you kids get offa there!" We would simply scamper back to the sidewalk and waited for another opportunity with the next truck.

The thrill was not just riding the tailgate, but launching ourselves toward an unknown destination which might be quite distant. Then, of course, the challenge was to find our way back by tailgate again. My fellow riders had done this many times and were quite nervy. A single outing might require three or four different truck rides. The trick was to sense when the truck was heading in the wrong direction and hop off before it was too late.

Once, I got caught on a bad ride. Three of us hopped aboard a truck stopped for traffic at Crawford and Lake St. We rode along happy and carefree for about a mile. As the truck slowed for the intersection with Sacramento Boulevard, I suddenly found myself alone. My friends had jumped off, and by the time I realized that they sensed the truck was going to turn, it had already made its turn and picked up speed. I was stuck, sitting on the tailgate, watching my friends recede into the distance while I was a captive passenger as the truck sped along Sacramento Boulevard. At first, I tried to stay calm, expecting the truck to slow or stop soon, allowing me to get off and walk back to my friends.

Instead of slowing, the truck gathered speed and was traveling at thirty or thirty five miles an hour. It passed through the next intersection on a green light and continued on. Now, I was beginning to worry. How far would this damn truck take me? I now became a little desperate. I was in for a long walk. This was getting serious. Every turn of the wheels took me further from Lake Street and I might find myself many miles from home without the leadership of my pals to find a truck ride back. I began to feel desperate and scared.

I had learned from my gang that in a situation like this you could get the attention of the driver by singing this little ditty: "Al's on a truck and he can't get off, Al's on a truck and he can't get off... etc., etc." The idea was to sing it loudly enough to be heard by the driver who would bring the truck to a stop and enable you to get off. I decided to try it. At first, I was a bit timid and began singing at a normal volume, but soon realized I would never be heard over the road noise unless I began shouting the song and so I did. Nothing happened. As I sat there feeling helpless, I grew desperate to get off that truck.

I began to consider lowering myself from the tailgate and when my feet were close to the ground, test the impact to see whether I could run fast enough to avoid being slammed to the pavement. It was what I thought was an experiment and if I decided it wouldn't work; I would haul myself back up on the tailgate and sit there till the truck stopped. How stupid! How could I even think that a twelve year old boy or even a full grown man could run thirty miles an hour.

I gripped the edge of the tailgate in the space between the tailgate and the truck ~ about an inch or so. Then I slowly let myself down. As soon as my foot touched the asphalt I realized the impossibility of my scheme. My foot flew back with violent and frightening force. No ~ this would not work. If I had let myself down completely, my face would smack down on the street. To make the plan even more foolhardy, there was a car following the truck down the street. If I weren't killed or seriously injured by hitting the street, I would be finished off by the car running over me.

I had to get back up on the tailgate. This would have been difficult under any circumstances, but I now had the misfortune of snagging my sleeve on a screw head protruding from the back edge of the tailgate, just under my arm. Every time I tried to pull myself up, I was stopped by that miserable little screw head.

Now my plight was serious. I couldn't let go and I couldn't get back up. This had become a life or death dilemma. The only thing left to do was scream for help and I did, loudly and then at the top of my lungs, hoping the truck driver would hear me. The truck did not slow, but help came from an unexpected source. The driver of the car behind the truck, seeing my peril as I dangled from the tailgate, sped up and pulled alongside the truck. He must have somehow communicated to the driver, for immediately the truck slowed to a stop.

I got off and stood on the street, my legs feeling like they were made of rubber. Shakily I began to make my way to the sidewalk. I hadn't gone three paces before the angry truck driver came around the rear of the truck toward me. "You stupid punk!" he shouted. "You coulda' gotten yourself killed! Stay offa trucks, ya unnerstand?"

"Yessir," I said contritely, grateful to be back on solid ground again. I turned toward home and began the long slow trek back to our starting point, Lake Street. Forty five minutes later I was back. I was surprised, but happy, when I saw the guys in my gang still standing there. "Got stuck on that truck, dinnya?" I affirmed that was what happened and left out the dramatic details, since they didn't reflect well on my courage. Having to yell for help is not a gang virtue. But there was a lasting consequence. I never flipped trucks again.

Besides Steve Bodnar and his little gang, I was obsessed by steam engines. I was so fascinated that I wanted to learn their anatomy by reading all the books I could find on the subject, books that described the mechanical parts and how they work, books that described railroading, the history of American railroads and the life of locomotive engineers, switchmen, dispatchers, the operation of locomotives, their design and construction and books of photographs, photographs of workday steam engines pulling freight trains, high-speed engines racing along, hauling glamorous trains; the Empire State express, the Santa Fe Chief, the Northern Pacific Empire builder and the Illinois Central city of New Orleans, lowly yard engines or switchers as they were also called, round house operations and shop operations where steam engines were dismantled, worn parts replaced and the engine given a complete overhaul.

I didn't just read these books. I studied them. In time, I came to know the names of all the working parts and how they moved. One day, browsing the magazine rack of a local drugstore, my eye was caught by the title of a magazine: "Railroad". As I scanned its pages, I saw railroad fiction, articles devoted to aspects of steam engine operation, Westinghouse air brake systems, injectors, booster's, reversing systems, and on and on. A treasure trove. I bought the magazine and took it home, eager to learn about the inner world of operating steam engines. From that day forward I became a regular reader of "Railroad Magazine". My dream was to get into the cab of a steam locomotive and watch the crew as they operated it.

This passion for steam locomotives led to a discovery. The Chicago and Northwestern Railroad mainline lay about six blocks north of our home. It ran close to Kinzie Street. I discovered that by standing at the fence near the embankment I would have a front row seat for the glorious spectacle of steam locomotives of all kinds passing within 20 yards of me ~ hauling freight trains, rushing along with short five car commuter trains, making their dignified way with first-class passenger trains. Occasionally, a lonely engine, not pulling anything, would occupy the mainline heading east ~ doubtless to the downtown Northwestern Depot ~ to be hooked up to a train.

I would take up my position after school and patiently wait ~ in all kinds of weather ~ for an engine to come along. Usually an engine would pass every 20 minutes. The reward of seeing this dramatic sight made the long wait worthwhile. I returned countless times over a period of several years till I discovered an even better observation post. Just north of my father's Tavern on Pulaski road was a viaduct over Crawford Avenue. I decided to investigate. On the far side was a small yard where the railroad stockpiled unused wooden rail ties. It was open to the street. Curious, I walked in and discovered it was adjacent to an embankment of tracks that led to the main Northwestern yards. This was not a mainline for fast-moving trains, like the ones along Kinzie Street, but the yard line for engines entering and leaving the yard. As I stood there, a large freight locomotive chugged slowly along and wondrously stopped directly in front of me, emitting all the exciting sounds of a steam engine, the rhythmic thumping of the two air compressor pumps mounted on the side of the huge black boiler, the hissing vents and the powerful sound of steam emitted by the smokestack. Here was this mechanical creature not ten feet away, stationary and alive ~ and there was no fence between me and the locomotive.

Gradually, I climbed up the embankment toward the steam engine till I was within three feet of the wheels. I stood there studying the familiar components, now visible clearly, and felt a thrill mixed with apprehension; would the engineer yell at me to get away from there? But instead, one of these heroes leaned out of the window of the cab and said, "Hello, kid." Neither he nor any of the locomotive crews who saw me standing and watching ever uttered a harsh word to me. They saw me as a kid fascinated by locomotives, clearly not bent on mischief.

One day, as I stood by the tracks, one of the giant steam engines stopped, apparently waiting for a signal to enter the yard. The engineer, obviously good natured, seeing me studying his engine intently, said,

"Wanna come up in the cab, kid?" My heart leaped. "Sure," I said and climbed the steps leading up to the cab.

I held tightly to the hand rails. Without them, mounting the nearly vertical steps would have been impossible. When I reached the top and stepped inside the cab, I was thrilled. At last, my dream come true! It was a dirty, grimy place, but my attention was focused on the plethora of gauges, dials, valve handles and the engineer's controls; the throttle lever (a long handle extending diagonally from the boiler), the two sets of air brake controls (one for the engine and the other for the train), the long rod for the reversing gear (controlling the travel of the cylinder valves for timing the admission and exhaust of steam from the cylinders) and the rear face of the boiler where the firebox doors were mounted.

After a few moments spent taking in the complexities of the steam engine's operating controls, I got up enough nerve to ask the engineer a few questions. It was clear that I knew something about steam engines. The fireman picked up his shovel (called a scoop) and held it out to me, saying, "Wanna throw a little coal on the fire?" "Sure," I said and confidently took it from him. I was not unfamiliar with shoveling coal ~ I had done it often in my cousin John Kurland's coal yard in Muscatine, Iowa. He pointed to the small portal in the coal car (called the "Tender") and I scooped up a shovelful of coal and swiveled around so I was facing the firebox doors. But they were closed and I didn't know how to open them. The fireman smiled at me indulgently and said you have to step on that pedal to open the doors. But then he noticed that I was left-handed and was holding the scoop on the wrong side of my body. "You have to hold the scoop on your right so you can push down the firebox pedal with your left foot." I

My locomotive drawing from memory of
a 2-8-2 MacArthur Type with coal car coupled (age 13)

My locomotive drawing from memory of
a 2-8-2 MacArthur Type without coal tender (age 13)

shifted the scoop to my right hand and, holding it on the right side of my body, awkwardly stepped on the heavy steel pedal. The two halves of the firebox doors swung apart, pivoting from the top and opening like an inverted V, revealing the white hot coal fire burning inside. I heaved the scoop toward the fire and its contents landed somewhere on the fire.

"You'll make a good fireman someday, but you 'gotta' learn to shovel from the right," said the fireman, taking the scoop back from me. "We've got a green," said the engineer and I knew my time in this place of dreams was up. I thanked both of them and carefully backed down the steps to the ground, holding tightly to the railings on both sides. The engineer gave me a farewell wave as he opened the throttle and the huge steam engine chuffed away.

My fascination with steam engines found expression in drawing. I made meticulous drawings of locomotives, depicting all the parts; the boiler, the steam and sand domes, the cylinder box, the piston rod, the connecting rods to the wheels, the reversing mechanism, the eccentric rod, the valve controls and their lubrication mechanism, the air compressor, the generator, the running gear and, of course, the whistle and bell. I took satisfaction in making the drawing as accurate as possible. These drawings were viewed with respect by my classmates.

My interest in drawing had actually begun much earlier when I was around six. I would sit at a table with a pencil and paper and draw anything that struck my fancy; faces, sailing ships, cows, horses, cowboys, Indians, airplanes. Often I would be inspired by a photograph in a magazine, but my drawings were poor imitations of the original. I recall one effort to draw the heavyweight boxer Jimmy

Braddock. His face turned out as a lumpy, misshapen representation of poor Mr. Braddock.

In the third grade the school began trying to teach art. One day a week, for one hour, we were encouraged to draw with colored chalk on heavy, coarse grained paper. Usually, the teacher assigned subjects, e.g. Halloween pumpkins, Pilgrims, Christmas themes and other banalities. There were two pupils in my class who were champs, compared to the others; me and a girl named Cherie Parker. But Cherie only wanted to draw horses, while I had the advantage of three or four years of generic drawing. I was soon recognized as the class artist.

When I was in fifth grade, our art teacher told us of a city-wide art competition. Each school could send two students to compete and the winners would receive a one year scholarship to the school of the Art Institute of Chicago, a prestigious museum and art center. Cherie and I were selected from Tilton School and on the appointed day we assembled at an outdoor area set up for the occasion with easels. We were given colored chalk to draw on a large sheet of art paper tacked to the easel. We were told that we had two hours to draw anything we wanted. The ten winners would be selected by judges from the Art Institute. I was one of the fortunate ten based on a pastel I had made of a tugboat passing beneath one of the bridges across the Chicago River.

Now I was drawn deeper into the world of Art. Every Saturday I rode the bus from our apartment on Washington Boulevard downtown to the Art Institute. After showing my student card, I made my way down to the basement where the classrooms were located. Almost immediately, I was struck by the pungent scent of oil paint. As I walked down the corridor to my classroom, I would glance through the doorways of the other classrooms and saw art in the making; young men and women standing at easels, working at charcoal sketches of models, and, in other rooms, students intently painting with oils on canvases mounted on easels.

In my class, our instructor had us working on trying to capture the three dimensionality of objects; the use of light and shadow not only to portray shape, but also the roundness and depth of the object. She taught us the techniques of drawing perspective and the subtleties of line. All of this was, of course, dedicated to realism. In later classes, I was introduced to the basics of expressionism. In one class we were asked to draw our impressions while listening to Ravel's Bolero.

After every class I wandered through the galleries of this great museum of Art, looking at Renaissance Art and contemporary American Art. I began to develop an intellectual appetite for the history of Art. In my readings, I was somehow captivated by the work of the Italian Renaissance painter, Giotto, probably due to his use of intense blues.

My boyhood was dominated not by Art, nor by steam locomotives, nor by the adventures with Steve Bodnar, but by reading. At an early age, probably seven, I discovered the Henry Legler Branch of the Chicago Public Library and obtained my library card. The card number is still imprinted in my memory: 92011. I read my way through the juvenile section and then, with the complicity of sympathetic librarians and over the next five years, read deeply in the adult section. Mostly I read fiction, though I did read some non-fiction; for example books dealing with sailing ships and steam locomotives. I read all the children's classics; the work of Mark Twain, Robert Louis Stevenson and the seagoing adventure books of Howard Pease and then moved on to adult fiction; Dickens, De Maupassant, O. Henry, William Saroyan, John Dos Passos, William Faulkner and others, now forgotten.

My reading was eclectic and unguided. It provided me with a large vocabulary and an intimate familiarity with English usage. All of this was deployed in my spoken and written schoolwork. Since my schoolwork put me near the top of my class, inevitably there was some tension with my gang mates. I resolved it by dumbing down my language and adopting their patois using "dese", "dem" and "dose", for the standard articulation of the "th" sound. It was a disguise to conceal my double life.

As I reflect now on those years I have trouble understanding my motivation. I was, of course, a creature of two cultures; the Jewish culture and the majority non-Jewish culture of the country. I tried to bridge the cultural gap by adopting the outward coloration of the Christian culture. But it went deeper than that. I was also trying to establish my masculinity by pretending to be one with the roughnecks.

These were the Tilton School years; kindergarten through eighth grade ~ 1933 through 1941. My young life was enlivened not only by steam locomotives, Art and reading, but also by playing the violin, by Hebrew School, by summer camp, by summers spent at my cousin's in Muscatine, Iowa, by the movies and by my father's tavern.

The violin became part of my life. It began when a violin teacher was allowed to address the students about taking instruction on this instrument. I don't know why I decided I wanted to play that instrument. I hadn't been interested in playing the instrument before, but it struck me as something I would like to do, particularly after I heard the instructor, Mr. Tiverofsky play a sweet solo. He offered lessons at $10. Violins could be purchased from him for modest monthly installments or the student could acquire an instrument independently. His sales pitch to the school was that he could form a school orchestra, using his violin students together with students taking lessons on other instruments. The idea of a school orchestra appealed to the school authorities. I took the sign-up sheet home and presented it to my parents. Perhaps thinking their son might be a musical prodigy (the violin had a long history in the Jewish world), they signed.

Well, I turned out to be no musical prodigy. In fact, I was a mediocre violin student. I always found a reason to postpone practicing till the day before my lesson. A conscientious instructor would have told me to quit. But Tiverofsky, who was a nice, patient man, also had to make a living and I suspect he couldn't afford to reduce his student enrollment.

Though I became acquainted with the works of Lehar, Gounod, Massenet and other classical composers, I actually knew little about classical music. We had no phonograph and I attended concerts only a few times. The last piece assigned to me by my teacher was the Mendelssohn Violin Concerto, which I struggled with. I was able to play only the first movement.

In High School I played in the Roosevelt High School orchestra and became familiar with the less difficult pieces. But even here I was mediocre, mainly because I could never concentrate on keeping time. My real introduction to classical music began when I was living in a fraternity house at the University of Chicago and a room-mate had an LP player. One day I listened seriously to the Brahms Violin Concerto and was swept away. That began my serious interest in music. It deepened when my friend Lawrence Friedman took it on himself to acquaint me with Bach. It opened my ears to what is arguably the greatest composer of all time. Since then, I have become an avid Bach listener.

When I was around nine or ten, my parents enrolled me in a Hebrew School. They called it by its European name: "Cheder". Here, the purpose was to teach Jewish boys (not girls) to read the classical prayers and the bible, the "Chumesh", in Hebrew. There were no English translations. In time it dawned on me how empty it was to read and recite aloud passages in Hebrew with no understanding of their meaning. Since this long predated the founding of the State of Israel, biblical Hebrew was the only Hebrew we knew, there was no conversational or vernacular Hebrew. Our teachers made a perfunctory effort at translation. In fact I suspect they themselves didn't know the language well enough to translate. But their objective was to give us the ability to participate in Synagogue services. Indeed we went there as a class on "Shabbas" (Sabbath) and sat there in rows of hard wooden pews among several hundred odiferous men (women were relegated to the balcony). The men held their prayer books, "Siddurim", praying aloud, most not even bothering to look at the books because they could recite the prayers from memory. While there was a leader on the podium, he was generally ignored while the men, mostly elderly, mumbled or chanted, all the while bobbing back and forth. There was no effort to synchronize and the result was a general babble of sound. When we students attempted to join in at the few points where we could determine what page they were on, even the most proficient of us were quickly left behind as the elderly worshippers sped along, barely pronouncing the syllables on the printed page. It was a challenge to try to keep up with them, even for short periods.

The spectacle made little sense and the classes at Cheder were not much better. My classmates and I were not caught up in any of it. We regarded the synagogue scene as disconnected from the life of America as we knew it and we resented having to attend Hebrew School every afternoon from four to six as an infringement on our freedom, especially since our Gentile schoolmates had no such intrusion on their lives. This resentment brought on a sullen antagonism toward the school and its teachers, manifested by disruptive and unruly behavior in the classroom. In contrast, many of these same miscreants were obedient and well-behaved in the secular public schools.

Years later, when I had the maturity to think about it, I concluded that the misbehavior was acting out of anger at being forced to attend the school, especially as it was so disconnected from American life. No one spoke Hebrew in America and our parents did not attend religious services at the synagogue except for the two or three days a year of Rosh Hashanah and Yom Kippur when almost all Jews crowded the synagogue. None of us were infused with religious belief ~ at least I saw no evidence of it among my contemporaries. Most of us joined a synagogue as adults, usually because we had children who had to be prepared for their Bar-Mitzvah and in the fifties, Judaism adopted the practice of confirming girls as well as boys in the equivalent ceremony called a "Bat Mitzvah". So both sons and daughters had to be put to this trying experience.

The Bar-Mitzvah was the only reason we attended Hebrew

School ~ we were being prepared for that all important rite of passage in which Jews everywhere for over a thousand years celebrated a son's attaining the age of thirteen. The Rabbis had determined that at this age a boy had attained manhood (a complete fiction) and could take his place among the men of the congregation.

In practice this meant that he not only had to recite the prayers, but also to mount the podium (the bimah) and read from the Torah, inscribed on a parchment scroll, in Hebrew without vowel signs. A Torah portion was the section read that day. (A succeeding section was read every day till the end was reached, when it started over again from the beginning.) The boy also read the commentary on that section (called the Haftorah). Adding another layer of difficulty, the Bar Mitzvah candidate had to chant both following musical symbols ~ of ancient usage.

None of this was taught in Hebrew School. A tutor was engaged who practiced all of it with each boy. Finally, the candidate had to prepare a speech ~ an exegesis on the section of the Torah he had read. This was usually prepared with the assistance of the tutor, though occasionally an originally-minded aspirant would insert his own thoughts. And it would always include words of appreciation to his parents and to his teachers for having gotten him through the Bar-Mitzvah.

Like my contemporaries, I too went through the ritual unquestioningly. On the great day my fears dissolved as I stood on the bimah and launched into the ancient chants. I recall actually enjoying being the star of the show. The "coup de gras" was my memorized speech. I have no recollection of its content, but I recall the Rabbi hugging me and my mother and father beaming with pride. I was aware of the magnitude of the event, if only because of the gifts piled high on the table at the rear of the banquet hall that night and the many envelopes stuffed with cash handed to me ~ a total of $800.00. In addition, there were numerous key chains, tie clips, ties, shirts and sweaters. But the gift I prized the most was a Kodak Brownie camera. The year was 1941 and I could not have foreseen that this would be the genesis of a love affair with photography that would blossom into a serious passion in 1975.

The Bar Mitzvah may have had other long-term consequences. I think it convinced my father that I had a gift for oratory and led him to believe that I was destined to be a lawyer. Like all the boys in my Hebrew School class, I dropped out of Hebrew School after the Bar Mitzvah. Judaism was not entirely erased from my life ~ just shrunk to a bare minimum ~ the Jewish Holidays. The big ones were Rosh Hashanah and Yom Kippur and, of course, Pesach or Passover. The last was not celebrated in the synagogue, but in the home. My mother was observant and attended the synagogue on the High Holidays, sitting in the women's section. My father never went to shul (synagogue), I think, because he associated it with the backward, closed world of the Jews of Russia. Instead, he embraced American life, its modernity, its style, its pastimes; sports, politics, cars and city life.

But the High Holidays did have some meaning in my boyhood; I would always get a new suit, with long pants for the occasion. And I stayed home from school and went to the synagogue and endured the meaningless chants of the praying men, broken by periodic operatic performances by the Chazzan (Cantor). Cantors were stars and commanded large fees. Famous cantors drew large crowds. When I reached the limit of my endurance I would go outside and join other boys gathered on the sidewalk near the synagogue. But we never wandered far from the "Shul" lest this be interpreted as abandoning your obligation as a pseudo-worshipper. Yom Kippur had a special feature: fasting. The kids would challenge each other: "Did you fast today?" Some did indeed fast, others lied and some confessed to eating.

The other major holiday of the year was Pesach, or Passover. In preparation, mothers engaged in furious housecleaning and unpacked their special Passover pots, pans, dishes and silverware which had been stored away for this occasion. Pesach lasted eight days and was highlighted by the "Seder"; the ritual dinner celebrating the biblical story of the Exodus. The Seder revolved around the reading of the Haggadah, the Passover prayer book. The meal itself was a ritual with ceremonial dishes and special foods. I hated Passover because the eating of bread was forbidden for eight days; instead we ate Matzos, a large square baked like a cracker. It was a fixture of Passover that I heartily disliked.

The entire experience of the holidays left me feeling distaste for what seemed like an archaic and foreign practice. At the age of fifteen I stopped going to the Synagogue, even on the High Holidays, and this central mandate of Judaism faded out of my life, leaving only the remnant of not going to school or working on those days. Yet I could not entirely escape my Jewish identity. It was part of me and buried deep within me. The issue would arise because, although my features did not look typically Jewish, my name, "Ziontz" raised Gentile suspicions that I might be Jewish. Often I was asked, "What nationality is that?" It must be recalled that my boyhood years were the 1930's and 1940's when Jews were commonly objects of scorn or worse, as

"Christ killers", especially in working class neighborhoods like ours. Derogatory words and expressions like, "kikes", "Jewing him down" were in common use. When the question of my nationality was put to me, I was in the uncomfortable position of either announcing my Jewishness, or concealing it. Even when I didn't speak out, ethnically derogatory remarks were hurtful. In that period and before, Jews were perceived as a pariah class ~ from Shakespeare to Dickens and beyond.

In my neighborhood I could masquerade as a Gentile boy. But only with my family or in Jewish circles did I feel comfortable in my Jewish skin. But outside those circles I was uncomfortable living in two worlds. Sometimes I wished my name was "Goldberg" and that I had an unmistakably Jewish nose. Being a Jew was not a source of pride but of shame. Stereotypically the Jew was seen as pusillanimous, weak, cowardly and greedy. Our heroes were the boxers, Max Baer and Barney Ross, the star quarterback of the Chicago Bears, Sid Luckman and the baseball player, Hank Greenberg. Growing up in a world where the male ideal was to be strong and athletic, to be perceived as weak and a bungler at sports reinforced the Gentile stereotype and left me with a lasting sense of my male shortcomings.

One may ask whether the intellectual accomplishments of the Jewish people counterbalanced these ethnic slurs. They did not. For Jews living in large American cities, there was no shield against the anti-Semitism which seemed to pervade the entire Gentile world. The military accomplishments of the State of Israel and the widespread knowledge of the annihilation of the Jews at the hands of the German Nazis as well as their Polish and Ukrainian accomplices have muted but not entirely silenced the voices of Anti-Semitism. But a new voice has been added: Islamic anti-Semitism, provoked by the existence of Israel.

So I, like almost every Jew, grew up aware that I was not a fully equal member of the body of American citizenry. Rather, this was a country of Christians ~ many kindly disposed toward their Jewish fellows, but for us Jews, there was a feeling of "otherness" which never entirely dissipated.

While I was growing up, during the Tilton years especially, I was acutely conscious of that "otherness". The Christmas season heightened that sense of otherness. We all had to sing Christmas Carols and I remember one in particular that was painful; "O Come All Ye Faithful" and the lyric, "O come let us adore him, Christ the King." Most of the other carols also were odes to the Christian narrative. I guess there was no "sensitivity" policy and the idea of separation of church and state would have been unthinkable in the context of Christmas ~ a national holiday. Challenging it would have been an incendiary undertaking.

There were other reminders. Near Tilton elementary was a Catholic School, St. Mel's. The teachers were all nuns whose long black robes and white cowls set them apart from lay people. Their large crucifixes worn prominently on their breasts were, to me, a symbol of Jew hatred. I knew they believed and taught that we had killed the man they worshipped.

Another consequence of feeling a social pariah was sexual. The ideal of female beauty was a Gentile appearance; snub nose, blonde hair, symmetrical calves, thin ankles and full lips. She was the typical movie star. Such a woman could be lusted after but never attained by a Jew. At least that was the sense I, and probably most Jewish boys and men had. Of course, this was not true, but we couldn't know about Woody Allen and Arthur Miller, prominent cases of Jewish men who attracted Gentile women. Nor did we know about Jewish women who represented the ideal of feminine beauty. Who knew that Hedy Lamarr was Jewish? Nevertheless this sense of sexual separateness continued throughout my adolescence. Particularly then, because I attended a High School with a predominantly Jewish enrollment and few, if any of the girls in that school matched the ideal of feminine beauty. By contrast, when I was at a Gentile High School, for swim meets or to attend a football game, the grounds seemed to swarm with these delectables; blonde hair, cute faces, great legs ~ the stuff of male fantasies. It wasn't till I had reached college age that I found I was attractive to girls ~ even Gentile girls. But that came after the Tilton years, which left a lasting sense of separateness. There, I was immersed in finding myself and I experienced the strains of maintaining a dual identity ~ a sensitive Jewish boy with an outward pose of "acting Gentile".

Early on, I was aware of my sensitivity and my exceptionalism. None of my schoolmates demonstrated any interest in Steam Locomotives, or the world of Art, and few if any devoured books with the appetite I did. When I spoke in class, the words came effortlessly to my lips. Contrary to the popular view of the importance of parental involvement in their child's schooling, my parents had no involvement at all. Nor could they. My father spent most of his waking hours working at his tavern and my poor mother, who never read a book, would occasionally attend a P.T.A meeting at my urging, but never otherwise involved herself in my schooling.

The Tilton years dominated my life. As the only Jew in my class, I felt isolated; uneasy in my identity, living in a state of tension with my classmates. I was frequently confronted by the superior strength and aggression of the boys in the class. They developed a custom of delivering a sharp punch to the upper arm of other boys. There was no hostility involved, everyone did it. Apparently it was a demonstration of masculine virility. Yet it hurt. And it was meant to hurt. Usually it resulted in a black and blue mark at the site of the bruise. Once I realized this was an established practice among boys and was not a prelude to a fistfight, I adopted the custom myself, punching other boys on the arm. The punch was delivered in a short, sharp jab. Sometimes the targeted boy anticipated the punch and evaded it by dodging out of range. It was all part of a game.

In the classroom we were taught spelling, composition, arithmetic, American History, civics, science, art and music. There was also gym; games and strength and balance exercises. We also studied geography. Our textbook was published around 1930 and it depicted the external world as it was seen by Americans in the 1920-1940 era. During that period there was almost no immigration so we had no contact with anyone other than Americans. There were no blacks or Asians in my school, nor had I ever met anyone from another country. Our conceptions were formed by our geography books and the movies. So all Mexican men wore sombreros and Chinese men pigtails. Generic Middle Eastern men wore turbans and those outside of Europe, e.g. Asia and Africa were pre-modern, if not primitive.

My art class assignments at Tilton were to draw people and scenes from these exotic lands. No one we knew had actually traveled abroad. That was for wealthy people or explorers, all of whom wore pith helmets and jodhpurs tucked into high boots. They usually were shown in the movies carrying a pistol in a holster, to fend off bandits or tigers. There were no black or other children of color in my school, or for that matter, anyone from another country; a result of the restrictive immigration laws of the time.

Air travel was on DC-3's; a twin engine transport that carried 21 passengers, two stewardesses and a 2-man flight crew. This was still a man's world and women were relegated to teaching, secretarial work and nursing. When we saw photographs of women in the U.S.S.R driving trucks or other such work, we thought it was barbaric.

I lived in a tight little insular world and for me, Chicago was its center. Oh yes, we knew about New York, but it was a distant reality having no substance in our lives. All travel was by car, bus or train. Gas was sixteen cents a gallon and "filling stations" gave away free highway maps. Traveling out of the city by car was an exciting experience. Leaving the city behind and entering the "country" was seeing an entirely different world. Unlike the city, buildings were spread out over the land, houses were different, streets became roads and there we saw barns, horses and cows. The roads were two-laned, with a tarred center line. The car speeds increased to fifty, fifty-five, and as high as sixty miles an hour. The highways were inherently dangerous; cars crossing the center line to pass another vehicle; cars crossing the highway from intersecting roads, farm equipment crawling along, sharp curves suddenly appearing requiring skillful use of brakes and steering. Tires were rubber and couldn't be relied on to grip the road, especially if the pavement was slick with rain or snow.

The towns and villages had a distinctive character, viewed as we slowly drove through them. Through the window of the car we saw feed stores, tractor dealers, small hotels and grocery stores. Occasionally we traversed railroad crossings with their distinctive crossed arms, and bridges over rivers. The traveler in a car moved through these places slowly ~ not like present speeds of 70 miles an hour on a freeway bypassing towns. The pre-freeway auto travel allowed the traveler to absorb the images of small town America spread across the flatlands of the Midwest. Cross country travel was often boring but occasionally enlivened by highway signs and billboards. The most distinctive were the signs for Burma Shave and their sometimes clever jingles.

CHAPTER FOUR

MUSCATINE AND DRIVING

Now I must write about Muscatine. I spent every summer from 1935 to 1940 in Muscatine, Iowa. My parent's fear of polio led them to take extraordinary measures. They wanted me out of the city each summer; the polio season. During the middle 30's polio was the scourge of childhood. As an only child, and a treasured one at that, my parents were fearful that I might contract this dread disease. They "tsittered", in Yiddish. In English, they trembled at the thought. My mother had a cousin, Fannie Kurland (originally Kurlandsky) who lived with her husband John (an unJewish name) in a small town in Iowa with the highly unusual and delightful name of Muscatine. They arranged for her and me to spend the summer with them. So, from age to seven to eleven, my summers were spent in this little town on the banks of the Mississippi which was populated by 18,000 Iowans.

Fannie and John had no children, but Fannie had two brothers, Sam, who lived in Muscatine with his wife Ethel. Sam had a retail coal yard ~ actually a competitor of John and Fannie's business. The other brother Max, was mentally ill and was in a mental hospital when I spent my first summer there. John Kurland, Fannie's husband, operated not only a coal yard but also an auto salvage business. He was the only Jew I ever knew named John. John had massive, muscular arms and was never without a cigar stub in his mouth. John was American born, while his wife Fannie came from Russia.

Coming from Chicago, Muscatine seemed quaint in its smallness. The Kurland's house was a wood frame two-story built in the style of small town single family homes. There was a front porch with a hanging swing, a front door with an oval glass window, and inside, a Living Room, Dining Room, Kitchen, and a stairway that led up to the second floor. Upstairs were two spacious bedrooms and a bathroom. The house was adjacent to the coal yard, in front of which was a sign: "Economy Coal Co". The yard adjacent to and behind the house was immense. Half was devoted to storage of coal and the other half to junked cars and auto parts.

In preparation for our Muscatine stay, my mother had bought me a pair of bib overalls with shoulder straps and copper buttons. I had never worn such a strange item of clothing. The material was so stiff that I wasn't able to button the fly. My mother had to do it. Wearing them I felt different than I did in Chicago, more ready to get dirty. The afternoon we arrived, I couldn't wait to put on my new overalls, and when I had them on, out I went to the coal yard. Just inside the entrance there was a mound of coal six feet high. I immediately started climbing toward the top. After numerous missteps due to sliding coal, I got there. Triumphant, I spent the morning enjoying the coal mound. Finally, my mother became curious about my whereabouts and came out to look for me. She walked into the coal yard and soon saw me, my face smudged with the black of coal and my brand new overalls more black than blue. She gasped in horror at my appearance and ushered me into the house to take a bath. This was my introduction to Muscatine.

As the summer wore on, I discovered more of the delights of this Iowa town. The heat was almost unbearably stifling, but somehow did not detract from the novelty of my Muscatine experience. At night the grownups sat out on the front porch and I and Cousin John swung back and forth on the swing. The night sky was ablaze with stars, unlike anything I had ever seen in Chicago. And there were fireflies, tiny glowing specks of light moving through the air. The silence too was unlike Chicago, where you never escaped the sound of cars, trucks and trains. Here there was only the sound of crickets, which I had never before heard. Then there were the Iowa thunderstorms, louder and more violent than anything I had seen in Chicago.

During the day I explored the neighborhood, walking for blocks in every direction. Fanny and John's house was at 816 E. 5th Street, a corner house at the intersection of E. Walnut Street. Directly across Walnut was a factory; the Barry Gear and Pulley Company. During the day the sound of the factory machinery was constant. Down Walnut ran railroad tracks ending at the factory and another set of tracks ran alongside the Economy Coal Company's yard. At intervals, switch engines would bring empty box cars to the Barry Company plant to be loaded for shipment, and on a separate track, Gondola cars filled with coal for John's coal yard.

John's methods were primitive by today's standards. He had a Diamond T Truck for deliveries, but it wasn't a dump truck, so the coal had to be shoveled out by hand. John always had two or three laborers working for him and these men shoveled the coal out of the truck and then into the basement bin of the customer. When a fully loaded railroad gondola car was delivered with coal for his yard the car had to be shoveled out by hand to his truck parked alongside and then the truck was driven into the yard where it was shoveled into piles according to the size of the coal; broken, chestnut or pea.

One summer I saw the men working in the gondola with John shoveling the coal over the side into the truck and I climbed up into the gondola. John looked at me and smiled; "wanna help, kid?" "Sure," I replied, confident I could contribute to the monumental job of emptying the entire car of its contents. John handed me a spare scoop and I began shoveling. I must have been ten or eleven and not very muscular, but I attacked the coal vigorously. After two or three shovelfuls I developed the rhythm; shove the scoop into the coal, using your body to help push the scoop into the coal, pull it out and then with one hand on the handle and the other near the neck, lift the scoop and in the same motion swing it over the side. The men in the crew had been at it for several hours, but in less than an hour, I was exhausted. John, smiling through his cigar, said, "I think you've done enough," and took the scoop from me. I was proud of my contribution and climbed down from the car.

There were a few other Jewish families in Muscatine. Across the street and down the block from Fannie and John's was a big house with a porch running across the front and curving around the side. Here lived the Starks. They had a boy, Eddie, and his older sister, Roxanne. I struck up a friendship with them. Roxanne was lively and easy to know. Her younger brother, Eddie was quieter, perhaps because his fingers on one hand were fused together. We played together and I soon was introduced to the horse barn in the rear yard. The Stark grandfather, who probably owned the big house, stabled his horse there, while an empty wagon stood in the yard outside. The Stark kids led me into the barn. It was dark and smelled of horse manure. Then I saw the horse standing in his smelly stable. He looked enormous to me.

Their mother was a pleasant woman named Sarah, who looked like the witch in the Wizard of Oz, and her husband, Phil, who worked as a mechanic and attendant at a Texaco station. Very unJewish. He usually wore a shirt with a Texaco Logo on the right chest. Mr. Stark was very American, spoke with no accent and was always friendly. I saw the grandfather only rarely, when he led the horse out of the stable and harnessed him to the wagon. I never knew what he did with the horse and wagon; probably bought old clothes or scrap iron. But for me, the barn, the horse and wagon, and the wrap-around porch were a novelty. Once the three of us, me Eddie and Roxanne, picked up the shafts of the wagon and pulled it about fifty yards. It was harder than it looked and we soon abandoned the effort. One year, when I was leaving to return to Chicago, Mrs. Stark presented me with a book, a detective story called, "The Skeleton Talks". I still have it.

I did form a close friendship with a boy who lived about six blocks away. He was my age, very poised and intelligent. His name was Marvin Kolpack. His parents owned an auto parts store in downtown Muscatine. Kolpack Auto Parts. They did very well and were rich, compared to my relatives. Like the Starks they were Jewish. Marvin was very cool and quite bright. He and I adventured all over town. He took me fishing in a garbage strewn pond. Not surprisingly I caught nothing. He took me out to the town golf course and I swung a club futilely at the golf ball. All I got was blisters on my hand. He let me drive the family Ford down a hill and only by luck did I avoid a crash at the bottom. We spent hours talking, about what I don't know.

His older brother Leo had a Piper cub. Once when we were at a picnic at a local state park, he buzzed over us at about 200 feet, with the side panel open, waving to everyone. They were a very self assured family. In 1981, when I was teaching at the University of Iowa, we took a short trip to Muscatine. Kolpack Auto Parts was still there. Leo was now the manager. I introduced myself, but he had no memory of me. I asked where Marvin was, and he told me Marvin was a Doctor practicing in Beverly Hills. I looked him up on the Internet and found he was a radiologist. I got his phone number and called him. It proved to be a disappointment. Though he had been an important figure in my life for several years, he barely remembered me. What is worse, he was cold and distant. It was obvious he had no interest whatever in renewing our relationship, and didn't even want to spend time talking to me. Well, sometimes sentimentality only runs one way.

Muscatine had character. The Mississippi River was a presence even when it was out of sight. The business center of the town was only a block or two west of the river and the main street was called Front Street. Downtown was a quiet place during the week, but on the weekends the farmers and their families came to town to shop and downtown buzzed with people. My mother bought my first model airplane kit downtown. I took it back to the house eagerly anticipating the pleasure of actually building a plane that looked like the one on the box ~ a Taylorcraft.

North of downtown was a sash and door factory ~ the Huttig Sash and Door factory. It was big and I remember an enclosure for a conveyor belt running over the street. On weekdays, there was a constant whine of the saws cutting into wood that could be heard blocks away. Another industrial building housed the Muscatine Pearl Button factory, making pearl buttons out of the shells dredged from the river bottom. A few blocks east of downtown was the courthouse. A stately granite building, it stood in the center of a park-like square. At each of the four corners stood Civil War Cannons with a triangular stack of cannon balls next to the cannon. And of course, the courthouse was topped by a cupola with a clock face on each of the four sides. I saw all this with the eyes of a little boy from Chicago who had never seen such things. They shaped my feelings about American small town living for the rest of my life.

The Illinois Central mainline ran alongside the river and passed in front of the downtown business district. There was also a passenger depot, though it never seemed very busy. But around seven in the evening the "City of New Orleans" arrived and stopped for passengers at the train station. My cousin John once proposed driving down to the depot to watch the train come in and I eagerly accepted. I rode down there in his '37 Ford sitting in the passenger seat. When we arrived there were ten or fifteen cars already parked there to watch the spectacle of the arrival of the "City of New Orleans". We parked and waited.

It seemed an interminable wait, but finally, in the far distance I saw the engine's headlight on the tracks and it grew nearer and nearer. Finally, the glorious steam engine, ground to a halt just past the depot. Behind it was the baggage car, and following it were seven or eight passenger cars, in orange colors with the title, "City of New Orleans" boldly painted on their sides. I found it thrilling.

The train paused only for a short time and then the engine whistle blew, signaling the imminent start of the train. The first blast from the smoke stack followed and the locomotive began to move, its connecting rods pulling the huge driver wheels around and its eccentric rod following in its complex circular movement. Soon it gathered speed and the entire train moved away to the south and finally disappeared from sight.

At that point, John started his engine as did all the other cars parked to watch the train and we left, together with some ten or fifteen other cars. It reflected the humdrum character of small town existence that the appearance of a train, commonplace in Chicago, would attract a gathering of watchers. Small town life.

John was a man of few words, very manly and quite muscular. One day he asked if I had ever played ping-pong. I hadn't. So he led me down to their basement and amongst the clutter was a ping pong table. John handed me a paddle and showed me how to use it. Then he went to the other end of the table and served the ball to me. I waved the paddle at it and missed. We kept it up till I could hit the ball, but it rarely landed on the table. We played some more and I improved but not enough to make a game of it. It was just another first for me.

One night John took me across the street to meet a neighbor. I was a little surprised to see a large, muscular black man stand up to greet us. It was clear that John and the man were long time friends. "Alvin," said John, "meet Kid Gaddis. Kid Gaddis was a professional boxer and a pretty good one at that, but he's retired now." I shook the massive hand of Kid Gaddis. Then John said, "Show my cousin from Chicago a few moves in boxing."

Kid Gaddis smiled and said, you have to be low, like this, and he went into a boxer's crouch. I emulated him, and then he said, "Get your fists together in front of your face." When I did, he said "you're left handed so you have to jab with your right, like this," and he demonstrated a jab. I tried to do as he did, but it was awkward. Kid Gaddis said, "That's how you begin and now you have to keep practicing." I said I would, though I had little desire to box. After five or ten minutes our meeting ended. Kid Gaddis smiled and said, "Nice to meet you kid" and we parted. Another first.

One of the wonders of Muscatine for me was its public library. I had asked Aunt Fannie if there was a library in town and she told me there was and gave me directions to walk there. It was quite a long hike, but I was young and didn't mind it. When I got there I found a large brownstone building with an imposing entrance. Climbing up the flight of front stairs I found myself in a near empty library. It was quite cool inside compared to the blistering heat outdoors. The librarians were very friendly and helpful and in response to one of my questions led me to a shelf containing the book "Smoky", by Will James. I had never heard of the book or the author. It only took a few minutes to issue me a library card and I headed back to Fannie and John's with "Smoky" under my arm.

Back at the house I began reading it and was soon absorbed by the story of a horse running wild and then tamed by a cowboy. What made the book so engrossing were the illustrations by the author. They depicted life on a ranch in all its dynamics, beautifully illustrated by the author's drawings. I could not put the book down and read it from cover to cover. As a pencil artist, I was enthralled by the drawings in the book. After finishing it, I returned to the Muscatine Library to see whether there were any more works of Will James. There were and I read three of four of them. After that I found the "Penrod" novels by Booth Tarkington as well as other fiction in the library, books I never found in my Chicago branch library.

I often sat in this precious place for several hours reading. That Library was a gem and I loved it. I felt it was a discovery that I made and it added another dimension to my delight with Muscatine.

Muscatine was a river town. The Mississippi was more than a mile wide there. Although I saw it often, I never really experienced it till I was ten. I had seen paddle wheel boats on the river occasionally, but one day I was walking downtown and saw signs advertising a "Moonlight Cruise" on a paddle-wheel boat. I immediately grew excited. I had read "Tom Sawyer" and "Huckleberry Finn" and the idea of going out on the river in an old fashioned paddle wheeler was irresistible. The cruise was aimed at young couples and included music and dancing. It was two days off and started at seven o'clock in the evening. Plenty of time for me to implore my mother to take me on the boat. Obviously my mother would have to accompany me; since I thought it unlikely Fannie or John would go. Initially my mother was reluctant; going on a boat carried a whiff of danger. But after persistent nagging, she finally agreed.

On the day of the cruise, John drove us down to the river and there she was: "The City Of Memphis", moored at the foot of Cedar Street. It was a breathtaking spectacle; a long white riverboat with red paddles in the rear, and multistory decks topped by a wheelhouse with a scalloped red trim around the roof. There was a long gangplank leading from the concrete riverbank to the lower deck. I could hardly wait to go up that gangplank and get on the boat.

As might be expected, the line of people waiting to board was predominantly made up of young couples. In fact, there were no mothers with children, and my middle aged mother and I attracted curious stares. My mother paid the fare at the ticket booth and we walked up the gangplank and boarded the boat. I was so excited I didn't know where to go first. The lowest deck was apparently for freight and we climbed up a flight of stairs to the next deck. It appeared to be a dance hall, so we made our way out to the railing and sat down on a couple of chairs. After what seemed an interminable wait, the steamboat whistle blew long and loud and we began to move.

As we sat there the sun went down and sure enough a moon appeared. About then, the boat's orchestra started playing dance tunes and the dance floor filled with dancing couples. My mother and I sat at the railing watching the river below us. After about a half hour or so, time began to weigh heavily. I was bored. I had noticed a door on our way to the railing that read, "Engine Room" and I decided to try to go for it. I told my mother I wanted to walk around the boat ~ a half-truth. With a dutiful "be careful" she gave me leave to go. I found the small door to the engine room and since no one challenged me, I opened it. There was a platform at the head of a stairway leading down to the engine room. The rhythmic pounding of the steam engine left me in no doubt that this was the place I wanted to see.

The engine room was a huge chamber filled with machinery and dominated by two long horizontal cylinders alongside each other. Each had a long thick piston rod moving back and forth, in and out, turning a crank which led to massive rods connected to the paddle wheels. The noise was deafening and steam hissed from the cylinders with each stroke. I was fascinated. From my familiarity with steam locomotives I could fairly well understand the mechanism. No one noticed me and after about ten minutes I had seen all that I wanted and left through the door that admitted me.

I returned to my Mother sitting on the deck patiently enduring the ride, which must have been rather boring for her. The two of us were a curiosity among the couples who had taken the trip for the dancing; a middle-aged woman and a 10 year old boy. But we didn't care and the trip ended finally as we made a landing around 10:30 that evening at the Muscatine shore. Mother and I went downstairs to the lower deck and got in line to disembark. Down the gangplank we went. Another Muscatine adventure.

The yard of John and Fannie's company was used not only for coal, but also for auto salvage. There were always six or seven junk cars awaiting disassembly. They made marvelous playthings for me; I would climb into the driver's seat and pretend to drive, turning the huge, thick wooden steering wheels and manipulating the metal levers used to control the spark and the fuel mixture. The cars were very old models, the upholstery smelled musty, and the windows were discolored by age. John would tackle the job of disassembly while I watched. There was a large wooden barn-like building where he stored the parts; generators, radiators, pistons, valves, spark plugs and distributors. Periodically he would have a customer for a car part and he would go out to his store house and bring it in to the customer. I became familiar with the look and feel of these parts from handling them in John's yard, though I never assembled or disassembled the cars. But it was another first for this boy from Chicago.

A more important first was learning how to swim and here again Muscatine was the site of my first venture into actually swimming and not just wading or jumping up and down in shallow water. This episode involves Fannie's brother, Max. He wasn't present in the house when I first went to Muscatine, but there was an air of mystery surrounding him that I gauged from the guarded remarks about Max.

The third year in Muscatine, I met Max. He was about thirty, nice looking and very quiet. Over time I learned that he had been in a state mental hospital and was now home on a trial basis. He stayed in one of the houses that Fannie and John owned, but he came to the office every day and did some paper work. Fannie assured me he was harmless and he did, in fact, seem quite mild mannered. He would run errands for John and drove John's pick-up truck. Max often invited me to come along for the ride, since I loved riding in trucks. Then one day he told me he was going for a swim at the Y and asked if I wanted to go with him and go for a dip in the pool. Though I didn't know how to swim I enjoyed the water, so I got my trunks and Max and I drove downtown to the Y.

The Y was in an old building and the pool was in the basement. Max and I changed into bathing trunks in the locker room and went out to the pool. The pool was small; twenty yards long and ten yards wide. The room was dingy; dark and smelling strongly of chlorine. There was a pipe on the low ceiling which discharged a steady flow of water into the pool and produced a continuous loud splashing noise ~ a noise that filled the room.

I intended only to wade, but the shallow end was chest deep. I began experimenting with holding my breath and ducking under the water. After a while I stayed underwater while I held my breath and became accustomed to this underwater existence. I had never done this before and was thrilled by my new ability. Max and I went to the pool several times and each time I tested my underwater skill until finally I decided to swim underwater using a breaststroke. It worked! I was swimming. Max was alarmed at the length of time I stayed submerged, but I assured him I was okay. Finally he acknowledged that I was swimming underwater. I was able to swim underwater the entire width of the pool ~ not very far, but far enough to enjoy the sensation of swimming. That was the beginning of swimming for me. Later, I learned how to use my arms and legs to swim on the surface, but I had conquered my fear of the water in that basement pool at the Y in Muscatine. Unfortunately, the following year Max had a relapse and had to return to the state mental hospital.

Fannie was always very sweet to me. She was an affectionate woman generally and seemed to enjoy our presence as her houseguests. She was responsible for another Muscatine first ~ fried chicken. My mother never fried her chicken; it was always boiled or baked. I had never tasted fried chicken before Fannie made it and I found it delicious. She and John were thoroughly comfortable with the Iowa culture, even though they were among only a handful of Jews living there.

I never heard any anti-Semitic remarks in Muscatine but there was one incident that left me feeling quite uneasy. One evening, in 1938, my mother, Fannie and I were walking near the downtown area and passed a tavern. Inside was a meeting of the local chapter of the German Bund. The tavern was crowded with men wearing brown uniforms and armbands displaying the swastika. They were singing loudly and I paused to watch. Fannie quickly urged me and my mother to move on, saying in Yiddish that these men were Jew haters. At the time I knew nothing of the Nazis and their venomous anti-Semitism. But the sight of this band of brown shirts left me with a permanent memory that was jarring. Here in America this Nazi doctrine had followers, even in a little town like Muscatine. My encounter with small town American Nazis was in 1938 or 1939, before Hitler had begun his European sweep. I had heard of Hitler, but not of the death camps. But I, like most Jews, knew of the open Jew hatred of the Nazis. Seeing it in Muscatine was a jarring experience.

I don't like to finish the discussion of my Muscatine memories with this hateful incident, since otherwise I felt a warm glow of affection for the town and the many growing up experiences I had there. But it cannot be overlooked. On the other hand, there were so many pleasant memories. It was small town America totally different than Chicago and I have relished the experience ever since.

In the fall was Tilton School. Of course, none of my dangerous exploits were known to or even guessed at by my parents. They could be called naïve, but their image of Alvin was of an intelligent boy, a good student with many respectable talents; art, violin and reading and above all, a nice Jewish boy. Nice Jewish boys didn't do the things I did, and indeed they were out of character for me. I don't fully understand it myself. I can only say that my reading and my experience growing up in a Gentile world attracted me to "adventures" and even danger. This side of my character may explain why in my life following Tilton, I was attracted to work as a construction laborer, a warehouse worker, a cab driver and ultimately to leave Chicago behind and take up life in a distant little-known city ~ Seattle. It may also explain why I decided to acquire a pilot's license and fly a plane, and even why I spent most of my career defending the rights of Indian Tribes.

When I reached the age of fourteen I was hungering to drive a car and a legitimate opportunity soon presented itself. My Dad had a '41 Chrysler, a "New Yorker Highlander". The designation must have been dreamt up by the Chrysler sales department to give the car some panache. The "Highlander" theme was carried out by Scotch Plaid cloth upholstery panels surrounded by red leather seat covers. The interior was actually stunning and the car was large and luxurious. The hood seemed to be eight feet long. My Dad was attracted to big cars, perhaps because he was just over five feet tall himself and could barely see over the dashboard.

Top: 1941 Chrysler Highlander New Yorker
Bottom: Interior of the Highlander New Yorker tartan seat fabric

I began badgering my father to let me drive. Because the car did not have the traditional gear shift, requiring coordinated use of the clutch pedal and the gas pedal, it was well suited to a beginner. The Chrysler had what it called, "Fluid Drive", a mechanical arrangement that allowed the driver to operate the car without shifting gears, except for reverse and low gear. My Dad was very generous in allowing me to drive the Chrysler. I would ask to drive every weekend when I was home from school and he was driving to the tavern, only six blocks distant. But there were other, longer trips requiring navigation through the heavy Chicago traffic. I soon demonstrated enough skill that he felt I ought to get my license. We went to the licensing office and he stayed in the car while I went in to take the written exam to be followed by a driving exam. I found the written test easy and passed with a high grade. Then I had to wait for an examiner. Soon a short paunchy man called out my name and when I responded he asked, "Where's your car?" "Parked right outside," I answered and we both walked out to the street. My Dad saw us approaching the car and got out to greet the examiner. Then, in a friendly tone of intimacy, he said, "Don't worry. He knows how to drive. He's a good driver," and handed the examiner a folded ten dollar bill. Without a word, the examiner, took the bill, stuffed it into his pants pocket, and said, "He passed." Then he signed some form and handed me a temporary driver's license and said, "He'll get the permanent one in the mail," turned and left. That's how you did business in Chicago.

Not long after, my father allowed me to drive his Chrysler alone. Soon I had developed the skill to maneuver through Chicago traffic. Driving in Chicago presented unique challenges. Almost all the arterials had streetcar lines. The streetcars ran on tracks and the space between these large lumbering streetcars and the cars parked at the curb was just enough to allow a car to pass between them. The maneuver took nerve and skill. One had to have a good sense of the width of the automobile and the steadiness to maneuver it past the moving streetcar while avoiding contact with the parked car. It was a necessary skill unless you were willing to follow behind the streetcar at 25 miles an hour for miles.

Chicago presented other challenges to the driver ~ winter. The neighborhood streets were not plowed and often cars were two or three feet deep in snow. Getting a car out sometimes required shoveling the snow behind and in front of the wheels and then rocking the car so it could get momentum to go over the snow berm, not a simple task because it required rapid movement of the shift lever from first or second gear to reverse, sometimes repeated several times till the car broke out of its snow bondage. The arterials were often packed with snow and sometimes icy, so steering and braking required an almost sixth sense of the car's path and a quick and delicate correction once a skid began. I learned how to do all these things. During the thirties and forties, when I was growing up, I was, like most boys, keenly aware of cars. I knew every make by its grille and I was proud of my skills at driving.

I was also fascinated by airplanes, but they could be seen only in the sky. To see one on the ground was only possible when my father drove South on Cicero Avenue for about fifteen miles to the Chicago Municipal Airport. From the road one could see the parked DC-3s that made up the American transport fleet. It was the standard airliner of the thirties and forties. It looked huge; its characteristic pointed noise tilted up to the sky, its long fuselage resting on a small tail wheel beneath the vertical and horizontal stabilizers. One year my father went to New York to see his mother and his sister. For some reason he decided to go by plane instead of the train, I can only say he was an adventurous guy and achieved some glory, since in 1938, it was the rich folks and the movie stars who were the common travelers on commercial planes. Most of America traveled by train.

My mother and I went to see him off. I was excited. My dad would actually ride through the skies in an airplane! We were tense. Air travel was much more hazardous in 1938 ~ planes crashed for no apparent reason. The tension rose as we went through the terminal at the Chicago Municipal Airport. His plane was parked on the tarmac in front of the terminal. It was a Boeing 247. At the time it represented the most advanced aircraft in service in commercial travel. The name Boeing was prominently painted on the tail. I had never heard that name before.

Finally, the loudspeaker announced the imminent departure of the flight to New York and my beloved father walked those fateful steps out to the aircraft. I knew nothing of the 247 at the time but have since learned that it had a passenger capacity of 10 people, one flight attendant, two members of the flying crew and a cruising speed of 188 miles an hour. What I didn't know was that it was soon to be replaced by the Douglas planes; first the DC 2 and then that workhorse of the world, the DC 3. I watched as my dad climbed the boarding steps to the passenger door and then entered the cabin. In a few moments there he was ~ his face at the window, waving to us. We watched anxiously till the pilot started the first engine. The three bladed propeller began to turn and then there was a frightening blast of smoke from the exhaust pipe as the engine caught and the propeller began to spin at a faster and faster rate. Then the second engine went through the same procedure.

Did the bluish gray smoke of the exhaust mean the engine wasn't working right? Apparently not, because the exhaust smoke ceased and the plane slowly turned away from the terminal and headed out to the runway. We continued to watch the flying machine till it reached the far end of the airport and began speeding toward takeoff. I couldn't take my eyes off it even after it was airborne and finally disappeared from sight. The experience was dramatic and after we got home I took out my drawing book and drew a clumsy image of the Boeing 247 flying. I still have that drawing and a copy is shown below. The name "Boeing" can be seen faintly on the vertical stabilizer. I was 10.

Well, my Dad arrived safely in New York and several days later flew back to Chicago. Afterwards, we regarded him as an adventurer. Who flew? Not many. But to me he was an unusual and heroic figure. Traveling by plane was only a part of who he was, but our relatives and, no doubt many of his customers and business acquaintances saw him as a bold man. Flying in 1938 was a high risk way to travel.

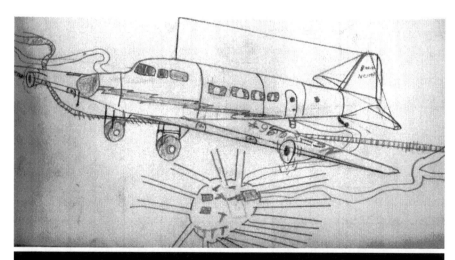

My drawing from memory of the Boeing 247 that my father flew in to New York in 1938

The only images of airplanes I saw as a boy were in the movies or photographs in magazines in the school library. In these magazines we could see photographs of Pipers, Taylorcraft, Stinsons, Beechcraft, Ryans and Lockheeds. Our fascination with these colorful craft was expressed by building models from kits. These kits always had full color photographs of the actual in flight on the front of the box. These inspired the young model builder to plunge into the arduous work of assembling the model from the components in the kit. We painstakingly pinned thin lengths of balsa wood along the lines of the plan provided. Then we glued cross pieces to complete the fuselage. The ribs which would form the wings had to be carefully cut from outlines on a sheet of soft balsa wood with a razor blade. Finally, we assembled the tail and attached the wheels to the landing gear which was then glued in place. The last stage was wrapping the fuselage in thin paper and, voila! It looked like a miniature of the real thing. I built my share of these models and spent many happy hours immersed in the work of making a model airplane. Actually piloting an airplane was an impossible dream. No one knew any of these elite adventurers. But it remained a dream of mine.

In 1941 the United States went to war. We knew the Germans had overrun Poland and ultimately France and the Low Countries. We also knew that they hated the Jews and were horrifically abusing them. What we didn't know was their program for extermination of the Jews. The radio and the newspapers carried almost no information about the death camps. We knew that Hitler and Tojo of Japan were the avowed enemies of our country and we knew that hundreds of thousands of men were being drafted into the military but the news media and the President were mostly silent about the victimization of the Jews of

Europe. Only after the war did we learn that the absence of news of what the Germans were doing to the Jews was a deliberate policy. Our government knew but chose to remain silent. The reason was official and unofficial anti-Semitism. President Roosevelt felt that sympathetic opinions about the Jews would not be well received by the American public, the military wanted to avoid issues that might divert their efforts to defeat the enemy and our State Department contained many upper class anti-Semites. We knew none of this. We also didn't know that the heads of the major Hollywood film studio, many of whom were Jews, chose to avoid making films that would antagonize the German government because this would jeopardize a lucrative market for their movies. When this all came to light, most of the principals were dead, but their record is shameful and so is the record of the upper crust of the U.S. State Department that denied refuge to European Jews who were trying to save their lives from the Nazi onslaught.

As for us kids, the war was brought home by constant campaigns to buy War Bonds, occasional aluminum drives to contribute aluminum to the government, and most of us had relatives who were drafted into the Army. Later, as Americans got killed in the war, a new symbol appeared; the gold star flag hung in the front windows of the bereaved. My cousin, Sidney Barr was killed in Europe in battle. His remains were never found.

The most far reaching change in civilian life was the suspension of new car production. After 1942, only used cars were available to car buyers. This struck at the heart of the American lifestyle. And then there was rationing. Gasoline was rationed and distributed on the basis of special needs. Cars had a decal in their windshields showing their category. My Dad's car had an A decal, meaning ordinary use. I suppose Doctors and policemen had different letter decals and access to more gasoline.

We saw the headlines, heard the radio broadcasts and saw the movie newsreels. All portrayed America as righteous and destined to win this war. President Franklin Roosevelt, already the hero of all but the business and wealthy classes, commanded the unalloyed support and loyalty of the great mass of citizenry. But for a thirteen year old boy growing up in Chicago, the war was remote and my life was largely untouched by it.

Meanwhile my life outside of school consisted of violin lessons, art school and Hebrew school. I wasn't very good at any of these. I took violin lessons from a middle aged Jewish violinist by the name of Edward Tiverofsky. I walked to his home every Saturday to perform the exercises he had assigned and the musical pieces I was working on. The last one before I stopped lessons was the first movement of the Mendelssohn Violin Concerto. Playing the violin was devilishly difficult and I soon developed an aversion to practicing. The week would fly by and suddenly I was faced with my Saturday lesson. I would begin practicing on Thursday or Friday and went to the lesson grimly prepared to perform badly. My instructor kept me on, I suppose, because he had to make a livelihood and his students were his main source of income.

I took these lessons from age twelve till seventeen ~ five years. I developed some proficiency, and the four years of violin studies did acquaint me with a few of the classics, but I was largely ignorant of the vast body of classical works that were the gems of western culture. I stopped taking lessons after I was seventeen, though I continued to play in the Roosevelt High School orchestra. The experience gave me an understanding the basics of music and left me with an appreciation of violin artistry.

At the same time I was attending the School of the Art Institute of Chicago; a consequence of an award in a citywide competition. There I learned the mechanics of perspective and shading. More important for me were my wanderings through the Museum that exposed me to the great classics of European and American Art. I had art skills, but no great talent. When I began high school and saw the imaginative work of some of my fellow students I realized my limitations and abandoned any thought of serious art work after my first year of High School.

CHAPTER FIVE

A NEW CULTURE

In 1942, I graduated from Tilton Elementary School where I had spent my formative years. I was 13, short and quite immature. Bowing to my parent's wishes I enrolled at Roosevelt High School many miles away, using a false address ~ my Aunt Gertie's; 4628 Monticello Avenue. My mom and dad wanted me to go to a school with a large Jewish enrollment to get me away from my Gentile friends at Tilton, whose exploits they only imagined but knew were reckless. It meant that eventually my parents would move to Albany Park ~ a long drive to my Dad's tavern. But they were willing to do it and moved during my sophomore year in High School.

Going to the high school under a false address never presented a problem. The big problem was that it took almost an hour to travel to that school from our home on the West Side of Chicago. My daily journey began with a four block walk to the nearest street car line; Pulaski Road. There I stood and waited for the red, lumbering, trolley car to arrive. During the winter months, I shivered in the cold despite a warm jacket, gloves and earmuffs. The trolleys had an open rear platform for entry; and boarding the streetcar meant stepping up on

At age 15 as a camp counselor
at Camp Horner in Round Lake, Illinois

a car stair while holding a black metal grab bar. Often the car was so crowded that there was no room inside and I had to stay on the open rear platform till enough passengers had gotten off to create some room inside, where it was warm.

The cars were crowded with working people, bundled up in their winter clothes, often giving off unpleasant smells. I would stand in the aisle with one hand on a handle at the back of each seat, carrying my books. Usually, when the crowd thinned out, I made my way through the car doors to the front platform where the operator, called the motorman, operated the controls; the power control handle, the brake lever, the sander lever, the warning bell and the door opener. There I took up a position at the front window, just to the left of the motorman, where I looked out on the passing street, the traffic and the neighborhood buildings and stores.

The trip from Washington Boulevard, on the West Side, to Lawrence Avenue, on the Northwest Side, took over forty minutes. Every major street along the route was a familiar name to me; Lake Street, Chicago Avenue, Augusta Boulevard, Grand Avenue, North Avenue, Fullerton Avenue, Diversey Avenue, (with the Olson Rug Company waterfall on the left) Belmont Avenue, Addison Street, Avondale Avenue, Irving Park (almost there), Montrose Avenue and finally, Lawrence Avenue. Here I got off and crossed Pulaski to wait for an eastbound streetcar. Once on, the trip was a short ten minutes or so to Kimball Avenue. There followed a two block walk to Wilson Avenue and the sight of Roosevelt High School.

It was a huge sprawling building, compared to Tilton Elementary School. My first impression was that I was now among

At age 16, Roosevelt High School

adults, not kids. In 1942, my freshman year, the senior boys wore long overcoats in the winter, sport jackets, white shirts and ties. The girls wore mid length skirts, tight sweaters (which emphasized their breasts), ankle socks and "saddle shoes". I was a stranger, knowing no one.

On the first day of school all incoming freshmen were sent to the auditorium to be seated in assigned "Divisions". I was in Division 101 and after locating its seating, found we were seated alphabetically. Since my name began with the letter "Z" I was seated in the fourth row. Next to me was a boy named Jimmy Winston, who despite the Anglican sounding name, was Jewish, like most of the kids at Roosevelt. Jimmy was outgoing and friendly and we soon struck up a friendship.

I was short, shy, introspective and sensitive. Like many kids, I felt that I lived in a shell; an outwardly normal teen, inwardly a withdrawn, fearful and shy boy. During four years of High School I went out with girls only four or five times. As the high school years drew to a close I was thinking only of what lay ahead, not social life. So, I was taken completely by surprise when one day, in my senior year, after chemistry class, a girl in the class came up to me, smiled and said she wanted to talk to me. The girl was Bettylene Welsh. Bettylene was considered a bit odd. She had transferred to our school in our second year and although she was pleasant and friendly, she seemed to have no close friends and no one seemed to know much about her.

Bettylene achieved sudden notoriety because of an incident in the auditorium. A group of boys who were sitting in the row behind Bettylene were being loud and raucous. One of them kept talking about black people, using a term now regarded as insulting. This was 1944 and it wasn't unusual to hear that word. But Bettylene turned around

My Prom date, Bettylene Welch and I (age 17)

and faced the boy. She told him the word was offensive and asked him to stop saying it. In 1944, it was unheard of for a girl to confront a boy like that, especially over the issue of race. The boy decided to treat this as a challenge, and when she turned back to the front, he again began using the word, only louder. Bettylene turned around again and, reaching back, gave him a hard slap in the face. This was not just unusual, it was shocking. The story flew around the school. Many said she must be a Communist. This reflected white attitudes toward race at the time. And it was she who wanted to talk to me.

Bettylene asked if I was planning to go to the Senior Prom. I shook my head, "no." The Senior Prom was a huge social event. The girls wore evening gowns and the boys wore tuxedos. The boy was also expected to give the girl a corsage. The dance was usually held at a big hotel and afterwards, groups of couples went on to a nightclub. It definitely involved dancing. I did not dance nor did I have any girlfriend to take to the prom and I had no thought of going to the event.

Bettylene then shocked me. She said, without hesitation, that she wanted to go to the prom and she asked if I would take her. She was quick to explain that she had a boyfriend, but he was in the Navy, and since she very much wanted to go to the prom, she had asked me. She made it plain that she thought I was a nice guy but there was no romantic feeling involved. Before I could say anything, she made it difficult for me to refuse by saying she would pay for everything; the tickets, the corsage and even my tuxedo rental. How could I say no? Such boldness was unheard of in the 1940's. Girls never asked guys for a date and certainly never offered to pay for everything. But this was Bettylene. She seemed very sincere and really wanted to go, so I agreed.

The prom was still more than two months off, but it was the custom to go out with the girl at least once before the prom if you had never gone out with her. I decided to ask Bettylene to go to a movie. She cheerfully agreed. I needed her address, since I was going to meet her at her home and return after the movie. The location of Bettylene's residence had always been part of the mystery that surrounded her. No one seemed to know where she lived. When she gave me the address I understood why. It was far distant from our high school. I wondered how she even came to attend our school.

We had a nice platonic evening at the movies and when I brought her back home she invited me to come up to the apartment and meet her mother. Her mother was very pleasant, but soon went to another part of the apartment, leaving us alone in the living room. Bettylene cheerfully said that since we would be dancing at the prom, we should practice a little. I dreaded this since I didn't know how to dance; I could only shuffle clumsily, holding the girl awkwardly.

After she put a record on the phonograph, it took only a few steps for Bettylene to realize that I couldn't dance. She stopped dancing, smiled at me and said, in a kindly way, "You don't dance, do you?" I abashedly acknowledged what was obvious. But Bettylene was not a girl to accept defeat. She said, "We'll have to do something about that." I did not say anything, but I doubted that anything could be done about it. Two of my female cousins had tried to teach me to dance without success. I was resigned to going to the prom and having a very uncomfortable evening.

Two days later at school, Bettylene came up to me in the hall and said excitedly, "Look at this!" She showed me an ad she had clipped out of the newspaper for the Arthur Murray Dance School. It offered a special price ~ lessons for two people for the price of one. She said, "Why don't we go and since I don't need the lessons, you get the two lessons while I sit and wait?" Again, she said, "don't worry; I'll pay for it because I really want to have fun at the prom and I want you to be able to dance." Again, I agreed.

The next week, we traveled downtown together and went up several floors to the Arthur Murray School. We were greeted by a very elegantly dressed guy wearing blue suede shoes. Bettylene wasted no time in telling him exactly what she had in mind. "We've got a prom coming up in five weeks and I want him to be able to do the foxtrot, jitterbug, waltz and rumba. Can you teach him that?"

The guy said, "Well, he'll need lessons and lots of practice." Bettylene was very firm. She said, "You give him the lessons and show him the steps and I will practice with him." The guy agreed, Bettylene paid him some money and we went right into a studio for my first lesson. Over the next five or six weeks I had lessons with the dance instructors at the school. Between these lessons Bettylene and I practiced. I found that once I knew what the steps were it was not difficult to move to the rhythm of the music. The night of the prom arrived. I wore my tuxedo. Bettylene wore a brilliant green gown with the corsage I gave her pinned in place. We danced the whole night. Nevermore was I afraid to go on a dance floor. And that is how I learned how to dance. I owed it all to Bettylene.

Throughout my first three years in High School I had been, at best, an average student. For some reason, when I began my senior year, I decided to work harder; to study my textbook assignments, to do the exercises and speak up in classroom discussion. I was no longer content to be average. I finished with very good grades. I had even acquired some of the social graces. I could speak with girls more confidently, though I was more comfortable with boys. But I was never a leader, always a follower. Although I was never adept at athletics I did develop a good swim stroke and in my sophomore year became a member of the Roosevelt High School swim team.

My career as a competitive swimmer was not a glorious one. Although the "Australian Crawl", now called Freestyle, was my best stroke, I learned and practiced the back stroke and the exhausting stroke called the "butterfly". In the "butterfly", the swimmer whips his arms over the water and pulls them down through a modified breaststroke. It takes a lot of arm strength to pull yourself forward with each stroke, and my arms were not strong. I really didn't like the breaststroke and didn't have the stamina to swim two lengths of the pool using this stroke, but for some reason, our coach entered me in the breaststroke event in our first swim meet. Had I known that, I wouldn't have asked my Dad to attend the meet. He did and I finished a distant fourth. He left after my event and never spoke of it. As a horse player, he knew what a last place finish meant.

I did find myself accepted into a small circle of guys. They had formed a fraternity; the "Zell Zorians". I have no idea what the name meant, but the group provided a circle in which I had a place. I never thought my conversational contributions, mostly adolescent gossip and witticisms, commanded any respect. Only some sixty years later, when Lennie and I traveled to Chicago and spent an evening with many of them, did I learn that my classmates listened to me with respect.

In 1943, when I was fifteen, my parents thought I would enjoy a summer in New York, staying with my father's sister Minnie and her daughters, Annie and Esther. Her third daughter, Mollie, was married and lived with her husband. Annie had visited us in Chicago and though she was four or five years older than I, we soon established a kind of brother-sister relationship. I scarcely knew Mollie or Esther, but their mother, Minnie was my aunt and she was very affectionate toward me. I stayed in the cramped apartment where Minnie and her daughters lived on Amboy Street in the section of Brooklyn called, "Brownsville". It was the very same apartment that family had occupied since the thirties, the apartment I described when Minnie was living with her then husband, Willie Marcus. He had long since passed away and Minnie had found a very nice man named Meyer Livner. They were married and now the apartment was home to him as well.

I spent two months of my fifteenth year as a guest in Minnie's home. Those two months gave me a firsthand experience of life in the Jewish ghetto of Brooklyn during the 1940's. Everyone spoke with a powerful Brooklyn accent. Their attitudes were shaped by what seemed to be a "Brooklyn culture". I became accustomed to the sights and sounds of tenement life; the dingy foyers, the mothers sitting by the open windows keeping an eye on their offspring, everyone sitting on the front stoops of the building, the "candy store" serving as the modern equivalent of the local convenience store: candy, cigarettes, soda, and snack food.

My aunt Minnie and her daughters, Esther and Annie were very kind to me and so was Meyer Livner, even though we were not related by blood. The Second World War was on and Annie was engaged to a young man who was then in the Army stationed in the South Pacific. His name was Joe Skope and Annie eagerly awaited his return.

Annie and Esther both had jobs in Manhattan, but on the weekends Annie and I spent time together, even renting bicycles and riding out to Coney Island. My sixteenth birthday was coming up on August eighth and the family planned a party for me. All of the family were there, even Esther's fiancé, Paul. I was surprised that they were doing this for me and I was completely surprised by their birthday gift ~ a gold ring with a huge gemstone, sapphire in color, in its center. I thanked them in an awkward adolescent way and put the ring on my finger. It seemed massive. I have no idea why they thought this was an appropriate gift for a sixteen year old but I suspect it was actually a mark of their respect and affection for my father, who had helped support them when they were in need. It served as a dramatic high note to my stay in the Amboy Street apartment in Brooklyn.

My adolescent years were spent in a kind of masquerade; outwardly acting the part of a boy no different than my friends, inwardly seeing myself as sensitive, highly introspective, uncomfortable in social settings and preferring reading, art and solitude. But during this period I was comfortable in my own skin, feeling little angst. I happily drove my Dad's car from time to time, navigating all over Chicago, occasionally shooting pool with my friends, going to the movies, to the Art Institute and, in the summer months, to the beach and often sitting in a neighborhood drug store with my friends sipping sodas. My constant reading gave me some insight into the broader world and the lives of men and women outside my family,

Mother and I (age 16) at Garfield Park, Chicago

My Mother was so devoted to me and so indulgent that I became a brat ~ self-centered and willful, accustomed to getting my own way and ignoring my Mother's imprecations. In fact, she was deeply committed to my dad, Harry, and would do anything for us ~ and I knew it. When my father had financial difficulties she went to work as a seamstress for a furrier. Looking back, I knew that I loved her, but I took her for granted. With my father, things were different. He too was affectionate and indulgent with me, but I felt he was a more weighty person; a man of substance and I respected him. Both of them had only the equivalent of a fourth grade education and at an early age it was clear that I was far more intellectually advanced than either of them.

CHAPTER SIX

WORKING

Most of the kids at Roosevelt had jobs; either after school or on weekends. In my freshman year, when I was fourteen, I got a job as a stock boy in a women's shoe store. The store was on Madison Street, the big commercial street near our apartment on Washington Boulevard. It was part of a large chain called, "Berland's". The year was 1942 and many of the men were in the military. This opened opportunities for teenagers like me to fill their places.

The Berland's store was big. It had a deep entryway; twenty feet or so back from the sidewalk with display windows on both sides. All the shoes in the window had style numbers posted so customers would come in and ask for a particular shoe by number. Inside, were two long rows of customer chairs ~ double rows with chairs back to back. In front was a display counter for purses and hosiery. There was a stock room in the rear where all the shoes were stored by number. Almost all the shoe sales people were men except one young woman. In front, at the hosiery and purse counter, all the sales people were young women. Our manager, the boss, was a portly fifty year old; Mr. Parker.

My job was to go out on the sales floor and pick up the shoes and shoe boxes left by the sales people and return them to their proper numbered boxes in the stock room. My pay was fifty cents an hour and I worked from six to nine on weekdays and all day on Saturday till closing time at nine o'clock. The job was tedious but I enjoyed having money to spend, even though it meant giving up some of my freedom.

After a few months, Mr. Parker came to me and said, "Hey kid, think you can sell shoes?" Even though I was uncertain, I said, "yes." It meant sixty five cents an hour plus bonuses if the customer also bought purses or hosiery. So, I, a blushing adolescent, went out on the floor and prepared to greet my first customer ~ an adult woman. It was surprisingly easy for me. The customers often had a specific style number in mind, or else a general style; closed toe or open toe pumps, closed or open heels, sandals, loafers, saddle shoes, or "baby dolls" ~ a low heeled, closed toe shoe with ankle straps. I knew the styles from having worked with them in the stock room, so it was easy for me to go back into the stock room and bring out what they wanted.

It took some time for me to be at ease in fitting shoes onto the feet of girls and women. At times it was difficult when the shoe was too small for the woman's foot, especially when the customer insisted, "I always wear a seven," and it was obvious a size seven was too small for her foot. I developed a line of talk with such phrases as, "These run small, let's try a seven and a half or an eight." Soon I could deliver flattery, "Oh, those look stunning on you."

Dealing with women and girls of all ages and kneeling at their feet in time created a sales mentality; these women were "customers" and the relation was defined by the setting; a large shoe store for women. Of course, at age fourteen and fifteen sexuality was beginning to occupy my thoughts and looking at and handling the legs of females certainly had a potential for prurience. But I still felt myself to be a "kid" and acting on any such thoughts was out of the question. As for the girls and women I dealt with, none encouraged any kind of intimacy, although I was probably too naïve and inexperienced to recognize it if they had. After all, I was a callow teenager.

I worked at Berland's for three years, selling shoes. After the first year, the novelty wore off and in its place there was a state of restlessness. I hated being cooped up in the store when I would rather be outside. Finally, I had enough of kneeling at the feet of women and selling shoes. I started thinking about an outdoor job. I wanted to do physical labor ~ a job done by men. Though I wasn't especially muscular or strong, I was a healthy, robust seventeen-year old. The summer vacation was coming and I didn't want to spend the summer in the confines of a women's shoe store.

My classmate and friend Jerry Handler had an uncle who owned a small construction company. I asked him to see if his uncle if would be willing to hire me as a laborer. A few days later, Jerry said his uncle wanted to see me before committing to a job. Mr. Handler was a short, stocky middle aged man. When we met, he looked me over and said in a kindly way, "Being a construction laborer is hard work. Think you can handle it?"

I replied with a confidence I did not feel, "Sure!" He smiled and said, "Okay, I've got a job on north Kimball near Damon. I'll tell the superintendent to try you out. Be there Monday morning at eight ready to go to work." After giving me the address, we shook hands and parted.

I immediately went out and bought a pair of work boots. So early Monday morning I showed up at the job site in my jeans and boots, looking forward to a new work experience, more masculine and more in keeping with my eagerness to use my body and my strength in a more rugged job than kneeling at the feet of women and talking about their shoes.

The job site was a typical construction site; raw dirt, stacks of lumber, piles of cement sacks, and most prominently a cement mixer. In 1945 concrete was mixed on the job, rather than delivered by a mixer truck as is done today. There was also a trailer parked on the site, containing the office. Here I met the superintendent who had been told of my hiring. After filling out some forms and recording my social security number, he pointed out a grizzled older man standing near the mixer and said, "That's Tom. He'll show you what to do."

I walked over to Tom who gave me a perfunctory greeting and then pointed out the wooden foundation forms in the ground and said, "We'll be pouring concrete in there and we have two guys working in the foundation to spread the concrete around. Our job is to keep the concrete coming. You ready?" I nodded and Tom pointed to a large mound of sand and a large mound of gravel, both of which had shovels protruding and said, "You want to shovel sand or gravel?" The sand looked easier to shovel and so I said, "Sand."

The mixer was a big yellow machine on wheels, consisting of a rotating barrel and a large scoop resting on the ground that could be raised to empty its contents into the barrel. It was connected to a hose which added water to the mix. He pointed to the sand pile and said, "twenty-five shovels of sand" and then he walked over to the gravel pile and yelled, "Fifty shovels of gravel," and began shoveling gravel onto the scoop, which had been lowered to the ground. He nodded for me to begin shoveling sand and my career as a laborer had begun.

I knew how to use a shovel from shoveling coal in Muscatine, so I felt comfortable plunging the shovel into the sand, pivoting and emptying the contents onto the mixer scoop. It was even fun. But by the tenth or fifteenth load of sand, my arms were beginning to ache and lifting each new shovelful seemed to take more effort. I glanced over at Tom and he was shoveling gravel steadily and showing no sign of weariness. "Damn!" I was not going to be outdone by this old guy and attacked the sand pile with renewed determination. When I had reached the twenty-fifth load, I stopped gratefully to catch my breath. Sweat was pouring down my face. Tom was still at it, shoveling in a steady rhythm, without a break. When he saw I had stopped, he said, "Go over there and grab a sack of cement, break it open and pour it onto the scoop." Glad for the change, I went to the pile of cement sacks to pick one up.

"Damn!" it was heavy. I was barely able to drag it off the pile, sling it on my shoulder and carry it to the mixer. It weighed over ninety pounds. Tom came over and tore it open and poured its contents into the scoop. He returned to the gravel and I returned to the sand. By this time the Chicago summer sun had begun to take its toll. I was sweating heavily and it was running into my eyes. Tom, seeing my plight, said, "Go over to that hose and wet yourself down." The cool water was delicious and brought welcome relief.

Tom had finished his fifty shovels of gravel and pulled a lever on the mixer. The scoop was pulled up and dumped its contents into the revolving drum. I thought we would stop and rest, but I was wrong.

He lowered the scoop and he went right back to shoveling gravel.

"How does he do it?" I asked myself and came up with the wrong answer. Maybe it's easier to shovel gravel than sand. So I said, "Hey Tom, how about switching. I'll work on the gravel and you take the sand."

"Okay," he replied and walked over to my sand pile. As soon as I started shoveling the gravel I realized my mistake. It was harder to work than sand. More effort was needed to plunge the shovel into the gravel and it was just as heavy, maybe heavier, to lift than sand. Tom finished his twenty five sand shovelfuls and came over to help out with the gravel. It was going to be a long, hard day.

Someone had started the motor that rotated the mixer drum and I stood with Tom watching our joint contribution to the mix being converted to concrete in the mixer. Our respite was brief because Tom pointed to two empty wheelbarrows and said, "Get one of those and wheel it up the ramp." One of the other laborers had laid a plank to serve as a ramp leading from the mixer to the top of the foundation forms. I grabbed the handles of the barrow and wheeled it into position, stopping just below the mouth of the mixer. A metal trough was attached at the mouth of the mixer and when Tom pulled a lever the barrel tilted and wet concrete poured down the trough into my wheel barrow. When it was full, Tom raised the mixer, cutting off the flow.

Now came another test of my strength; I had to lift the wheelbarrow and push it and its contents, wet concrete, up the ramp to the foundation, then lift the handles dumping the contents into the space between the wooden forms. Straining, I lifted the barrow and with a mighty grunt, began shoving it along the ramp. When I got to the top one of the other laborers came over and helped me lift the handles into the air so the contents would pour out into the forms. Then it was back down the ramp to position the barrow for another load.

Once again I strained and grunted to move concrete from the mixer to the foundation forms. On my third trip disaster struck. As I wheeled the heavy, unstable wheelbarrow up the ramp, suddenly I felt the barrow tilting to the left. Despite fighting with all my strength to right it, the tilt continued till all the contents spilled out on the ground. I was horrified at the sight of wet concrete all over the ground. But Tom took it in stride and without any recriminations, picked up a water hose and washed away the spill. His casual, matter of fact, response told me this was not a rare occurrence. I was ashamed at this demonstration of my weakness, but grateful that no serious damage was done and even more grateful it didn't result in my being fired on the spot.

I worked at this site for about a week till the foundation work was finished and then I was assigned to be a carpenter's helper on a store remodel. This was a lot less strenuous; carrying lumber, holding components in position, bringing fixtures into the store and generally making myself useful to the carpenter on the job. I spent the entire summer working for Handler Construction Company at eighty five cents an hour, an increase over my pay at Berland's shoes. The experience stood me in good stead and I worked as a construction laborer during the summer months for the next four years, except for one summer when I worked as a warehouseman.

In the summer of 1947, when I was nineteen, Handler Construction had no job for me and I went looking. Again, I sought physical labor and one day spotted an ad in the newspaper, "Warehouse laborer. Good pay. Flexible hours. Call Lawrence Warehouse Co." I called the phone number in the ad and was happy to learn the job was still open. All they wanted was my Social Security number. The location, however, was a real surprise. The warehouse was in the yards of the Chicago and Northwestern Railroad on Kinzie and Pulaski Road, the very same yard adjoining the rail line where I had spent hundreds of hours observing locomotives. I had always been curious about what was inside this gigantic yard that was the destination of so many locomotives and freight trains. But getting into it would require climbing over a fence, crossing the tracks and then possibly confronting a hostile railroad employee. No, it would remain off-limits. Now, I could enter it legitimately and see for myself what was inside.

The warehouse official on the phone simply said, "You know where the Northwestern Yards are?"

"Yeah," I replied.

"Okay. Come up the stairs under the viaduct on Pulaski Road and about a block ahead of you is our warehouse. The foreman is Louie and just give him your name. He'll be expecting you. Be there at eight tomorrow morning."

Getting this job was absurdly easy. Later I came to understand why. The next morning I found myself mounting the stairs to the Railroad yard ~ an area that had been a mystery to me for years. Finally, I would be allowed to enter the yard without risk of challenge as a trespasser. Once in the yard there were tracks everywhere and strings of railroad cars sitting stationary, as though waiting for an assignment. Ahead I saw a large structure. That had to be the warehouse. Why put a warehouse in a railroad yard? I didn't have any idea, but it struck me as incongruous with its surroundings. Then as I got closer I saw tracks leading into the building. It really wasn't so much a building as a large shed, with both ends open. I entered through one of the open ends and saw two box cars sitting on tracks in the building. There was a group of men unloading one of the cars and I walked up to them. One of them, a short stocky man with impressive biceps, looked at me and left the group to approach me.

"You Alvin?" he said to me. I nodded and he said, "I'm the foreman, Louie. Here's the deal, you'll be working with a crew of six guys loading zinc into a car out in the yard. For today, you'll be helping unload this one here and tomorrow we'll load zinc out there. The pay is by the carload. One car, twenty bucks a man. Two cars, forty bucks. We pay every day. When a crew finishes a car, it can go home or do another car. Once a car is started it has to be finished or no pay. Understand?"

This was far more money than I had ever made in construction and the job sounded easier. But the work was actually backbreaking. They paid daily because few of the workers stayed more than a week. The company sent a truck to the Skid Row regularly to enlist new workers to replace the ones who had quit. That explained the appearance of my fellow laborers ~ itinerants, alcoholics and drifters who worked only to earn enough to get by.

The first day I worked in the warehouse unloading a boxcar holding large cases of soap. Not bad. But the next day we were led to an area of the rail yard where a stack of zinc ingots was piled in a square eight feet high. Louie had the crew bring over a heavy steel conveyor ~ a fifteen foot long steel conveyor consisting of rollers mounted on side rails. It took two men to lift it into place.

An empty box car stood on a track directly in front of the ingot pile. Louie supervised the placement of two sawhorses near the box car and then laid two wooden planks across them making a platform two feet below the sill of the freight car door. He had the crew put one end of the conveyor on the pile of ingots and the other end sloped down to the platform. Then he set up another heavy steel conveyor inside the boxcar, with one end raised on some two by fours and the other leading to the interior of the car.

Now it was clear how we were going to work; two men would work on the pile, lifting ingots onto the conveyor, two would work on the platform at the entrance to the car lifting the ingots off the conveyor as they rolled down and lifting them onto the conveyor in the car and two would work inside the car stacking the ingots on the floor of the car as they came down the conveyor.

I was the youngest in a six man crew. The others had worked with their hands all their life and they were tough. They all had nick names and to all of them I was, "kid". The routine began as the two men on the pile dropped the first two ingots on the conveyor and they began rolling down toward me and my partner standing on the opposite side of the conveyor. I bent down to pick up the first ingot. It was not difficult to get a grip on it because the top surface of the two foot long metal slab was longer than the bottom, making a slanting front and rear edge. The ingots were topside up so picking one up was only a matter of grabbing the front and back edge and lifting. Ah, lifting.

Each ingot weighed about forty pounds and lifting one took some effort. They were coming down the conveyor in a steady procession and each ingot had to be quickly lifted and placed on the conveyor in the box car and the two man crew inside had to promptly bend down to pick up the next one and lift it. To prevent an ingot from dropping off the end of the conveyor, we stuck one vertically between the last two rollers. The work was a non-stop effort of bending and lifting. My partner and I alternated but we had to be alert to avoid having our fingers smashed by the next ingot coming down the conveyor.

The constant bending and lifting began to take its toll. After an hour or so I began to doubt that I could keep this up all day. Again, the Chicago summer sun was beating down and I regularly had to wipe the sweat out of my eyes. There was another, unanticipated problem; soot. I think it came from the dust in the interior of the box car and soon my throat was dry and dusty. When I cleared it, my spittle was flecked with black. The work was grueling but I simply gritted my teeth and worked ~ harder than I had ever worked in my life. The other men in my crew were sweating too, but never slowed their pace.

About ten in the morning we took a short break. A food truck drove into the rail yard and stopped at our car. Several of us went over and bought a pint of milk. Some bought sandwiches, but I had brought my lunch. Around noon, we stopped for lunch. I sat on our platform, almost exhausted, and ate my lunch, guzzling the entire pint of milk. I wanted to sit there as long as possible, feeling drained of strength. Finally, one of the men who worked on the pile said, "O.K. boys, let's get going."

My crew resumed our labors. As the afternoon wore on, I wondered if I could endure much more of this. By now I was operating

116

on sheer will power. There were two other piles of ingots nearby and other crews were working on them. I looked over at them and they looked wearier than we did. About three thirty in the afternoon we finished loading our car. Somebody called Louie over. He looked at the interior of the car to satisfy himself that it was fully loaded and then said, "Okay, boys, you can start a second car if you want, or you can call it a day and go home."

Wow! Finishing work at three thirty was new for me. When our crew unanimously decided to quit for the day I was happy, though exhausted as I had never been before. I seriously considered quitting the job and not returning the next day. But a stubborn voice in me said, "No." So I did return the next day and the next and the next for the rest of the summer.

I was tougher and stronger than I had ever been and took pride in my tenacity at sticking with the job. After working there for ten days I was the most senior employee in the yard, but for Louie, the foreman. All the rest had quit, to be replaced by new recruits from skid row.

One Saturday, I joined some of my friends from Roosevelt High School at a local drug store when three former high school classmates, all big guys and athletes came over to me and asked about my job. They had heard about this high paying job and wanted to know if they could be hired at Lawrence Warehouse. I told them it was likely they would, because the company was constantly looking for laborers. I gave them the number and told them who to ask for. The following week I was pleasantly surprised to see the three of them bending and lifting on a pile of ingots near ours. It seems my crew was tougher and faster than theirs, because we finished at two thirty and began walking out of the yard. My school mates, looking weary and drenched in sweat stared at us enviously. They were far from finished with their pile, either because they were slower than my crew or took more breaks. I'm not proud to admit it, but I was secretly pleased that I had out-performed these athletic types. They quit two days later. Call it schadenfreude.

Working as a warehouse laborer and a construction laborer gave me what I wanted; a manly sense of self. Over the years I continued to work as a construction laborer and it provided me with the money to finish law school in later years. I was confident in my strength and fitness and I knew something about construction job protocol. It also gave me the ability to relate to the "common man", a facility that stood me in good stead the rest of my life.

With pals at Roosevelt High School at age 17. I am at the far right.

CHAPTER SEVEN

TOWARD ADULTHOOD

In 1946 I graduated from high school. I was not a stellar student, nor a stellar athlete, but I grew from a shy, introverted boy to a more confident and accomplished adolescent. Now it was time to take the logical next step; college. Very few of my classmates had families able to send them out of state to fancy universities. A few went to the University of Illinois in Champaign-Urbana, about a hundred and forty miles south of Chicago. Most chose to go on to a local city Junior College; Wright Jr. College on the Northwest Side of the city. This was the most practical and easy step and that's what I did. Like most, I had no idea what career I wanted, nor did I have any notion of what a college curriculum looked like. I just went.

Wright was one of three city-operated two year colleges in Chicago. The main attraction was that it was free, or almost free. I started in February 1946. The Second World War had ended six months earlier and hundreds of thousands of veterans took advantage of the GI Bill and flocked to colleges around the nation. Wright had been occupied by the U.S. Navy as an electronics training facility during the war and was turned back to the city only a month or so before the opening of school. It was amusing to see painted on the toilet doors, "Enlisted Men's Head," giving evidence of the school's previous occupant.

Two of my friends and I took a bus to the college and arrived to find the place swarming with young men and women, many of them veterans. It was the first year of civilian operation of the college and the atmosphere was hectic. There was a makeshift set of arrangements with hand lettered signs taped to the doors of many of the offices. One large sign read: "Registration in The Gymnasium." In the gym were large crowds waiting in lines to register. The administration had set up three tables at one end of the gym with signs: "A to L, M to R, and R to Z". At each table sat a counselor with registration forms. There was one chair for the registrant.

I duly took my place in the line leading to the "R to Z" table. Everyone had sent in applications so the counselors had some idea who we were. By the time I reached the counselor's table it was apparent that he was already weary, but when I sat down at his table, he asked if I knew anything about the College's basic curriculum. I didn't, so he proceeded to explain to me that it was based on four required core courses: Physical Science, Biological Science, Social Science and Humanities. These had to be taken during the two years of study. Beyond these there were many electives the student could choose.

I had no preference, so he said, "Let's see. We'll start you with Social Science I, Biological Science I and you can take two electives. How about English?"

"Okay," I said.

Then he said, "You should take one more. How about History?"

"What kind of History?" I asked.

"American or European," he answered.

"American," I quickly decided.

"Early or late?" he asked.

My response was one which generations of friends have since laughed at. I said, "Well, I don't like to get up too early, so put me in late."

The counselor looked at me in disbelief. Then he put down his pen and looked at my file. He was scanning my grade point average and then said, "Since you graduated, I have to assume you have average intelligence. Early American History covers the discovery period up till the Civil War. Late covers the Civil War to the present time."

Embarrassed at my ignorance, I quickly said, "Early."

Thus began my college career.

My next two years at the college led to an intellectual awakening. The course in International Relations introduced me to the principles of national sovereignty. I felt this was the touchstone to understanding international conflict. The United Nations was then in its early, formative years and was seen by some political groups as a threat to American national sovereignty, particularly on the far right.

At age 18, Wright Junior College

I certainly never dreamed it would have any application to American Indian affairs -- the field in which I ultimately spent my career.

I found myself studying hard in the social sciences and the result was a political awakening. My reading introduced me to what seemed the anti-progressive force of the National Association of Manufacturers - a lobbying group aligned with the interests of large corporations. I came to understand the struggle for political dominance of competing visions of America; the laissez-faire or free market forces and the New Deal philosophy; government which was humane and did not hesitate to restrain business in the interest of human values. I was a product of the Roosevelt Era, an era when the nation expected the federal government to be activist and protective of the working class. These values were part of my outlook before I went to Wright, but my reading gave them factual force.

I discovered that not only politics, but all my other studies were stimulating. I delved into the then new field of General Semantics and read S.I. Hayakawa and Alfred Korzybski. I took a math course, a subject that had been my nemesis in High School and decided to test the hypothesis that my disinterest and poor performance were a result of laziness. So I worked hard, did all the math problems, even the optional ones, and received an "A" in the course. But rather than convincing me that I could, if I chose, be an engineer, it convinced me of the opposite, because I saw how easily some of my classmates mastered the subject while I had to work extra hard to get that "A".

I took courses in Psychology, Sociology, Social Psychology, Political Science, Biological Science, Physical Science and Humanities. While all of these studies shaped my intellect, the one that left a lasting legacy was the course in International Relations. It was taught by a youthful, tall young instructor named Hymen Chausow. He provided such a clear picture of the forces that governed international relations that I never forgot them. The most important lesson concerned the concept of national sovereignty; the absolute right of a government to act as the supreme law maker over its territory.

Swimmers repeat as state champs

Bottom row (L. to R.): Arnie Glass, Coach E. R. Bradley, Bill Rix, Herb Klein. 2nd row: Don Fahrback, Tony Kozakiewicz, George Jorgensen, Chuck Svendsen. Top row: Al Ziontz, Al Glass, Joe Wapotish.

With junior college swim team at age 19.
I am in top row far left.

This was the first time I had heard of the centrality of this ancient idea. The principle was very timely, since it was then the subject of heated political controversy. Remember, this was 1947 and the United Nations was in its early formative years. The political right smelled a left wing plot to subordinate our government to an international body. The John Birch society, a right wing organization that suspected Communist conspiracies everywhere, quickly launched an attack on the U.N. as a threat to U.S. sovereignty. The argument escalated and resulted in a proposal to amend the U.S. Constitution to prohibit any treaty or rule of an international body from superseding American law. The proposed amendment was later introduced by Senator John Bricker of Ohio, and came to be known as the "Bricker Amendment".

I became fascinated by the concept of National Sovereignty, particularly as it explained the sources of conflict between nations. The issue remained a subject of political controversy till 1954 when the Supreme Court ruled that no international treaty could override the Bill of Rights. The Bricker Amendment quietly died.

My instructor in International Relations, Mr. Chausow, became my ideal. He had served in the Army Air Force in the Second World War and was decorated for heroic action. After being discharged, he attended the University of Chicago where he received a Master's Degree in Political Science. His lectures were so clear and insightful that I wanted to follow his example; go to the University of Chicago, study political science and become a college instructor. It seemed to settle the question of what I would do in life after college.

My years at Wright were also years of athletics; the swim team and the track team. On the swim team, I practiced and competed, never winning a race but usually placing second or third. Why track? Well, I found that I enjoyed running and wanted to be better. After time trials, the coach said, "Ziontz, I'm putting you in the two mile run."

"The two mile run?" I asked.

"Yeah. You're too slow for the other events and you don't need a lot of speed for it, just endurance. If you train hard you can do it."

The message was clear and correct; I was too slow for any other event. So I began training for the two mile run. It was hard. Grueling is the better word. Many times I was running the second mile around the oval track and wanted desperately to stop. But I stuck with it and ran the event in several meets, finishing third, fourth or fifth, but at least finishing. When I look back, I see once again that something was motivating me to show that I was, if not athletic, at least not weak.

Meanwhile, my father made a momentous decision, one that proved to be his undoing. In the final years of the second world war, his tavern was prospering and he began to think of acting on a vision that he had for several years: to open a barbecue restaurant. Barbecued spareribs had become a very popular item at the time and having eaten at several barbecue restaurants, he thought that he could make money running such an establishment, even though he had no experience operating a restaurant.

An A&P grocery store a hundred yards south of his tavern on Pulaski Road had just become vacant. He was moved to act on his dream and rented the store. Now came the hard part. He didn't have enough capital to finance the extensive interior construction for the kind of restaurant he wanted; one with an authentic brick barbecue oven and an attractive interior. So he borrowed $30,000 from a finance company and began.

I saw the design that the architect had prepared. It called for a rectangular interior with booths along the sides, a cashier's post in front, and a large kitchen, featuring a brick barbecue. The only feature that was at all distinctive was the glass brick for the front wall of the exterior. It was this that gave my father the idea for a name: "The Glass House".

Since his tavern, "The Economy Club", was doing very well, he felt that he could operate both. Having two businesses meant he was no longer a simple tavern owner and perhaps could lead to more expansive business undertakings. But he certainly had to have somewhat grandiose ideas to think he could operate two separate and different businesses successfully, even though he had never operated a restaurant.

He was very excited about the barbecue restaurant and spent most of his time there. The Glass House opened to large crowds of customers, filling the restaurant and even waiting for an empty booth. It seemed to validate his vision. But he soon encountered the woes of every restaurant operator; unreliable and even dishonest kitchen workers, turnover in waitresses and busboys and absence of any controls over his cash flows. He was operating as he always had; without records and only a general sense of profitability.

Occasionally, I worked at the Glass House; as a cashier and also driving a delivery van, a Jeep he bought for home deliveries of orders of ribs or barbecue sandwiches.

In its first year, the Glass House seemed to do very well; there were plenty of customers and it attracted Chicagoans from distant neighborhoods. But that was mainly because it was a novelty. Harry knew lots of people and they heard about his new restaurant and came.

One night two customers with an ominous aura came in. They were members of the Chicago mob, known as "the Outfit". I was there and my dad quietly told me who they were. One was Paul "Needle nose" Labriola, and the other was known as "Marty the Ox". They had parked in front of the restaurant in a long black Cadillac, a car popular with important mobsters. Each wore long black overcoats with silk collars and carried themselves with the confidence of power.

Labriola was a member of the Chicago Mafia and like others, he was a murderer. Marty was a gang strongman; an enforcer, physically intimidating because of his size and known for beating up people severely. Word quickly spread and soon everyone knew who those two men were. They were waited on by one of the prettiest waitresses. This was not lost on them and Labriola began a flirtatious conversation with her. After finishing their ribs, Labriola had a quiet conversation with the waitress, causing her to smile flirtatiously. Of course, I had no idea what passed between them, but Labriola being somewhat of a Don Juan, I thought it was likely that he set up some kind of meeting with her outside the restaurant.

After the first year, the novelty of the "Glass House" seemed to wear off and there was a noticeable drop off in the business. In the meantime, it seemed the income from the tavern was also declining and my father decided it needed full time attention. So, he made a second mistake; he leased it out to two guys. After a year under their management the business of the tavern had declined so much that my father had to decide: either keep the Glass House and sell the tavern or keep the tavern and sell the Glass House.

Whether it was pride or bad business judgment I don't know, but he decided to sell the tavern and keep the restaurant. This was a second mistake and it proved to be disastrous. The income from the Glass House continued to decline and its profits dwindled till he was in serious trouble with his creditors. Soon he was able to get restaurant supplies on a cash only basis. The end was foreseeable, but he continued to hope for some kind of turnaround. It never came. Finally, the day arrived when he had no more cash to pay suppliers or workers and there was no alternative. The Glass House closed. It was 1949.

CHAPTER EIGHT

TOWARD A CAREER

As I approached the midpoint of my second and last year at Wright Junior College, I had to begin thinking of a career. My interests were clearly in the field of political science and my model was my former instructor, Mr. Chausow. That was it. I would become a teacher of International Relations. Still, my career choice was somewhat vague and I had no idea what school to go to, maybe Roosevelt College in downtown Chicago, or the University of Illinois, although this was financially beyond the reach of my parent's income and I had no idea how I could do this. Going to The University of Chicago was a daunting idea. Chicago was known as a school of extremely bright students and no doubt was also expensive. While these thoughts were taking shape, the whole issue suddenly became complicated.

One afternoon my dad asked me, "Well, sonny, what are you going to do after you graduate from college?"

When I told him my idea of becoming a teacher, he made a face and said, "A teacher! You'll starve. There's no money in teaching. You should be a lawyer."

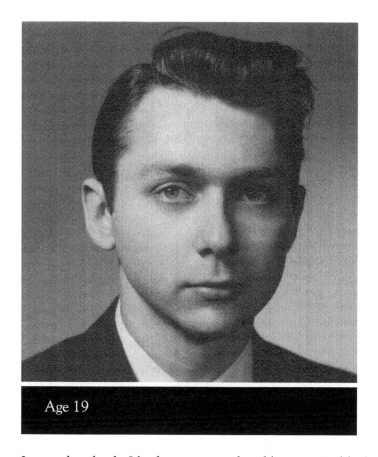

Age 19

I was taken back. I had never considered law as suitable for me. My conception of lawyers, admittedly more hypothetical than realistic, was that they were a reactionary group. Lawyers conjured up an image of bombastic, argumentative egotists. Either that or pettifoggers; men who spent their professional lives fussing over obscure passages in documents. Neither appealed to me. I was a highly idealistic young intellectual ~ interested in work that improved society. So I said to my Dad, "Dad, I'm not cut out to be a lawyer. It's not for me."

He was not so easily put off. "Alvin, you're a smart boy and you have a good mouth. I think you would be a fine lawyer. Besides, you can make a good living, maybe even big money, practicing law."

Our discussion about my career didn't end with this exchange. It went on for weeks. Finally, I said, "Look, Dad. They have a scientific way of measuring how good you would be as a lawyer ~ they have tests." I was thinking of aptitude tests, which I had taken in High School and which had accurately predicted that engineering was not for me. So he said, "All right, take the test." I pointed out it was not so simple. I had to find out where I could get the testing and it would cost some money. He responded, "Okay, find out and I'll pay. If the tests show you should be a lawyer, will you study to be a lawyer?" I could hardly say no, but responded, "If the tests show I'm not cut out to be a lawyer, will you accept that?" He shrugged his shoulders in acquiescence.

After a bit of searching I found that the Psychology Department of the Illinois Institute of Technology administered vocational aptitude tests. The cost was $150. My father somehow came up with the money and I scheduled an interview at the college. A psychologist discussed my reasons for wanting the test and then gave me a date to begin the testing which would require three days.

On the appointed date I sat down in the testing room and began filling out an extended and intrusive set of test forms, asking questions such as, "On entering a party, do you join the crowd or find a chair in a corner." Of course I answered "find a chair in a corner." I thought I could detect the purpose of the questions and my answers were designed to show I was not a "hail fellow well met" but a shy introvert ~ a personality type ill-suited to be a lawyer. The tests covered spatial analysis; reading comprehension, personal values and tastes and life goals. I was confident I had presented a picture of one suited to the life of teaching and not law.

At the end of the exhaustive testing, a staff member told me my responses would be evaluated and I would be given an appointment with one of the psychologists to explain the meaning of the scoring. Three days later I received a manila envelope in the mail containing a sheet showing my test scores on a graph with lines corresponding to my abilities and values relative to mean values in various fields of work. With it was a letter summarizing the meaning of the graph in succinct words. The key part was the summary: "You are best suited to a career in Law, Journalism or Business."

I was stunned. What about teaching? It was not mentioned. I called and asked for an appointment with the grading psychologist. Three days later I sat in the office of a pleasant woman and explained my quandary. She went through the various tests and explained that they showed unequivocally that while I was a young man of high intelligence who could do well in almost any field I chose, my values coincided most closely to those in the three identified fields. Since I still seemed dubious, she asked, "Why don't you come back and take the Law Aptitude Test?"

I did and got the results: 96th percentile. The psychologist said the test had proven predictive value. There was nothing more to argue about. The issue was settled; I would become a lawyer.

Now I had to go about selecting a school. There were six law schools in Chicago: The University of Chicago, Northwestern, Loyola, De Paul, Chicago Kent and John Marshall. The last two were out. Loyola, though secular was a Catholic school with little distinction. John Marshall and Chicago Kent were not held in high regard.

Northwestern and De Paul law school required either an undergraduate degree or three years of college. They were also expensive.

I sent for catalogues from Northwestern, Chicago and the University of Illinois, even though the latter was out of my reach because it was not in Chicago but in Champaign-Urbana, a hundred and forty miles south of Chicago. Like the others it required an undergraduate degree. But when I studied the catalog of the University of Chicago Law School, I found they had two programs; one requiring an undergraduate degree followed by three years of law school and the other admitting applicants with only two years of undergraduate schooling followed by four years of law school. To qualify for admission to this program, however, you needed a high grade point average in undergraduate studies and passing an entrance examination.

In 1948 I applied to the University of Chicago four year law school program in hopes of starting law school without having to find a local college and going to school another year or two. Apparently my grades at Wright were good enough to warrant consideration and I was asked to take an entrance exam at the Law School.

A trip to the University of Chicago campus from Albany Park involved a forty five minute ride on the "El", including a change of trains and a bus ride. The bus took me to 55th Street and University Avenue and from there it was a fifteen minute walk to the campus. In my eyes, the buildings of the University were a spectacular sight; Gothic stone structures scattered over a ten block area. It was nothing like the rest of Chicago. The Law School was in its own building; a large gothic stone affair announcing its identity on a bronze plaque: "The Law School of The University of Chicago".

I was directed to an empty class room and there I took the admissions test. A few days later I received in the mail the cheerful news that I had passed and would be admitted as a first year student in the class of 1951. I also received an application and a financial needs form. Since my father's business was bankrupt and we were surviving on my mother's earnings as a seamstress, it was clear I did not have the ability to pay the established tuition. A week or two later I received a letter announcing I had been awarded a scholarship for my first year. Renewal of the scholarship was contingent on my grades.

Classes at the University of Chicago began in September, but I had graduated from Wright in February. So I was looking at a seven month hiatus before I could start on my law education. I didn't want to waste this much time without any schooling and besides, I felt was not adequately prepared for Law School. Having some money saved from working, I decided to attend the University of Illinois at Champaign Urbana for a semester, taking courses which might be germane to law school.

My time at Illinois was far more meaningful than I would have predicted. I enrolled in two courses; Logic and Criminology, both appearing relevant to law. But first I had to find a place to live. The campus was bulging at the seams with returning veterans as well as the normal volume of students. After some searching I was directed to a student rooming house in Urbana ~ the twin city to Champaign where the main campus of the University was located. The house was located on Main Street and was called "Main Manor". It was an old residence that had been converted to student housing. There were rooms on each of the two floors and a room which had been constructed on the glassed in front porch. It was then available and I took it.

Graduation from Wright Junior College

The landlord had told me that my room was equipped for two roomers and that I could expect a roommate when another renter showed up. Meanwhile I had it to myself. The rooms had been occupied by students before, as I discovered when I sat down at the desk. Tacked to the wall over the desk was a penis skin, removed from a cadaver by a previous occupant. It was an ugly thing and I carefully removed it and threw it in the garbage. I was alone only about a week when my new roommate showed up. He was a taciturn Air Force veteran who had very little to say to me. Though we occupied the same quarters for three months, we might as well have been strangers. The only communications were his loud and frequent belches, a result of some digestive disorder.

The other tenants were not nearly so distant. All were older than me and drank beer, constantly it seemed. There was a pay phone on the main floor just below the stair well and many of my neighbors used the coin slot as a beer bottle opener. As a result, the beer that splashed on the coin slot created a sticky surface, so that often when a coin was inserted, it would stick and not fall down the chute. Other users would put in more coins which also stuck, until the weight of the accumulated coins caused them all to fall at once, creating a kind of slot machine, with the lucky caller cashing in on five or ten coins.

Most of the other tenants were in this university town to carouse, rather than study. On the weekends some would stand on the second floor stairs and throw empty beer bottles down into the stairwell creating a hideous crash of breaking glass and a pile of bottle shards. Later, some of these guys or some janitor cleaned up the pile. And the phone company removed the phone because of its misuse.

I too experimented with drinking and went to a local beer hall with some of my neighbors. We drank what was then a popular beer called, "Glueck's Steit". It must have had a high alcohol content, because after two or three bottles I walked back home unsteadily through an alcoholic haze. One weekend we had a beer party at the house, which was called by my fellow roomers, not Main Manor, but Main Manure. The beer party featured a keg in the basement. After everyone was sufficiently sloshed, someone suggested a snake dance out of the house and down the street. About twenty of us formed a line, holding one hand on the shoulder of the guy in front of us and we went dancing out, doing a kind of Conga. We emerged onto the sidewalk and danced about twenty five yards down the sidewalk till one of the drunken geniuses spotted a parked car whose doors were unlocked. He opened both rear doors and the entire line danced through the car, entering on one side and emerging on the other.

It soon was apparent that most of my housemates were not serious students but were there to party and drink. One of these lived on the second floor and I occasionally stopped by his room to chat with him. He had a typewriter on his desk but I never saw him use it. I had never learned to type but the thought occurred to me that if his typewriter was sitting idle, maybe he would let me practice typing on it. He cheerfully agreed and I got an instruction book from the local bookstore and began practicing. After a couple of weeks I had developed some proficiency.

One day, as I was sitting in his room practicing my typing, I heard loud voices coming from the room next door. At first it was just background noise, but then I began to listen more carefully and it seemed there was some kind of argument going on and one of the speakers had an Italian accent. I was intrigued and went out into the hall to listen more closely. The argument seemed to start and stop. My curiosity overcame my reluctance to intrude on the privacy of a stranger and I knocked on the door. In the doorway stood a slender young man, clearly an American, looking friendly. When I told him I was listening to the argument he broke into a laugh, saying there was no argument; it was only him. He was rehearsing a scene from Mark Twain's "Innocents Abroad" in preparation for a radio show, he told me, and it was his voice speaking first as an American and then as an Italian. Then he introduced himself, "My name's Don Walker, what's yours?" I introduced myself and a friendship was born.

Don spoke with a country twang and I learned he had grown up in a small downstate rural town called Morrisonville. He smiled easily and was a bubbly, outgoing, self-confident young man. I later found out he was one of the University cheerleaders and he was also the entertainment manager of the Student Union Club, arranging for shows, booking acts and functioning as the Master of Ceremonies.

He was friendlier than any of the other occupants of Main Manor and the two of us spent a lot of our free time together. One day he told me he was going home to visit his mom and sisters in Morrisonville the following weekend and invited me to join him. It was an attractive idea and I accepted.

Morrisonville was about eighty miles south of Champaign, sixty miles north of St. Louis. It was in what Chicagoans called "downstate" Illinois. I packed a light overnight bag and the morning of our departure met with Don. I had no idea how we were going to travel there. Don, in his typical jaunty way, said, "Oh, we'll hitchhike.

It's easy. Done it many times."

He was right. First we got a ride to Decatur Illinois and then a second ride to Morrisonville. We arrived about eleven in the morning and began walking down the main business street of the town. Everyone seemed to know Don, one shop owner saying, "I heard you're on the radio in Champaign." In five or six blocks we arrived at his family home where I was expected and greeted warmly by his mother. After sitting at the kitchen table and talking for a while, Don said, "Hey, how would you like to go to my uncle's farm with me?" I had never been on a farm and enthusiastically accepted.

His mom said, "Why don't you take my car, Don." Together we drove some ten miles or so out of Morrisonville and turned up a dirt road leading to a farmhouse. Inside three or four women were working in the kitchen and greeted Don and me warmly. Don introduced me. They were his aunts and cousins and were preparing a mid-day meal for the farmhands who were due to arrive shortly. When they did, we all sat down at a huge table in the kitchen completely covered with dishes of food; ham, fried chicken, gravy, potatoes, biscuits and pies. I had never eaten such a huge mid-day meal, but the men who had been working in the field scarfed down almost everything in sight. They were hungry and the women who had prepared their lunch knew what to expect. After lunch Don introduced me to his uncle who owned the farm and invited me to go out to the fields with him, riding on his tractor. This was great fun and I now saw firsthand the life of those who worked the land. It was an education.

That night Don and I went out and met some girls in town. The girls were jolly and far more forward than the Jewish girls I had known in Albany Park. Don later laughingly told me that small town girls were not shy and there were lots of hi-jinks between the boys and girls in Morrisonville.

Don Waker (left) and I in Morrisonville, Illinois 1949

The following morning was Sunday and that meant church. I asked Don whether it was acceptable to have a Jewish guy attending services in a Christian church. Don cheerfully assured me it was not a problem. Everyone in town knows about you and they will treat you nicely. I had never attended a Christian church service before and tried to conform to what everyone in the congregation was doing; standing when they stood and singing when they sang. But I had a problem; we had stayed out late the night before and rose early Sunday morning, so I was sleepy. When the pastor began to drone on in his sermon, I struggled to stay awake but occasionally nodded off. Don would awaken me with a sharp nudge of his elbow and said, "Hey; they all know you're Jewish and it wouldn't look good for you to be sleeping during the service."

So I straightened up and tried to be alert. But I nodded off once again and was awakened by the sound of the worshipper in the row in front of me standing up. So, I too stood up. But Don grabbed my sleeve, and hissed, "Sit down. The pastor is calling for volunteers to do missionary work. You don't want to do that, do you?"

I quickly resumed my seat. Don was right about one thing; everyone greeted me cordially as I exited with the Morrisonville church goers. It was an enlightening experience.

The semester in Champaign-Urbana was notable for one other experience: I lost my virginity. I was nineteen and had never experienced the sexual act. But one of the guys in Main Manor, with whom I had become friendly, an older guy, said to me, "I'm going to Danville this weekend to get laid. There's a house there with prostitutes. Wanna come with and get laid?" My heart leaped. I never dreamed of such an opportunity. "Sure," I said. "How much does it cost?"

"Twenty five bucks. Not too bad." I had the money and we agreed to leave Saturday evening. There was an electric tram running from Champaign to Danville, a town about twenty five miles east. I was nervous, but my companion, who had obviously availed himself of the Danville women before, was quite nonchalant.

When we got off the tram my friend walked confidently several blocks down a residential street till we reached a house that was actually marked by a shining red light on the porch. We entered a living room with eight or nine women sitting in chairs around the room. The madam collected our twenty five dollars and said, "Take your pick, boys."

None of them were attractive and they all seemed to be thirty five to forty years old. I was too nervous to look carefully at all of them and simply chose the first woman I saw, who smiled at me. The woman, in her late thirties, with dyed dishwater blonde hair and a lumpy body, led me upstairs and into a bedroom. She quickly perceived my nervousness about the coming event and asked me, "Have you ever had sex with a woman before?"

When I said, "No," she smiled and looked at me benignly and said, "So this is your first time?" When I affirmed that it was she moved toward me and in a kindly way said, "Go ahead and take off your clothes. What did you say your name was?"

When I told her, she opened her dressing gown and stood before me stark naked. I was unprepared for the sight. She was not reticent about allowing her nude body to be seen in full display and this, perhaps more than the body itself, stunned me. I was not expecting such nonchalant, matter of fact, female nudity. But on reflection it was obvious she had disrobed innumerable times before men and nudity was familiar to her.

I don't think I ever learned her name and it didn't really matter. The entire transaction was almost impersonal. After she examined me closely for evidence of venereal disease and applied a condom, she laid down on the bed, smiled at me and said, "C'mere honey."

The act was joyless and over in less than five minutes. So this was sex, I thought. It was a far cry from the sexual ecstasy I had long fantasized. In fact, the experience was tawdry. When I arrived back at my rooms in Urbana, I immediately took a long hot shower, to cleanse myself from the sense of contamination I felt.

Meanwhile, I was studying the texts and attending classes in Criminology and Logic. Criminology was not what I had expected; a course in the investigation and evidence of crimes. It was instead a subfield of Sociology, describing the varieties of population groups who engaged in criminal behavior and theories of the root causes. Still, I found it interesting and learned some lasting lessons about crime in America. I received an "A" in the course. Logic was a different story. Although I had no difficulty understanding the principles, I seemed to have a poor grasp of their application. I was dismayed to receive a "C" in the course. Oh, well. I was already admitted to Law School and I did not think the course would have any bearing on Law School studies.

Donald Neil Walker 1926 - 2012

I had kept in touch with Don since 1949 and visited him in St. Louis where I argued a case to the 8th Circuit Court of Appeal in April 1990. I took this photo of him during this visit.

CHAPTER NINE

THE UNIVERSITY OF CHICAGO LAW SCHOOL

I began to study the Chicago law school catalogue closely. In the first year I would take courses in Torts, Contracts, Property and something called "Elements of the Law". I had only a vague understanding of the meaning of these terms and no understanding of the content of "Elements of the Law". Nothing I read in the catalog promised intellectual excitement or connection to the real world. They all seemed to deal with the self-contained world of "the law", a world foreign to me. But, with a certain degree of excitement, I plunged ahead. At the University Book Store I bought the large, leather bound "casebooks" for Torts and Property. The books for contracts and Elements were bound copies of mimeographed pages. Elements ran to three thick volumes.

At home I leafed through these tomes, finding them at once strange and daunting. While the text on Contracts contained pages and pages of court opinions in cases involving contracts, the Elements books were compilations of essays by Aristotle, Plato, economists and court decisions on a wide variety of subjects. This, I thought, would be an interesting course.

Law school began in September and when I finished my studies at the University of Illinois in June, I needed a job. I found a construction job on the south side of Chicago in the summer of 1948, again working as a laborer, but the work was not nearly as strenuous as the previous Chicago jobs had been. I was earning eighty five cents an hour, which was a good wage for laborers. Though I had saved some money, it was not enough, even with the scholarship.

My first University of Chicago Student ID,
still living at home with my parents on N. Harding Ave.

In September the first day of my new career began. I was entering the University as a law student. My first class was in Torts. The course on Torts was taught by a Professor Gregory, followed by Contracts with Malcolm Sharp and Elements of the Law with Edward Levi. I arrived at the law school on the first day of classes lugging my heavy Torts case book and the first volume of the three volume Elements treatise. I had looked through these books but, based on my college experience, I expected reading assignments would be given in class.

Each of the two main classrooms was constructed in amphitheater style; curving rows of wooden desks on each side of a center aisle descending down to the front of the room. Below was the instructor's desk in front of a large blackboard. I took a seat in the very last row and looked around at my new classmates. They were a varied lot; many older than me, probably veterans, two women sitting together and another, a Japanese woman, sitting apart. There was also a Japanese man and two black men. One of the Japanese women was Patsy Takemoto, later Patsy Mink, who became a distinguished member of Congress from Hawaii, and one of the men was Abner Mikva, later to become a Federal Judge and then legal advisor to President Clinton.

The professor, a pleasant looking middle aged man in a tweed jacket, entered, walked down to the desk in front of the room and introduced himself.

"I'm Professor Gregory and I'll be teaching the Torts course." With that he began, "Anyone have any idea what the court meant in the Helverton case when it spoke of 'apprehension'?"

I was shocked. Here he was, beginning a discussion of a case I hadn't read. How was I supposed to know which case would be covered in class? I was shocked further when five or six hands went up and one of the students began spouting his opinion. How did he know which case to study? I opened my Torts case book to the first case and there it was: Helverton. But the entire first page of the opinion of the English court was in Latin! My God! Should I have taken Latin in college to prepare for Law School? I was somewhat relieved when I turned the page and the remainder of the opinion was in plain English, though in stilted language and interspersed with mysterious unknown phrases, no doubt known to law types. Later I learned that the reading assignment had been posted on the school bulletin board. I had never thought to look there. This was a sorry beginning.

Later, we were seated in alphabetical order and I found myself next to a student named John Wolf; a serious but pleasant guy without any pretensions of intellectuality. All the Professors conducted their classes using the Socratic Method; questions with no hint of the correct answers. This was hard for me to follow, but apparently not to most of my classmates whose hands regularly shot up in the air with volunteered comments. They seemed to be a confident and verbose lot.

I kept my mouth shut. Taking notes on a Socratic dialogue was difficult but I felt I had to do it, so my notes largely recorded questions and answers. The problem was making sense of all this ~ trying to understand what the rule of law was when the discussion bounced around the language of different court decisions like a ping pong ball. Our professors derided the idea of learning the actual rules of law, what they called "hornbook rules". Instead, we were supposed to extract those principles from the cases we read and discussed.

I found the subject matter of the law a far cry from the lofty ideas I had arrived with. It seemed dry and technical, concerned not with large social questions but only with how to determine who wins and who loses a contest over money. In one of my courses, Property, the professor seemed to think the law should be learned by studying 18th and 19th century English property concepts. I was not doing well in these studies. I had to force myself to read and try to understand these cases, but my mind often roamed elsewhere.

During that first year I attended a family function ~ a wedding or something ~ and a fellow somewhat older than me came over and introduced himself. He said he heard I was attending the University of Chicago, as was he. His name was Bernie Alpert and he had a specific purpose in meeting me. He wanted me to join his fraternity on the campus; Phi Sigma Delta. A fraternity! I associated Fraternities with wealthy playboys, but Alpert quickly explained that at Chicago, fraternities accepted only graduate students, not college kids. So it was actually a graduate student men's club, and Phi Sigma Delta was a Jewish Fraternity. I told him that I was a scholarship student and couldn't afford a fraternity membership.

"No problem," he said and explained that the fraternity could employ me at one of several jobs in the house to cover my expenses. He went on to tell me about all the camaraderie and social benefits of living there. I agreed to come to the house and meet the members.

The following week I traveled to the campus and walked to the Phi Sig House at 5625 Woodlawn Avenue. It was a three story brick residence that looked quite elegant. Indeed, Woodlawn Avenue was a gracious, tree-lined street with stately old homes on each side of the street. The fraternity house had been converted from an upper class home to a student residence. Traces of its original status were clearly in evidence; servant's stairs to the second floor, a large kitchen and a very large living room with a fireplace. I was met by a small contingent of members, intent on showing their friendliness and attracting me to join their ranks. The living quarters were on the second and third floors. I was shown a large room with desks and double deck bunks on the second floor. This was the room which had an opening for a new member. It was undeniably attractive and I really wanted to live on the campus and feel a part of the rarefied atmosphere of the University of Chicago. The fraternity charged monthly dues and served lunch and dinner, prepared by a congenial black woman named Linda. When they offered me an arrangement where I would be in charge of the "Commissary", doing the grocery shopping, setting the tables and bussing them after each meal, as well as keeping a record of how many meals each member ate, in exchange for which I would receive room and board without charge, I agreed to join.

In the fall of 1948, I moved into the Phi Sig fraternity house on Woodlawn Avenue where I was assigned the upper bunk in the second floor bedroom. My two roommates were congenial and the fraternity house atmosphere was a new experience. There were no hi-jinks, but rather, frequent serious political and philosophical discussions. The rigors of the University set the tone for my fellow residents.

During my first year in the Phi Sig House I experienced an unexpected musical awakening. One of my roommates had a high quality phonograph system and a collection of classical LP's (Long Playing) ~ then a new technical advance over the old vinyl types. They offered an improvement in sound quality as well as the convenience of being able to listen to musical selections without having to frequently change records. Ordinarily, I would have little interest in listening to classical music because I was not musically well-educated, despite having played the violin for six years. But one day I found myself listening to the Brahms Violin Concerto on an LP record. For the first time, I was emotionally caught up in the music, in a way that I had never experienced. In our home there was no phonograph and the only source of concert music was the occasional radio program heard on a small, tinny sounding radio speaker. My violin studies had exposed me to only a limited repertoire of violin music, and even my High School orchestra never performed lengthy, complex music. So although I was at the University to study law, I had gained a cultural dividend by living in the fraternity house, one that made me a classical music lover the rest of my life.

There were other benefits as well. Living in the Hyde Park neighborhood of the University introduced me to a side of life I never knew before. Bookstores, Jimmy's Tavern, liberated young women quite different from the middle class Jewish girls I knew in High School, and high powered intellectual young students who lived in the apartments of the neighborhood. For the first time I began to feel like an adult, not like a child on leave from my parent's home.

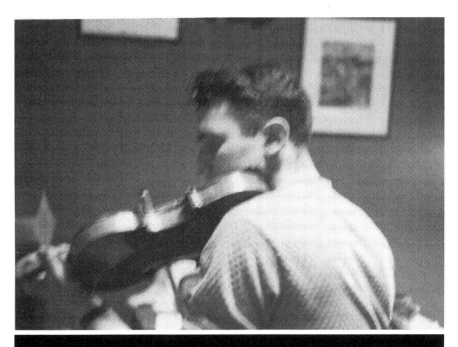

Playing the violin while living at Phi Sig House on campus at the University of Chicago

It was about this time I met George Rothbart. George was nominally a Sociology major, but actually he was a permanent student whose interests ranged far and wide. George had an apartment and a car and earned money delivering sandwiches to students in frat houses and apartments. When I visited him I was exposed to a cultural style that I had never experienced.

George was short and spoke in a deep ponderous voice. He always seemed to have a cigarette dangling from him lips, the smoke curling up into his eyes. He was an intellectual and led the life of an intellectual. It seemed he had read everything and had strong iconoclastic beliefs. Sarcasm was his style, often accompanied with a short guttural laugh. Visiting his apartment was a revelation.

First, he introduced me to his phonograph equipment. In those years there was no high fidelity audio, only mass produced phonographs like Zenith, RCA, and Magnavox. High fidelity was a specialty indulged in only by a small population of audiophiles. George was one of these. He had built a custom speaker cabinet with speakers, including "woofers" and "tweeters" that reproduced almost the full range of sound frequencies. I had never heard such realistic and magnificent sound.

I learned that George was a gifted craftsman and a knowledgeable electronics buff. In response to my questioning he told me that as a boy he had dealt with a malfunctioning radio by disassembling it and learning radio electronics. He had gone on to build a short wave radio and had obtained a Federal ham radio operator's license. This was not the only talent of George Rothbart; he had become a gourmet cook, prowling the ethnic neighborhoods of Chicago to get just the type of coffee he wanted, and other exotic, foreign food items. He was a meticulous and imaginative chef, preparing Greek and French dishes that were outside the realm of my eating experience.

On the wall of his living room hung an original oil painting of a nude young woman, her back to the viewer and looking boldly over her shoulder. I had never been in a home with an original oil painting, let alone a nude. All of this introduced me to a world different from my bourgeois life in Albany Park, or for that matter, anything that had gone before. The cumulative effect was to show me a world of culture and intellect that opened my eyes to a life different than middle-class Jewish life in Chicago.

George and I became good friends. That friendship was jeopardized by an incident when I tried to be a Good Samaritan. The fraternity was having a party and I invited him to come. It turned out there was a problem. The party was for couples and while I had a date, George didn't and what's more didn't think he could get one. So I volunteered to find a girl for him.

There was a nursing school on the South Side, not far from our campus and I had accidentally discovered it as a rich source of dates. Many of the nursing students were from small towns or farming communities and were happy to be invited out on dates. I had dated one of these young nurses and I was confident she could find someone for George. When I asked her she was happy to oblige and told me she had a girl in mind that had a "terrific personality". That should have told me that this girl was not attractive. But it was not till the night George and I picked her and my friend up that I saw how unattractive she actually was.

Her name was Mona Posephny; she was short, fat, had thick ankles and wore a skirt almost of floor length. Her worst feature was her face. Poor Mona had an oversized, misshapen nose, resembling a banana. When George and I saw her, I could tell George was completely put off by her.

When we arrived at the frat house and entered the living room, George mumbled a few words and ambled off to the kitchen. There he stayed the rest of the evening, making spaghetti and sauce, staying busy and away from poor Mona. Out of pity for her, I tried to engage her in conversation and even danced with her once or twice, for which her girlfriend beamed at me. George emerged from the kitchen only to bid her goodbye and I drove her and my girlfriend back to the nursing school dormitory. When I returned to the Phi Sig house George accosted me in the stair well, grabbed me around the neck and proceeded to engage in a mock choking.

"Al, you son-of-a-bitch, how could you do this to me?" he said. He was not serious, but the little charade expressed his resentment at a disappointing evening. George and I remain good friends to this day. But he has never forgotten or forgiven me for fixing him up with Mona Posephny, or, as he persists in calling her, Mona Posephoney.

Meanwhile, my poor father was for the first time in his life unemployed and without an income. My mother had little difficulty finding work as a seamstress working for a furrier and her earnings were the only money coming in. My dad called on old friends trying to find employment as a clerk in a liquor store or anything in the liquor business, without luck. Finally, his sister Minnie, in Brooklyn, called him and said, "Why don't you come to New York. You can stay with us and look for something here. I'm sure you'll find some kind of job." Somehow, he scraped together the money and took the train to New York.

For three weeks he took the subways and looked for work. I was acutely conscious of his pain and wrote him a letter, telling him how much I admired his courage in the face of such adversity and encouraging him in his search for employment. My mother told me that he treasured that letter and it meant everything to him. He was in his 50's and without any formal education. His job prospects were poor. He returned from New York without a job.

Meanwhile, I needed money too. That winter I heard the Postal Service was looking for extra help at the main post office to handle the annual flood of Christmas mail. I intended to apply and told my dad he could apply there too. He did and we ended up working side by side in the main post office for two weeks, sorting mail. Finally, he found a job as a clerk in a liquor store in Chicago. But it was on Blue Island Avenue, on the far southwest side of Chicago, requiring a long series of streetcar rides. The commute was long and tiring and he desperately needed a car. I borrowed $500 from one of my wealthier fraternity brothers with the assurance that it would be repaid, and gave it to my father to enable him to get a car, telling him I had borrowed it from a friend and promised to repay it. He was deeply grateful and promptly went out and bought a used 1942 Packard Clipper.

The car was a four door sedan with a very long Packard hood, and, as it turned out, it was a "beater" ~ a tired old car. But he had always liked big cars and it was inevitable that he would choose another one. I also try to remember that in the immediate post World War Two era, it was hard to find good used cars. The last year of new car production was 1942 and this one had seen seven hard Chicago winters. It took ten months, but he repaid the $500 loan.

In the meantime, I was struggling with the cases and the Socratic method of teaching at the Law School. It was not going well. I almost never volunteered to answer any of the professor's questions and lived in dread of being called on. The content of my law courses dealt with the closed world of legal discourse and we were somehow supposed to absorb its methodology by reading the opinions of courts in diverse fields using language that seemed to obfuscate the issues and often headed in one direction only to end up in the opposite one. This was not my ideal of social justice and I had to stifle the dangerous thought that maybe, just as I had thought, I was not "cut out" to be a lawyer.

The school operated on a system of an annual comprehensive examination. There were no exams prior to the annual comprehensive essay exam. So I could procrastinate and avoid studying in the expectation that somehow, at the end of the year, I could cram all this law into my head. My growing aversion to the "law" led to more procrastination and avoidance, even though I knew this was dangerous. The final exams lasted three days and I quickly saw that my cramming had not brought any clear understanding of the subject matter. Sure enough, when the final grades were posted, I had a "C" grade. Barely good enough to stay in school but not good enough for my scholarship to be renewed.

Now I faced a real financial problem if I wanted to continue. So even though my rooming and food at the frat house cost me nothing, somehow, I had to find a source of income to pay my tuition, buy textbooks and support myself without asking for aid from Mom and Dad. But I was determined not to drop out of law school, an act that would bring enormous disappointment and pain to my parents.

I needed a job that would allow me to attend classes and work during the off hours. I found such a job ~ a strange and unpleasant one working for a large furniture store on the South Side. The store sold furniture to poor black families on a plan calling for weekly payments as small as two dollars. My job was to go to the homes of these debtors and collect their payments. The store gave me a large stack of cards showing the payments made and balances due from each customer. They also gave me the use of an old car to drive to the homes of these furniture buyers. My boss told me I would hear all kind of excuses for not making the required payment, but to be tough and threaten repossession in order to exact payment. But, he added, the last thing the store wanted to do was repossess. It was a threat to be used but rarely enforced.

The neighborhood of these customers was the "Colored South Side" as white Chicagoans knew it. I was one of those white Chicagoans and the neighborhood was foreign to me. I was apprehensive. It might even be dangerous. Yet, I was curious and wanted to see with my own eyes how these people lived. Black people were absent from my world, from my schools, stores and streets. We rarely saw any; they stayed in their own precincts. But I did feel they were victims of injustice and deserved better.

So, on my first morning of work, I drove to an address on my list with a mixture of fear and curiosity. I entered an old apartment building and climbed the stairs to the third floor where I knocked on the door of one of the apartments. I heard the voices of children inside and then the door was opened by a husky black woman who stared at me with curiosity. When I explained that I was from Greenblatt's Furniture she noticeably relaxed.

"Just a minute, I got your money for you," she said and walked into the interior of the apartment. In a minute or two she returned with her purse and took out three dollars, the amount of the weekly payment. I thanked her, wrote down the payment on the customer card with the family name on it and left. There was no animosity, indeed, she was courteous and clearly expected the collector. As I called on other customers I realized that all were familiar with collectors coming to their doors to get the installment payments. It was the way the business was done. But this method was unique to black communities. White customers buying furniture on the installment plan made their payments by mail or at the store.

But not all the customers were so easy to deal with. Many did not answer my knock, even though I heard voices inside. In some cases a woman, always a woman, came to the door and told me she was not able to make the payment that week, to come back next week. In many cases the front door was opened enough for me to see the poverty of their lives; newspapers covering the windows, shabby, worn furniture and wide-eyed children, often wearing only diapers or soiled, torn clothing.

One day I knocked on an apartment door and the mother came to the door, with a gaggle of little ones behind her, and told me she not only didn't have the money for the furniture payment, but she said, "My man done left and I don' have money for food for the kids."

I was moved and took four dollars out of my wallet and gave it to her. The poverty was everywhere and often I accepted any excuse for inability to pay and left without money. After two weeks, my employer called me in and told me I was through.

Finding another job was imperative. A friend told me there might be a job driving a school bus for a Yiddish school near Hyde Park. I had never heard of the Sholem Aleichem Schools, but there was one on Drexel Avenue. I walked over there and met with the director, a kindly middle aged Jew. He explained that the school met five times a week and their students had to be bussed from their homes to the school after their regular public school day. The pay was modest; twenty dollars a week for five work days that began at two thirty in the afternoon when I left to pick up the kids, and ended when the kids got out of the Yiddish school at four thirty and had been delivered to their doorsteps. During the hour and a half the kids were in class, I was free. He explained that the school owned a Ford station wagon and would provide the gas and maintenance.

The kids' homes were in apartment houses scattered over the South Side and it took thirty to forty minutes for each trip. So actual working time was about three to four hours a day, five times a week. It worked out to about a dollar an hour. Not bad. Especially, when he said I could keep the car when I was not ferrying students and was free to use it for my own purposes, within reason and so long as I provided my own gas ~ then twenty cents a gallon.

My chauffeur's license, required to drive a school bus

These Sholem Aleichem schools were entirely secular, teaching only Yiddish language and culture. They had originally been founded by the Socialist Workers Party but had long since severed any political connections. It was a perfect job; allowing me to attend my law school classes and even do a bit of studying during the time the kids were in class. I kept this job for a year and a half, even using the wagon when I took girls out, though the large bold lettering on the door attracted attention: "Sholem Aleichem School No. 3".

Towards the end of my first year at Law School, the program made a significant change. The Law School terminated the four year J.D. (Juris Doctor) degree program in which I was enrolled and brought the school into conformity with all other American law schools; requiring a minimum of three years of undergraduate study followed by three years of law school. To accommodate those of us who had enrolled in the four year program, they offered the opportunity to take three courses during the summer. We would then be in a three year law school program and receive a J.D. on graduation. There was really little choice. So I attended summer school the summer of 1949. Fortunately, I was able to schedule morning classes and keep my school bus job.

In the fall, there were other changes. Within the fraternity house, a room became vacant on the third floor and I took it. It was a one man room and a very interesting one. It was a bit like a garret; the ceilings were sloped and the main window was a small one, actually a dormer window with round arch top. The room had character and I liked it.

Soon after I moved into my new quarters, two new neighbors moved into adjoining rooms. They were European Jews, who were what is now called Holocaust survivors. Next door was a twenty seven year old economics major named Jacob Mincer. Down the hall was a twenty nine year old named Edward Stankiewicz, a scholar of Slavic Linguistics. Both had been born in Poland. They were mature, more mature and more serious than most of the members. I was fascinated by them and over time learned about their life and near death experiences.

Jacob Mincer was not tall and his body was compact and muscular. His room was next door to mine and because I was always curious about foreign born people, I invited him into my room often and we had long conversations. He had a logical approach to everything, no matter how mundane. Over time I learned about his harrowing life.

He came from a small city in south eastern Poland near the Russian border, called Tomaszow, in which the majority of the population was Jews. There he attended a public elementary school and later, after passing strict entrance exams, high school. He developed a love of reading and music. Jacob was a highly talented student with exceptional intelligence. Yet, when he applied for entrance to a Polish university, he was rejected, as were almost all the Jewish applicants. This came as no surprise and his father told him to apply abroad. He applied to universities in Denmark, Italy and Czechoslovakia. Only the Technical University of Brno, in Czechoslovakia, accepted him and it was there he went. While he was a student there the German army invaded Czechoslovakia. The year was 1939 and Jacob was 17.

In Brno, Jacob was arrested by the Gestapo and imprisoned. Thus began six years of suffering as he was moved to various prisons and finally put to hard labor in a quarry. In 1945 he was liberated by the arrival of the American army. For the next two years he worked for the U.S. military government in Germany in their efforts to prosecute Nazi war criminals. Then, after working for the American Joint Distribution Committee, helping refugees trying to resettle in Europe and America he was granted a fellowship by the Hillel Foundation to study in America. In July of 1948 he arrived in New York. He received a scholarship to Emory University in Atlanta and spent the next two years there, majoring in Economics. Then he went to the University of Chicago where we met. We spent two years in close friendship. He and I played Bach together on our violins and ping pong in the basement of the frat house. Two years later Jacob served as best man at my wedding in New York. But such a life changing event was far from my mind then.

Jacob Mincer 1922 – 2006

My close friend, Jacob at his home in New York. This photo that I took of him is now used as the definitive image of him found in text books on his theories.

Jacob studied at Chicago for two years and then moved to New York where he received his Ph.D. in economics from Columbia. Even as a student he was recognized as brilliant and original. Later he went on to pioneer the study of Labor Economics, devising equations to model wages as a function of different variables. These equations are still in use and are known as the "Mincerian Equations". He is now recognized as one of the major economists of the twentieth century. My good friend Jacob died in New York August 20, 2006.

Edward Stankiewicz my other neighbor lived down the hall from me. I remember him as a slight, hollow cheeked man, who laughed easily and often, a laugh that did not entirely conceal an underlying experience of tragedy. I cannot do the story of their lives during the Nazi period justice because it is one that challenges belief.

Edward, like Jacob was from Poland, had been born in Warsaw and as a youth showed a flair for both poetry and painting. When the Germans invaded Poland, he fled to Russian controlled Lwow (Lvov) to continue his schooling. He supported himself by painting portraits of Stalin, Marx and Lenin. When the Germans took over he was confined to the Ghetto and survived by using his artistic skills to forge documents. After two years of living under the constant threat of death or deportation to a concentration camp, he escaped to Russia. Shortly after, the Germans overran that part of Russia and he was betrayed by Ukrainians to the Nazis. Ultimately, he was sent to Buchenwald ~ a death camp for Jews. He survived by using his linguistic skills in German, Russian and Polish to satisfy the guards' demands for detailed written records of the prisoners. When Buchenwald was liberated by American troops, he went to work as an interpreter for the U.S. Army and ultimately made his way to America. He had spent a good deal of his time in Buchenwald and after liberation, in Europe, writing about his theories of Slavic Linguistics. Somehow he found his way to the University of Chicago and there, in 1949, we met.

Edward Stankiewicz
1920 – 2013

(Photo by Michael Marsland)

Edward was a warm and friendly man, who gave little hint of bitterness. We got on immediately and he remained a friend even after I left the University in 1952. On later trips to Chicago I visited him in his apartment in Hyde Park where he was living with his new wife; Florence. He was probably working on his doctorate at the time. I last saw him in 1953 and never saw him again. But I heard from other sources that he had gone on to a distinguished career at Yale. I just looked him up on the internet and was saddened to learn that he died at age 92 on January 31, 2013. He is described in his obituary as one of the leading Slavic linguists in the world.

Both Edward and Jacob were sponsored by Hillel and neither paid any room or board to the fraternity. Both gave evidence of their intellectual prowess, and each achieved the highest level of scholarly eminence. Jacob is described as one of the world's greatest economists of the twentieth century and Edward was considered one of the leading Slavic linguists in the world. How extraordinary that I was thrown together with such powerful minds when I was a callow, but curious twenty one year old. Many times I have thought that the Holocaust destroyed six million Jews, many of whom could have contributed to the world as Jacob and Edward had. These two men illustrate the world's loss.

I was now in my second year of law school, having traversed courses in Torts, Contracts, Property, Elements of the Law, Legal writing, and Negotiable Instruments (Checks, notes, and bills of exchange.) None of it excited me. I struggled to understand the material, let alone master the cases. Gone was my idealism and with it any enthusiasm for the career I was pursuing. Nevertheless, I did manage to develop some understanding of Legal Reasoning and some ability to do legal writing. But I was so disengaged from the substance of Law that I often sat passively through the classes, barely listening. I was so bored with the subject of Civil Procedure, that I went to the class once and never did again. My case book was pristine; I never opened it.

So what was I doing with myself living on the campus while nominally a law student? Reading. Reading the classics, avant garde literature and playing ping-pong whenever I could get someone to come down to the basement and join me in a game. I was also browsing in campus bookstores and occasionally buying books and joining in serious political discussions. Occasionally, I would be overtaken by a fit of conscience or fear and I would sit at my desk with a law casebook, underlining and taking notes. I knew that I was in serious academic danger and the day of reckoning was approaching ~ the year end comprehensive final examinations.

Many of my classmates joined "study groups" ~ groups of three to five students reviewing the subject matter of the classes. I was a "loner" and was never invited to join one of these groups. But it was my good fortune to have a good friend in the class, a young man named Lawrence Friedman. He had short blondish curly hair and a voice that tended to sound whiny. Lawrence was extremely bright and cruised through the legal materials at the very top of the class. I discovered that his interests were broader than law; he composed music, wrote short stories, and was a student of languages, including Arabic and Old French. He spoke with a noticeable Yiddish sing-song voice pattern. That may have come from his time working as a proof reader at the Yiddish newspaper, "The Forvitz" (The Forward).

I don't recall how we came to establish a friendship or why he found me an interesting friend. He was a member of the law school elite: the Law Review, and he was friends with many other members of the class, but we enjoyed each other's company and stayed friends. Lawrence soon saw that I was not studying and was on a self-destructive path. Then he did something extraordinary: he took it on himself to tutor me in all my courses. Several times a week we would meet and spend an hour or two while he clearly and patiently explained the principles of law in each course subject. He was an excellent teacher, reducing complex ideas and cases to their essentials. Without his help I would not have passed the final exams. But I did, although with a "C" grade. The gift he gave me was priceless; the ability to complete law school and become a lawyer. He was to become a distinguished legal scholar and a professor at Stanford, writing the first history of American Law.

Lawrence M. Friedman
1930 –

Photo:
© Stanford University. Stanford, California 94305

Lawrence also gave me another gift, an appreciation of the music of J.S. Bach. I had rarely listened to Bach's music and when I did, didn't find it to my liking; too choppy, short and mechanical sounding. But one day Lawrence took me into a record store that had listening booths, where the customer could select a record, go in and listen to it in a sound proof booth without distraction. He selected Bach's Toccata and Fugue in D minor and started the record. As it went on, he pointed out the wonders of this piece and gradually I understood. From that day to this I have been a Bach lover and I think of Lawrence frequently as I listen.

I was living the life of a student on campus, seldom traveling to my parents' home in Albany Park, though we spoke often on the phone and my affection for them was deeply ingrained. In fact, I was puzzled by how many of the students I met on campus spoke of the bitter relations they had with their parents.

Meanwhile, my father hooked up with an old friend to partner in the opening of a bar and liquor store on West Madison Street near the old Chicago Stadium. The neighborhood was almost completely African-American and the area was regarded as crime-ridden and dangerous. My father was the only white face behind the counter usually working with an African-American man or woman. I visited him in his new place of business occasionally and found the atmosphere intimidating. The customers looked at me in a way that made me feel I was out of place. Yet, somehow, my father could joke and make friendly conversation with all of them. It was clear he had established himself as a white man who was accepted. I never felt comfortable there, particularly because the neighborhood seemed so menacing. The parking strip between the sidewalk and the curb was solid broken glass and the men and women who walked by were often rowdy and loud. It was a mean place, but my father held his own with his customers and I never heard of him being threatened or menaced.

CHAPTER TEN

THE SUMMER OF 1950 - SEATTLE

My second year of law school came to an end in the spring of 1950 and I was considering my choices; I needed to make money to support myself and pay for school but I also had a yen to travel. My real desire was to visit Europe, but the cost of such a trip was beyond me. I next began to think of traveling to some distant part of America, a part I had never seen, and try to find work there. Somewhere I had read an article about the Pacific Northwest; describing it in almost mystical terms. It became one of my preferred destinations. But I was also considering Los Angeles and New Orleans. I made inquiries of government agencies regarding the job market in each of these cities but the opportunities for an unskilled worker were poor in all of them, perhaps a bit better in Seattle. I decided on Seattle. That summer was to be a life-changing experience.

First, I had to find a way to travel to Seattle. That city was almost two thousand miles to the west ~ and I did not have the money to fly or travel by train. One day I was speaking to a friend, Ray Birndorf, a medical student, and when I asked him about his summer plans, he told me he planned to go to Los Angeles, get some kind of hospital job and work there all summer. How was he going to get there? Drive his car. Well, I began to tell him about the glories of the Pacific Northwest and ultimately convinced him to drive with me to Seattle. Then he told me he was going to be traveling with a fellow medical student, Manfred Wallner. I knew Manfred slightly. He was a blonde haired, sleepy-eyed pleasant fellow and I felt the three of us would be good travel companions.

My mom and dad were uneasy about me making such a long trip and working in a strange city, but by now I was quite independent, so there was no question I would do as I thought best. I did, however, assure my father I hoped to make enough money to support myself the following school year.

So, one fine spring day, the three of us left for Seattle, heading west out of Chicago. None of us had ever seen the west and when we reached the badlands of South Dakota, we were excited at the raw beauty of these eroded cliffs and bluffs. Then we reached the overpowering sight of the Mount Rushmore sculptures ‑ the enormous stone faces of George Washington, Thomas Jefferson, Abraham Lincoln and Theodore Roosevelt carved high up in a mountain. We now fully realized that this was an experience of the rugged west, not to be found in the plains of Illinois, Indiana or Iowa. Our route took us through Yellowstone National Park ‑ a set of glories that we had not imagined. We traveled through the Bitterroot Mountains and finally reached the Cascades, the last range between us and the Pacific Ocean.

The West gave me a vision of rugged country, winding mountain passes and breathtaking scenery that was entirely outside my experience. I had never seen mountains and traveling across the continent before the days of freeways, on two lane highways, winding up and down mountains was exciting. My western adventure had begun. I didn't dream it would change my life, as it did, nor did I give great weight to a radio announcement we heard as we traveled through the West ~ North Korea had attacked South Korea across the national boundary and a war had begun. That war would later change my life in unforeseeable ways.

As we approached Seattle we traveled across a large lake on a floating bridge and entered a tunnel with an inscription at its entrance: "Seattle. Portal to the North Pacific". What a dramatic way to announce a city! We were here! None of us had ever been in Seattle and had no idea where to stay. We somehow ended up in the seedy area of downtown and selected the first large hotel we encountered, the Frye Hotel. We got a room and found that we were in a third rate facility when we realized there was no shower or bath in our room and we had to use a common shower down the hall. Oh well.

The following day we checked out and decided to find living quarters in the University District. We went to the University of Washington campus and headed to the Student Union building to see if they had any housing listings. Yes. There were a number and we selected a student rooming house at 4717 17th Northeast. The house reminded me of the Phi Sig House; a dignified older brick house, once a residence of an upper class family, now converted to a student rooming house. On entering we met the owners, John Hedlund and his wife, congenial middle aged people, who showed us the rooms that were available. Ray and I chose a double room and Manfred a single room. We were ready for Seattle.

The first priority was getting a job. I thought I would try to find a summer job in a Seattle law firm. How naïve I was. This is not the way it is done. Résumés are normally sent with an application letter long before the desired start date and then the applicant waits for an interview date or a rejection letter. You don't just stroll into a law office and ask for a job interview. But that's what I did. After several perfunctory interviews, courteous but negative, I understood that I was not likely to find a job in a law office that summer. So I turned to my standby job experience, construction laborer. Luckily, my landlord John Hedland was a construction carpenter and when I asked him if he knew of any construction jobs, he told me that there might be an opening at the site of the University of Washington football stadium construction project.

Our boarding house was only a few blocks from the campus so I walked across the campus till I saw the massive structure of a football stadium in the distance. As I approached I could see it was a construction site; piles of lumber, large yellow loaders, piles of steel beams and steel stadium parts. I asked one of the workmen where the labor foreman was and was directed to a trailer office. Though I was wearing my construction jeans and boots, I was fearful that I would not pass muster as a laborer. Inside the trailer I asked for the labor foreman and a middle aged hefty man in jeans said, "I'm the labor foreman. Did they send you down from the hiring hall?" Quickly picking up on this, I unhesitatingly lied and said, "Yeah."

"O.K. go over there to the timekeeper, show him your union card and he'll put you on the payroll." Union card? I had no union card, but improvising I went to the timekeeper and said I had just arrived from Chicago and forgot to bring my union card along but it was being mailed to me. He was not troubled by the absence of the card and only said, "Bring it by here when it arrives." Then he took my name, address and social security number and entered it in some kind of roster. With that, I was hired by the Strand Construction Company.

After the paper formalities, the labor foreman led me out the door and pointed me to a pile of construction junk scattered around the site; planks, lengths of cable, steel clamps, fasteners, bolts, hangers and miscellaneous construction detritus. "Hey kid, I want you to clean this up. Put them all on that pallet over there so we can organize the site."

I cheerfully assured him I would do it and he left me to my work. It was hard. Some of the planks were long and heavy and it took my full strength to lift them. But I worked diligently and without respite till two or three in the afternoon when the cleanup was finished. I went back to the foreman to report the completion of my task and he went over and looked at it. He was obviously pleased at my diligence because he gave me another assignment; removing nails from wooden planks. This work lasted another day or two, but I could see that the work remaining on the ground was dwindling.

Other laborers were working high up on the structure, inside each of the two silo-like cylinders that formed the core around which ramps wound their way to the upper decks of the stadium. I dreaded being assigned to that work, which was dangerous and required climbing up wooden scaffolding within the silos and wielding a crowbar to pry loose wooden forms from the drying concrete of the

Coming home to the rooming house after a day's work as a laborer on the Husky Football Stadium, Seattle 1950

inner walls. I knew it was inevitable I would be sent up there, since there really wasn't much work left on the ground.

It wasn't long before the labor foreman approached me saying, "I need some more guys working up in the silo. Does it bother you to work high?"

"No," I lied, fully aware that a yes answer would probably mean the end of my employment. So now I was fated to work 120 feet off the ground, something I had never done before. The "silos," as I called them, were an architect's creation to provide a continuous winding ramp leading to the upper decks of the stadium, instead of the conventional zig zag series of ramps. There were two of them, each providing landings at the upper levels of the stadium. They were hollow cylinders, about 120 feet high, each having an entrance doorway at ground level. They were made of poured concrete and were shaped by forms composed of wooden planks, thin enough to bend and held in place by metal ties between the inner and outer walls of the wooden forms.

Within each of the cylinders was a forest of wooden scaffolding. Teams of laborers worked high up on the wooden scaffolding with crowbars and pipes, snapping the ties then prying the boards away from the dried concrete. Doing this made it necessary to lean forward over the open space between the scaffolding and the wall and then working the crowbar till the plank came loose. Since the planks were held in a circular shape they were under tension and when they came loose they popped out away from the wall. We simply allowed them to fall to the ground below. This made entering the silo hazardous, and I quickly learned to look up to be sure no planks were falling before entering the silo. Our job was to remove these forms as the concrete dried, higher and higher up the wall of the silo.

My first day was terrifying. I looked up at the levels where the men were working and realized I would have to climb up there on the scaffolding. There were no ladders or stairs; one simply had to hold onto the cross bracing and walk up a cross brace to reach the next higher level. When I had reached the second level, about twenty feet up, I was afraid to keep climbing and simply held onto the vertical posts till I had girded myself to continue to the next level. It must have taken me twenty minutes to reach the level the crew was working on.

In fact, there were two crews in each silo; one on each side of the circle. When I finally reached the level being worked, one of the foremen handed me a crowbar and pointed to the concrete wall, saying, "Might as well start there."

I lifted the crowbar and then realized I had to lean forward over open space to reach the wall. I was standing on a single plank, about two feet wide, with nothing in front of me and only two by fours nailed as cross bracings behind me to guard against a fall. Since the three other men on my level were doing it, I gingerly leaned forward and reached out with my crowbar. I was scared. But after about twenty minutes of prying loose planks my confidence in my balance rose and I was working at the same pace as the others. By the second day, I was a seasoned high worker, climbing agilely up the scaffolding and working with my crowbar to loosen the form boards. Soon, I was able to ignore the height and felt at ease. My confidence was shaken the second week when one of the laborers working on the same silo, but on the opposite side, somehow lost his balance and fell. Luckily he caught himself on one of the bracing planks and hung on till rescuers reached him. He went to the hospital with broken ribs. It served to remind me of the danger inherent in the job.

As I reflect on this method of construction work, I realize that no construction company would be permitted to operate this way today. Railings would be required at every level of work and ladders or steps would be required for workmen to ascend to the high levels we did. But for me it was a "macho" experience. Every day I went to work enthusiastically, working high and enjoying the camaraderie of my fellow laborers.

At noon, I would descend ~ a process that took ten or twelve minutes and walked across a pavilion to a lunch wagon parked in front of Hec Edmundson Pavilion, actually an indoor athletic arena. There I usually bought a sandwich and sat on the steps of the Pavilion I ravenously ate my lunch, washed down with a pint of milk. Then I noticed a large red convertible parked there almost every day. Once, I asked one of my co-workers if they knew whose car it was. "Oh, he said, its Hugh McIlhenny's car."

Hugh McIlhenny was the star running back of the Husky football team and the car was one of the emoluments, no doubt provided by a wealthy member of the Alumni Club. I later found out that he too was on the payroll of Strand Construction Company, though I never saw him on the job. Another emolument.

In time, the work on the inside of the silos was finished and we were moved to two high concrete walls on either side of the silos. Here again, we were working high on scaffolding, but there were no wooden forms, only snap ties protruding from the concrete. Our job was to fit a short length of pipe over the tie, bend it down and twist it off. This left a small depression in the wall, but others would come with cement and fill it in. I rather liked the work because I could turn around and from the heights look at the dramatic views; Mount Rainier and the waterways of the Montlake District. I was proud of myself.

Again I was walking along a plank without any railings, but I felt no fear. The snap ties were in easy reach except those at the very end of the wall, beyond the end of the planks. The planks were not nailed down but were stable because of their weight. To reach the snap ties beyond the end of the planks, I would have to stand on the end of the plank and reach out for the ties. One day, as I reached, I suddenly became aware that the snap tie seemed to be moving higher. "What the Hell!" Then I realized that the plank was slowly tipping down from my weight at the far end. The tie wasn't growing higher; I was going down. Quickly I stepped back and the plank returned to its level position. I had narrowly avoided a fall, from a height that would have been fatal.

I enjoyed my work on the Husky football stadium that summer and made enough money to finance my coming school year. My construction job was a small part of my Seattle adventure, but there were other new and exciting things in store for me. One day I was in the laundry room of our rooming house doing a wash and met a fellow roomer there. He was short, with a hairline moustache and had a strong Latin American accent. I promptly began a Spanish dialogue with him and we soon established a relationship. He was Jose Duran Montaño, a Bolivian architecture student and we soon became fast friends. Pepe, as he was called, was lively, witty and seemed to know all the Latin American students on the campus. I met them all and found that these guys were very popular with the women. They all seemed to have a glib line of flattery and they all played the guitar and sang.

My friendship with Pepe paid many dividends. For one thing it led me to discover Pacific Northwest architecture. Pepe was taking a class or two but also worked for an established architect in downtown Seattle. I was introduced to him one day. He was a dignified, rotund Frenchman named Roger Gotteland. Pepe took me to some of the houses he was working on and the architecture of the Pacific Northwest convinced me that this was where I wanted to live.

The houses were wood structures with stone fireplaces, floor to ceiling glass windows, clerestories and ultra-modern staircases. All of them were sited so they seemed part of the small forests that surrounded them and they all had views. VIEWS! Views of the lakes, mountains and dramatic landscapes framed by the windows of the house. There was nothing like this in Chicago. For one thing, in Chicago there were no views, nothing except other houses or apartment buildings. The word "view" was never used in Chicago because it had no referent. I knew I could never hope to live in a house like these in Chicago.

One of the houses he had helped design was on Mercer Island. I had never heard of Mercer Island. The island was reached by driving across a floating bridge! I had never heard of a floating bridge, but the real thrill was Mercer Island. Here was an island in the middle of a huge, beautiful lake, almost in a pristine state, heavily wooded and just across a bridge from the city. Unbelievable!

The summer of 1950 was the first year of a Seattle celebration called Sea Fair. The city seemed alive. There were hydroplane races on Lake Washington. I had never heard of hydroplanes. In conjunction with this festival, several ships of the French Navy came to Seattle. Roger Gotteland was honorary French consul and he considered it his duty to entertain their officers. Pepe and I were invited to be Roger's guest at one of the best Chinese restaurants in what was called Seattle's International District. I sat down to a meal like I had never eaten before. The only Chinese dishes I had known in Chicago were Chop Suey and Chow Mein. But Roger knew Chinese food and he ordered dishes that were exquisite. My head was swimming.

Meanwhile, my friend Pepe asked if I would help him buy a car and teach him how to drive. We went car shopping and he selected a used blue Studebaker (alas, a brand no longer in existence). While we had some harrowing experiences when he was behind the wheel, eventually he became proficient enough to drive the car around the city alone. One night he and another of his Latin American friends were out drinking beer when someone suggested a visit to the Washington Social and Athletic Club. As we drove, one of them explained this was a club for African Americans, located in the heart of the Central District (as the black neighborhood was called) at 23rd and Madison. But, they said it was o.k. because many white people also went there. Because of Washington's peculiar liquor laws, this was a "bottle club" which meant they didn't sell alcoholic drinks, but only mixers – you had to bring your own beer or whiskey. When we entered the club I learned that they maintained the façade of being a club and required a nominal membership fee. So "clubs" could host drinkers and entertainment, so long as the customers brought their own alcoholic beverages.

For reasons, I can't recall now, we were all wearing sombreros and attracted a lot of good natured teasing from the patrons, most of whom were black. That night the club was featuring a nationally known black singer who sang rhythm and blues as well as Jazz. She was Nelly Lutcher; and I had heard of her. Probably because of the Seafair weekend she was in town and performing that night. We drank our beer and listened to the exciting music and Nellie Lutcher's distinctive style for about a half hour, when she took a break and stepped off the stage to sit at a table with some friends. As I glanced at her I noticed her looking at me and then, to my alarm, she got up and walked over to me. "Hey, white boy," she said, "Want to dance with me?"

"Sure," I answered and got up, took her by the hand and walked out on the dance floor. We danced and danced and I loved it. She was a natural dancer, perhaps having danced professionally, but in any event, we did all right. When the song ended, we parted gracefully; I thanked her and returned to my friends, who now looked on me with new respect. Dancing with Nelly Lutcher! Seattle!

I made friends with some of the other boarders in the house and one of them suggested a visit to Vancouver, B.C. Always eager for new experiences, I happily joined a group of three. We left late and didn't arrive in Vancouver till eleven at night. As we got into the city center we saw an amazing sight. The streets were crowded with young revelers. I thought it must be a celebration or holiday. But the crowds seemed concentrated in the central section. Once we passed through it, the crowds disappeared. I told our driver to turn around and go back to the lively Vancouver we had first encountered. But by the time we returned, the crowds had largely vanished. We pulled over to the curb and asked a bystander, "Why the crowds?" His answer was simple, "The bars all close at eleven and everyone comes pouring out into the street. Then they leave to party elsewhere." Vancouver liquor laws. We were downcast at having missed all the fun. As we drove into the city, we passed a streetcar, and looking up saw two young women sitting inside. They looked nice and, driven by young male hormones; we did something I would never dream of doing in Chicago. We began to smile and gesture at them to join us. To my amazement, they disembarked at the next stop and got into our car.

After introductions, one of them said she knew where there was a party but we would have to stop at a bootlegger's and buy some beer to take to the party. Again, Vancouver liquor laws; no beer sold in stores or bars. Following their directions, we found the bootlegger, bought the beer and drove to a house where a party was in progress. There was dancing, drinking and some necking. I had connected with one of the girls from the streetcar and we were getting along just fine. Then, with no intention except flattery, I commented on how nice her hair was. My remark brought on a completely unexpected reaction. She burst into tears.

Immediately she rose from the arm of the chair where she was sitting and rushed through the apartment to the rear door leading to an outdoor porch. I was totally flummoxed; what in the world had caused her such distress? Out of empathy, I followed her out the back door and found her standing on the porch, sobbing. I put my arms around her and asked solicitously, "What's the matter?" She raised her head and swiftly removed a wig from her head, revealing it to be completely bald. Then she told me she suffered from a condition causing all her hair to fall out so she had to wear a wig. I was at one and the same time shocked but sympathetic. I tried to comfort her, but the evening was ruined for romance. I simply could not overcome the image of a completely bald female.

We left the party around two in the morning and since we all had brought sleeping bags, we drove around looking for a park where we could spend the night. Not knowing our way around the city, we drove rather aimlessly looking for a park. It was very dark, but we finally found a park. The three of us got out of the car and looked for a level place to lie. I found what seemed like a path, soft and level and there I stretched out and went to sleep. I had drunk too much beer and fell into a drunken sleep. I was awakened in the morning by a strange sensation. It was a horse, nuzzling my face. I opened my eyes with alarm and saw a woman riding the horse. Her first words were, "What are you doing sleeping on the bridle trail?" I got up with a jerk and quickly removed my sleeping bag from the trail. I apologized to the smiling rider, who rode on. My friends were either luckier or smarter than me and had laid their bags off the trail. I felt rather foolish but put it all down to adventure. It had been an exciting night.

Seattle continued to enthrall me. Lake Union, Lake Washington, Mount Rainier, the western skyline defined by the snowy peaks of the Olympic Mountains and the eastern skyline by the peaks of Cascade Mountains. Houseboats! One evening I went with a few friends to a party on a houseboat and as the evening wore on and the liquor created a sense of wild freedom, someone suggested skinny dipping in Lake Union where the houseboat was moored. Several jolly boys and girls, stripped, went to the front porch and dove into the lake. I was shocked at the casual nudity but taken by the novelty of diving into a lake right off your front porch. Seattle!

None of my adventures prepared me for what was coming. One day Pepe invited me to join some of his friends at a party in Bellevue, a suburb across Lake Washington from the city. The party was on a Saturday night so there was no work the next day and I happily agreed to go. He added, almost as an afterthought that before going to the party the Latin Americans had to make an appearance at a dance being held at Spanish House. Spanish House, he explained, was a university dorm set aside for high school Spanish teachers and at Spanish House they spoke only Spanish all day. There was an understanding that Spanish speaking students at the University would attend, or at least make an appearance for a short time. This would not, he assured me, interfere with our going to the party in Bellevue afterwards, in fact, several of the guys said that if they found an attractive woman there, they would take her to the party. I had the impression that these guys had been to those affairs before and considered it a kind of obligation to do this. The guys told me with a wink that all the residents were older women ~ between thirty five and forty five. So I was prepared to simply be chivalrous ~ not romantic.

On entering the room where a dance floor had been cleared, I glanced around at the faces of the women there. None appeared attractive to me and I resigned myself to spending a short time at this dance and then moving on to the party in Bellevue. The women, on the other hand, appeared eager to be get a partner for a dance, and so each one I invited to dance quickly responded and went out on the dance floor with me. My conversation with them was stilted and forced. I really didn't relate to any of them.

When there was a break in the music I walked over to the wall and sat down to smoke a cigarette. I didn't have any idea how long we were going to have to be there. The other guys seemed to be dancing enthusiastically and were being charming Latin Don Juans. Just what these teachers wanted. I could not pretend to such language of flattery or flirtation. I just sat there, waiting till we could leave. As I sat there I became aware that an older woman sitting opposite me was smiling at me. At first, I thought the smile was intended for someone else. It couldn't be me. I didn't know her. But there was no other male in my vicinity. She had to be at least forty and I was twenty two. But each time I looked in her direction, her smile was more direct, even flirtatious. "Okay," I thought, "she wants to be asked to dance." So, conscious of our role at the dance, I stood up and asked if she would like to dance. She greeted my invitation with a warm smile and, taking my hand, led me out to the dance floor. As we danced she held me in a tight embrace, holding her body against mine intimately. I took a closer look at her. Her face was very ordinary but her figure was shapely. "My name is Marge. What's yours?" she asked.

After telling her my name I asked where she taught. She was a Spanish teacher at an Auburn High School. I told her I was a law student working that summer on the construction of the addition to Husky Stadium. When the music stopped, she gave no sign of wanting to leave the floor and stood poised to dance again. So, we did, and again and again.

Pepe then came over and said most of the guys were leaving to go to the party and asked if I was ready to leave. I had spent so much of the evening dancing with Marge that it was too late to try to find a new partner, so I asked her if she was interested in joining the group at a party in Bellevue. "Oh, yes," she replied enthusiastically. When Pepe told me that they were leaving in their car, she said, "I have my car here and we can drive there if you have the address."

I asked Pepe if he had the address and he went to one of his friends and got it, returning with a small piece of paper containing the address. Marge said she would have to notify the dorm chaperone, and while it might take a few minutes it would not be a problem. I said to Pepe, "You guys go ahead and leave without me and this lady and I would join them in Bellevue later." Pepe waved farewell and left.

In a short while, Marge said she had talked to the chaperone and we could leave as soon as she got her coat. When she left to get her coat, I felt I had got myself into an uncomfortable fix ~ going out to a party with an older woman, a woman whose age and appearance made us an unnatural pair.

Marge returned with her coat and, taking my arm, led us down the stairs and out the dorm building. It was a summer evening and night had fallen. She led me across a parking lot to her car; a Plymouth coupe. To my surprise, she handed me the keys and said, "Why don't you drive?"

I was agreeable and after opening the passenger door for her, got in on the driver's side, slid behind the wheel and put the keys in the ignition. But when I pressed on the starter, I heard the familiar and sad noise of a weak battery, barely able to turn the engine over and then stopping. A few more efforts to start the engine left no doubt that this Plymouth was not going anywhere that evening. My first thought was, "Damn, we're going to miss the party in Bellevue." When I turned to my companion with the bad news, I was not prepared for what followed. She turned to me and with a smile that left no room for doubt; she leaned forward and kissed me. Now I understood all that had gone on in the dance hall; her smiles, the dance embrace and the proposal to go in her car.

My head was spinning. I had never experienced the amorous embraces of a woman her age; forty or more. As we sat there in her car, in the darkness of the parking lot, she continued her advances, and I did not resist – though I could have, I suppose. But she was becoming more openly sexual and the entire event was turning into a sexual adventure. Clearly, this was what she was after, and I found myself in the totally new and unfamiliar role of the recipient of sexual advances by a woman. What a night!

Afterwards, she embraced me affectionately and said, "I can see you don't have much experience with women. I can teach you if you're willing to learn." I promptly affirmed my willingness to be her student. Marge smiled at me seductively and said, "Al, I have an apartment in Auburn, and if you come by next Saturday, I'll have my car fixed and we can spend the afternoon together there. O.K.?" "Sure," I said enthusiastically and escorted her back to her dorm.

As I left her and walked back to my rooming house, my head was spinning. It had been a surreal experience. When I got home, my friend Pepe was waiting up for me, dying with curiosity to find out what had occurred between me and the High School teacher. When I described our tryst in her car, he giggled with prurient delight. He assured me that I had a far more enjoyable evening than he and his friends had at the party in Bellevue.

During the following week I had an opportunity to reflect on the strange relationship I had gotten into. On the one hand I felt it was bizarre for a twenty two year old to have an affair with a woman who seemed more like an older relative than a romantic partner, but on the other hand there was lust. Lust triumphed, so the following Saturday I called her and we arranged to meet for a tryst in her Auburn apartment.

Thus began a summer of pure carnality; uncomplicated by emotion, but with a deep sense of unease at what seemed an unnatural relationship. Yet, Marge, seemed to enjoy the opposite of what I found disturbing; the opportunity to have a young, vigorous lover. As the summer wore on and the novelty of sex with this woman wore off, I became more and more convinced that I should end our arrangement. I was increasingly uncomfortable at being seen in public with her. One night, after one of our trysts, I returned to our house and again found my friend Pepe waiting up to hear the latest details of my romantic adventure. I tried to explain to him why I felt such discomfort. His comment was typical of his wit, "Ahlveen, you should not feel bad. You are like a boy scout. You are being kind to old ladies."

The comment did not soothe my feelings ~ quite the opposite. It convinced me that I must end it. The following week, after a painful meeting with Marge, I told her I would not be seeing her again. The hurt she felt was obvious, but there was no turning back. The adventure was over.

By then, the summer was ending and the beginning of the next school year was approaching. It was time to return to Chicago. Seattle had been magical; the mountains, the architecture of the homes, the dramatic hills and lakes of the city, the construction work, the Latin Americans and their music and finally the affair with an older woman had broadened my horizons beyond anything I anticipated when I set out for Seattle in the spring of 1950. Ultimately, my summer in Seattle changed my life and set me on a course to a career as a lawyer for Indian Tribes, something I could not have imagined in my wildest dreams.

CHAPTER ELEVEN

GETTING MARRIED AND BECOMING A SOLDIER

I returned to the fraternity house on the campus. One of the residents in our fraternity house was a rather unpleasant, arrogant fellow named Gene Borowitz. He was tall, handsome and athletic. In fact he was a pitcher on the university baseball team and had even pitched in the minor leagues. One day he mentioned that a friend of his cousin, Judy Friedman, whom I had met, was coming over to the house and bringing with her a friend ~ a girl I might want to meet. I was always interested in the possibility of new relationships with girls so I agreed. The two girls arrived, Judy accompanied by a slender girl, with a pretty face and long hair, named Lenore Guralnick. Lenore immediately told me she preferred to be called, "Lennie", and that became the name I was to use for the next sixty years.

Lennie was only sixteen, but displayed a maturity beyond her years. She was attractive and obviously bright. Her voice was sultry; like the voice of an older woman. I was put off at first by her youth ~ she was a teenager, but she was a scholarship student in the college and chose her words carefully. As we spoke, I saw in her a kind of beauty and a quality that was responsive to my thoughts and ideas. I

Lennie at age 16 on the campus of the University of Chicago
I kept this photo in my wallet for many years.

invited her to join me in a game of pool at the Student Union building and that was our first "date".

If I thought this was merely a brief diversion, I was wrong. I called her for another meeting and soon we were seeing each other regularly. Our relationship deepened and became serious. It became more difficult to devote time to my studies as I found my life intertwined with hers. Lennie had matured from a teenager to a thoughtful young woman and we were a couple. Below is a photo of Lennie at seventeen at the University of Chicago. From this distance in time I see the irony; from a relationship with a woman twenty years my senior to a relationship with a young woman six years my junior.

In the fall of 1950, the Sholem Aleichem School closed and my driving job was ended. Without any source of income, I was forced to move back home with my parents and find a job while I finished my last year of law school. Finding a job proved easy. I applied to the Yellow Cab Company to be a taxi driver and was promptly hired. For the next eight months I drove the streets of Chicago from four in the afternoon till two or three in the morning. During the day I attended classes at law school followed by a long trip on the "el" to Albany Park, where the Yellow Cab garage was located. I usually took one or two of my casebooks along so I could do some academic reading in the rare times when I was idle. But my studies suffered and my standing in the law school became more precarious.

Driving a taxi at night in Chicago provided an experience of life in the city unparalleled by anything that had gone before. At that time Yellow cabs had no radios so we cruised the streets till we were hailed by someone. The riders were from all classes and colors; rich, poor, working class, playgirls and boys, drunks and disabled, elderly and young. I sometimes had lively conversations with my passengers, frequently no words were exchanged. My pay was 40% of the total on the cab's meter plus whatever I received in tips. The hours were long and the work always had a potential for danger, but I chose to ignore it and picked up anyone who hailed me.

One night, though it was two in the morning, I decided to make one more run before turning the cab into the garage. I cruised up and down Broadway, a busy arterial where there were many clubs and bars. A man in his thirties stepped out into the street in front of a club and hailed me. He was carrying a newspaper folded up under his arm. As I stopped the cab, he opened the rear passenger door and then two more guys stepped off the curb and followed him into the cab. I hadn't noticed them when I saw him, but didn't think it was significant.

He gave me a street address about two miles away. It was a residential neighborhood and I suspected nothing untoward. The street was dark, lit only by one street light as I pulled up in front of the address he had given me. When I stopped I shifted the manual gear shift lever into neutral and asked the other passengers if they were all getting out here. One of them said, "No, we're going on to the North Side." So I moved the gear shift lever into first gear and held the clutch pedal in, prepared to drive on after the first guy got out. Suddenly, an arm whipped around my neck and pulled me up and back over the top of the seat. At the same time, the other two men got out and pulled open the doors in the front of the car, one coming in from each side. The guy on my right held a razor blade over my face and said, "One wrong move and you get sliced."

The guy on my left went for my shirt pocket and pulled out the wad of bills I had there – about thirty or forty dollars and then reached in my back pocket, taking out my wallet. All this time I was locked in the chokehold of the guy in the back who kept pulling me up and back. I was trying to keep my left foot extended; holding the clutch pedal to the floor, lest releasing it would cause the car to begin jerking forward. I tried to explain this to my captor, but was not able to get words out because of the grip around my neck and under my chin was choking me. Finally, there was another yank on my neck and I was pulled so far back that I could no longer reach the floor with my foot and it slipped off the clutch pedal. Immediately, the cab began jerking forward and the three thieves panicked and fled the cab.

I was angry. A whole night's earnings gone. The three robbers had run; two had run to the back yards of the house on one side of the street, one on the other side. In a rage, I started up the cab and raced around the block hoping to catch them in the alley. I honestly intended to hit them with the car if I caught them. They were nowhere to be seen. Gloomily, I drove back to the garage and reported the theft to the manager. While he sympathized, he told me of the company's policy. I would still be liable for 60% of the fares rung up on the meter, even though I didn't have the money. The missing 60% was deducted from my paycheck. I quit the next day.

Predictably, law school was going badly. Between spending time with Lennie and trying to study while driving a cab, I had only a perfunctory grasp of the material being taught. My worst course was Federal Income Tax and it turned out to be my downfall. After the comprehensive final exam in June, I had barely passed all my courses but one: Federal Income Tax. I was not surprised to see that I had gotten a "D" in the course; a failing grade. The dean told me later that week that failure to pass the course on Federal Income Tax left me with insufficient credits to graduate. I was offered the option of taking a law course during the summer, and if I were successful, I would receive my J.D. in August. I took a course in Insurance law that summer, got a "B" and graduated with a J.D. in August.

With fellow fraternity members at the Phi Sigma Delta House at the University of Chicago, 1949. I am far right middle row.

Finally, I had completed law school, received my degree and the question was "what now?" I had enough of law and didn't want to pursue a career in this unappetizing field. My first love had been International Relations and I thought perhaps I could find something in that area. The Foreign Service? But I knew I needed some schooling beyond law school for that. I decided that I would try for admission to the Master's program at the law school and seek a degree in International Law.

To gain acceptance required submitting a proposal for a Master's thesis. I chose my favorite topic: "The Divisibility of National Sovereignty". I submitted a carefully composed essay on the importance of this question and my plan for a thesis. It was accepted. I found that though I had to take a Law School course in International Law, I was free to choose any other courses outside the Law School that seemed relevant to my project. I spent two quarters that fall as a Master's student, taking International Law and courses in the Political Science Department on International Relations. After my dismal experience as a dunce in Law School, I found studies once again enjoyable and experienced the satisfaction of receiving "A"s in my courses. My confidence was restored. As for finances, I had no alternative to getting a student loan from the University.

That summer of 1951, Lennie and I decided we wanted to spend our lives together and marry. When this news was conveyed to our families, planning commenced for a June wedding in New York the following year. I was still in graduate school and Lennie was still a scholarship student in the college. I had no definite career plans but the coming wedding loomed large. It was carried off with the usual travail over guest lists between Lennie's parents and mine. The question of a honeymoon was easily resolved when Lennie decided on going to Cape Cod for a week. Afterwards, we would return to Chicago where we had rented an apartment in Hyde Park and I would resume my thesis work.

My handwritten caption on the back of this photo:

"In April 1951 Al & Lenore plan to have Al go to New York to meet Lennies parents. Al & Lennie sell their blood to finance the trip. This photo taken that morning."

With my bride, Lennie at our wedding in New York 1952

Our parents were happy with our choices, though Lennie's father Dave could always be counted on to make unpleasant, sarcastic and critical remarks. The wedding was a glorious affair in the Bronx, at a place named the Concourse Paradise Catering Hall, a venue for weddings, Rabbi included. He even produced a Ketubah, a traditional Jewish marriage contract which Lennie and I signed. Many of my relatives came from Chicago and, of course, the Guralnick family was there in force. My friend Jacob Mincer was my best man and looked elegant in a white dinner jacket. Lennie wore a bridal gown designed and made especially for her by the father of her friend, Judy Friedman and she looked ethereal. Like most wedding participants, we felt an air of unreality about the entire evening.

On our honeymoon at Cape Cod following a bicycle-ride. Lennie said that she was too exhausted to go any further.

Following a delightful week on Cape Cod, driving Dave's loaned Dodge Wayfarer to get there, we returned to our apartment in Chicago in June of 1952 to begin married life. I resumed work on my thesis and Lennie, to help with our finances, took a job with a giant printing company, the R.J. Donnelly Company, the company that printed the nation's telephone books. They made their money by selling advertising in their "yellow pages" and Lennie's job was to work with their outside salesmen taking their orders and coordinating the sales and production functions.

With Lennie in Asbury Park, New Jersey 1952

By August of 1952, Lennie began to suspect she was pregnant. Her doctor thought she was indeed pregnant. I had asked Lennie to get a written confirmation from the doctor for my Draft Board. The Korean War was in full swing and men were being drafted all the time. I was vulnerable, because though I had a student deferment while I was in Law School, that ended when I graduated and I was now in category 1-A, the most likely to be drafted. Fathers were in a different category. Each day I went to our mailbox looking for the letter from the doctor until, finally, after about a week, it came. But there was another letter in the same mailbox ~ a notice from my draft board to report for induction into the U.S. Army.

My first thoughts were the pregnancy will cancel out the draft notice. There was an appeals process and I sent in a notice of appeal, confident I would succeed in having the induction notice cancelled. I was given a hearing date with my draft board ~ a group of five citizen volunteers who ran the process. Surely they would see that the notice to report arrived the same day as the proof of my wife's pregnancy and this whole thing would be straightened out. Instead, I encountered a hostile reception. The only comment was sarcasm, "How pregnant is she; five minutes?"

This was followed by a motion of one of the members to deny my appeal; unanimously agreed to by the board and my appeal was ended. I was stunned at the injustice and even more by its implications; I was on my way to two years in the Army.

Being drafted into the military changed everything. I had to abandon my work on the Master's Degree, and more disruptively, Lennie could no longer continue living in our apartment. She was pregnant with our first child and could not continue working beyond her fifth or sixth month. Where would she go? My parents invited her to move into their apartment, assuring her she was welcome and they would help her as best they could when the baby came. For a time she tried to keep up with her studies, but it soon proved to be impractical; there were too many distractions and she gave up. Her college schooling ended before she had gotten a degree and was not to be resumed till she was thirty five, seventeen years later.

We were both worried about the uncertainties ahead. The Korean War was bloody and our troops were being killed and wounded there daily. Lennie faced the prospect of two years alone, at a time when she needed me. She was nineteen and frightened. Meanwhile, I was concerned with the physical rigors of soldiering. Was I up to it? I had spent three years living the sedentary life of a student. I had to start a program of physical conditioning and so I began daily runs in nearby Jackson Park, running longer distances each day till I was covering a mile or so. Finally, the date of my induction into the Army arrived and in late September, 1950, I reported to the induction center in downtown Chicago and was shipped to Fort Sheridan, an army base close to Chicago. Wearing the uniform that was to be my identity for the next two years is shown in the photograph.

The next two years had an air of unreality; my life was lived in a completely foreign environment; the military. As I was writing this story of my life, I decided to read some of the letters I had written during that time, so I went out to our garage and took out several bundles of letters we had saved. My army anecdotes are excerpted from those letters.

In U.S. Army uniform at Fort Sheridan, Illinois 1952

Here is one of the first, describing my journey from Fort Sheridan to Camp Gordon, Georgia, where I would undergo the transformative rigors of Basic Training ~ a two month period of intensive discipline and introduction to the weapons and techniques of war. The date of my letter to Lennie was October 4, 1952.

"On a Thursday morning we were marched to a bus which took us to a train; seven Pullman (sleeper) cars and one Army kitchen car, pulled up on a siding. At eight thirty, the train began to move. The cars were not modern, but comfortable. We crawled slowly toward Chicago, passing familiar neighborhoods, Lawrence and Cicero and then Crawford near Lake Street, teasingly close to my home and life on the West Side. At fifty First Street we stopped for about an hour while they serviced the train and substituted a Diesel engine for our steam locomotive.

We pulled out of Chicago at 1:30 P.M. Then we really began to move. Our route was straight south along the Illinois-Indiana border. Toward evening we crossed into Indiana. The trip was quite pleasant and at times even exhilarating. The train was all Army ~ no civilians except porters, who made a pretty penny going through the cars and selling candy, cigarettes, etc. We lined up and went through the kitchen car where we were served buffet style on paper plates; one paper plate, one cup and one spoon. Everything was slopped together on one plate. The food was bad; no other way to describe it. This actually worked to the porter's benefit; they were doing a brisk business selling snacks. In the meantime, the cooks weren't overlooking any opportunities to make money either. Although strictly forbidden, they were selling beer and liquor.

Meanwhile, as luck would have it, I was the first one to enter our car and so took the first seat by the window. The seats were actually intended to form a compartment to be used by two passengers, one for the upper berth and the other for the lower berth. But two of my acquaintances followed me and seated themselves opposite me, unaware of the compartment arrangement. That night, matters came to a head when the porters arrived to make up the berths. We ended up flipping a coin. I won and got the lower berth. One of my friends was disgruntled and went across the aisle and began arguing with the two seated there, claiming that since he had gotten into the car before them, he was entitled to one of the berths. This escalated into a heated argument and might have gone to a fist fight, but I intervened and somehow cooled things down. At this point one of the porters appeared and resolved the problem by assuring them they would have berths in the next car, which was occupied by the porters.

Finally, my berth was made up and I crawled in. It was delightfully comfortable. You have no idea how much more bearable a train trip becomes when you are lying in a Pullman berth. You can lean back and look out the window to watch the night scene fly by. Despite the fact that I was pretty sleepy, I forced myself to stay awake and enjoy my luxurious bed. And even after I had fallen asleep, I awoke several times to stare out the window. Once I awoke as we were passing through Kentucky and I was rewarded by a memorable sight. The moon was very bright and it illuminated a large rolling field and there, in one corner was a group of horses. One horse jerked his head up at the sight of the train and galloped off at full speed across the field, leaving a trail of white dust rising behind him.

About three in the morning, I opened one sleepy eye and saw a sign showing we were in Nashville, Tennessee. I was up and out of bed at six a.m., feeling more refreshed than I had been during the previous two weeks at Fort Sheridan. As I was dressing, I looked through the window and saw were in Georgia. The land was rolling and wherever the earth was bare, the dirt was red; the color of rust. We were passing cotton fields and sharecropper's run down shacks, a sight I had seen only in movies.

I walked out into the vestibule and stood at the doorway, leaning out of the open top half. I stood there for over an hour watching Georgia roll by. The train was going like hell, blowing its horn almost constantly and the wheels were pounding out an exciting rhythm on the rails. As we passed, people in the fields and small towns stopped what they were doing to watch the train. I waved, and they grinned and waved back. Most of these people were blacks, some of them whole families picking cotton in the fields. The children were running barefoot and some of the girls were clad in what looked like flour sacks made into dresses. There was an old black man I saw, plodding up a steep hill on a lonely country road, wearing a floppy straw hat, smoking a corn cob pipe and leaning on a crooked cane. It didn't seem real that this was 1952 and I was observing Southern rural life."

This section of my letter goes on to describe our arrival at Camp Gordon and the beginning of a hellish two months of physical and psychic intimidation. The atmosphere is described in the next two excerpts.

"Singing Jody. Whenever we march we sing and it's amazing how it lightens the burden. There are many Jody songs, almost all semi-jazz. I'll try to remember some of them and sing them to you when I see you in Dec. One of them goes: 'Ah don' know but ah believe, ahll be home by Christmas Eve.' Then the sergeant sings out: 'Am I right or am I wrong?' And we shout, 'You're right, so right!' This is followed by the sergeant shouting, 'Sound off!' We respond, 'One two.' Then the sergeant again shouts; 'Sound off!' And we respond, 'Three four!' To this the sergeant sings out: 'Bring it on down!' The troops respond, singing loudly, 'One two three four, one two three four, one two and a short pause, then a quick, 'Three four!' It surprises me but the morale in my company is high, despite all the shouting and cursing directed at us by the cadres." ("Cadre" is an army term for the non-coms assigned to control each company of soldiers. They have only disciplinary responsibilities, not teaching. That is done by others.)

There were some ugly events and one of them is described in my letter of October 12, 1952. One of the nastiest of our cadres was our field sergeant, Sgt. McManus. A Southerner, he constantly addressed us in curses. The man is only about five feet eight inches tall, but he looks heavily muscled and acts as if he is ready to fight anyone. From my letter:

"He has a darkly bearded face, a jutting square jaw, high cheek bones and blue eyes that gleam from beneath his helmet in a strange way; a combination of evil and 'I don't give a shit' glint. He's about 25, from North Carolina and has never seen combat, despite acting as though he had. Both cocky and vicious, he managed to get all of us to despise him.

One afternoon, we were marched to a building for some kind of interview, and since it was raining heavily, the cadres told us to go inside to wait. The building was a long, narrow, empty army structure. There were about 200 of us and we sat down on the concrete floor. After about two hours, we were quite bored and uncomfortable sitting on the concrete floor. The two cadres who were in the room with us had stretched out on a table and appeared to have fallen asleep. Two of the men in our company, both black, lay on their backs, stretched out on the floor. Then McManus walked in. Without a word, he pulled his helmet off and flung it at the two black men lying on the floor. It hit one of them in the stomach and both immediately sat up. McManus strode over to them and yelled, 'Sit up!' Then, looking at one of the men, said angrily, 'What were you laying down for? You tired?' The man looked directly at McManus and said in a challenging voice, 'Yeah.' McManus pressed the matter further, 'Why you so tired?' The soldier, unintimidated, replied, 'Didn't get no sleep last night.' McManus, determined to maintain his dominance, sneered, 'Now, isn't that sad. That's tough shit!'

The black soldier glared at McManus who attacked again, 'Whatchoo lookin' at? Don't you gimme them smart-assed looks of yours or I'll break yore dam arm.' The black soldier stared straight at McManus and said quietly, 'That can work both ways.'

McManus exploded, 'I know your kind, you're one of those smart guys.' That brought this response, 'I ain't no smart guy but you can't walk on me.' 'God dam it, don't you talk back to me! McManus snarled.

In the meantime, complete silence had fallen over the whole room as all two hundred troops listened to the confrontation. McManus had fallen silent and turned his back on the black soldier. But the soldier continued to stare at him. McManus started to walk away and as he walked it was apparent that he was considering his next steps. The guy had refused to back down and, in effect, his bluff had been called. The problem facing McManus was how to maintain his dominance and fighting posture. All eyes were glued on him. If he merely continued his verbal tirade, or threatened the guy with KP, he would lose face. There was only one course of action open to him. He whirled around, stalked over to the guy and said, 'Looks like you lookin' for some of my ass. Well, we'll see if you can get any of it.'

With that McManus walked toward the rear of the room where the latrine was located. As he walked he unbuttoned his jacket and whipped it off. When he reached the latrine door he turned around and said, 'C'mon in here with me, God dam it! An' take off your jacket.' It was clearly an invitation to a fight.

The black soldier was slightly taller than McManus and looked very muscular. McManus walked back toward the latrine and turning to the black soldier said, 'Come on in here with me, God damit! And take off your jacket!'

The latrine was behind a plywood partition which didn't reach to the floor and the occupants could be seen beneath the lower edge of the partition and their heads above the upper edge. Their conversation was clearly audible to the entire body of soldiers sitting on the floor.

When the two were in the latrine, McManus shut the door and said, 'Go ahead, you think you can get some of my ass? Just try it. Go on! Swing at me!' To this the black soldier replied, 'I got more sense than to swing at you. You think I want to go to the stockade? I got more sense than that.'

McManus goaded him, 'You ain't got no god dam sense! Ah got just as much sense as you have. You swing at me first. I'll kill you!' His opponent replied, 'You think you can? And McManus answered, 'Ah know I can. So go on and swing then.' The black soldier refused the invitation saying, 'Ah got more sense 'n that. You just hit me.' Then they went silent and glared at each other for what seemed a full minute when McManus said, 'Looks like you don't want none a my ass.' The black man replied, 'Looks like you don't want none o' mine neither.'

Complete silence had fallen over us watching this contest of wills. Following this exchange, there were long periods of silence, broken by the same kind of exchanges, McManus inviting his opponent to swing first and the other repeating the invitation to McManus to swing first. This went on for twenty minutes till finally the black soldier said, 'Shit!' in a disgusted tone and started to open the latrine door to leave.But McManus slammed the door shut and said, 'You don't leave till I tell you!'

Finally, when everyone of us had gotten bored, the latrine door opened and the black soldier walked out with a grin and sauntered over to the spot where he and his friend had been sitting and sat down. The latrine door remained open but McManus did not come out. Two minutes later he emerged, looking abashed. He walked over to the table picked up a clipboard and began studying it intently. He knew he had lost face.

After the incident, McManus was a changed man. That night he appeared in our barracks without any apparent purpose, told jokes, demonstrated Judo holds and seemed to be trying to make friends with everyone. From this point forward, he made a show of talking tough, but you could tell his heart wasn't in it. He had 'painted himself into a corner' and when his bluff was called there was no way out for him. Hitting the enlisted man first would have meant losing his sergeant's stripes and who knows what other disciplinary consequences he would have faced.

The entire incident was bizarre and it seemed to me to result from Sgt. McManus' southern bigotry. It showed the determination of a southern white man to establish his dominance over a black man but it also showed that the black man understood this and was willing to risk a dangerous confrontation to preserve his own dignity."

I spent eight weeks at Camp (Now Fort) Gordon, Georgia undergoing what was called Basic Training. Although 1 was in the Signal Corps, the training was combat infantry training, presumably on the theory that every soldier has to have the skills of infantry combat. So, I, like all my fellows in the training units were assigned our own rifle, an M-1 Garand, semi-automatic weapon. Semi-automatic means its capability to fire repeatedly from a clip of eight rounds without the need to manually pull the bolt or to insert another round. We carried our rifles on our shoulders with us everywhere except to the mess hall. It weighed about nine pounds and almost became an appendage. We were trained in disassembling and cleaning the gun and later taken out to the firing range and instructed in aiming and firing from three positions; standing, kneeling and prone. I concentrated on developing the skill of hitting the target and eventually was graded "sharpshooter", a level below "marksman".

The training also included use of the smaller and lighter "carbine" and later, the very heavy machine gun, used with a tripod, the "bazooka" and the rifle grenade. We had the somewhat frightening experience of practicing the use of a hand grenade, triggered by pulling out a pin and quickly hurling it toward the target. It was frightening because there had been casualties during training when the soldier dropped the grenade or it slipped from his grasp when he was in the process of throwing it, or the soldier held it too long after triggering it.

Combat experience was replicated by "live fire" drill and by bayonet drill. In the former, we crawled on our bellies beneath a network of wires some two feet above our heads to prevent our standing up as machine gun fire was directed over us. I vividly remember the sound of bullets whizzing through the air as I crawled and even the coppery glint reflected from them.

But it was bayonet drill that drove home the dark message that all this training was for the purpose of killing other humans. In this drill, we fixed our bayonets (a long knife) to our rifle barrels and were instructed in combat techniques, including charging across a field at mounted sandbags and thrusting our bayonet into this simulation of a human body, all the while yelling at the top of our lungs, "kill, kill!" I'm not inventing this, it actually happened. When I started across the killing field I was too embarrassed to shout out the unnatural words, but as I ran and continued the thrusting, I too joined in the yelling of these words of killing. In the end, I knew what the Army was up to, but I doubted that I could actually kill someone.

Basic training hardened my body. We marched and marched,

miles and miles. We ran, we ran holding our rifles over our heads, we engaged in wrestling matches with our fellow soldiers in programmed combat, we learned the techniques of camouflage and use of the compass to find our way cross country through wilderness. We went on "bivouac" (what a strange word!) setting up two man pup tents in the wild and living there for days.

During these eight weeks I missed Lennie terribly and wrote to her almost every day. On Sundays, I would have an opportunity to telephone her, but since I had very little money, I had to "reverse the charges", a practice I later learned infuriated her father, Dave. In fact, her letters told me that he was constantly denigrating me in the way only he could do; poisonous, pointed attacks. I was angered and later, when I began to think of the possibility of my child being raised in the environment of the Guralnick home, I became irrational and even considered going AWOL to rescue my child or to confront them. But, as events played out, this proved unnecessary.

Finally, my eight weeks of basic training came to a close and I anxiously awaited the orders that would determine where I went next; would it be Korea ~ a bloody battlefield ~ or would it be some Signal Corps base in the U.S.? One day we were called into formation and a sergeant passed out to each of us a single sheet of paper with our name on it containing our orders. I looked at mine and felt overwhelming joy when I read, "Fort Monmouth Telephone and Teletype School". By word of mouth I learned that it was regarded as a campus ~ a school with a reputation as one of the Army's nicest facilities. Many of my friends were envious, especially those being sent to Korea. I was jubilant. Telephone and teletype were a complete mystery to me and

I had no idea why the Army thought I was suited for such a technical job, but the ways of the Army are mysterious and one quickly learns not to seek rationality in its decisions.

Leaving Fort Gordon we were bused to a nearby military airfield where we boarded a chartered C-46 and flown to New Jersey. Here we boarded buses that took us to our new post, Fort Monmouth. I reported to the orderly room of a training company where I presented my orders and was given bedding and assigned a bunk in a nearby barracks. It was eleven at night so I groped my way through the dark till I found an empty bunk, leaned my duffel bag against the wall, made the bed, undressed and crawled in to spend my first night in New Jersey.

The next day I joined the hundred and sixty men of my company and stood in formation as a sergeant explained we would be marched to school. All of us would begin with a basic course in electricity and its applications. As we marched I looked around and the Fort looked more like a college campus than a military base; certainly nothing like Camp Gordon with its identical, pale yellow wooden two story barracks buildings everywhere you looked. There were no shouting cadres and the soldiers were all wearing stylish green belted trench coats, instead of the heavy woolen army overcoats issued to us in Camp Gordon. The troops didn't wear helmets but "campaign hats". Troops strolled along the walkways that crisscrossed the grounds. Most importantly, there was no atmosphere of intimidation.

The most exciting development came with an announcement at our noon formation; all married soldiers were eligible to live "off-post". That meant Lennie and I could rent an apartment and live together while I was getting training at the Fort. There was more good news; married soldiers living off-post received an off-post financial allowance and were eligible to shop for groceries at the Army Post Exchange, or PX.

As soon as I could, I called Lennie in New York, some ninety miles away and told her we could live together here in Ft. Monmouth. She was overjoyed to know that we would reunite and her first question was, "How soon can I see you?" Her parents agreed to drive down to Eatontown, a town close to the base. We agreed to meet Saturday evening at the Blue Jay diner and to spend the night together at a motel nearby. The soldiers at Ft. Monmouth were free on the weekends so I could look forward to a weekend with my young, pregnant wife.

I arrived by bus earlier than the appointed hour and stood outside the diner in my heavy Army wool overcoat, waiting. Finally, I saw the Guralnick Dodge Wayfarer, the one I had driven to Cape Cod for our honeymoon, pull up in the diner driveway. Lennie squeezed herself out of the rear seat and ran to me. It was the first time I saw her protruding midriff, a strange sight. But we embraced and kissed passionately. She was shy and embarrassed by her pregnant body – a body I hadn't seen before. But we spent the night in each other's arms in a motel, reveling in the intimacy that we could only have imagined during the previous two months.

The following day we found a house in Long Branch available for rental, fully furnished and within our means. We carried our meager belongings into our new home; an old two story wooden structure on Atlantic Avenue, within sight of an inlet of the ocean. Lennie's parents said they would return the following weekend with the rest of her things; the crib they had purchased for the coming baby and books. The house was rather bare; had no phone and was heated by a coal fired furnace in the basement that sent hot air up through a grate in the living room. The rest of the house was chilly and uncomfortable, but we didn't care, we were together.

Despite living miles away from the post in a civilian house, I was still in the Army and Monday morning I had to report for duty at seven o'clock. I had to be up at five thirty but it was a delightful novelty to sleep in a civilian bed with my wife for the first time in months.

At the Fort I was assigned to a training company, essentially students, who would all be attending classes together. We had a company sergeant named Donnelly, who called us to attention, took the roll, and then led us on a march to the school area. His face bore the unmistakable marks of an alcoholic; it was prematurely aged and haggard. He was an old timer – he had risen to Master Sergeant and been "busted" down several times. He was long past having any illusions about the military, but he had a commanding presence and when he shouted out, "Forward, harch!" the entire company strode off in unison.

It was a distance of about a half mile to the school area and we marched as on parade, with the lead corporal carrying "the guide on" – a pole bearing the pennant of our company. As we approached the street of the school, we heard the unmistakable sound of martial music. I couldn't believe it; an Army band to ornament a parade of trainees to school? Yes, it was so and we paraded past a reviewing stand where commanding officers stood and saluted as we swung past.

Once having arrived at the school area, our grizzled old Sergeant Donnelly shouted a command I had never heard before: "Hippity hop, Company stop!" The group broke up laughing at the Sergeant's open ridicule of Army protocol. We were then sent to class in separate buildings. My first class was "Electricity Basics". Here we were introduced to wiring diagrams and wiring tools as well as the fundamentals of electric circuits. Later, I and the others were set to work soldering connections on a circuit board. Army manuals were distributed dealing with electric circuitry. I found it interesting and not difficult.

In our next class we were seated at benches and in front of us was this curious machine called a teletype. That machine had served as the foundation stone of both military and civilian communications for forty years. It was basically a typewriter activated by a signal sent over wires. The signal was translated into key strokes and the machine produced printed messages transmitted by the sending teletypes. It is, of course, a museum piece today, replaced by the internet and computer printers. But as a critical element of written communications in the days before computers, the military needed technicians to maintain and repair these clumsy, clattering machines. That was going to be my job.

Each day I attended classes, studied the manuals on the teletype, tried to memorize the names of its parts, and struggled to understand the circuitry of telephone relays. At the end of the class day, we marched back to our company area, stood in formation and listened to announcements, got our mail and then were dismissed. Most of the men headed to the barracks, some to the PX for a beer, and I to my wife in Long Branch.

Our life in Long Branch was comfortable, but isolated. The house next door to our right was rented by a Sergeant married to an Italian woman who spoke little English, and on the left a Sergeant's wife who spoke only German. So we had no neighborly relations. The biggest problem was keeping the fire going in our furnace. I had never fired a coal fire and at night the fire had to be banked. It never worked for me. Despite my best efforts, overnight the fire would go out and inevitably we awoke to a freezing house. I would have to go down to the basement to start the fire every morning and make sure it was going strong enough to last the day. Sadly, I wasn't very good at it because often when I came home, Lennie would tell me she had to go down to the furnace and shovel more coal on the fire. Since she was five months pregnant, this was ill-advised. But the alternative was to shiver in the cold all day.

Our pleasant life was suddenly upended one night when Lennie found she was bleeding – not just a stain, but copiously. We had both been rather indifferent about medical care. Now we both realized this was a medical emergency. Since we were living off-post, I simply assumed it was my responsibility to get a civilian doctor to see her. Running to a phone booth in front of a bar two blocks away and looking in the phone book, I called the office of an obstetrician and described the problem. The doctor was nice enough to come to our house and examine her. First he administered a drug to stem the bleeding and then spoke to us.

"Since she is just beginning the sixth month of the pregnancy, it would be very hazardous to the survival of the fetus if she were to go into labor now, particularly since she informs me that her blood is RH Negative. That could require a complete blood transfusion if the baby is RH Positive. I have stopped the bleeding from the uterus, but it is extremely important that she remain completely immobile to avoid another bleed. She must stay where she is, on the couch. Use a bedpan, but she is not to get up from the couch. If she begins to bleed again, get her to a hospital as soon as possible. They should provide care at the Fort Monmouth Hospital since you're on active duty."

I paid him and thanked him and he departed, leaving us frightened and feeling a little foolish for not getting her prenatal care at the Fort. I began to think what I must do. No more Lennie shoveling coal, but who would attend to the fire? What about meals? The next day, I asked to speak to our company commander and explained the situation to him. He told me the regulations authorized emergency medical leave for a maximum of two weeks and he promptly gave orders so I could be home with her.

For the next two weeks I was a house husband, preparing meals, keeping the house clean, the furnace going and, of course, attending to Lennie. But at the end of this leave, I had to return to the Fort and classes. Lennie assured me she would be o.k. alone and I had no choice but to leave her. On the weekends her parents came and stayed with her.

One day when I came home from the post Lennie said, "We have a mouse." "What! A mouse!" I said in disbelief. She described the creature dashing across the living room and hiding under the furniture. As I sat in the living room I saw a fast moving dark object cross the room and I knew it was the mouse. Now I had to figure out how to catch the little creature and get rid of it. By the second day I had spotted it in the kitchen. I never thought of a commercial trap. Instead

I decided to try and quickly trap it under a metal waste basket and then figure out how to dispose of it. I waited patiently in the kitchen and finally it emerged from its hiding place and froze, motionless when it saw me. I moved swiftly to cover it with the waste basket. The trapped mouse tried to crawl out beneath the basket but I planted the basket firmly to the floor.

My plan was to somehow cover the bottom of the basket and carry it down to our basement and then fling the mouse into the furnace fire. Easier said than done. After slipping a sheet of cardboard beneath the wastebasket I gingerly carried my live cargo downstairs. A roaring fire was going and now I had to think of a way to hurl the mouse into it without giving it an opportunity to dash out when I removed the cardboard. It was a challenge to move quickly enough to accomplish the fiery execution of the mouse, but I somehow managed it. Any doubt that the mouse was in fact incinerated was erased when a strange unpleasant odor arose from the living room heat grate.

Lennie was now in the sixth month of her pregnancy and we felt we simply had to keep her immobile till she went into labor three months hence. But everything suddenly came to a head one Saturday night. Her parents had visited earlier in the day and had returned to New York. That evening, Lennie said to me with alarm, "Al, I'm bleeding again." I knew what that meant. An emergency run to the hospital at the fort. We needed an ambulance!

With no phone available I again had to run two blocks to the phone booth outside the bar. Frantically, I searched the telephone directory for an emergency number and found it: The Long Branch Emergency Rescue Squad. When I called and explained the crisis to the operator, she said, "Oh, no. You picked a bad night for an ambulance run. Tonight is our annual dance and everyone is there. But don't worry; we'll get an ambulance to your house."

I thanked her, hung up and began running back to our house. As I neared the house I saw flashing red emergency lights. When I arrived at our house there was a fire engine and two ambulances in the street outside. I ran into our living room and there were three men, large guys, wearing white coveralls with "Long Branch Emergency Rescue" embroidered in red letters. They were standing over Lennie, who was lying on the couch, frightened. One of them assured me they had already called the Fort Monmouth Hospital and her admittance was approved. I was allowed to ride in the ambulance with Lennie for the fifteen minute trip to the hospital.

At the hospital, I showed my military ID and signed the necessary forms. The admitting nurse asked where Lennie had been getting her prenatal care. I sheepishly admitted she had not had any. The nurse's look told me of her disapproval. They wheeled Lennie away to a room and the nurse, after writing down the name of my military company, told me I could leave and they would call when there were any developments.

For eight days she was kept immobile while they administered a drug to inhibit the onset of labor. Meanwhile every day I went to class. Each time the phone rang in the classroom I thought it was the hospital, but it wasn't. When the baby arrived I learned it in a typical Army way; we were marched back to the company area at noon and stood in formation while routine announcements were made and then the Sergeant called out, "Ziontz!"

"Here!" I yelled, and he said simply, "You're wanted in the orderly room." After being dismissed I hurried to the orderly room where our fat little company clerk was sitting at his desk.

When I identified myself, he said, "Oh, Yeah. They called from the hospital. Your wife had a baby." I was excited at this news and immediately asked him, "Boy or girl?" He responded indifferently, "I think it was a girl. Oh, maybe it was a boy. I don't remember. Anyway they said you could visit her now."

I took a bus to the hospital. Inside, I was directed to her room. She lay looking tired but happy. I hugged her and then asked, "What was it, a boy or a girl?" Lennie was surprised I hadn't known and said, "It's a little boy. But he's so tiny. They have him in an incubator. I think you can go down the hall and see him." I walked to the nursery window and joined other fathers and relatives looking in on their newborns. There must have been five or six and I didn't know which one was ours till I saw the name tag on the incubator and there he was, my first born. It was February 13, 1953, Lennie's birthday. The boy, whom we named Jeffrey, was born in the seventh month of Lennie's pregnancy. He weighed three pounds, two ounces. I looked at his squashed little face and tiny body. He looked like a little frog. But he was ours and it was the beginning of a new chapter in our lives.

I left the nursery area aware of the significance of the moment. First, I had to call my parents with the news, then Lennie's parents. After completing these calls I felt aimless. I didn't know what to do. I felt I had to do something to mark the event. Then it occurred to me. I would go to the PX, buy a box of cigars and pass them out to any one I knew on the post. After buying the box I looked around to see if any of my acquaintances were sitting at any of the tables in the fast food area. Then I spotted my grizzled old Sergeant, Sergeant Donnelly, he of the "Hip hop, company stop," fame. He was working at the PX. I strode over to the counter where he worked and said, "Hey, Sarge! Congratulate me, I'm a father." With this I handed him the box of cigars. He took one and said, "What was it, a boy or a girl?"

"A boy," I responded while he lit up one of the cigars. "How much did he weigh," was next and I told him, "Three pounds, two ounces." He took the cigar out of his mouth slowly and said, "Three pounds two ounces and you call yourself a father?"

It was typical of Donnelly's humor and I wasn't offended. I continued to circulate around the PX handing out cigars until I couldn't find any more takers, so I went home to our empty house.

It was six weeks before the hospital would allow us to take little Jeffrey home. So we went to the hospital every evening and looked at this tiny baby, whose features looked like a caricature of my face. In the meantime we had moved to a nicer, roomier house that was centrally heated and had a separate room for the baby. We bought all the accoutrements: a crib, bottles, blankets, diapers and a pacifier. Finally, the day came when his weight reached five pounds and we could take him home. Lennie had just turned nineteen and had no experience or training in the care of infants, but we were naively confident of our ability to parent our baby.

Taking care of a newborn premature infant was harder than we had imagined. Jeffrey spent most of his hours sleeping, crying and excreting. We had to bottle feed him and this proved to be difficult.

Holding my first born, Jeffrey in Long Branch, New Jersey 1953

He would begin sucking on his nipple but before he got very much milk, he would fall asleep. Lennie and I would jostle him and jiggle the bottle in and out of his mouth to encourage him to wake up and take more milk. It didn't work very well. At night he would awake crying at two or three in the morning and one of us would try to bottle feed him, with limited success. He cried without stop, so to soothe him I would carry him on my shoulder as I walked back and forth through the length of our apartment. He would cease crying for the first few minutes and then start again. I finally devised a method which seemed to soothe him; I would run ~ not walk ~ with him from one end of the apartment to the other. The bounce of the run seemed to soothe him and he would stop crying. This would often have to be repeated through the night, so by the time I had to leave for the post in the morning, I was haggard from lack of sleep.

I guess my face showed the effects of loss of sleep because one evening at formation, tough, grizzled old Sergeant Donnelly looked at me and said, "Hey Private, you 'oughta' put a Band-aid over your eyes before you bleed to death."

After we were dismissed, he came over to me and said, "Whatsa matter, aint getting enough sleep?" I told him of our difficulty in feeding our newborn. Then he said, with surprise, "Have you poked a hole in the nipple?" "Poked a hole in the nipple! I thought they came with a hole," I exclaimed.

Well, the old Sergeant knew a thing or two about nipples, saying, "Sometimes they're too small and you have to take a hot needle and push it through a couple of times to enlarge it." I was ecstatic and could hardly wait to get home to tell Lennie about this exciting discovery.

Once home, we promptly put the Sergeant's marvelous idea to use and enlarged the holes in all the nipples. At his very next feeding, poor Jeffrey began sucking with his accustomed effort and was surprised with the gush of milk that ran down his little chin. He soon adjusted to the new nipple flow and our night time feeding sessions went far more smoothly. The next day I told the Sergeant about the success of his advice and thanked him. He smiled slightly. Who would have thought that this grizzled old Army veteran was an expert on baby nipples!

Classes went on and I gradually learned about more complex circuits and telephone relays. Looming in the future was the question of whether after completing my training I would be sent to Korea. Meanwhile, Lennie and I were living the Army life. This meant shoe shining, belt buckle shining and ironing dress uniforms for Saturday inspections. Lennie helped with the ironing, leaving the shining for me. Then, one day I received a telephone call from my mother in Chicago informing me that my dad was going to have gall bladder surgery and asking whether I could get leave to be with him and her at the hospital. There was a procedure in which the Red Cross verified the nature of the emergency and facilitated emergency leave. So, for the second time I got emergency leave and went home to Chicago.

I was disturbed at my father's condition in the hospital. He had not recovered well and was in critical condition for a week. But I stayed by his bedside as he gradually improved. By the time my emergency leave expired he was on the road to recovery and I returned to Ft. Monmouth. But each time I had emergency leave, I was removed from my class and on my return had to join a class several weeks behind mine.

The result of these absences was that I did not cycle through the training program in the normal time, which would have been about eight months. Instead, it was almost a year before I finished the training. This was fortunate, since it was the Army's policy not to ship a soldier to Korea who had less than nine months remaining before discharge. After finishing at the School, I would have about a year remaining of my two year term. Now the question was where would they assign me? I and my classmates nervously awaited the posting of orders for assignment. After a week, it was up on the bulletin board.

I scanned the list and found my name. Next to it was "Sacramento Signal Depot". Yeah! It was not Korea.

Many of my friends did get sent to Korea, but some got exotic assignments such as Brussels, Paris, Italy and other European posts. I felt no envy. With a stateside assignment, it was likely that Lennie and Jeffrey could join me. Not only Jeffrey, but now Lennie was pregnant again and there would be another Ziontz in a few more months. The news that Lennie was pregnant again depressed her. Soon she would have the responsibility of caring for two children. It spelled the end of any hope she might have had that she could finish school and have a career. She would be locked into motherhood for years.

I had no idea what a Signal Depot was, but I asked around and learned it was a huge repair and overhaul facility for Signal Corps equipment of all kinds, radios, telephones, teletypes and relay panels. Though I wasn't much of a repairman on teletypes, I was happy with the assignment. We would be living in Sacramento, California.

CHAPTER TWELVE

SACRAMENTO AND THE SEATTLE DECISION

Leaving Fort Monmouth I boarded a plane in Newark and flew to San Francisco, then rode a bus to Sacramento. As I stood in the Greyhound station in Sacramento I had no idea of how to get to the Signal Depot. I spotted another soldier with a Signal Corps patch on his shoulder in the bus depot also looking uncertain. I asked if he was going to the Depot and he affirmed he was, happy to find a kindred soul in the same predicament. The fellow was short with a somewhat swarthy complexion and spoke with an accent. He was Greek and we soon became friends. I offered to call the Depot and when I reached them told the duty officer there were two of us needing a ride from downtown Sacramento out to the post. The guy grumbled a bit and finally said he would send a jeep out to pick us up. Meanwhile I and my Greek friend became better acquainted. Both of us had come from Fort Monmouth, though I was from Chicago and he was from Fresno, California. After about an hour a jeep arrived outside the bus station and we cheerfully loaded our duffel bags into it and climbed aboard.

My new friend and I sat in the rear seat of the Jeep as we drove through the city toward its southern edge, where the depot was located.

It was a warm, balmy night and the sight of palm trees along the streets reminded me that I was in California. California! I had never been in the state and I was eager for another new experience. I have always been experience-hungry; an appetite for people, places and new states of being and doing.

The ride seemed very long. Finally we turned down a wide street and after a few minutes I saw the depot. I was expecting a single building but instead saw what looked like a huge industrial complex; many buildings arrayed in a line and other similar looking buildings in rows behind them. It was like the grounds of a huge manufacturing complex; something you would expect if you visited the Ford Motor Company factory. In front of the main building, facing the street was a large billboard announcing that this was, "The Sacramento Signal Depot", Colonel somebody or other "Commanding".

The Jeep stopped at the guard shack where an MP stepped out to check our entry. We drove past these long industrial buildings and after passing three rows of them the roadway led through a vast open field. Finally, I saw lights ahead and we entered the area I later learned was called, "the troop area". This was where the troops were quartered.

After the usual routine of presenting my written orders I was issued bedding and directed to one of the Quonset huts that lined the street outside the Company Headquarters. I made my bed and got out of my uniform. There was a moment of strangeness as I lay in my new bunk and contemplated the idea that I was actually in California.

A loudspeaker blaring the familiar trumpet call of Reveille awakened me. It was six thirty. After shaving, washing and dressing, about two hundred of us fell into line in the morning formation and stood at attention while the Platoon Sergeant took the roll and then made the routine announcements. I expected that somehow we would be transported the mile or so to the Depot and was surprised when all my fellow soldiers walked to two nearby large shop buildings and went in. I turned to one and asked, "When do we go to the Depot?" His answer stunned me. "We don't go to the Depot. That's run by civilians." I didn't understand. Why were we here? He elaborated. "The civilians don't want any of the troops up there, so we stay in the troop area and do whatever we want in our shops."

I followed him into a large shop building with work benches and work areas cluttered with communications equipment. I was directed to the teletype area. There sat four machines in various stages of disassembly. Five men were sitting on work stools chatting, with no apparent interest in getting on with the work of assembling the teletypes. We introduced each other and I asked one of them, Hank, how the system worked. He explained the depot would send down some machines for us to overhaul, but then they would go right back to the depot to be overhauled again by the civilian workers. It seems that these were sent to us only to keep us busy and with no expectation that they would be sent into active service by us. Later, I learned that the depot had been built during the war and was staffed by soldier technicians but after the war they were replaced by civilians. For some reason, the Army held onto the troop area but seemed not to know what to do with the troops, so we were consigned to "make-work" projects.

Later I learned that there was an auto shop in the building and several of the men were working on their cars there. There was also a woodworking shop and one of the guys in my section made it all plain, "You can work on anything you want here. If you want to make furniture, we have all the tools and equipment."

Our platoon sergeant said we should finish overhauling the teletypes so others could be sent over from the depot ~ a meaningless cycle of equipment just to keep us occupied. I had experienced mindless exercises in the Army but this was beyond anything I could conceive. The watchword was, "Look busy. If you can't find anything else to do, clean your tools."

Not only were we about a hundred and eighty highly trained communications equipment repairmen, but to support us there were also another two hundred troops assigned to the mess hall, the armory, the motor pool, the headquarters staff, even barbers. As all of this sank in I thought; what a monumental waste of public money. In fairness, some of the radar techs would periodically be sent out to National Guard units to service their equipment, but that was sporadic and hardly justified the existence of our "Signal Maintenance Battalion". No, it was an Army boondoggle and nothing more. From time to time I thought seriously of writing to my Congressman to expose this misuse of public money, but on second thought, I had other ideas. If this was disbanded, where would I be sent ~ to Korea? No, best to keep my mouth shut and live with the system. When I got out of the Army I would take some action, perhaps writing to Secretary of Defense Mac Namara, he of the efficiency reputation, and no doubt, he would act swiftly to put an end to this Army charade.

Since I would be here indefinitely I decided to gamble on the odds and ask Lennie to come out with the baby and we would live off-post. I had to find a house and tell Lennie to come out to California. She was happy at the prospect of our reunion, especially when she considered the pending arrival of our second child.

After looking through the ads in the paper I found a rental in South Sacramento, about two miles from the depot. It was a very simple wood frame house, with a living room, two bedrooms, a bathroom and a kitchen. There was bare furniture, but it would do for us. Below us, in a basement apartment there was another family living, the Speases. In time we found them to be a very warm and welcoming family who offered to help with anything we might need.

Lennie and Jeff arrived on the train and I drove down to the station to meet them and welcome them to our new home in Sacramento. Lennie and Jeff moved from her parent's home to mine in Chicago while she awaited word whether I would remain at Sacramento and not be shipped elsewhere. We had been separated only about a month when she stepped off the train. I was happy to embrace them and I was also eager to show her our new Chevy ~ the first car I had ever owned. Like me, Lennie had never been in California and this was an adventure for her.

As we drove from the station to our rented house, she commented on the palm trees and the balmy weather even though it was December. She liked the house and quickly set about making it into a home. For one thing it meant buying another crib for the new baby who was coming in February. Our meager furnishings were shipped by the Army from Fort Monmouth to Sacramento and were waiting for us in a warehouse shortly after I arrived.

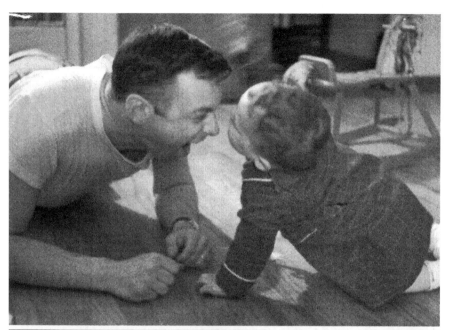

Playing nosey-nosey with Jeff at home in Sacramento, California 1953

We quickly settled into our new living routine; Lennie at home with Jeffrey and I driving my yellow Chevy into the depot each morning for the morning formation. But life at pretending to work and trying to "look busy" became tedious. Then one day there was a change. I was called to the orderly room and our commanding Captain informed me that I was being assigned to TI&E; Troop Information and Education. It meant that I would have a small desk in another building on the post where I would process enrolling interested soldiers in education courses and on Saturday mornings I would deliver a talk on assigned topics. My talks had to be based on official literature. Examples were, "The Strategic Air Command, It's Mission", "Our Mission in Germany" and "The Global Threat of Communism". The challenge was to keep over a hundred men awake and interested in my presentation while they were actually impatient to get off the post and go into town. Occasionally, I showed Army films. For this I had to drive an Army Jeep to Mc Clellan Air Force Base, just outside of Sacramento ~ or "Sacto" as we called it, to pick up films. I enjoyed the freedom and the Jeep. Later, for some reason, I was given an orientation and then a license to drive an Army two ton truck. Since it had an automatic transmission the driving was easy; just a matter of adjusting to the size and dimensions of this large vehicle. On weekends, Lennie and Jeffrey and I would get in the Chevy and drive downtown, do some shopping and go back home.

But as the year deepened into the summer months, scorching temperatures made life in Sacramento more and more difficult. There was no air conditioning in our house and during the day the heat made the indoors almost unbearable. Our only relief was weekend drives out into the countryside with the windows rolled down and the wind flowing through the car.

One weekend, our recreational drive became a nightmare. The day was a Sunday and I decided to drive out toward Jackson, some forty miles away. I had no intention of going all the way to Jackson, since it was too far and there was nothing there of any interest; it was just a direction for a Sunday country ride. Jeff was ensconced in a car crib mounted between the front and rear seats, sleeping.

The countryside was barren; no farms or houses, and after we passed a gas station we went for miles with no sign of human habitation. Suddenly I heard an unusual sound from the engine. This was followed almost immediately by a bizarre event; the windshield wipers both swept back and forth once, then stopped. So did the engine. I knew this meant serious car trouble. I pressed the starter pedal and the starter did something even more bizarre. Instead of its usual slow grinding action it whirred like a high speed electric motor, but the engine didn't start. We sat motionless on the highway with a dead engine. We were miles from anywhere and we were in trouble.

I got out of the car and opened the hood, not having the slightest idea of what to look for. Dear Lennie called out the window, "Would a screw driver help?" "No," I replied through gritted teeth, knowing the problem was something beyond fixing with a screwdriver. I saw nothing obviously out of place in the engine so I knew it would take a mechanic to get my car running again. In the meantime it was sitting stock still in the middle of the road. I reluctantly decided that the only thing to do was push it off to the side of the road and for Lennie and me to cross over to the other side and hitch a ride back to a gas station so I could call, our downstairs neighbor, Lou Spease and his older son to come out and get us.

First I had to push my car to the side of the road; something I thought was well within my ability. I told Lennie to get behind the wheel, though she had never driven a car, and simply steer to the side when I got it rolling. Once she was behind the wheel I went to the rear trunk and began pushing. Nothing happened. No movement at all. I pushed harder. Still no movement. Must be in gear I thought. So I went to the driver's side, opened the door and wiggled the gear shift. It was in neutral. I looked at Lennie accusingly and said, "Were you stepping on the brake?" "No, of course not," she answered. I returned to the trunk and again pushed with all my strength. Nothing. Now I was determined to put my whole body into it; turning my back to the trunk, lifting the rear bumper, digging in my heels and pressing my back against the trunk with all my might. The Chevy didn't budge. Since it was on a level roadway, the immovability of the car seemed to defy the laws of physics.

Our first car bought in Sacramento, California

Finally, I had the brains to walk around to the front of the car and look at the front wheels. There it was! A rock in front of the right front tire was effectively blocking the car. After removing it, I told Lennie simply to turn the wheel to the right once I got the car rolling. She nodded. I returned to the rear and again exerted my back against the trunk. This time I was rewarded with movement. The car was rolling. As I stood there watching, I was horrified to see the car roll off the road to the right and continue rolling till it reached a ditch, where it gently settled, leaning to the right, tilted into a ditch. Fortunately, it didn't roll over and Lennie emerged, lifting Jeffrey out of his car bed and carrying him to the highway. It was my fault. I had instructed her only to turn to the right without explaining she had to straighten the wheel after the car was off the road, so she held the wheel in the turned position and didn't let go while the car headed straight for the ditch. Oh, well. Disaster averted.

Now we had to try to find a generous soul to give us a ride. We stood by the side of the road, Lennie, obviously pregnant and holding our baby, Jeffrey, and me. There were few cars and when we saw one approaching we faced it with our thumbs up, giving the classic hitchhiker's sign. I had been naïve enough to think it would be easy. Who could turn down a couple with a baby, standing across the road from a disabled car in a ditch? But that car whizzed by without even slowing. The same thing happened again and again as the time slowly passed. The most painful part was when the occupants looked back at us after they had sped by. What were they thinking ~ that we were some kind of roadside curiosity?

I was getting worried. My expectation of a quick ride was obviously not happening and we had been standing at the side of the road for over an hour. But there was no alternative. Finally, a car with only the driver and one passenger approached. It slowed and I was thrilled to see its brake lights come on shortly after it passed us. We hurried to it and were gratified when the passenger opened the front door for us to enter the two door car. The two men were ordinary looking and courteous. As we squeezed into the rear seat both of us were alarmed at what we saw. On the floor were two rifles. I immediately thought: Folsom Prison escapees! Well, my imagination had run away with me, because their behavior was calm, friendly and they simply wanted to know where we were going. I told them about the gas station I had noticed and explained I was going to call for help with my disabled car. They said they would take us to the station and let us out there. And that's what happened. We thanked them and they left.

Happily, when I called the Spease apartment, Bea answered and immediately understood our predicament. Her husband Louie had a truck and she said she would dispatch him to us without delay. In about a half hour he arrived. We got in the truck and went back down the road to the pathetic sight of my Chevy tilted over in the ditch. Louie took out a chain and hooked it up to my car. In a matter of minutes he had it out of the ditch and turned toward Sacramento. With me at the wheel controlling the speed of the car to insure it didn't hit Louie's truck when he slowed or stopped, we made it to a garage in town, where Louie knew the owner. It took only a few minutes for the diagnosis: the timing gear had been stripped. Once that happens there is nothing to move the cam shaft and activate the cylinder valves. They remain in the open position, ergo, no compression, ergo whirring starter. It took only a day to replace the timing gear plus seventy five dollars for the repair. Life returned to normal.

Meanwhile, Lennie's pregnancy was advancing. The expected date of delivery was some time in February. She would have to go to the nearest military base with obstetric facilities, Mather Air Force Base, some fifteen miles from our house, twelve miles out of the city. Our friendly downstairs neighbor, Bea Spease assured us she would be ready any time of day or night to take care of Jeffrey when Lennie had to go to the hospital. But I had no confidence in our Chevy and decided we needed a newer and more reliable car. I bought a 1948 Hudson from a used car lot; a pretty car with blue embossed leather trim around the doors, chrome steering column and chrome trim around the windows. It ran fine and I felt confident about taking Lennie to the hospital in it.

On February 15, 1954, two days after Lennie's twentieth birthday, at two o'clock in the morning Lennie awakened me saying she was having labor pains and we better get going to the hospital. After taking Jeffrey downstairs to Bea and leaving him with her, we got into our Hudson and started out for Mather. This baby was going to be full term and there was no sense of emergency, but still, with labor beginning, I wanted to get Lennie to the hospital as soon as possible.

As soon as we left the city and started down the highway to the air base the only light was the beam of my headlights. We had been underway for only about twenty minutes when suddenly, without warning, my headlights went out, leaving us in pitch darkness. There were few other cars on the road, but I felt it would be dangerous to continue without being able to see the edge of the road. I decided to turn around, wait for a passing car and follow its tail lights to the nearest gas station. I felt confident we had blown a fuse and it could easily be replaced.

Soon, I saw the lights of an approaching car, pulled out and followed him. Guided only by the tail lights ahead, I proceeded several miles till we reached a gas station. It was somewhat tricky but it worked and I pulled into the station and told the attendant the problem. Did he have fuses? Yes, he did and I bought one for fifty cents and he popped it into place. The lights went back on; I thanked him and took off again for Mather, this time a little less cool than I had been. I went only a few miles when the lights again went out. Now I knew what I had to do. I repeated the maneuver and followed another car back to the same gas station. This time I was nervous. How many times would this happen? I excitedly told the attendant that my wife was in labor and we were on our way to Mather, there was no time to lose. He went behind the counter, brought out an entire box of fuses, put one in and showed me where to insert them. I bought the entire box. "Good luck!" were his parting words as I sped off down the highway praying that the new fuse would not fail.

The fuse held and we arrived at the hospital on the Air Force Base. I led Lennie into the admitting area and told the on-duty nurse that she was in labor. They promptly put her on a gurney and wheeled her down the hall to the obstetrics ward. Me, they told to wait till they had some idea of how soon she would deliver. After about twenty minutes a nurse came out and said she would not be delivering that night, but probably some time the next day. I could check by phone and return to visit her and see the new baby then. The following day, February 16, after two phone calls were met with a "not yet", at around 10:30 the next morning, my call produced the news: she had delivered a little boy, weighing about seven pounds and she was doing fine. We named him Martin.

Lennie, Jeff (left) and Martin (right)
in our backyard in Sacramento, California 1954

After the excitement of a new member of our family, life
returned to normal, with double the work load for Lennie, taking care
of both a one year old and a newborn. Martin was born one year
and three days after Jeffrey, making it convenient to remember their
birthdays but giving Lennie the hard work of handling two infants.

Meanwhile my discharge date was only seven months away and
I had to start thinking of what was I going to do. I had a law degree,
but my legal education had been very spotty and now I had been away
from the law for almost three years. Did I really want to be a practicing
lawyer? The idea of working for a lawyer or a firm in a downtown
Chicago building, probably on La Salle Street, the street of lawyers,
was repugnant. How about my long standing interest in international

relations? Well, the only career possible without an advanced degree, was working in the Foreign Service. The idea of working in a bureaucracy was not an appealing one. I couldn't see myself fitting into a large structured government department. Despite my parents' assurances that the family would send me legal work, I thought that starting a solo law practice was not a practical idea, especially because I knew nothing of the actual practice of law, a subject not taught in law schools, particularly the University of Chicago Law School. No, I had to go back to Chicago, study hard for the bar exam and look for some kind of a law job.

I began my preparation by getting an Army manual on Business Law and reading it carefully. I found it far more satisfying than law school because it laid out the fundamentals of such subjects as Contracts, Sales, Negotiable Instruments, Corporations, Partnerships, Agency and the like, without the vagueness of the Socratic Method and the Law School's disdain for clear cut rules of law. I soaked up this body of information easily, since most of the ideas and language were familiar to me.

On reflection, it is surprising that I decided to become a practicing lawyer. My experience with Law School had been, for the most part, miserable. I had entered a bright eyed, young idealist, excited about the world of ideas and left a deflated and confused twenty-three year old, deeply disappointed in the ideas that the Law School embraced: Free market economics was the predominant theme. Meanwhile, it seemed to me that law was devoid of social ideals.

Returning to Chicago seemed only natural; it was the city of my childhood and young adulthood, and most important, that was where my Mother and Father lived. Oh to be sure, I hadn't forgotten Seattle, but it seemed a dreamy place, beyond my practical reach and it didn't figure in my plans after discharge from the Army. All that changed as a result of an unexpected event.

On an ordinary day in June, I received a call from the Captain, the commanding officer of the Base. He wanted to see me at Headquarters. I went over, was admitted, saluted and waited to hear the reason for the meeting. The Captain was friendly, told me to sit down and then proceeded to inform me that he was sending me to New Jersey. I was alarmed, since we had moved from New Jersey to California and I hoped I wasn't being reassigned. He assured me that this was a brief mission and afterward I would return to Sacramento. Then he explained that the Depot was shipping some highly classified equipment, called IFF, which was an electronic device to identify friend or foe. While it was being shipped on a cargo flight, regulations required it be accompanied by an armed guard and that is what he wanted me to do; be an armed guard and stay with the equipment till it was delivered to the authorized Signal Corps people at the Newark Airport. I would be armed with a .45 caliber pistol which I would carry at all times in a holster. When I asked when I would depart, he said, "Tonight." I hesitated to complain, but then told him we had planned to have dinner guests that evening and such an abrupt trip was going to cause my wife to be unhappy. He said,

"Call her right now and tell her you're leaving the base at seven this evening. Now I want you to go over to the armory and pick up your pistol and holster. Because I understand this is causing your family some inconvenience I will authorize ten days TDY. Dismissed."

Our meeting was over and I headed to the phone booth outside of the office building and called Lennie to tell her of this unexpected development. She took it in good spirits and simply wanted to know what clothing items I needed for the trip.

TDY is army jargon for temporary duty and meant I had 10 days of leave. I began planning to stop in Chicago on my return to see Mom and Dad and spend some time with them. When I reflected on why the base commander had chosen me for this military assignment. I could not think of a single reason. I was not aggressive, nor physically prepossessing. I had no experience in shooting the pistol. The mission didn't involve legal training. I could only surmise he must have thought me a mature and cool headed soldier.

I went to the armory and picked up the .45 caliber pistol; a weapon I had never handled before, feeling only its weight and its menace. Placing it in a holster I took it home and packed for the trip. Back at the base I left the Hudson parked and walked over to the headquarters building where a small Army truck awaited. In it were two large containers wrapped in canvas with prominent lettering: "U.S. Army Signal Corps. To be handled by authorized personnel only!" There were two men in the cab and the driver told me we were going to San Francisco Airport where the cargo would be put aboard a plane.

At the San Francisco Airport, we negotiated various gates and went to the air freight loading area. We were directed to a large hangar and instructed to place the freight items on the floor till our flight was ready. The driver and I lifted the boxes, which were not heavy, and placed them on the floor of the hangar. My driver bade me "so long" and departed. At this point I thought my status as a guard required that I put the holster and the gun onto my belt. I had never worn a gun or a holster before and felt somewhat like an actor pretending to be an armed guard. None of the airport people came into the hangar and I finally sat down on one of the boxes to await developments. As time wore on, I became bored and impatient and worse, cold, in the dropping San Francisco night temperatures.

After two hours, a guy came over to me and said my flight would be preparing for departure in about a half hour. He said the airport crew would come over with a forklift to load my boxes on the plane. At last! Developments. Eventually, this did happen and I rode the forklift out to a waiting DC-4, a four engine transport. It had no windows and was clearly a cargo plane.

The flight crew were already in their seats in the cockpit when I climbed up the stairway to the cargo compartment in the rear of the aircraft. We were the only people aboard. The co-pilot came back to the rear, carrying two blankets.

"Sorry," he said, "These are all we can offer to sleep on. When you get up, come up front and we can get you some breakfast to eat." The interior was cold and dark and filled with cargo held in place with cargo straps. I spread the blankets on the metal floor and laid down on them. Getting to sleep was easier than I thought. It must have been about five in the morning and I was tired. I awoke, chilled and stiff from sleeping on a hard metal floor. I made my way forward to the cockpit and got a cheery "good morning" from the pilot, "Howdja sleep back there?"

"Okay," I replied as I sat down in the jump seat behind the crew. Then the copilot stood up and went to a small refrigerator, saying, "How about some breakfast?" "Sure," I replied and he took out a tray covered with foil and stuck it into some kind of microwave. In a few minutes handed me the tray with scrambled eggs and bacon. Then he got me some plastic utensils and offered me coffee from a large thermos. I gratefully ate this airborne breakfast and then turned my attention to the instruments and controls of this large plane.

After watching for a few minutes I began to ask the pilot questions and in response, he explained the various mysterious dials and switches. Each explanation led to more questions till finally the pilot said, "Hey, why don't you get in the first officer's seat and try flying this thing?" I was somewhat overwhelmed by such an invitation, but I didn't hesitate and slid into the seat next to the pilot, while the copilot switched places and got into the jump seat. I grasped the control wheel and at the pilot's suggestion banked the plane left and right. It was a thrill.

I noticed a large knurled wheel between my seat and the pilot's seat and asked about it. "It controls the trim tabs," he said. "Wanna see how important that is?" When I nodded affirmatively, he said "Hold onto that control wheel hard, cuz I'm going to trim its nose down and when you see the nose start to go down, you pull back on the wheel just as hard as you can, got it?" Again, I nodded and he began to roll the wheel forward. Immediately, the nose of the plane tilted downward, alarmingly. I pulled back on the wheel as hard as I could, but couldn't bring it back up. "Pull harder!" he yelled. I braced my two feet against the instrument panel and pulled back with all my strength. The nose didn't come up. The pilot laughed and then said, "Okay, I'll take it." I let go the control wheel as he confidently rotated the trim wheel backward and the nose obediently rose. "Now you know what the trim tabs do," and he explained. It was a powerful demonstration.

After I returned to the jump seat the copilot said, "We'll be in Denver in about thirty minutes. We're landing there and your cargo will be transferred to a United flight to Newark."

That's what happened and after a brief stop in New York to visit my cousin Annie, I caught a flight to Chicago and was embraced by my Mom and Dad. After spending the day with them, I borrowed my Dad's Chrysler and drove out to Hyde Park to visit some of my U. of C. friends. There weren't many around. Lawrence Friedman, like me, had also been drafted and was in the army and so was George Rothbart. I decided to visit another old friend, Burt Ditkowsky.

Burt was older than me and a businessman, having inherited his father's Laundry business; the Hyde Park Laundry. He had a large flourishing business laundering uniforms and clothing. Burt invited me to come over to his house and we sat in his kitchen drinking coffee and talking. Then he asked me, "So, what are you going to do after you get out of the army?" "Go back to Chicago, I suppose, take the bar exam and try to start a career in law," I answered. "What happened to your dream of living in Seattle?" he asked, provocatively. "Oh, maybe some day after I get started, I'll move to Seattle," I said airily.

Burt, being a smart and direct friend, shot this down quickly. "You're kidding yourself. Once you start a law practice in Chicago, you'll never be able to move. Lawyers are not mobile and they can't take their connections with them. If you really want to live in Seattle, you should start your career there."

Thoughtful in Sacramento 1953

Suddenly, I realized he was right. If I was ever going to live in Seattle, I had to make my move directly out of the Army. It was a moment of enlightenment. I simply hadn't thought the issue through carefully, but Burt's advice made it crystal clear: I would go to Seattle and not return to Chicago.

When I arrived back in Sacramento, I sat down with Lennie for a serious talk about our future plans. I told her about my conclusion after talking with Burt Ditkowsky; that I would not be going back to Chicago and instead head up to Seattle to try to find a job there. There were serious problems with this decision: my parents would be deeply hurt that Lennie and I and their grandchildren would be two thousand miles away. There was also the fact that we knew no one in Seattle and I had no idea about getting a job with a law firm there. But she had heard me speak of Seattle many times and had some idea of why this place was so attractive for me. She agreed ~ we would go to Seattle and make a life there.

A friend on the post, a nice guy; Tom Pargeter, was from Seattle and I had the idea of starting my job search with the Yellow pages of the Seattle phone book. Tom was going home on leave and I asked if he would be willing to tear out the pages of Attorney's listings and bring them back to me so I would have a way to start. Tom was nice enough to do it and soon I was poring over names of lawyers, trying to make an enlightened guess which might be a good possibility for a job. I picked out sixty, prepared a resume and an application letter and sent copies to my selections.

My plan was to take leave and go up to Seattle for interviews with any lawyer or firm that showed interest. I soon received fifty or so replies; most saying they had no openings, but some saying they would be glad to meet me. This was encouraging enough to warrant a trip to Seattle.

On my arrival in the city of my hopes, I took a room in the downtown YMCA. In hand I had a typed list of the firms and individuals that seemed like possibilities and this was my working tool. I began telephoning for interview appointments and soon had four or five appointments. It was my first introduction to the lawyers of Seattle.

For two days I walked around the office buildings of downtown Seattle, taking the elevator up to the suites of my prospects. The lawyers were courteous, respectful and even friendly, but I did not even receive a glimmer of a job prospect. I was becoming discouraged.

I hated the thought of returning to Sacramento empty handed, but I was determined to move to this city even if I had no job. But it was one such interview that led to a chain of events and a law job.

One of the lawyers I had an interview with said he had seen an ad in the Seattle Journal of Commerce, a business publication, seeking a young lawyer to do collection work. When I asked where I could find a copy of this publication, he told me to go to the King County Law Library. They would surely have one. He also told me something that turned out to be a key to my future. He said, "You might want to talk to the Law Librarian ~ an old fellow by the name of Bob Jarvis. He often hears of openings in law firms and he might be a good source of information for you." I thanked him and left.

Determined to follow every lead, I walked over to the King County Courthouse, where the library was located, took the elevator to the sixth floor, walked down the gloomy marble corridor and found the doors to the library. It was a very large room with rows and rows of shelving for law books. Along one side, next to a wall with large windows, were study tables, a few of which were occupied by lawyers reading law books. At the front of the library, behind an oak railing sat a rotund elderly man, with prominent double chins, wearing an old fashioned high collar and looking like a character out of Dickens. This was Mr. Jarvis, the librarian, whose name even sounded Dickensian. I introduced myself, told him that I was in the Army and looking for a position with a law firm when I got out the following month. Old Mr. Jarvis hemmed and hawed and finally said, "Just a minute. I think I might know of someone who is looking for a young feller like you. His name is Jerry Hile and he's a damn good lawyer. He's leaving his firm and I heard he wants to hire a young man."

With that he turned around in his oak swivel chair and dialed a number on his phone. After a brief conversation, he swiveled back and said, "I just spoke with Jerry and he'd like to meet you. You go on over to the Dexter Horton Building. He's expecting you."

After thanking him profusely, I walked one block to the Dexter Horton Building, a fifteen story undistinguished office building dating back to the 1920's. In the lobby I looked up Jerry Hile. There it was, under the firm name of Hile, Hoof and Shucklin. Sounded very lawyerly. I rode the elevator to their floor and entered the prosaic interior of an office. The secretary told me that Mr. Hile would be out to see me in a few minutes.

After a short wait, a tall man in his sixties emerged from one of the offices and introduced himself to me; "I'm Cliff Hoof." I was momentarily confused. I had been expecting Jerry Hile. But I followed him as he ushered me into his office, thinking perhaps the interviewing assignment had been given to someone else in the firm. As I sat in his office across the desk from Mr. Hoof we began a friendly conversation. Two minutes later, the door burst open and another older man entered, saying, "Just a minute, Cliff, he is here to see me!" Mr. Hoof excused himself for thinking I was there to see him and I followed Mr. Hile into his office. From being without any hope of a job it seemed I was now being fought over by two lawyers. I sat down in Mr. Hile's office and the interview began.

It was strange. It seemed as though I was interviewing him. He spoke almost non-stop, telling me about himself, his origins in Oklahoma, his career as a United States Attorney. Garrulous is an understatement. I didn't know what to make of it. Jerry Hile was in his late fifties or early sixties, with tight white curly hair and a broad, flat nose. I was struck by the fact that he wore a string tie and didn't look or sound like the traditional lawyer. But heck, this was Seattle and maybe lawyers here were a lot more informal than Chicago. He told me that he had a very successful practice and one of his clients was a brilliant developer by the name of Buford Seals who was going to build a world class market. He also said he was leaving Hile, Hoof and Shucklin and going into his own practice, for which he needed an experienced lawyer with at least ten years of experience and a young neophyte, to do research, write memos, briefs and do the leg work. It was clear that I was a candidate for the neophyte position. He had quickly scanned my résumé and had few questions except for asking whether I was married and had children. The tone of the exchange was going well, and I sensed that I would probably be hired by him.

Then his phone rang and he said, "Send him in." In walked a short, nice looking young man who was seated in the other chair in the room. To my shock and horror another job interview began with this guy, named Ken Hobbs. Hobbs was a Harvard graduate who had actually practiced for a short time in Boston, and had a broad Boston accent. Could he be considering which of the two of us he would hire? But Hobbs' interview was going badly. He kept trying to tell Hile of his practice experience in Boston, and Hile responded by telling him in loud, aggressive tones, "Look, no lawyer is worth a damn till he's been at it for at least ten years."

Unfazed, Hobbs resumed his recital of his experience, not sensing apparently that he was getting Hile angrier. Finally, it reached a point of open hostility from Hile and he ended the interview. Hobbs left and I felt the threat to my job left with him.

Hile then told me he was relocating to an office in West Seattle, saying, "The doctors have all left downtown because the parking is impossible and the lawyers who stay in the downtown district will find their clients will leave them too. I have beautiful offices being prepared in a new building and we'll be relocating there as soon as the facilities are ready. Now what is the minimum amount you need to live on?"

I felt that I was in no position to bargain, what with my poor law school record and the difficulty I had in trying to find a position. So I made a serious tactical mistake and said, "Two hundred dollars a month." I should not have opened with my lowest figure and said at least said two hundred and fifty, but I had heard that big firms were paying three hundred a month and thought I would make Hile an offer of a low salary that he would find attractive. He did and said, "Okay, then that's our deal. Two hundred a month. When do you get out of the Army?" "Next month," I said.

"Good," said Hile and then told me to come up to his office when I got settled in town after I was discharged. I could hardly wait to call Lennie and tell her the news. I had a job and we could move to Seattle.

On my return to Sacramento we began making preparations for the trip to Seattle. I built a bench to be placed on the floor in front of the rear seat of our Hudson. We would place bedding on it and on the rear seat so as to create a roomy platform for Jeffrey and Martin to play and sleep on during the long trip up the coast. I sold the Chevy to another guy on the post so now we were committed to the Hudson. In September I was sent to Fort Ord to process for discharge and on my return I had my discharge papers in hand. I was out of the Army.

On one sunny morning we put the two babies in our car, waved goodbye to our neighbors, the Speases, and started out for our new life in Seattle. The Army took care of shipping all our furnishings to Seattle where they would await my pickup at a freight house. Now we looked forward to a scenic two day drive to Seattle where we would have to find an apartment and I would begin to build my life as a lawyer.

CHAPTER THIRTEEN

TRANSITIONING TO LIFE IN SEATTLE: TROUBLE IN PARADISE

I eagerly awaited the first sight of the magic city so Lennie could see what I had found so captivating. Unfortunately, the morning we reached the southern edge of the city, it was grey, overcast and raining. Not a good beginning. We found a nice, modest motel on Highway 99 and decided to stay there till we found an apartment. It was called the Blue Haven Motel ~ an inviting name. We spent our first five days there while we searched for an apartment. Since Mr. Hile had said his new offices would be in West Seattle I scanned the want ads for apartments there. One sounded intriguing; "Roomy, airy two bedroom apartment on Puget Sound. Furnished." We decided to look at it.

I had never been in West Seattle before, and, indeed, had only a vague idea of where this part of the city was. The address of the apartment was 10109 51st Avenue S.W. It turned out to be a remote and difficult place to find. After much searching and consulting our Seattle map, we were led to a street that descended down a steep cliff in tight, winding turns. At the bottom was a block long street along the shore of Puget Sound. The house looked out on Puget Sound and across to the Olympic Mountains. Wow! This clearly vindicated my claim that Seattle was a picturesque city.

10109 was the last house on the block; a brown, shingled two story house just up from the waterfront. The owners lived in a small house below it just behind a retaining wall at the water's edge. They were an elderly couple and the wife showed us the rental apartment. It turned out the description in the ad was not exactly accurate. The main bedroom was actually a glassed in front porch. But there was another small bedroom, a bathroom, a kitchen, a large living room with a fireplace and an area that could serve as a dining room. We were charmed and rented it.

After picking up our shipped belongings (a bookcase and books, two cribs, a baby carriage and some linens) we settled into our new home. Mr. Hile told me his new office quarters were not yet ready and he had a temporary office in the Georgetown neighborhood, near Boeing field. I reported for work there and Hile gave me a legal research assignment and told me I should go to the King County Law Library, since he had no law books in his office yet. Dutifully I took the bus to downtown Seattle and went to the Law Library and began to re-familiarize myself with the methods of legal research.

Reading cases quickly brought back my understanding of the language of the law. In those days, before the era of computers, we used a publication called Shepherd's, which listed every case that cited the one we were interested in. So we "Shepherdized" to find our way through a body of law. If the case had not been cited in any other case, I had to go to the treatises; one of two encyclopedias called "American Jurisprudence, or Am. Jur." or another more comprehensive one, "Corpus Juris Secundum, or simply, "Corpus Juris". After a week or so, I became intimately acquainted with the library and able to find answers to my assigned questions.

There was another and more daunting challenge ahead of me: the Bar Exam. I had a law degree but I was not a licensed lawyer, so until I was "admitted to the bar", my work was limited to research and writing memos and briefs. It was September when we arrived in Seattle and the rules of the Bar Association required residency in the state for 90 days to be eligible to take the Exam. The next scheduled exam was in early December and I would not be eligible till late December.

On the advice of Jerry Hile I applied for a waiver of the 90 day requirement on the ground that I had been in military service and could not get here earlier. The waiver was denied. It was just as well because I needed the extra time to learn the law, especially Washington State Law, some of which was unique to the state. But not taking the December exam meant my next opportunity would be June of the following year and since there is a lag of a month or two till the exam was graded and announcements of the names of those who had passed was made, it meant that almost a year would elapse from the beginning of my clerkship with Jerry Hile till I was useful as a full-fledged lawyer. But he never complained about the length of time that I could work only as a clerk.

In the meantime, I was taking a "Bar Review Course", given in the evenings, to prepare for the exam. While their classes were held only three nights a week, I spent other nights in the Law Library studying legal materials and case law to help me prepare. This was not like law school. My job depended on passing the exam and these no longer seemed like abstract rules or boring court opinions; they were the stuff on which my livelihood would be based.

One day, Hile said his new offices were almost ready and we

could move in shortly. He was driving over to West Seattle to look it over and asked if I wanted to see our new, and as he put it, "beautiful" quarters. "Sure" I said and we rode together to West Seattle. The office was located on the main commercial street, California Avenue, in a corner building near the corner of Oregon Street. We walked to the front entrance at ground level, two doors down from the corner. It looked like an ordinary store front. He unlocked the front door and we walked in. Fronting the sidewalk was a tall plate glass window, floor to ceiling, just like any store. Inside was a large empty room and to the right was a corridor leading to the rear. We walked down the corridor and immediately to the left was a door opening into a spacious office. "This is going to be my office," said Hile. Further along the corridor was another door opening into a similar space. "This will be the office of the lawyer I'm going to hire," said Hile. The corridor opened into a rear room containing a bathroom and a rear exit door. There were no other offices. "Where is my office?" I asked, and his reply left me disappointed and angry. "Oh, we'll put a desk back here for you," he said. Hile's plan stunned me. An office in the back of a store. The quarters were not, "beautiful", they were an ordinary storefront, and now I was being told, I would have a desk in the back of the store. So this is where my career as a lawyer would begin. It was a humiliating beginning. I swallowed my pride because I had no alternative.

When we "moved in" a week or so later, a desk was placed in the front of the office for a secretary. The front was spacious enough for a reception area and a couch was placed there for waiting clients, Desks were also installed in each of the two offices. In the back room bookcases were installed to contain American Jurisprudence. a multi-volume encyclopedia of American Law, and a set of the Washington Statutes, called, R.C.W. Those were the only legal sources we had.

But one couldn't do legal research without the collected decisions of the Washington Supreme Court, called "Washington Reports", nor without Shepherd's. I could see that I would have to keep going downtown to the King County Law Library. The worst feature was the card table; a flimsy folding card table and folding chair in the back room. "We'll get you a desk later," said Hile. I couldn't help thinking of how my parents would view this beginning of my career. They would be mortified.

Two weeks later, a tall, dignified fellow came into the office and Hile came out of his office to greet him. Then he introduced him to me. "This is Bob Juhl," he said, and went on to tell me that he was the lawyer with experience that Hile was looking for. We shook hands coldly. Juhl occupied the second office. I soon learned that he had been a Lieutenant Commander in the Navy and he continued to act like one. From the outset he treated me as an insignificant inferior. Well, that's what I was. A law clerk who was expected to be not only a "gofer", but, I learned, also a janitor. My duties included emptying all the wastebaskets and once a week, washing the front window. For some reason, I didn't resent these lowly tasks. I guess I hadn't yet assumed the air of importance and dignity that a lawyer is supposed to have.

Meanwhile, Lennie and I were trying to survive on $200 a month. We couldn't. In the end we gratefully accepted monthly checks of $50 from Dave and Anne, Lennie's parents. I had only one white shirt and didn't have enough money to buy a briefcase. Instead, I used a manila expanding envelope to carry my legal materials downtown on the bus. That was my routine; drive to the office in the morning; meet with Hile to discuss my assignment and board a bus to the King

County Law Library. The routine was unvarying.

But after three months things began to change. Hile seemed to act more and more subdued and soon he was closeting himself in his office for the entire day. Once I needed to discuss a case with him and entered his office to find him reading a paperback mystery and eating a candy bar. He was obviously flustered at being found so disengaged from law practice and made it clear that my presence was unwelcome. I disposed of my question quickly and made a prompt exit. The situation grew more bizarre. He discouraged any contact and finally, one day he didn't come in at all. The days passed and he absented himself completely. When our lone secretary, Mrs. Brown, called him at home about an office matter, he told her he had the flu.

Then I got the welcome news: I had passed the Bar Exam. Soon after, I was sworn in and now I could call myself a lawyer. My name was painted on the window below that of Gerald D. Hile. Then Mr. Juhl, the Lieutenant Commander, announced he was leaving to go into practice in Bellevue. That left just me and the secretary, Mrs. Brown. I did not feel I had any right to go into Hile's office and rummage through the files on his desk, so I kept working on the cases he had already assigned me to research, but clearly this was coming to an end with no new assignments. I didn't know what to expect. Though I was technically a lawyer, I had never spoken to a client, initiated any court action or even spoken in court. That was all about to change.

We continued living in the waterfront apartment. While there was a certain charm in living on Puget Sound, there were serious problems with this apartment that we could not have foreseen. Our apartment was on the ground floor of a two story house and above it was another apartment occupied by an older, childless couple, the Parmeters. We rarely saw them and when we did their greetings were brusque. But over time we discovered that they were heavy drinkers, if not alcoholics. This was manifested on the weekends when they apparently went on drinking binges. The following day they would be extremely grouchy and became highly annoyed at any noise made by our children, especially Jeff who would rock himself to sleep at night by banging his head on the headboard of his crib.

The Parmeters communicated their irritation not by words, but by thumping on their floor ~ our ceiling. I tried to deal with it in a friendly way; I went upstairs and knocked on their door and when the husband responded, I said I was very sorry they were disturbed by our kids, and I would do what I could to keep them as quiet as possible, but kids are kids and there was bound to be some noise. I was relieved when he said he understood and there was no problem.

I thought the issue was resolved, but I was wrong. It got worse and even escalated. Any noise resulted in furious banging on their floor. One night, Jeffrey began to cry in his crib. I went into the children's bedroom, lifted him out of his crib and began to walk around the apartment with him, rocking him and patting him on his back till he stopped crying. Then I gently deposited him back in his crib and went back to bed. I was sound asleep when Lennie and I were jolted awake by a huge BANG! It came from above and sounded like a bomb. Since Jeff had been quiet for several hours this could only be retaliation.

The problem was now serious. I went to the landlady. She was old and in poor health and clearly did not want to get involved.

We would just have to live with it. About a week later, I came home from the office and was standing in the kitchen talking to Lennie as she prepared dinner, when there was suddenly another nerve rattling crash above.me. In a rage, I grabbed a broom and jabbed the broomstick up into the ceiling. Of course it punched a hole in the plasterboard. Our feud with the Parmeters became a war and one day I lost all control, ran outside and shouted up at my neighbor to come down and fight if he wanted to continue the war. He didn't.

In a calmer moment, I reflected, surely there must be a legal remedy. But after some research all I could find was that I was entitled to move without notice on the ground of constructive eviction. That was no help. I didn't want to move. I decided to take drastic measures. Outside our rear door there was a small enclosed porch and on the wall were the master switches to the power for each apartment. The next time Parmeters slammed something on their floor; I walked out to the power box, pulled the switch and left them in the dark. I smiled grimly as I heard them staggering around in their apartment and cursing. Eventually, I heard Mr. Parmeter coming downstairs and fumbling with the power switch. He discovered it was off and he turned it back on. But it didn't bring an end to his banging and led to a war of the power switches; each of us turning off the other's power. Since it was easier for me to simply go out my back door and pull the switch than for him to go downstairs, go around the house and walk up on the rear porch, I had an advantage. Parmeter switched tactics. One day I went out to the rear porch to put the kids in their carriage and discovered he had placed three large dog turds on the floor and smeared one on the wheel. It was amazing that he never talked to me or shouted; just did these stupid, childish things.

The Parmeter problem was not the only drawback to our living in this remote site. The steep winding road that led to our street was the other. Lennie did not drive and to get out of the house she had to walk down an unpaved, muddy street and then push a baby carriage up a hill that would test the fitness of an athlete. She simply couldn't do it. The consequence was the poor girl was stuck in our apartment all day long. We had no television, only a radio. There was a dramatic view of Puget Sound out our windows and she could take the kids out to the front yard in good weather, or walk across the road and talk to a woman who had a five year old. Otherwise she was a prisoner of the house and had only the babbling of our babies for conversation. To make matters worse, her eyesight was bad and she needed new glasses, but we didn't have the money to pay for them, so she couldn't even read comfortably.

Meanwhile, I was entirely dependent on my Hudson to go up the hill to the office or shopping or anywhere. But the Hudson was developing serious mechanical problems; it was harder and harder to start once the engine was shut down. Finally, I had to bring it into a garage to have a mechanic work on it. They kept it for three days, forcing me to take a bus home from work. While there was a bus stop two or three blocks from the street leading to the hill, one first had to climb the hill in the morning to get to the bus. On the first day I labored up the hill, arriving at the top breathless, sweating and exhausted. When I got home that evening I walked down to the end of our street and found a gate on which a sign said, "Private Property - No trespassing". I decided that the next morning I would brave the consequences and enter that property, knowing that the other side opened onto the bus line. As I walked toward the gate, I encountered a group of three or four dogs on the other side of the street. All of them eyed me and began approaching me, barking in a menacing way. I tried the friendly approach but they came up to me, snarling and forcing me to back up against a fence. They circled me and I finally yelled, "Go home!" as loudly and as commandingly as I could. They backed off enough to allow me to walk through to the gate.

I was unnerved. I had never felt so threatened by dogs. I needed something to deal with this pack of dogs if I encountered them the next morning. I decided to buy a squirt gun and fill it with ammonia. When I came home that evening, I was wary of the dog pack but fortunately they were nowhere in sight. I asked Lennie if we had any ammonia but she said we didn't. The closest thing she could suggest was vinegar. So I filled my squirt gun with vinegar and hoped its odor and the fluid would keep them at bay.

The next morning I walked down that road with my hand on the handle of the squirt gun, ready to confront the dogs. I was disappointed when they didn't show up. I was looking forward to giving them an unpleasant surprise if they came at me again. But, in fact, I was relieved as I took the bus to our office. The unpleasant surprise was mine as the odor emanating from my raincoat, and the sensation of wetness told me there was a problem. I reached into the pocket and found all the vinegar in the gun had leaked out. When I arrived at the office, I told our secretary, Mrs. Brown, the only other occupant, the story of my dog confrontation. When I got to the story of my squirt gun, which was still in my raincoat pocket, I pulled it out and playfully pointed it at her and squeezed the trigger on what I thought was an empty squirt gun. To my horror, there was a residue of vinegar in the toy and a stream of vinegar struck her in the face. I rushed over to her and hastily pulled out my handkerchief to wipe the liquid off, but she had already deployed a Kleenex and was wiping her face. I apologized profusely, but Mrs. Brown had a sense of humor and thought the whole thing was funny. The squirt gun episode was the final straw and shortly after, we found another rental house in West Seattle and moved out of the increasingly problematic, scenic apartment.

With the departure of Lt. Commander Juhl and the absence of Jerry Hile, I was left to run a law practice alone; a neophyte with no one to turn to for help. I had no idea of what to charge for my services or even how to file a lawsuit. I was more than a little scared. One of the first things I had to do was get a raise in my miserly $200 a month salary. We simply could not survive on that income. I had thought that when I passed the bar and became a licensed lawyer, Jerry would voluntarily increase my salary. When that didn't happen I had no alternative but to go to his house and tell him that I needed more ~$350 a month. I was not looking forward to intruding on him in his illness, but as I thought about it, he had little alternative if he wanted to keep his office open. I called, spoke to his wife, Millie, a nice woman, and told her I had to speak to Jerry about an important matter and would it be all right if I came over that afternoon. She said yes and I drove over to his house.

He looked bad; pale, withdrawn and clearly in no mood to argue. When I presented the issue to him he promptly agreed to my request. Since he seemed disinterested in further conversation, I thanked him and left. I breathed a sigh of relief and looked forward to telling Lennie that we wouldn't have to pinch pennies quite so much from now on. The first thing we did was get Lennie a new pair of glasses. Soon after, Hile's wife, Millie, called me and revealed that Jerry was suffering from manic-depression, a serious psychological disorder, and that he was under treatment by a psychiatrist. She begged me not to disclose this because she hoped he would recover soon and resume his legal career. Public knowledge that he was manic depressive probably would spell the end of that career. I promised her I would protect his secret, a promise that became more and more difficult to keep after he returned to his practice and became manic again. In the meantime, I was alone with the practice. He didn't return for almost a year.

During Hile's absence, an increasing number of clients called and asked for me. The sign on our door read: "Law Offices of Gerald D. Hile and Alvin J. Ziontz" and if anyone asked for Hile, they were told he was not available but I was. As time wore on, fewer and fewer asked for Hile and I slowly developed my own law practice. With no law books except American Jurisprudence and the Washington Statutes, serious legal research meant continuing to take the bus to the King County Law Library.

My parents came out to visit and see their grandchildren. My position was a little more respectable, now that I had my own office, but I still didn't own a briefcase ~ a lawyer's badge. Before they left, my father bought a briefcase for me.

In 1956 we traveled to New York to visit Lennie's parents. A visit with them was always unpleasant, mainly because of Lennie's father; Dave Guralnick. Dave Guralnick was a man who left a legacy of distaste, comedy and bitterness. He was my father in law and for most of our married life we lived separated by three thousand miles. Yet he was a presence always and remains so today.

Dave was the only boy in a family of girls when he was growing up in Russia, an area called Mogolov Podolsk, in the Ukraine. Because he was the only son, his parents never disciplined him and even as a small boy he was spoiled, egocentric and cruel. He would torture any village dogs he could and soon earned the accolade in Yiddish, "Die malchemovis foon hynt", the avenging angel of dogs.

Lennie and I with my nemesis Dave, Lennie's father (left), in Asbury Park, New Jersey 1952

Dave was very bright and perhaps this contributed to his narrow vision. He came to America during the Great Depression and acquired the penny pinching ways that defined him for the rest of his life. He quickly acquired a very good command of English and a polished writing style. This, no doubt, enabled him to get a job in New York with the Russian Trade Agency, Amtorg. During this period he professed a belief in Communism, which made him an acceptable American employee.

After several years in that job, at a low wage, he went to night school and got a degree in Psychology. From that point on, he never sought a job in the private sector ~ only government jobs. Because of his excellent mind and his writing skills, he could always score high on any Civil Service Exam. He began a lifetime career in psychological counseling. It was during this time he met Lennie's mother, Anne, a quiet girl who had only a high school education. Because Dave was a college man, who even smoked a pipe, she idolized him and they married.

The Guralnicks lived in the Bronx; Dave, Anne, Lennie and her younger brother, Eddie. When Lennie and I began to go together in Chicago, I asked about her parents, and her cool response told me something was wrong there. When I first met them, I tried a friendly, "son-in law to be" style. While her mother was relatively warm, Dave's remarks displayed an obvious undertone of hostility. My overtures were met by sarcasm, and more frequently, he simply ignored what I said and continued on his own conversational path. That monolingual attitude was Dave and never changed.

My parents were quite different. They quickly became loving in-laws and thought Lennie was wonderful. In our first years in Seattle, we went back to Chicago two or three times for a visit. Our departures each time left them sad and nearly heartbroken.

In 1957, our daughter Ellen was born and that same year we bought our West Seattle house. It was an older, carpenter-built two story wooden frame house, located at 2616 50th Ave. S.W. in West Seattle. The previous year we had traveled to New York for a visit with Lennie's family and her father surprised me with a generous gift; he gave me his 1954 Dodge. My old 1948 Hudson was on its last legs so the gift was timely and made our lives much more pleasant. Dave bought an Oldsmobile to replace his Dodge.

Lennie with our third child, Ellen in West Seattle 1957

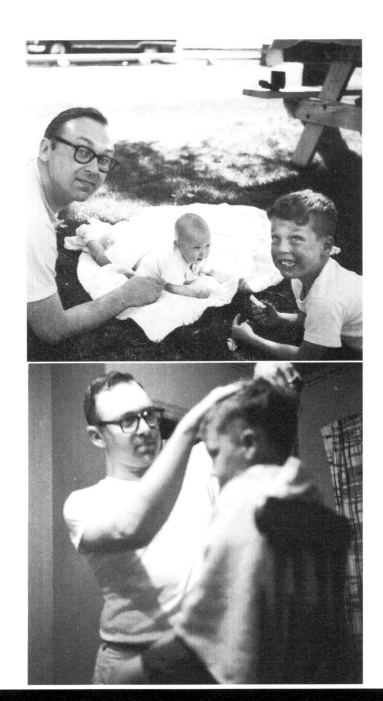

Top: With baby Ellen and Jeff, picnicking in West Seattle 1957
Bottom: Giving Jeff a haircut at home 1957

1961 was a momentous year. My parents, Harry and Rose decided to move to Seattle to be closer to us and their grandchildren. I went to Chicago to help them with the move. My mother was going to fly because her doctor advised against a strenuous car trip due to a bad heart, but Dad wanted to drive his Pontiac to Seattle. He had never seen the West. I was looking forward to his reaction to the mountains. There was no interstate highway system then and most of the trip was along two-lane state roads. He was duly awed by the spaciousness and grandeur of the West. But his reaction to mountains was entirely unexpected. We had stopped for gas at a station in Montana and the attendant, noticing our Illinois license plates, asked my father how he liked the countryside. "Well," he replied with his familiar gesture of thoughtful consideration, "These mountains are dangerous and someday they'll find a way to get rid of them." He may have been unsophisticated but he was certainly an original thinker.

We rented an apartment for them quite near to our house. They had a small amount of savings and my dad hoped somehow to open a store to sell wine and mixer, or, alternatively, a beer tavern. I didn't have any financial reserves to help them. But we were happy to have them in Seattle. Our children stopped at their apartment every day on the way home from school and everyone was delighted with the arrangement.

Meanwhile, my parents too had to make adjustments. Life in Seattle was strange to them. After the flatness of Chicago, Seattle's hills seemed positively dangerous. We had to become reacquainted after a separation of nine years. My father began looking around for a business opportunity. He took Lennie along wherever he drove to show him how to get to the different parts of the city. The two of them

Top: Dad on a fishing trip after moving to Seattle catching his first salmon

Bottom: With Dad after returning on a fishing trip not long before his death

got to know each other and my father told me that she was a girl with "sechel", the Yiddish word for practical wisdom. My father wanted to go out to the track to see horse racing and Lennie and I took him out to Longacres. He bought a Racing Form and with his usual perspicacity picked three winners. His winnings were modest but we all had fun.

The highlight of his new life was a salmon-fishing trip with a client of mine, Jerry Crangle. There were four of us on the small cruiser as we motored out into Puget Sound. Jerry provided fishing gear and baited Dad's hook. All of us were trailing lines in the water as we trolled for salmon. Suddenly, there was a strike. My father had hooked a large salmon. Jerry told Dad how to reel it in and he was thrilled to see a ten-pound silver salmon emerge from the water. His excitement was obvious and I was happy for him. We continued fishing, but no one else caught anything. Then Dad had another strike; another salmon. When we returned to the dock after a long day of fishing, only Dad had fish to show for it. Everyone was congratulating him on his beginner's luck. Sadly, that was the last day of happiness for him.

He had been complaining of fullness in his stomach. I took him to our family doctor and after testing he was diagnosed with stomach cancer. He had only been in Seattle four months when he died following surgery. My mother had come all the way to Seattle and had become a widow here. She suffered the anguish of loss ~ they had been married forty-five years. I was devastated by the sudden loss of my father. My mother became extremely close to Lennie and her grandchildren. But her life was cut short tragically by a heart attack and she died two years after my father's death. It was a hard blow for me. In the space of two years I had lost both my parents. Their move to Seattle brought tragedy and their happiness here was short-lived.

West Seattle 1961 -
Top: Lennie, Ellen and my Mom
Bottom: Jeff and Martin wearing suits for some reason

We lived in the house on 50th for seven years and our family lived a middle class life there. Judaism was almost entirely absent from our lives, but not completely. Though we did not belong to any Jewish Synagogue, we both expected that our children would go through the Bar Mitzva ceremony in their thirteenth year. In the meantime we were entirely irreligious. The only thing we did that had any connection to Judaism was to keep our kids out of school on the High Holidays. But since we had no Jewish calendar, we had to rely on the newspapers to inform us when the holidays occurred.

But in 1962 we somehow missed it. That September I found out that the High Holidays had already passed. I was horrified. How could we have made such a dreadful mistake? Was it too late to rectify? I got hold of a Jewish calendar and there it was—both Rosh Hashanah and Yom Kippur were past. I frantically scanned the calendar for the next closest Jewish holiday and there it was: The Fast of Gedaliah, practically coinciding with Rosh Hashanah. I pointed it out to Lennie and said we would keep our kids out of school on that day. Both of our boys were attending Lafayette Elementary School and we kept them out of school, telling them it was for a Jewish Holiday. The following day we sent them to school with notes saying that they were home in observance of a Jewish holiday. Somehow it made me feel better. I had kept the basic rule of Jewish life; observe the holidays.

Several weeks later there was an open house at Lafayette School and Lennie and I went. After chatting with the boys' teachers, the principal came over to me and said his assistant principal would like to talk to me. This kindly gentleman, named Joe Frankel, came up, smiled and shook my hand. Then he said, in a friendly manner, "I see you kept your children home because of a Jewish holiday two weeks ago, may I ask what Holiday that was?" I replied confidently, "The Fast of Gedaliah." "Oh," he said, "You see I'm a cantor and I never heard of anyone observing the Fast of Gedaliah before. Very interesting." He smiled and walked away, leaving me feeling exposed and foolish. I later learned that the fast of Gedalia was not a significant Jewish holiday, indeed it was practically unknown in the Jewish community. In later years the story of keeping our kids out on the Fast of Gedaliah made the rounds of the Jewish community and became a joke ~ at our expense. In the end we joined the Herzl Congregation and all our children attended Hebrew School there and ultimately went through their Bar Mitzvahs. We never quite lived down our Fast of Gedaliah fiasco which became a kind of joke in the Jewish community and it became a part of our family lore.

Living in the old two story house in West Seattle, our three children grew up. Jeffrey, our oldest, was chubby and cheerful, but always seemed to be the butt of bullying by his playmates. Martin, or Marty as we called him, on the other hand, had friends and playmates and always seemed more physically coordinated than Jeff. Ellen was a charming toddler.

My mother had long had heart disease and high blood pressure. So when she died of a heart attack in 1963, it was not a complete shock. After her death, my cousin Adele told me that a cousin, an older man whom I vaguely knew, had recently visited the Soviet Union and made contact with my mother's sister, Basia. This was extraordinary because few outsiders ever were permitted to enter that hermetically sealed country. I can only guess that this cousin was permitted entry because he was a member of the American Communist Party.

This news was startling, since my mother assumed that her entire family as well as almost all the Jews in the Ukraine had been killed by the invading Nazis. My first reaction was deep regret that my poor mother had not lived to hear of this, since she had always grieved over her lost family and would have been overjoyed to learn that one of her sisters had survived. My thoughts turned to making contact with my aunt Basia. Adele's cousin had given her Basia's address in Kiev and I began to consider how to communicate my existence to her.

The only thing that came to mind was a letter. But in what language? Of course I knew no Russian, and for that matter didn't know anyone who did. Indeed, the Communist government had been so efficient at sealing up its people inside its borders, that very few Russians found their way to America. Few Americans had even heard the Russian language spoken. So, what to do? I decided that since they were Jews they would be able to read a letter written in Yiddish. I knew a woman in Seattle who was fluent in Yiddish and she agreed to write a letter for me in Yiddish. I wrote the letter in English and it went something like this:

"Dear Aunt Basia,

I am the son of your sister, Rachel Bolasny. Her married name is Rose Ziontz. She would have been thrilled to learn that you survived the War. Unfortunately, she passed away last year. I would like to get in touch with you. Please write to me.

Alvin Ziontz"

I gave her the address of our new house on Mercer Island ~ we had just bought it in 1964. Then I waited, and waited. But no reply came. As the months passed I assumed the letter had been intercepted or gone astray, or that she couldn't read Yiddish. In time I forgot about it. The answer came 25 years later, but that is a story that has to wait in this very long narrative.

My handwritten caption on the back of this photo :

RAZIA (Rose) in 1965 with her cousin(?) brother(?)
Morris Feedman of Los Angeles. He visited
the U.S.S.R. in 1965 and carried with him my
letter to Basia, Razia's cousin. I gave him my
letter in Chicago in May of 1964 and he transported
it. It was the link that led to our reunion. Morris
died shortly after this photo was taken.

CHAPTER FOURTEEN

THE WEST SEATTLE YEARS, MEETING JFK

Leaving for the office in the morning, August 1957

At the time of my father's death in 1961, I had been a practicing lawyer for six years. All of my practice was in West Seattle in the offices of Jerry Hile. Starting with his first absence in 1955, he suffered from recurring episodes of Manic Depressive behavior. Now it is called Bipolar Disorder. I grew familiar with the cycles: a short period of two or three months of normality followed by increasing symptoms of his illness; supreme confidence in his ability to win any case, belligerence toward opposing lawyers and an increasing sense of grandiosity and then ~ the crash into depression. Depressed, he would stay home and disengage from everything in his law practice; leaving cases unfinished, trials pending and appeals started but all work on them abandoned. These periods of depression lasted from six to nine months. I once calculated that he had been present in the office a total of twelve months of the seven years I worked for him. The remaining time he was absent and I alone conducted the practice.

It's hard to convey the anxiety I lived with constantly during the early years of law practice. I was alone, without adequate research tools and no confidence in my ability to give legal advice or argue motions, much less conduct trials or appeals. I lived with anxiety, even fear. My cigarette smoking increased to three packs a day ~ long cigarettes, Pall Malls. By the end of a day my throat was burning and I knew I was probably harming my health, but I was addicted and the cigarettes buffered the tension. The pressures mounted on me. Even though I had passed the bar exam, I remained in doubt that I was a real lawyer. It was another masquerade.

I have described the first time I had to appear in Superior Court for a client in my book, "A Lawyer in Indian Country". I won't repeat it here. But it was typical of my experiences in those early years;

1955 to 1957. Where the issue was clearly governed by Washington Statutes which were in our office, I could act with some confidence. But more often it was a matter of contract law or case law where I had no clear guidelines. In those cases I acted using a combination of vague recollection of legal principles and phone negotiations with opponents. It would be accurate to say I was "winging it".

Within the first few months of my novitiate, I was confronted by a client who wanted me to take legal action immediately to seize property of a debtor of his ~ a subject about which I knew nothing. This client's name was John Brown ~ his actual name. Brown had for many years owned and operated a moving and storage company; the West Seattle Transfer and Storage Company. His warehouse was a mile or two down the street from our office. John was a quiet, almost mousy little man. I had dealt with a few minor legal matters for him, when he called me one morning, and, in an agitated tone of voice, said it was urgent that he meet with me right away. I told him to come right over.

He launched into his grievance. "Al, I have to do something about this woman, Jean Norberry. You may know of her; she owns a beauty shop down California Avenue near Fauntleroy. About a year ago she broke up with her boyfriend and had us move her to a new place. We had done a move for her once before; same situation. She was slow paying, but eventually we got paid. Not this time. It's been over a year and she owes $1,400. She ignores my bills and when I called her she got real nasty on the phone. She told me she owed other people too, but had some problems and couldn't pay anything now. Then she warned me; 'Don't think you can collect in court. If you start anything, I'll go right into bankruptcy and you won't get a dime.' Then she hung up on me. I talked to a few other people in West Seattle that had done business with her ~ same thing. They were all stuck with her bills because they were afraid of this bankruptcy thing."

John went on. "If it weren't for this bankruptcy threat, I'd just send it to collection and forget about it. But now she has me good and mad. See, she has this big blue and white Cadillac Coupe De Ville and she drives it every morning down California Avenue right past my warehouse. I see it out the front window of my office and every time I see her going by in that big Caddie, my blood pressure goes up. I finally decided bankruptcy or no bankruptcy, I want to take that Cadillac. Can't we do that? After all, she owes me $1,400."

My mind raced. How does a creditor seize the property of his debtor? Somehow the word, "attachment" popped into my head. But I had no idea how to go about an attachment. So I told John, "I think we can attach her car, but I have to check out the procedure. I'll call you this afternoon."

John seemed pleased that there was a legal remedy for his distress and said, "Good. I don't care how much it costs; I just want to take that Coupe De Ville." We shook hands and he left.

Now my work began. I went to our shelf of the Washington Statutes hoping the subject of Attachment was there. It was. I saw there were two kinds; pre-judgment and post-judgment. If a creditor tried to attach property before he had a judgment in his favor, the law set a series of obstacles in his path. If he could show there was an immediate risk of the debtor absconding with the property plus a liquidated, i.e. a documented, fixed monetary obligation, then a writ of attachment was easily obtained. That was not us. If it was not a case of a documented, fixed obligation, like a promissory note, then the only way to attach the debtor's property was to enforce a court judgment. Hmm. That meant I would have to get a court judgment against Ms. Norberry before we could touch her Cadillac. It meant filing suit with all the attendant uncertainties, including the possibility that she would contest it and a trial would be necessary. I called John Brown and explained all this. He was unfazed. "Just do what you have to do," he said.

Launching myself into uncharted waters, I drafted a complaint against Ms. Norberry in King County Superior Court and gave it to a process service company and began the lawsuit. The summons gave her 20 days to appear by an attorney or serve a response to the complaint. I was certain an attorney would serve me with a notice of appearance. When more than 20 days elapsed without a response, I heaved a sigh of relief and went to court with a motion for an order of default, setting the groundwork for a judgment. The judgment against Ms. Norberry for $1,400 plus interest and costs was entered two days later. With this, the basis was now laid for a writ of attachment. I wasn't sure I knew what I was doing but it seemed to be in accordance with all that I had read.

After I had a judgment in favor of West Seattle Transfer and Storage against Jean Norberry, I wrote her a letter, enclosing a copy of the judgment and asking her to contact me regarding payment. My letter was ignored and I heard nothing from her. Now I had to venture further into the unknown and figure out how to get a writ of attachment to physically take possession of the Coupe De Ville. The Washington Statutes said the writ was to be executed by the County Sheriff on filing a bond in the amount of twice the value of the attached property.

I had no idea how to get a writ of attachment to the Sheriff or how to go about getting a bond. But a phone call to the Civil Division of the King County Sheriff's office and the helpful instruction of one their clerks told me what I needed to do. The writ of attachment was simply a form that specifically described the property to be attached. The bond form was easily procured at one of the bond offices around the courthouse on paying 10% of the estimated value of the property to be attached, or $280. John Brown was pleased to send me a check in that amount to expedite the seizure of the coupe De Ville.

After I filed the required bond with the Sheriff's office they told me a deputy would be dispatched to the location of the car together with a tow truck, but they insisted that someone, either the plaintiff or his representative, had to accompany the deputy when he made the attachment to insure the right property was seized. I would have loved to be the representative to accompany the sheriff that morning, but unfortunately I had an appointment that morning that could not be changed. I called John and he said he would be delighted to go with the sheriff for the attachment. We agreed that the attachment would take place at ten o'clock in the morning two days hence. The deputy would come by John's office in his cruiser, followed by a tow truck and John would bring up the tail of the procession as they drove to Jean's beauty shop, where her Cadillac was parked.

Now the gears of the legal machine were set in motion and if I had goofed, I would have to pay for it. When I awoke the morning of the great attachment, I was shocked to find it had snowed during the night and the ground was covered with a blanket of white. This was rare in Seattle. Naturally, I worried that it might affect the extraordinary event that was about to take place. I was at my office by nine and meeting with a client at 9:30. During the entire session I had trouble concentrating on the problem at hand, wondering what was going on at the Norberry beauty salon. At 10:30 I called Brown's office but was told he was out and would call me on his return. John didn't call but came into my office at 11:30. He didn't look as pleased as I expected and, in fact, seemed agitated. I soon learned why.

"Al, that was the craziest experience I ever had in my life," he said. I was afraid that my first effort at an attachment had gone awry, but I learned that was not the reason John was upset. Then he told me of the morning's events:

"Well, the Sheriff's deputy pulled up in front of my office at about a quarter to ten and I went out to meet with him. There was a tow truck parked behind him, which I was expecting. He told me to get in my car and lead the way; park in front of the beauty shop, point out the Cadillac and he would take over from there. So that's what we did ~ a little procession going down California Avenue till we got to her shop. There was an empty lot next to the beauty shop and that blue and white Coupe De Ville was parked out there. The tow truck backed into the lot right behind her car. The deputy went into the beauty shop and I waited outside. I could see the two of them; the deputy and Jean standing near the front window. He had handed her a paper, which I assumed to be the writ and then it looked as if they were arguing. Then the deputy came out and said, 'She wants to talk to you. If the two of you settle this, then it's over and you'll get a bill for the tow truck trip. But you better go in there and talk to her."

I really didn't want to get into any argument with Jean, but I did as the deputy asked and went into the beauty shop. First thing she says is, 'My attorney, Carl Pruzan, says you can't do this because I'm filing for bankruptcy.'

'Well,' I said, 'I don't care about bankruptcy; I'm taking the car now.' Then we had some more back and forth with her calling the deputy back in and telling him the same thing. He says, 'Lady, I got a writ here and unless I get a court order that says I can't execute it, I'm going to take the car.'

At this point she says, 'John I've been a customer of yours and I need to talk to you for a minute. Would you please come back to my office with me?' Against all my instincts I followed her to her office in the rear of the shop. The place was fairly busy and there were women sitting there, some under the hair dryers, all listening to this.

Back in her little rear office, she began telling me about all her problems, till I finally stopped her. 'Jean,' I said, 'I've got financial problems of my own. I have two girls in college and I have to pay for that besides all my bills. Now if you can come up with the $1400 or $1500 you owe me, I'll tell the sheriff to let your car alone. Otherwise, we have nothing to talk about.'

When she began whining about all her troubles, I turned to leave. That's when she scooted around me and locked the door. 'I won't let you leave till you promise to leave my car alone.' I said, 'Now, Jean, don't be foolish, let me out of here.' But she wouldn't budge and since she was holding the key in her hand, I grabbed the key and went to unlock the door.

She wrestled with me for the key but I was too strong for her and I unlocked the door and went walking out of the beauty shop. I was heading for the front door when she came running up behind me and jumped on my back. She had her legs and arms wrapped around me and I couldn't shake her off. So I did the only thing I could do. I kept walking out of the shop with her on my back. The eyes of the women sitting in the shop were fairly bugging out of their heads, but I ignored them and kept going till I got out the front door and onto the sidewalk. That's when she dropped off. I was relieved. I thought the whole thing was over, but it wasn't.

Next thing I know, she's going up to the deputy and asking if she can get her personal things out of the car. 'Sure,' he says and she walks over to the driver's door of the Cadillac. Before anyone can say Jack Robinson, she's got the key in the ignition and has the engine started. The deputy yells to the tow truck driver, "Hook her up!" The guy pulls down his hook and gets it under her back bumper just as she starts to pull away. Well, it was a good thing the ground was covered by snow, cuz' she traveled about three feet and the cable stopped her. She began gunning the engine, but with the snow on the ground, her wheels spun and she didn't go anywheres. She got out of her car, madder'n hell and was yelling at all of us, 'You'll hear from my lawyer.' Then she stormed into her beauty shop."

As I sat listening to Brown's incredible tale of the blue and white Coupe De Ville, I vacillated between a sense of the ridiculous and fear that I had somehow failed to foresee the consequences of the attachment. But I felt I had vindicated his reliance on me, especially when he told me that the sheriff had towed the car to his warehouse for storage. Even if Jean's bankruptcy robbed him of recovery of his claim, at least he would get storage charges out of it.

Fifteen minutes after John left, my phone rang. It was Jean Norberry's lawyer, Carl Pruzan. I later learned he was regarded as a tough and capable lawyer. Pruzan's tone was rough and peremptory. "Did you know she is filing for bankruptcy?" he asked. "She did say something to that effect," I acknowledged. "Well, she is. The bankruptcy petition is all prepared and I'm filing it tomorrow. Once the bankruptcy is filed, your attachment is null and void. But, I'm willing to give you $200 for the release of her car at this time. Is that agreeable?"

I knew nothing of bankruptcy law and certainly didn't know that it made my attachment null and void. But my instincts told me that if he was willing to pay $200 for the release of the car, the attachment was not something he could ignore. So I refused his offer. This provoked an angry response, "Okay, you'll be sorry you didn't make a few bucks when you had the chance. Now, you'll get nothing once the bankruptcy is filed." And he hung up. Fifteen minutes later he called again.

"Okay. We're willing to raise our offer to $250. Now will you release the car?" I was more sure of myself now, when I said no. I really didn't know what I was doing, but I figured that if he thought it was worth $250 to release the car we had leverage. Apparently he was really angry now. "Well, the hell with you," and he hung up again.

I was in deep water, but though I didn't appreciate it at the time, I had done exactly the right thing. I called a lawyer I knew who specialized in Bankruptcy who told me what to do.

"You're in the driver's seat," he said. "There will be a first meeting of creditors in Bankruptcy Court, and as a creditor with a secured claim, you will be entitled to be her trustee. Of course, you'll name me as the attorney for the trustee and I'll handle things from there."

That's exactly how the little drama played out. Jean stared daggers at me in Bankruptcy Court, but I was named trustee of her Bankruptcy estate. The Cadillac was practically the only asset available to creditors. It was put up for sale and brought $3,000. Out of this came my fees, the trustee's attorney's fees, and, of course, John's storage charges. The rest was distributed pro rata among the creditors. John ended up with enough money to cover most of the cost of the attachment proceedings and part of his claim and more importantly, the satisfaction of never having to see Jean Norberry drive the Coupe De Ville down the street each morning past his office.

The law practice settled into a routine of clients coming to see me and I was the sole source of income for the practice. My monthly salary of $350 was barely adequate to pay our basic living expenses. So, once again I went to see Jerry about a raise. This time his response was unexpected. Instead of a raise, he said since I was conducting a practice alone, he would allow me to keep all the fee income generated from clients coming to see me but would terminate my monthly salary. Since few, if any, clients asked for him, this meant he was subsidizing the cost of the office and I was keeping all the income. It obviously was a good deal for me, though I had to rely entirely on fee income, but it also allowed him to keep an office available for the day when he could return to practice.

Money was always a problem. There was a different problem

that created marital strains ~ my absence from the lives of Lennie and the children. Immersion in the work of developing into a lawyer, civil liberties work with the ACLU, all kept me away from my children and Lennie. I have many regrets about this period and the heavy burden it placed on Lennie.

Meanwhile I was learning more every day about the practice of law. Relating to clients came easily to me and I soon developed the technique of questioning a client closely regarding the facts of his claim. I was appearing before Superior Court Judges arguing motions and since I was a clear thinker and a good speaker I had more and more successful outcomes. I developed a wider circle of acquaintances among the downtown lawyers who came to know me as, "the guy from West Seattle".

Meeting with two League of Women Voters officers at my office in West Seattle 1957

I also had to face crises. For one thing, there was a stack of case files on Hile's desk that I was reluctant to disturb. Finally, I decided that there could be horrors hidden in that stack, so I began examining the files. There were horrors; three appeals and a Superior Court Jury trial, all requiring immediate attention. So far as I could tell, Hile had done nothing to prepare for any of these court cases; no appellate briefs had been written and no depositions had been taken in the trial case.

The first task was to begin working on doing the legal research for the appeals; one to the federal Ninth Circuit Court of Appeals and two to the Washington State Supreme Court. The state court appeals were run-of-the mill civil cases, but the federal appeal raised a thorny question of Presidential Emergency Powers. I had briefed the law on this case when it was before the Federal District Court and had some familiarity with the legal issues. The case involved the criminal charge of illegal possession of gold bullion. Our client was a businessman named Harold Bauer and I felt a responsibility to write the very best brief I could.

Bauer's criminal charge was unusual. In possessing gold bullion he had violated not a law, but an executive order issued by Franklin D. Roosevelt in 1934. The language of the order made it a criminal offense to possess gold bullion without a federal license. The President was acting under the authority of The Trading With The Enemy Act of 1917 which gave him authority to prevent the holding of gold in time of war. When Roosevelt came into office, the exigencies of the Depression led him to take the country off the gold standard and to implement this he had the old 1917 law amended to read, "... *in time of war or other national emergency.*" He then declared there was a national economic emergency and issued his executive order prohibiting the private holding of gold bullion. The problem for the government was that the national economic emergency had ended long before Bauer's action in 1954 and the legal question was whether an emergency order could remain in force after the emergency had ended. I argued the appeal to the Ninth Circuit and enjoyed a partial victory; the court remanded it to the District Court to make findings of fact on the question of whether the national economic emergency of 1934 had ended. I was confident I would win on this issue, but, as related in my memoir, the case was settled. The remaining appeals to the Washington State Supreme Court resulted in a split: I won one and lost the other.

There was one lesson about law practice that I found hard to absorb; that was the need to dissimulate, in other words to speak less than the truth. My instincts were to speak to an opponent with complete candor, holding back nothing. I learned in time that this was foolish, particularly in negotiations. One's opponent never was completely open or honest, usually overstating the strengths of his case, or minimizing an offer below the amount of a reasonable settlement in the hope of discouraging a fair price. It took a long time before I became able to practice this kind of dishonesty, justifying it only because it was the general practice. But I had one case where my opponent suffered the consequences of this general cynicism. It was Burr v. Fuqua.

I discovered we had a trial coming up in this case only after rummaging through the files on Hile's desk. The trial was only three weeks off! I had to suppress panic. I had never tried a case and wasn't even familiar with court procedures, especially the rules of evidence. I felt desperation at the prospect of walking into a courtroom and presenting a case to a jury. I called on an older lawyer; one of those I had interviewed with, and asked if he could recommend someone to take over the case. Instead he reassured me. "Try the case yourself. It will be a great experience."

When I got home that night I pulled out my law school casebook on Evidence and began frantically scanning it, hoping, if nothing else, to master the Hearsay Rule. Reading that book only added to my panic. There was no way I could hope to absorb this body of law in time for my upcoming trial, especially from a casebook -a compilation of court opinions dealing with the rules of evidence. But I had read of a new treatise on trial practice called, "Modern Trials," by a San Francisco personal injury attorney by the name of Melvin Belli. The next day I went to the King County Law Library and took home all three volumes of this work.

Belli's specialty was what he called "demonstrative evidence", and he hammered away at the theme that the job of the plaintiff's attorney was a "race for disclosure", in other words, get your evidence out there first. I read all the relevant parts of "Modern Trials" and afterward I felt confident I could try this case and make a presentation to a jury.

Our client was a police sergeant named Roscoe Burr. He was driving his car on an arterial and had stopped for a red light when the car following him crashed into his rear end, demolishing it and causing him to sustain a sprained neck. He did not need to go to a hospital nor did he miss any time from work. The value of his car was promptly paid by the other driver's insurance company, so there was no claim of damages for property, loss of wages or medical bills. My job was to prepare evidence of his pain and suffering and any financial loss it caused. The following car had been driven by a sailor in the U.S. Navy, stationed aboard a ship which had long since sailed and the defendant wouldn't even be attending the trial. It was an ideal case for a beginner. Yet I was unable to suppress my anxiety and didn't sleep a wink the night before the trial.

In preparation for the trial I spent a good deal of time questioning my client about the ways the accident had changed his life. For years he had purchased old, run down houses and remodeled them himself; doing all the carpentry, wall boarding, painting, plumbing and even the wiring. Then he would sell the house pocket the profit and start over again on another house. All of this was done during his free time, he said, and he loved doing it. After the car accident, he told me he could no longer do home reconstruction and was limited in his neck and head movement. Life had lost a good deal of its satisfaction, he said. I planned to present all this to the jury.

I had also contacted his doctor and received a two page report detailing his physical condition. There was one item in the report that attracted my curiosity; he had tinnitus – a ringing in the ears. I decided to meet with his doctor. The doctor was pleasant and cooperative – he liked Sgt. Burr. The doctor explained the physics of the violent movement of the head resulting from a rear end collision – what is now commonly called a "whiplash" injury, though that phrase was rarely heard in 1956. Then I asked him about Mr. Burr's tinnitus. "Oh, that," he said. "That has nothing to do with his car accident. It's a result of his spending time on the pistol range. Repeated exposure to the nearby loud sound of gunfire caused his tinnitus." I was disappointed because I had hoped he had suffered some permanent disabling injury. But the doctor said that because of the severity of his neck injury, he could have a permanent problem with the neck. So that was my injury case.

The night before the trial I slept little, anxiety keeping me awake. I went downtown to the King County Superior Court building the following morning and met my client there. All cases were dispatched to the trial courts by a presiding judge who sits in a huge courtroom. I sat there as though in a nightmare; this couldn't be actually happening, I thought. I would have to walk into a courtroom and without any knowledge of trial procedure or the rules of evidence, call witnesses and address a jury. It was my good fortune that no courtrooms became available that day and we would have to return the next day. That night I slept through the night and walked into the presiding judge's courtroom the next day feeling more refreshed. In the morning our case was sent to a courtroom and a judge. My legal career was about to take its first small step into maturity.

I had never spoken to anyone in the law firm representing our opponent; Williams, Kastner, Lanza and Gibbs. But I knew them to be one of Seattle's strongest firms defending against plaintiff's personal injury claims. I was surprised when I walked into the courtroom and found the case was being handled by Henry Kastner ~ a partner in that firm. This case was small potatoes for a firm like that. Why would they assign it to a big shot like Henry Kastner?

Kastner was tall, well-groomed and wearing a tailored, elegant suit and tie. He handled the trial with practiced ease, while I, a novice, wore a cloak of confidence that I did not feel. At the outset, Kastner informed the judge that they were admitting liability and the only issue would be damages. He also told the judge that his client was on active duty in the Navy and would not be attending the trial. Maybe that's why the case was given to Kastner; a trial with no client sitting in the chair next to him.

The procedure of jury selection was not familiar to me, but we got through it and ended up with a panel of twelve reasonably open minded citizens. There were only three witnesses; Sergeant Burr, his doctor and a doctor called by the defense. Having covered the ground of Burr's physical disabilities thoroughly with him, I confidently led him through his testimony regarding his neck and back pain and the ways in which it had changed his life. Burr, being a cop and familiar with being on the witness stand, successfully withstood the efforts of Kastner to trap him into admitting he was not suffering any serious consequences of the accident. When Kastner finally said, "I have no further questions, Your Honor," I felt we had scored heavily.

Next came our doctor who did a very good job of demonstrating the way in which the muscles and ligaments of the neck were stretched and torn by the violent head tossing caused by the rear collision. As he testified he had his two page written report in his hands and I took him through it point by point. When I got to the subject of tinnitus (ringing in the ears), I fully intended, in accordance with Belli's principles, to have the doctor testify that it had no connection with the auto collision; rather it was a result of the many hours Burr spent on the pistol range, exposed to the loud reports of the guns. But I never got to do that. Instead, to my surprise, Kastner leaped to his feet and shot out, "I object, Your Honor. Nothing was pleaded regarding hearing loss and it cannot be brought into the case at this late date."

I got to my feet and tried to explain, "But, your honor..." I was not allowed to finish my sentence. The judge said, "Sustained. Next question." I sat down and simply said, "No further questions, Your Honor."

By his cynicism and distrust of my motives, Kastner had hurt his own case, for when the jury returned a substantial verdict for us and I asked some of the jurors what had led to the verdict, one said, "We felt that the Sergeant's hearing loss had to be compensated." Burr v. Fuqua infused me with confidence that I could take a case to trial and argue it to a jury.

As time went by I became more confident in my ability to practice in almost any area of law. A lawyer friend urged me to join the American Civil Liberties Union. Although it was widely regarded as a radical left wing organization, especially by the followers of Senator Joe McCarthy, I joined. Soon I was appointed to the Board of the Washington State affiliate. At the time, the ACLU was a small struggling organization in Washington State. We barely had money to rent an office and hire a staff. Our work and analysis of constitutional issues were exciting.

My most important contribution to our work came when the board took up the numerous complaints we received against the Seattle Police Department. Abusive and racist behavior went on over the years despite complaints filed with the department by victims. We decided that the entire matter should be brought to the attention of the City Council. We sent a formal letter to the council demanding an investigation of the department. We attached ten sworn affidavits from victims and one from a former employee of the Department who described abusive behavior he personally observed within the headquarters office. A copy was released to the local press. As weeks passed without any response from the Council, the press began to badger the Council. What were they going to do?

The response was revealing. Their announcement evaded the issue of an investigation. Instead, they would afford us a hearing to produce our evidence. This was the action of a municipal council that was not going to give any credence to the ACLU or the many victims of police misconduct. Instead, they said, in effect, "prove it!" They had a strategy. They would allow us to present our evidence at a public hearing, but then they would call the Police Department to respond and rebut the evidence.

I was asked to present our case and I prepared as if for a trial. The hearing was held in the public chambers of the Municipal Building ~ a huge room. On the day of the hearing it was packed; the public and most importantly, the press looked forward eagerly to the contest.

We called our witnesses, one after the other; an African student at the University who was arrested because he was walking in a white neighborhood and couldn't produce satisfactory identification, a Bremerton businessman who was physically abused and arrested when he challenged two officers to give the reasons why he was stopped on the street of downtown Seattle, black men who were stopped in their cars for specious reasons ~ burnt out tail light, suspicious presence in a neighborhood close to their homes, and cases of citizens physically beaten for using such inflammatory expressions as "I have constitutional rights."

The most damning evidence was the testimony of the young man who was employed by the Seattle Police Department and worked in the property room ~ where confiscated or recovered property was stored. This young man testified that he had personally witnessed officers going through the wallets of men arrested for public intoxication, and removing money and putting it in their own pocket. More shocking was his testimony of seeing a young man brought into the station, strapped to a chair and then punched and slapped till he told the officers what they wanted to hear.

When our last witness finished, I addressed the council and told them the conduct of the Department cried out for an official inquiry. But the faces of the nine members staring at me told me that this body was not likely to take any action.

After increasing pressure from the public and the media, the council scheduled a hearing for the police department to respond. In that hearing the police department dismissed all the witnesses against them as liars and called up various luminaries to describe the department as, "one of the finest in the country."

I was shocked. But I learned an important lesson: police officers lie, they lie brazenly and with confidence that their lies will not be disputed. Recent history has borne out the truth of this conclusion. Police will lie to protect their jobs, to protect fellow officers or to protect the department. I saw that they were good at it; smooth and well prepared, with glib stories that fit legal defenses. Of course, not all police officers are willing to violate their oath to tell the truth, but sadly, too many are. So I have become cynical about police justifications.

But there was an event that occurred in Seattle not long after these hearings that revealed the truth about the relations between the Department and the black community. An argument in a restaurant between two off-duty police officers and a black man culminated in a police officer shooting and killing a black citizen. The black community was enraged and no police car could drive through the black district without hearing insults and even having rocks thrown at their cars. It marked the beginning of an era of change. The city government could no longer allow the Department to be a law unto itself and similar events in many of our cities led to basic reforms in police departments. For me, one consequence was that I was elected President of the Washington State affiliate of the national organization; a post I held for a year. For several years I served on the Board of the State affiliate and later on the special Indian Rights committee of the ACLU.

In 1957 I received a phone call that ultimately would change my life. The manager of the local branch of what was then called The National Bank of Commerce called me. I kept my checking account there and my balances were so modest that ordinarily the branch manager would never take any notice of me. But since I was one of four lawyers in the neighborhood, he felt a need to be friendly toward me. I still remember his name: Jack Gordon. Jack's conversation was short and to the point, "Al, there's an Indian gentleman in the bank and he's asking me legal questions that I think should be answered by a lawyer. He's here now, would you be willing to see him if I sent him over?"

I was surprised by a client referral from the bank. He had never sent anyone to see me. But I thought I understood his reason.

I was the neighborhood liberal; West Seattle Democratic Club and ACLU. But his reasons were irrelevant. I would be pleased to meet this new client. In about fifteen minutes my secretary said there was a gentleman waiting to see me. In walked a large, paunchy, dark skinned Indian. He introduced himself as Pat Wilkie, Sr.

Mr. Wilkie explained that his wife Nell was a member of the Makah Indian Tribe, of Neah Bay. He was a member of the Turtle Mountain Chippewa of North Dakota. He had come to Seattle during the Second World War to work in the shipyards. They had several children, and Nell had several children by a previous marriage, the oldest of which was Pat, Jr., called "Shine", short for "Sunshine".

Shine, he told me, had inherited an allotment on the Quinault Reservation from his grandmother, Ida Kallapa. The allotment contained valuable timber and the Bureau of Indian Affairs had gotten her to sign a power of attorney, authorizing them to cut the timber. The proceeds would go into her trust account, maintained by the government. They would contract the cutting to a logging company, which would charge for the work. The issue was that Shine wanted to log it himself and pocket the profit, instead of having it go to a logger. The Bureau refused, saying they had already contracted for the logging, relying on the Power of Attorney. The problem was that Ida Kallapa had died and the Bureau was still relying on her Power of Attorney.

I sat and listened attentively, all the while realizing I had no idea what an allotment was nor whether the Bureau of Indian Affairs had the power to cut timber. At the outset, it seemed to me that if the principal on a Power of Attorney had died, any claim of authority based on that document would lapse. But I wasn't certain and I told Mr. Wilkie that I would have to do some legal research and then I would contact him with my results.

At the Law Library I found that Indian Allotments were governed by Federal Statute, found in Title 25 of the U.S. Code. There I encountered a welter of statutory sections that made little sense to me. More research revealed the history of Allotments. They were the product of an 1887 law, called the Dawes Act, a law designed to break up Indian Lands into parcels assigned to individual Indians with the purpose of encouraging Indians to become farmers or loggers.

The law had an insidious purpose; to break up tribal landholding and declare all land not allotted as "surplus lands" to be sold to non-Indians. Since the parcels allotted were limited to 40 acres, there were large areas of tribal land not allotted and then sold to non-Indians. It was part of a scheme to deconstruct tribal life and convert Indians to non-tribal state citizens. The result of this law was the massive loss of Indian lands, and later, when some Indian owners, called "allottees", sold their allotments to non-Indians, reservations were broken up into Indian and non-Indian parcels. This was called "checkerboarding", and resulted in still further loss of the Indian land base.

All of this was found in cases cited in Title 25. When I read the cases I learned something of the history of Federal Indian Policy. I learned something else from these cases ~ something which was a complete surprise: from the earliest court decisions to the present, the courts had held that tribes were "sovereign". The word leaped off the page. Since my studies at Wright Junior College twenty five years earlier, I had been deeply interested in sovereignty. It was not classic sovereignty since the tribes were subject to the overriding power of the federal government, but as to the states they were self-governing and not subject to any laws but their own. This was important. How important I was to discover later.

My research did establish that in civil law, the death of the principal terminated the power of an "attorney in fact" under a power of attorney. So, I confidently sent off a letter to the Portland Area Office of the BIA informing them that the timber sale on the Kalappa allotment could not be consummated, because her grandson and heir objected and the power of attorney was now a nullity. A week later I received a letter from that office advising that this question had been litigated and there was a court decision holding that once a sale had been made under the authority of the allottee's power of attorney, it was irrevocable. When I read the decision I was ruefully forced to agree.

I called in the Wilkies and told them the bad news. They took it philosophically and said they appreciated my efforts. As it turned out this didn't hurt my standing with the Wilkie family, quite the opposite. In the following months other family members came to me with their legal problems. Pat's wife, Nell Wilkie, fell at work and was injured and I successfully prosecuted a workman's compensation claim for her. One of their little girls fell while swinging on the antlers of an elk head at Elks lodge and I got a sizable settlement for them. Shine was divorced and wanted sole custody of his daughter and I was able to convince a court that it was in the best interest of the child that she be placed in his custody. But the case that was to have long term implications for me was deceptively simple. It involved Pat's son, Bruce.

Bruce was 17 and a senior at West Seattle High School when he came to see me. He was a handsome, big, burly boy and, in keeping with his size, was on the football team. He had a kind of dignity and seriousness not typical for kids his age.

His legal problem was not complicated; he had bought a used car from a West Seattle dealer and the car broke down soon after he bought it. When he went back to the dealer, they refused to take any responsibility pointing out he had bought it "as is". Since Bruce was a minor at the time, it was clear to me that the purchase could not be binding. I called the dealer, pointed out that the contract had been signed by a minor without a parental signature and was void. After a short exchange between me and the sales manager, he agreed to take the car back and refund Bruce's money.

When Bruce came to my office again, we began to talk about Indians in America. He was a member of the Makah Tribe, though he lived in Seattle. It soon became apparent that Bruce had a good deal of repressed anger over the way Indians had been treated. I spoke to him about the idea of Sovereignty and the law holding that tribes were sovereigns. He was clearly fascinated and said he hoped some day to move to the reservation and work for his tribe, doing whatever he could to restore their rights. He and I had established rapport, despite the differences in our ages.

The Wilkies were the only Indians I had ever met and the research I had done on Federal Indian Law made me aware of some of the complexities of law and policy that had entangled the Indian people of America. Seven years after I last saw Bruce, and because of Bruce, my professional life entered a completely unanticipated field of law: defending the rights of Indian Tribes.

My law practice had never completely satisfied my idealism ~ New Deal idealism I had grown up with and never forgot. I met Democratic activists and joined the West Seattle Democratic Club ~ actually the 34th District Democratic Organization. After a few years I was elected President of the organization. I joined the Metropolitan Democratic Club ~ a downtown organization of professionals who had an intellectual commitment to the Democratic Party and its New Deal principles. These organizations led to personal meetings and conversations with some notable Democrats; Senator Henry "Scoop" Jackson, Adlai Stevenson and Eleanor Roosevelt.

In 1960 I was elected an alternate delegate to the Democratic National Convention in Los Angeles. The selection was made by vote of the King County Central Committee and I had to do some old-fashioned campaigning to get their vote. Lennie and I flew to L.A. and settled into a hotel near the convention center, the Los Angeles Sports Arena ~ a huge edifice. We were soon swept up in the hectic campaigning of the candidates vying for delegate votes. The leading contenders were John F. Kennedy of Massachusetts, Lyndon B. Johnson of Texas, Hubert Humphrey of Minnesota and Adlai Stevenson of Illinois.

I was a Stevenson supporter, but we were assailed by pitches from all the candidates. One night, as we were in our hotel room, I noticed a paper sliding under our front door. Picking it up I read a screed attacking Kennedy for his Catholicism and predicting he would be a doctrinaire Catholic in public policy were he elected. I found it disgusting and though it was unsigned, I took it to be a product of the Lyndon Johnson camp.

Inside the center there was a teeming mass of delegates, candidate supporters, and the press. The atmosphere was exciting, emotionally and visually. There were banners and pennants everywhere. The floor was sectioned off into areas by state, each state's area marked by a tall post topped by the state's name. At the podium a steady procession of speakers exhorted the delegates to support their candidate. After listening to these for a while, we got bored with their sameness and tuned them out, turning instead to our fellow delegates for discussion of the contenders. Periodically there were demonstrations for a candidate; processions of young people wearing hats with the name of their candidate, marching to the beat of small bands.

Of course, everyone was waiting for the main events; the nominating speeches. Each of the contenders was nominated by a luminary; a governor or senator, all describing their candidate as "a great American". Each nominating speech was followed by supporting speakers, seconding the nomination. It became tiresome. While all this was going on the candidates themselves were in their hotel rooms meeting with delegates and courting their votes. Then I got word that Senator Kennedy would like to meet with our delegation in his hotel room. Though I was not inclined to support him, I looked forward to meeting him in person.

Lennie and I joined ten or so members of our state delegation in the hotel suite of John Kennedy and took our seat on a couch facing two armchairs. We sat there chatting among ourselves for three or four minutes before I realized that sitting in the armchair opposite was Kennedy himself. In person he was more handsome and glamorous than his photographs. He was deeply tanned, and sat with an easy grace. I hadn't noticed him because he wasn't saying anything, just listening to one of our delegates speaking about federal farm policy. That was the way it went; Kennedy saying little and asking questions. Finally, he spoke, in his broad Boston accent, laying out his vision for a Democratic Presidency. He was impressive and though he may not have changed the commitments of delegates who were pledged to the support of other candidates, he did convey an easy mastery of the issues and a quiet way of telling us who he was. Not a word was uttered about his Catholicism, but he sounded totally presidential. We knew he was a highly likely candidate, but had no idea he would end up a historic president. When we got up to leave he gave me his senatorial business card and signed it. I still have it.

Meanwhile, my preferred candidate Adlai Stevenson was driving his supporters crazy with his dithering and indecision. He had a sizable number of delegates and there was a floor demonstration for his candidacy, but in the absence of an enthusiastic candidate, we were left feeling like bridesmaids without a bride. The more likely candidate was Hubert Humphrey, but somehow he didn't seem like a winner. In the end, Kennedy was the victor and the shock of the convention was his selection of the despised Lyndon Johnson as his running mate ~ a highly unlikely match. Thus the great event ended and the fate of the country was put in Kennedy's hands. No one dreamed that one day it would be in the hands of Lyndon Johnson.

CHAPTER FIFTEEN

FROM SOLO LAWYER
TO LAW FIRM

In 1961, Jerry Hile returned from one of his cyclical absences, subdued and soft spoken, and was easing himself back into the practice. By that time I had developed a sufficient body of cases that I felt I could support my own practice. I had long since concluded that if I wanted to have anything more than a neighborhood law practice I would have to locate downtown and it was only a matter of time before I left West Seattle and moved to an independent downtown law practice. That time arrived unexpectedly. Jerry came into my office a week or so after he returned and said he wanted to change our arrangement; he proposed that he and I become partners. I told him I would let him know my decision in a day or two. But in truth I had no doubt about the issue. I had no desire to be a partner with a manic-depressive who had already shown himself capable of bizarre behavior. I went into his office and told him that I regretted that our seven-year relationship had to end. There was no hesitation in my voice when I said, "Jerry, I appreciate your offer of a partnership, but I'm afraid my answer is no. I will leave the office and move downtown and I wish you the best of luck."

He seemed surprised but said he understood and we shook hands. On my last day, Jerry said to me, with emotion in his voice, "Al, I appreciate everything you have done to keep the practice going and I'm going to miss you."

I was leaving to set up my own office in downtown Seattle. I was surprised and touched by Hile's sadness at this news. It seemed he genuinely liked me and I was embarrassed by his flowery speech of appreciation for all I had done to keep his practice together.

The die was cast and I had to find an office in downtown Seattle. Finding an office downtown was surprisingly easy. I saw an ad for office space in the law offices of Arthur Grunbaum in the Dexter Horton Building. Grunbaum was a middle-aged lawyer who specialized in representing bonding companies. He had rented two of his offices and one of his tenants, a man I knew, Solie Ringold, had just been appointed a Superior Court Judge and his office was now vacant. There was a third renter, a soft-spoken fellow named Owen Johnson who primarily did personal injury work. Art Grunbaum was a very kindly, avuncular man, and we easily reached an agreement on terms, paying a monthly rental which included use of his secretary. It didn't take much effort to move. Art told me that Ringold wanted to sell his office furnishings and I could probably get them at a very low price. That's what happened and I ended up with Ringold's desk, swivel chair, two office chairs and a file cabinet. I bought only two items: an ashtray and a rolodex. So now I was established in my own law office; the office of Alvin J. Ziontz, 1201 Dexter Horton Building ~ the same building where Hile's old firm was located and where I had started my career seven years earlier.

Johnson was a rather distant fellow but Art was a warm and friendly man. I soon came to join him at a nearby cocktail lounge, "The Lamplighter", every evening after work where he met with three or four lawyer friends over a whiskey, while we waited for the evening rush hour to pass. All these men were much older than I and much more established in their law practice. Yet we enjoyed each other's company and conversation. I came to know the gossip about the lawyers in town and formed a bond with Art Grunbaum.

It was exciting to begin my own law practice; printing letterhead stationery and bills, setting up a bookkeeping system, sending out announcements and tasting the delights and fears of independence for the first time. I had a block of cases that came from West Seattle, but I didn't know how many clients would continue to retain me now that I was no longer so convenient, and I didn't know where my new clients would come from. While at first my income was skimpy since I no longer could count on walk-in clients, still my West Seattle base provided a livelihood. People knew of me and I began getting referrals from my clients. For two years I was a solo practitioner, making a living, but not a good one.

My seven years working as a lawyer in Jerry Hile's office gave me the confidence that the masquerade was ended ~ that I was a real lawyer. I had done almost every kind of case; divorce, child custody, personal injury, bankruptcy, creditors rights, drafting wills, drafting contracts, drafting leases, chartering corporations, litigation in Superior Court, in Traffic Court, one or two criminal cases, and appeals. In the course of that lawyering, I became somewhat known to a number of lawyers and judges. That's the only reason I can think of for the call that came from a prominent lawyer downtown asking if I would be willing to give a presentation at the upcoming Bar Association convention in Tacoma. The subject was the state's new Anti-trust law. I knew nothing about it, but felt I would simply study it and deliver a talk, so I agreed to do it.

About a week or so later I received the notice of the meeting, to be held at the Hotel Benjamin in Tacoma, It was still a month away and I had plenty of time to familiarize myself with this new statute. The field was familiar to me because I had a course on anti-trust law in Law School. Soon I felt ready to address an audience of lawyers on the subject of Washington's new anti-trust statute.

I had the date of my talk well in mind, but somehow I got the idea that it was to be at two thirty in the afternoon. That morning I arrived at my office and glanced at the announcement of the convention. My heart almost stopped. My panel was scheduled for that very morning at 9:30 not 2:30. How could I have made such a critical mistake? It was now 10:00. Could I get to Tacoma in fifteen minutes? Impossible.

I got on the phone and tried to reach the chairman of the panel but the hotel front desk knew nothing about the programs and it was impossible to reach the chairman of the panel. Driving to Tacoma was an hour trip. I would miss the entire panel presentation, to say nothing of my embarrassment. My mind raced. Was there any way to get to Tacoma in a half hour? I was wishing that somehow I could fly from downtown Seattle to Tacoma. Wait a minute. Fly!

I had seen float planes on Lake Union. Maybe I could charter a float plane and fly to Tacoma. It was a desperate idea but I could see no alternative. I called Lake Union Flying Service and asked if they could fly me to Tacoma. "Sure," said a voice. "It'll cost you thirty-five dollars."

"I'll be right over," I said and packed my briefcase. I ran to my car, carrying my briefcase heavy with copies of my talk, and drove as fast as I could to Lake Union. There it was: "Lake Union Flying Service". I quickly parked and entered a small, unimpressive office. Sitting behind a desk was a fat man in shirtsleeves who must have weighed over 250 pounds. "I'm the guy who called about a charter to Tacoma. How soon can we leave?" "Right now," he said and got up from his desk.

"Where's the pilot?" I asked. I was shocked when he answered, "I'm Ted and I'm the pilot," and led me out a rear door onto a dock. I had expected a pilot to look more slim and athletic, but now I was committed. As I walked beside him, I asked, "Where's the plane?"

"The Yellow one over there," he answered, pointing. Tied to the dock was a fabric covered float plane with room for only two passengers. Feeling the desperation of passing time, I quickly walked on toward the small plane, leaving my pilot behind me. As I started to walk down the wooden ramp toward the craft, I vaguely heard him say something but didn't clearly understand his words. At that moment my feet went out from under me on the wet, slippery ramp and I began to slide into Lake Union. I was just able to grasp a wing strut and stop the slide, but not before my left leg slid into the water. Ted, came up and said, "I tried to tell you the ramp was slippery." So that's what he was saying! "Climb in," said my pilot and I carefully set one foot on the float and opened the door to the cabin.

As I sat down on one of the two seats, I wondered how my behemoth of a pilot was going to squeeze in with me. I sat there holding my briefcase on my lap while Ted, turned some knobs on the instrument panel and then stepped on the right float. I was uneasy about the flimsy structure of the plane, expecting an all metal fuselage, I was uneasy about Ted and my unease grew when he gripped the wooden propeller and gave it a hard shove down to start the engine. The whole thing looked primitive, but the engine started. Ted heaved himself into the right seat, shut his door and said, "We're ready to go."

His massive bulk forced me to squeeze against my door. The door was light and flimsy. It provided little assurance that I was shielded from the outdoors. Worse yet, when I tried to shut it, there was no solid contact; instead there was a worrisome gap between the door edge and the door frame. When I asked Ted if the door was securely closed, he glanced at it and said, "Sure. Don't worry about it." With that he revved the engine and we began to taxi out into the lake.

It seemed to me, sitting in the cramped little cabin, that we were not moving very fast, in fact we were just chugging along and I began to worry about whether we would attain takeoff speed. Ahead I saw the shoreline at the end of Lake Union growing nearer and now I was certain we didn't have enough speed to lift off the water. Finally, in desperation, I said to Ted, "Shall I throw my briefcase overboard to lighten the plane?" Ted looked at me with amusement and said, "Hell no. We're just taxiing to roughen the surface, then we'll make our takeoff run."

Sure enough, after reaching the north end of the lake he turned the plane around and began taxiing back to our starting point. Once again he turned the plane around and this time opened the throttle fully so the engine began to roar, at least it seemed like a roar to me. Now, as we headed north, the little craft seemed to settle back on the rear of the floats and the nose began to point up to the sky. In a short time, we rose from the water and began flying. I was on my way. He banked the plane steeply to the left and began a u turn to the South. Our altitude couldn't have been more than 200 feet as we flew South over Lake Union, Queen Anne hill's houses just off our right wing. This was nothing like a commercial plane ~ it was flying at its most basic.

Slowly we climbed higher and soon were above the hills of West Seattle. As we flew south over Puget Sound, Ted turned to me and asked, "Where in Tacoma did you want to go?" I was confused by his question. It sounded like a taxi driver. Could he actually fly to the Hotel Benjamin? I told him the hotel name and he nodded, "Downtown Tacoma," he said. "I'll land at a downtown waterway and you can take a cab from there."

Thirty minutes later we could see Tacoma ahead of us. The little craft descended toward a waterway and we splashed down in the waters of Tacoma. My pilot taxied toward a dock and skillfully cut the engine as we coasted toward a floating platform. He opened his door and with surprising agility stepped out on the float and then, reaching down he picked up a mooring rope and pulled the plane to the dock. We had arrived.

I paid Ted the agreed fare of $35 and he pointed me toward a ramp that led to the street level. I stood there for a moment. Now what? Then I noticed a small office building nearby. Maybe I could phone for a cab there. I entered the building and found myself in a small office where three men were sitting. Breathlessly I told them I needed a cab immediately to get to the Hotel Benjamin. One of the men said, "I can call you a cab but it will probably be twenty minutes before he gets here."

When I explained that I was supposed to be at the hotel at nine that morning and was way late, one of the other men said, "I'm with the county coroner's office and I'll drive you there in our ambulance."

I had only a momentary qualm at arriving at the hotel in a coroner's ambulance, but I expressed my gratitude and we went outside where the ambulance was parked. As I got in I noticed the prominent marking on the vehicle: "Pierce County Coroner". Oh, well.

I ran into the hotel lobby, aware that my left shoe, socks and pants cuff were still wet. "Where is the King County Bar Association meeting?" I asked the desk clerk. "In Conference Rooms B, C and D," he answered.

Great. Now I had to guess which room they were in. I entered Room B, a cavernous room where over a hundred lawyers were sitting, listening to the speaker. I hastened toward the front of the room, as lawyers heads turned toward me, and only when I was near the podium did I realize that the panel sitting there was not my panel. Wrong room! I was too frantic about my lateness to be embarrassed and, whirling around, ran out.

Next, Room B. With relief I recognized the four members of the speaker's panel and walked quickly to the front of the room. "Well,

I see that Al Ziontz, one of our panel members has arrived. Just in time. Al, come on up here and let's hear your presentation." the panel chairman said.

Breathlessly I began, "You won't believe what it took to get here, but never mind," and I launched into my presentation, passing out the outlines of my talk which I had crammed into my briefcase.

The talk was not brilliant, but adequate and when I had finished, I sat down as the audience applauded the panel. What a day! Never again would I rely on memory for any important date.

I was working hard to keep enough income coming in to pay for the office and for our family to live on. Now that I had to pay my own overhead, my income was reduced. But I was committed to independence and new cases always seemed to make their appearance. I had been operating as a tenant of Art Grunbaum for a year when he suddenly had a heart attack and died. The other tenant, Owen Johnson, decided to move out and join another law firm. Mr. Grunbaum's widow told me she wanted to close the office, but if I wanted to continue, she was sure the building would accept an assignment of the lease to me and I could buy all the office equipment for a very reasonable price. But I had to act fast. Unless I acted, she was going to close the office in a month.

I was uncertain what to do. An older, very successful attorney talked to me about becoming his associate. But I had had enough of being an associate in another man's office. I wanted to have my own firm. The suite had three offices so I began to look around for two lawyers to join me. I quickly found a friend, Floyd Fulle, who was looking for another situation and he offered to join with me in a partnership. Floyd was a very nice guy and I liked him. He was a Columbia graduate and a good lawyer. But we needed a third and I had no idea who the third man might be.

Not long after my discussion with Floyd I was riding up the elevator in the King County Courthouse. There was only one other occupant. The fellow's appearance was striking; he looked like a short version of Abraham Lincoln and he was carrying a briefcase ~ a lawyer's emblem. I looked at him for a few seconds and said, "Hi, my name's Al Ziontz, what's yours?"

His response was cordial, "My name is Robert Pirtle. Pleased to meet you." We both exited at the ninth floor, a common destination for lawyers. Stepping out of the elevator I asked him, "Where do you practice?"

"Oh, I have my own office but I was with Perkins, Coie before that." I was immediately impressed. Perkins, Coie was one of the top firms in the city, representing Boeing among others. Anyone who had been with them had to be a very good lawyer. Maybe this was my third man.

I told my new acquaintance that I was looking for a third lawyer to join me in a partnership I was forming and asked if he would be interested. Pirtle lit up like a lamp. He was immediately enthused and wanted to know more about my new firm. At my suggestion we repaired to a coffee shop across the street from the court house and sat down in a booth. I told him about myself, my background, about Floyd Fulle and about our office in 1201 Dexter Horton Building. In return I learned he was a graduate of the University of Colorado Law School and had been recruited by Perkins, Coie. (The full name of the firm at that time was Marion, Holman, Micklewait, Perkins, Coie and Black.) After three years at that firm, he said he decided to leave and concentrate on the study of Philosophy but rented a small office to practice law for a time to provide income. He was married with two children and lived on Bainbridge Island.

This was an interesting guy and he seemed a good candidate for a small firm, but I was disappointed when he told me about his practice. He represented a collection agency and most of his work was enforcing vacuum cleaner contracts. Not an impressive practice. Still, I thought, he was just beginning and his background at Perkins, Coie loomed large in my thoughts.

The three of us, I, Pirtle and Fulle agreed to meet to review our financial records and client lists. Pirtle's income was the lowest, followed by Fulle. Fulle's client list included a taxicab company in Burien, but his income showed they were not paying their bills, nor were many of his other clients. My practice and income was the most substantial. Nevertheless, I had decided that I didn't want a partnership that split income in proportion to each man's fee earnings. Instead I opted for complete equality. My two erstwhile partners were taken aback by this announcement, apparently expecting a more formulaic sharing, but they were enthusiastic, feeling, as I did, that we would be bound together more tightly in a true partnership, rather than a cost and fee sharing arrangement. So the firm of Ziontz, Pirtle and Fulle was born. The date was June 1, 1963.

In its first years, Ziontz, Pirtle and Fulle struggled and we lived from month to month. The law firm didn't make much money and my household had to get by on a bare bones budget. Some months it was touch and go. I continued to serve on the Board of the state affiliate of the ACLU, grappling with policy positions for the organization and trying to find funds to support our staff. The organization was widely viewed as radical. The public and the press had difficulty distinguishing between the principles the organization fought to protect and the people whose deeds brought those principles into play. So the ACLU struggled too.

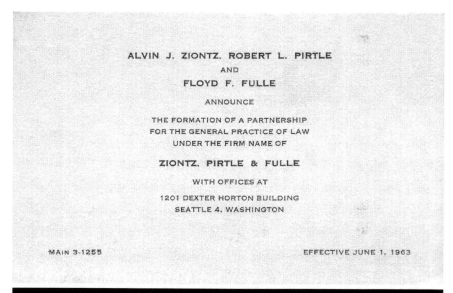

ALVIN J. ZIONTZ, ROBERT L. PIRTLE
AND
FLOYD F. FULLE

ANNOUNCE

THE FORMATION OF A PARTNERSHIP
FOR THE GENERAL PRACTICE OF LAW
UNDER THE FIRM NAME OF

ZIONTZ, PIRTLE & FULLE

WITH OFFICES AT

1201 DEXTER HORTON BUILDING
SEATTLE 4, WASHINGTON

MAin 3-1255   EFFECTIVE JUNE 1, 1963

Card announcing the formation of the law firm
ZIONTZ, PIRTLE & FULLE

Our first year was a financial struggle. The income was sporadic and meager. The following year, 1964, turned out to be a banner year ~ not for financial reasons but for other events that had long term consequences. The most important was a phone call from my former client Bruce Wilkie. I hadn't spoken to him in seven years. When he called he said, "Hi, Mr. Ziontz, remember me, Bruce Wilkie." "Sure," I said, "How the heck are you?" "Fine, fine," he answered and went on, "You know after I finished High School I went to the University of Puget Sound in Tacoma and got my degree. Then I kind' a knocked around for a while, did some traveling and ended up working for the Makah Tribe, here at Neah Bay."

"Wow! That's wonderful. You always said you wanted to work for the tribe." "Yeah. Now I'm what they call the Executive Director, sort of a city manager. Hey, Mr. Ziontz, I'll tell you the reason I called. For many years the tribe had a lawyer in Port Angeles as their tribal attorney. From what I could see, he wasn't much good. Usually, the tribe had to depend on the BIA for advice and their Solicitor's Opinions were never aggressive on Indian Rights. Now the tribal attorney has just got elected Prosecuting Attorney for Clallam County and he still wants to represent the tribe. The council decided that there would be too much conflict of interest and wanted to find a new attorney. They are considering two firms, one in Port Angeles and one in Seattle. But I suggested you. Would you be interested?"

His question sent a thrill through me. We had only one client on retainer ~ a collection agency, and that was barely profitable. To have an Indian Tribe on retainer would be a huge leap forward. "Yes, of course I would be interested," I replied. "Well, you'd have to come to Neah Bay and be interviewed by the Council," said Bruce.

The date of my interview was quickly set. It would be a Monday night of the following week in February of 1964. Pirtle and Fulle were excited at the development and Pirtle said he wanted to come with me. I told him it would be best that I meet the Council alone and that's what I did.

One evening in February I set out alone, driving along the coast highway to Neah Bay, an Indian fishing village at the furthermost Northwest tip of the continental United States. I arrived at night and I had no idea where the main office of the tribe was. Driving along the main street that fronted the bay, I spotted a small white cottage that bore the sign; "Makah Tribal Office". When I entered I found myself in a brightly lit office dominated by a large square glass topped table. The glass covered a geological map of the reservation. Around the table six men were seated; Bruce and five councilmen. They stood and greeted me with a smile and handshakes. Bruce introduced me. "This is our Chairman, Quentin Markishtum, and this is Hillary Irving and Ty Parker and Charlie Peterson and Joe Lawrence, Jr."

I was quickly informed that Quentin was called "Squint", Hillary Irving was called "Zab", Ty Parker's actual name was David Parker, and Joe Lawrence was called "Bobe". In time I learned that the Makahs are inclined to create nicknames for almost everyone. There was also a young woman seated in a corner with a notepad to take notes of the meeting. There was one file cabinet and a stack of cardboard boxes crammed with papers. This was the totality of the tribal governmental office. Bruce said to me, "Just tell them about your firm and anything you'd like to say."

With that I was on my own. Though I had never addressed a group of Indians, the atmosphere in the room was friendly and I easily launched into a description of my background and my ideas about the legal rights of Indian tribes. "I cannot claim to have a background in Indian Law, but I do know some important things that I think any tribal attorney should know."

Then I described my knowledge of tribal sovereignty under Federal Law and my own studies of Sovereignty. I gave them some idea of my experience in the trial and appellate courts and invited questions. What followed were some short, pithy remarks from several councilmen. "We are fishermen," they said, "But the State of Washington doesn't seem to recognize we have a treaty and our boys can't go out and make a living fishing, which is our legal right."

This was my introduction to the Indian Fishing Rights struggle in the State of Washington and I couldn't say anything helpful about it except I would try my best to protect their sovereignty and their treaty rights. The meeting lasted about an hour and at the end they all stood up, shook hands and thanked me for coming to talk with them. I did not feel confident that I had scored any points and given my lack of knowledge of Indian Law, I thought it very unlikely we would be retained as their attorneys. When Bruce called me the next day and said the council had voted to retain us I was stunned. Excited, joyful but stunned.

CHAPTER SIXTEEN

INDIANS, WINNING
AND FLYING

The Makah Indian Tribe was a major new client but the financial rewards were modest; $3,600 a year. Still, it was exciting ~ an Indian tribe! This would mean learning an entirely new area of law and who knew where it would lead? Fulle and Pirtle were impressed. We were, after all, a tiny firm; three lawyers struggling to pay the bills from a variety of ordinary, middle class clients. I did have some personal injury cases and they produced income from settlements, but nothing big.

The first major development with the Makahs came in the form of a phone call in 1964 from the chairman, Squint Markishtum. "Al, the BIA just told us there's going to be a very important conference in Washington, D.C. and they want all the tribes to attend. It has something to do with President Johnson's war on poverty and we want you to come with us."

I had no idea why a lawyer needed to be there, but this was a request I could not refuse. I agreed and made plans to stay in the same hotel as the Makahs. The big problem was the plane fare. We simply did not have the money for me to fly to Washington. I went to the bank in our building for a loan and after the loan officer looked over our balance sheet, he politely but firmly turned me down. I didn't know what to do. Then I thought of a lawyer who had been one of the drinking buddies of Art Grunbaum, George Toulouse, and went to see him. After I explained the nature of our problem, he generously loaned me $500. I was embarrassed but swallowed my pride; I could hardly explain to the Makahs that I was unable to go because we didn't have the money for plane fare.

The Makah delegation and I flew to Washington together. We stayed at a rather run-down hotel not far from the capital. The delegation consisted of four of the council members and an elderly Makah, not on the council, Art Claplanhoo. The BIA had distributed a program listing the scheduled meetings, the places where they would be held and the subjects to be presented. All of us had dinner together at the hotel and spent a pleasant evening in preparation for the following day of attending programs. The programs were about the War on Poverty, the Community Action Program, the Job Corps, Legal Services, Head Start, Housing and Vista. Since these were going to be presented at different locations, many at the same time, we divided up so as to have someone in attendance at each of the talks. Spending the evening with the Makahs gave me an opportunity to get to know them personally. Our talk was at times serious; at times joking, but always intimate.

The following day we dispersed to the various locations of the talks, agreeing to meet again that evening back at the hotel. At the end of a day of sometimes tedious descriptions of the details of these new government programs, we reunited in the lobby of our hotel. There was an air of cautious excitement among the Makahs. These programs promised a healthy infusion of federal money into tribal communities. There had never been anything like it.

TRIBAL DELEGATES MEET: SEATTLE TIMES FEB. 16, 1964

Indians Urge Federal Study Of Their Fishing Practices

By BOB MONAHAN

Representatives of 34 Washington Indian tribes yesterday urged immediate federal research into Indian fishing practices here.

The tribal delegates, meeting at Norway Center, also pledged united action in a public - relations campaign against policies of the State Fisheries and Game Departments.

Bruce W i l k i e, business manager of the Makah Tribal Council at Neah Bay, said the Indians might follow the lead of civil-rights groups in presenting their case to the public.

Indians here face their gravest crisis since "the extermination policies of the last century," Wilkie said.

"We feel that the good faith of our country is at stake," he added.

WILKIE, executive secretary of the National Youth Council, organized the meeting. About 110 persons, including attorneys representing various tribes, attended.

Most discussion centered on Indian fishing rights.

A number of Indians have been arrested by state game protectors for using gill-nets in off-reservation rivers. They contended they could do so under an 1854 treaty.

The Indians said their fishing practices should be studied by the federal government, "removed from the pressure of commercial and sports-fishing groups."

They said Indians had a vital interest in conservation and practiced it, although they acknowledged the need for more information.

Wilkie contended that Indians account for less than 5 per cent of the state's total salmon catch. About 70 per cent of the state's Indians rely heavily on fishing for their livelihoods, he said.

WILKIE AND others attacked a 1963 state law that gives the state jurisdiction over Indians in criminal, child-welfare, divorce and other matters.

Jim B. Hovis, attorney for the Yakima tribe, said he had been directed to challenge the constitutionality of the law.

Indian tribes take the position that they were sovereign nations and that the state government had no right to pass such a law without their consent, Hovis said.

Hovis said law enforcement has declined on the Yakima reservation since passage of the law. Local authorities have not added a single policeman despite their increased responsibilities, he said.

Among Indian leaders at the meeting were Harvey Moses of the Colville tribe and Quentin Markishtum, chairman of the M a k a h tribe. Alvin J. Ziontz, Seattle attorney, represented the Makahs.

Another inter-tribal meeting will be held in a few months, Wilkie said.

HARVEY MOSES
Colville Indian at meeting

BRUCE WILKIE

JIM B. HOVIS

QUENTIN MARKISHTUM

ALVIN J. ZIONTZ

Seattle Times article describing the beginning of public protest against State fishing laws, 1964

327

The Makahs were particularly excited about the Community Action Program since this promised funding for the operations of Tribal governments. The Makahs were governed by a five man council, all volunteers, since there was no money to pay them a regular salary. All but one were employed at daytime jobs, most working in the woods for the giant timber company, Crown Zellerbach. Art Claplanhoo was employed as a janitor at the local school. The council met as a body twice a month, in the evening. Most of their time was spent reviewing and then, for the most part, rubber stamping actions proposed by the local agency of the BIA. Law enforcement was under the jurisdiction of the BIA, logging on the reservation was conducted under contract with the BIA, medical services were provided by Indian Health Services, a federal agency. Roads were maintained by the BIA. Schools were funded and staffed by the local school district with county and state funds. Housing was ramshackle and dilapidated, the land was non-taxable and there was little money in the community. So the tribal government had few governmental functions. Many young Makahs moved off the reservation when they got married because there was no housing. The prospects of change in all this was a dream come true, but many Makahs, mindful of the history of broken promises, were skeptical.

We returned from Washington abuzz with suppressed excitement. Back at our office in the Dexter Horton Building, I told Frost (Floyd Fulle's middle name and his preferred name) and Robert about the War on Poverty and its potential for big changes in Indian life. Soon I got a call from Squint, The members wanted to know what had transpired at the Washington meetings so the council called a general tribal meeting to be held at the Community Hall the following week. He wanted me to attend and make a presentation.

Again I drove the winding road along the coast to Neah Bay and found the Community Hall at the West end of the village. It was an old structure, wooden and worn. It was built by the CCC during the Roosevelt administration in the late 30's. Inside, folding chairs held a growing number of Makahs who had come to hear about the new programs the government was starting. This was the first time I had ever appeared before the general membership of the tribe and the audience was mixed; young and old, men and women and children. They looked upon me with curiosity ~ I was the new tribal attorney. There was a long table at the front of the room with chairs for the council members. After twenty minutes of hubbub, Squint called the meeting to order and announced that everyone who had attended the Washington conference would address the members and explain what they had heard, starting with me.

I rose and walked to the center of the table and began. This War on Poverty was a new and bold program and would likely have a big effect on life at Neah Bay. Starting with the Community Action Program, I explained they would have to establish new tribal structures, for example a Makah Housing Authority to handle the construction of new homes and manage the federal funding to do it. The Community Action Program offered the promise of major federal money for tribal government, enabling the government to pay regular salaries to its employees. I then gave a brief description of some of the other programs and then sat down.

Squint then called on each of the delegates to describe what they had heard at the sessions they attended. The talks were tedious, flat and, judging from the audience reaction, boring. Lastly, he called on old Art Claplanhoo. Art had attended only one presentation and spent the rest of his time sitting around the lobby of our hotel. He was a very quiet and soft spoken man and I doubted he would have much to contribute. He stood up and his talk in its entirety was as follows: "Well, I went to the housing talk and they showed some of the houses they had built for them people over in Korea."

With that he sat down. To my amazement there was rousing applause. None of the other speakers had been applauded and I was mystified by the crowd's reaction to Art's few words. Then I began to understand. The government could build houses for foreigners but they hadn't built any for American Indians. Now there seemed to be promise. The Makahs would wait and see. Indian blunt speech.

Following our trip we set about working to implement these programs; drawing up the charter for the Makah Housing Authority, arranging for the construction of ten new houses, setting up a program for a Small Business Administration loan to construct 10 fishing boats, and coordinating with the government for the construction of a Job Corps Camp on the reservation.

Federal money flowed quickly, especially for the Community Action Program. This provided major funding for tribal governmental programs; supporting salaries for tribal employees in the fishery department, planning department, alcohol treatment programs, law and order employees, the tribal court system, cultural programs ~ in short, the functions that local governments typically perform in non-Indian communities.

The result was a rapid growth of job opportunities for members who wanted to work for their tribe. Tribal government expanded and became a real government; no longer a shadow of the BIA. Council members now received regular salaries and didn't have to depend on outside employment. Lyndon Johnson's War on Poverty brought about a profound change in the Makah community, and I am sure, on other reservations as well.

Meanwhile, our three man law firm was still struggling financially. There was one bright spot on the horizon: the Blodgett case. This was a wrongful death suit I had brought against the Great Northern Railroad (Now the Burlington Northern) on behalf of a widow and her surviving five children for the death of their father. The father's car had been struck by a Great Northern Train while he was attempting to cross the tracks at a rural grade crossing at a place called Milltown, some miles north of Stanwood, Washington. His destination was a nearby fishing site.

I drove out and carefully inspected the crossing. The tracks were on an elevated embankment reached by a gravel road. Going up the embankment put a car at a steep upward angle, making it difficult to see any oncoming train. There was no gate or lights, just the familiar crossed wooden arms. The ground alongside the embankment was covered by thick brush, obstructing any view up or down the tracks till the vehicle was practically on the tracks.

The railroad offered a paltry settlement, so with my client's approval we went to trial before a jury. The railroad's attorney offered in evidence photographs taken by a professional photographer purporting to depict the view North and South from the crossing. They appeared to show an unobstructed view at least a quarter of a mile in each direction. I was worried. That evening Lennie asked whether the photographs were taken at the height of a driver seated in a car. Such a position would clearly show the brush obstructing the view. Smart woman!

The next day I had the photographer on the witness stand and asked him; was he standing when he took the photographs. He said he was using his professional tripod and was standing. I asked him to produce the tripod on which his camera was mounted and he did. One glance was enough to show that the lens was at least four feet off the ground, far higher than the position of a seated driver. The brush had obstructed the driver's view and left him in a position of peril in trying to cross the tracks at that location. I called Mrs. Blodgett to the stand and she testified about the loss to the family of her husband's income and the loss of love and affection suffered by her and her children. The jury returned a verdict of $250,000 in our favor.

The Blodgett case marked a turning point in the fortunes of our firm. Our fee was over $80,000. With these funds, we were able to set up a reserve for future contingencies. More important we moved from our rather dowdy quarters in the Dexter Horton Building to a suite on the 31st floor of the then new Seattle First National Bank Building. Each of us had spacious quarters; there was an office for a potential fourth lawyer and a conference room which also served as a library.

The year was 1964 and it turned out to be an eventful one. The Indian Fishing Rights struggle was heating up. The brunt of the conflict was borne by the Puget Sound river net fishing tribes: the Puyallup, the Muckleshoot and the Nisqually. While the Makahs did some netting on the rivers near their reservation, and while they had won a court case protecting their right to net on the Hoko River, they were mainly an ocean fishing tribe. So it wasn't the Makahs that sent me to battle for fishing rights, it was Bruce Wilkie.

Bruce was an angry Indian from the time I first met him and he stayed angry. While he felt anger at the historic betrayals and injustices that the American Indians had suffered since the 18th century, his anger now was aimed at the State of Washington for its trampling of the fishing rights proclaimed in the treaties made with the United States in the 1850's.

Since statehood, Washington had legislated the Indians off the rivers. Only the sports and commercial fishing interests were protected by state fish managers. Indians who dared to fish with nets on the rivers were routinely arrested, their catch confiscated, and often their boats and motors seized. Their justification? The Stevens Treaties with the northwest tribes in 1854 merely guaranteed the same rights as non-Indians. Where was the Federal Government? Largely passive, unwilling to engage in a fight with the states of Washington and Oregon. But in 1957 one Indian, a Puyallup named Bob Satiacum, a World War II veteran, decided to challenge the state.

He went out on the Puyallup River, near Tacoma and openly set a gill net in daylight. He was, of course, arrested, but he and his attorney asserted immunity from State regulation, citing the Stevens Treaties, which purported to guarantee his right to fish at "all usual and accustomed places". The case went to the United States Supreme Court which ruled that the State of Washington could restrict his fishing in "the interests of conservation". Naturally, the State claimed that all its regulations were "in the interests of conservation" and did not change its practice of prohibiting Indians from fishing on the rivers.

But Satiacum's boldness had ignited a smoldering feeling of injustice and soon Puget Sound Tribes began defying State prohibitions. It was here that Bruce Wilkie found a channel for action. He joined with a friend, Hank Adams, an Assiniboine-Sioux who lived on the Quinault Reservation to launch what they called a "public awareness" campaign. Indians who were arrested for fishing were rarely covered by the press. When they were, the story appeared on the sports pages as a case of another Indian caught "poaching". Indian treaties were considered ancient documents with no present force.

Page 6—Port Angeles Evening News, Salute to Neah Bay, Friday, July 15, 1966

Makah Days 'New look' coming

The Makah Indians of Neah Bay are getting ready for their annual Makah Days celebration scheduled for Aug. 27-28.

It really is a two-pronged event for the Makah. First of all it gives them a chance to welcome a number of visitors to their community to join in the two-day affair. Secondly it gives the elders of the tribe a chance to train the youngsters in the traditional songs and dances.

One of the highlights will be the salmon barbecue with the Indians preparing the salmon in their traditional manner.

Another is the exhibitions of Makah Dancing both during the day and at night. Also included are a number of sports events for everyone, water events, a parade, a speaker and a flag raising ceremony.

A regular modern dance is also scheduled for those attending.

A training period for youngsters from all ages through the teenagers begins July 18 and will continue right up to the two big days.

They are taught the songs and dances of the tribe which have been handed down through the years. It also serves to keep the youngsters together and gives them an insight into the culture which has been their heritage for hundreds of years.

But there is one thing the elders might be a little dubious about. That is the traditional Indian bone game. It is a gambling contest that can go on for hours.

For the last two years, the youngsters challenged the old er tribesmen to a session of the bone game and have taken them to the cleaners both times!

Neah Bay could take on a far different appearance in the next few years, Makah Tribal Manager Bruce Wilkie says.

Wilkie explains it all began four years ago when the tribal leaders took a long, hard look at the reservation and decided some studies should be made.

The result was the analysis of the recreation potential, possible community utility systems, information on the use of forest resources and the fisheries resource.

Most promising of the possibilities are timber and development of the fisheries with an eye toward tourism and recreation.

On the immediate horizon is the development of a fish reduction plant. Wilkie feels this could revolutionize the fishing industry. With Neah Bay perched in the middle of the largest fishing banks in the world, he thinks it is a "natural" for the community.

He noted a large fleet of trawlers and dragger fishing boats headquarters at Neah Bay and a lot of their catch which is wasted now could be utilized in the new plant.

The proposal is so near reality that he hopes to see it established and operating by November.

The plant would be owned in part by the Makah Tribe. It would produce fish meal as a high protein dietary supplement for animals. When in operation it would provide about 100 jobs.

Wilkie says leaders in the proposal are keeping a close watch on a similar operation now beginning in Aberdeen.

Another good point about the operation is that it would cause no air or water pollution. The only end result other than the meal would be distilled water.

At this point, he grinned and remarked, "These people will not permit any kind of pollution in the harbor."

Another proposal now in the planning stage is a 60-home housing development in the west end of the community. Planned are two to four bedroom homes to fit the needs of the community, in each case, the individual would be given the chance to buy his own home.

Still another proposal is to take advantage of federal programs to provide low rental housing for the aged and others who could not afford other housing.

In September work will start on Phase I of a new water system. The source will be a series of wells with the water to be stored in a 250,000-gallon tank.

Phase II of the program includes the erection of another storage tank to serve the eastern section of the town.

Still in the future are plans for storm sewer and surface drainage systems along with sanitary sewers and a treatment plant.

A new contract will soon be let for a garbage disposal service. Wilkie says this will give better control of garbage disposal.

With an eye on the current boom in private flying, he says the council hopes to soon develop its own air strip. The only facility available now is a short, light plane strip at the air force station.

Wilkie has traveled about the country a good deal while working on Indian Affairs and he says the Makah Tribal Council is one of the most advanced in the nation.

TRIBAL MANAGER — Bruce Wilkie ... looks to future.

Tribal council governs area

The Makah Indian Reservation is governed by a five-man tribal council and manager similar to the governing setup of many cities.

Council members are elected in annual elections, two in one year, two the second year and one the third year.

Elections are held in December of each year following a nominations meeting held in November. The council elects its own officers and hires the tribal manager.

Bruce Wilkie, a graduate of the University of Puget Sound, has been the tribal manager for five years. He also serves as secretary-treasurer for the council.

Bruce Wilkie, executive director of the Makah Tribe, announces tribal development plans, 1966.

334

Bruce and Hank wanted to move the struggle into the public eye by "fish-ins", modeled after black sit-ins in the South, and by attracting celebrities to join with them. The first celebrity to join their cause was the well-known film actor, Marlon Brando. Brando came to Tacoma and went fishing in a boat with Satiacum. Of course he was arrested. No charges were filed because the local county prosecutor claimed it was all "a publicity stunt". But the "stunt" resulted in national publicity and the Indian cause had a new dimension.

Marlon Brando (left), the movie star, taking part in a demonstration for Indian Fishing Rights in 1964. Bob Satiacum (right), a Puyallup Indian and an Indian Rights Activist.

(Photo from the Seattle Post Intelligencer Collection, Museum of History and Industry)

Brando's visit to the Pacific Northwest even drew me into his orbit. In 1964, Marlon Brando was an international film star. I accompanied him to provide legal assistance if he needed it. After his demonstration on the Puyallup River, he went to the state capitol, Olympia and met with the director of the Game Department to plead the Indian's case. The director was unmoved, despite Brando falling on his knees to beg for recognition of the Treaty Rights of the Indians. The next day we headed for La Push where Brando would accompany some Indian fishermen in another demonstration. Afterwards, he told me he was feeling sick and asked if I could drive him back to Seattle where he was to take a flight to Los Angeles. Of course, I affirmed that I would be happy to take him.

During the next four hours together we discussed his feelings about Indians and I explained some of the legal aspects of their claims. The result was a kind of rapport. Since his flight was not scheduled till that evening, I suggested he stop at my house for dinner before heading to the airport. He said he would enjoy that. There was a minor problem ~ my wife and children had to be informed of this visit from a celebrity. When we stopped in Port Angeles en route to Seattle, I took the occasion to call my wife so she could make the preparations for such a visit. My oldest son, then eleven, answered the phone.

"Where's mom?" I asked.

"She's not here. She went to the store."

I had to rely on him to convey an important message.

"Tell Mom that Marlon Brando is coming for dinner, and

I want you kids to straighten up the house and put on your good clothes."

"Okay, Dad. I'll tell her."

But Brando spent an inordinate amount of time in the restaurant in Port Angeles chatting with fans and giving autographs, so we were going to be pressed for time to fit in dinner in time for him to catch his plane.

After driving for about a half hour, Brando said, "Hey, Al. I'm awfully sorry, but I'm feeling so sick that I'm going to have to skip dinner with you and your family, Maybe next time. Just take me to the airport" Brando actually had contracted pneumonia and entered the hospital in Los Angeles after arriving home.

There was no way I could communicate with my wife about this change of plans so I simply drove home after dropping him off at SeaTac Airport. When I pulled into my carport Lennie and my three children were all standing on the doorstep, dressed in their best clothes, prepared to meet the great Marlon Brando. Their faces fell when I stepped out of the car alone. All of them had been excited at this, Lennie more than anyone since she always thought Marlon Brando was one of the most attractive men in the movies. It was a great disappointment.

Meanwhile, the Indian fishermen were demonstrating on all the rivers, while the state simply hardened its stance, claiming their acts were a threat to the fish resource. The acts of a few grew into a movement which attracted the support of local churches and the

American Civil Liberties Union. The demonstrations escalated and soon there were violent clashes between Indians and state fisheries officers. No longer could the press treat these conflicts as the acts of a few "poachers"; now it had moved off the sports page of the local papers and was "news".

I have described this historic struggle and its epic climax in the United States Supreme Court in my memoir, "A Lawyer In Indian Country", but I must here relate the part I played in the court case that was the defining decision of Pacific Northwest fishing rights.

The case was U.S. v. Washington, a suit brought by the Justice Department against the state. It was the first and only case in modern times that presented to any court the history of Pacific Northwest Indian fishing and the reality beneath the claim of the State of Washington that their prohibition of Indian fishing was "necessary for conservation".

In September of 1970 the government filed its suit, acting on behalf of seven tribes (not including the Makahs). Immediately all the tribal attorneys of the Northwest saw the far reaching implications of this case. The tribes and their attorneys viewed the case with deep misgivings. All their eggs were in this basket and the tribes had no reason to trust the federal judge to whom it was assigned ~ George Boldt. He had no record of ever deciding a case involving Indian rights and his judicial record was extremely conservative

I was one of four lawyers who conducted the Indian side of the case. The trial began in August of 1973, three years after the filing of the suit. After three weeks of trial the decision was released in 1974. It was a resounding rejection of the arguments of the state and affirmed the continuing validity of the Indian Treaties. Judge Boldt was careful to lay down a strict definition of the word "conservation" and to require state government to recognize tribal government as co-equal managers of the fish resource.

It was an earth shaking moment in Northwest history and permanently elevated tribal governments to respected members of the family of governments. The court decision had other far reaching consequences. Although it was sharply questioned and even attacked, the affirmation of Judge Boldt by the U.S. Supreme Court in 1979 brought an end to the agitation against the court decision, and while there are still ardent rejectionists, the issue was now settled. The decision has been the basis of other court decisions throughout the United States. While I played a relatively modest role in the case, it brought me a measure of fame.

In the early years my firm's work was not heavily dominated by Makah issues. We had developed a general practice and Makah was a relatively small part of it. It was 1964 when we hired our first associate. 1964 was also the year I decided I wanted to learn how to fly. From boyhood I had fantasized about flying, but it remained a remote and vague goal, my only flying experience being at the controls of the four engine DC-3 in 1954. That was changed by one experience.

Driving from Seattle to Neah Bay was a tedious four hour trip. One day in 1964 I was asked by the Makahs to be at the reservation for a meeting at 10:30 in the morning. This would require either going the night before or a very early morning departure. I had heard there was a charter air service flying from Boeing Field in Seattle to Port Angeles. I wondered if they could take me to a field close to the reservation, cutting off two hours of car travel. The company was called Fairchild Air Service and they had a phone at Boeing Field in Seattle. I called them and the owner, Bill Fairchild answered. Yes, he could fly me to Sekiu, a fishing village about twenty miles from Neah Bay. The total flying time from Boeing Field to Sekiu was only about forty minutes. I could easily arrange for someone from the reservation to pick me up at Sekiu and drive me to Neah Bay; a trip taking thirty minutes or so. So the total travel time would be an hour and ten minutes instead of four hours. The cost was not exorbitant so I arranged for a charter flight the next day.

I met Bill Fairchild at Boeing field and liked him immediately. He was a clean cut man of about forty, somewhat on the short side, wearing sunglasses and a leather jacket. He looked like a pilot. He led me out to a twin engine Piper Apache parked on the tarmac. It was an older airplane. There was only one large door on the passenger side for both pilot and passenger. Entering required climbing up on the wing and sliding onto the front seats. Fairchild entered first and I followed. This was a new experience and I watched with interest as Fairchild went through the engine start and tower communication procedures. His professional familiarity with the airplane was obvious.

As we roared down the runway and rose off the ground, my fascination with the art of piloting an airplane kept me intensely interested in the cockpit environment; the instrument panel, the knobs, levers and buttons Fairchild was using to control the movement of the aircraft, to navigate and to communicate. Soon I began asking questions about all of it. Bill Fairchild seemed pleased to explain what he was doing.

Suddenly, he turned to me, smiled and said, "Why don't you take the control wheel and see what it's like?" There were dual controls and when I grasped the wheel on my side, he said, "Keep a light touch. You don't have to move the wheel unless you want to turn or raise or lower the nose. Remember, the airplane wants to fly and it doesn't need you to keep it flying. Just keep the wings level, that's all you have to do." With that he turned the control wheel over to me.

Holding that wheel, at first delicately, then confidently, gave me a sense of exhilaration. I was actually at the controls of a plane. After a minute or two Fairchild said, "Let's do a left turn. Bank the plane gently to the left and then straighten the wheel."

I did as he said and the craft responded immediately to the turn of the wheel. After repeating the maneuver to the right and then recovering to level flight, Fairchild took back the controls. I was hooked on flying.

After more questions and answers Fairchild said, "You ought to take flying instruction. There are plenty of flying schools around Seattle. All you have to do is sign up."

This planted the seed in my mind. Within a few days I went to the library and took out several books on flying. When Lennie saw them she asked, "Why are you taking out books on flying? You're not thinking of doing that, are you?"

My answer was disingenuous, but not completely dishonest. I hadn't yet decided to act on the idea of getting a pilot's license, but

I was deeply interested and intent on finding out as much as I could before acting. So, I said, "No. I'm just interested in it."

She knew me better than that and the following day said, "Hey, how about boating? You said once that you liked boats. Maybe we could buy a boat and then the whole family could go out with you."

So the following weekend we drove out to a local marina and started walking along the docks looking at cabin cruisers for sale. A salesman soon made an appearance and pointed out several boats that had sleeping accommodations. One of these was quite nice and Lennie and I went aboard and inspected the interior. We liked it. The salesman, sensing that his customers were warming up to the boat began extolling the pleasures of boat ownership. Then, he made a serious mistake. He said, "One of the best parts of owning a boat like this is that there's always work you have to do on the boat."

The thought of sanding, varnishing and painting was anathema to me and Lennie knew it. We thanked him and left. The following week, Lennie and I had a serious conversation about flying. Although I explained what I had read about the glide ability of light planes to fly without engine power and the overall infrequency of fatalities, she had deep reservations about something commonly regarded as risky. Finally, knowing how determined I was, she exacted a promise from me; never fly when pressed by the need to be somewhere at a specific time when there was a question of whether the weather was safe. I promised.

The next week I enrolled at the flight school of Renton Aviation located at Renton Airport and began the process of becoming a licensed pilot. I took the lessons seriously and ultimately passed the written and flying exams. It was a boyhood fantasy realized. I flew rented aircraft for ten years, had some close calls and some wonderful experiences. I took Lennie and our children with me on several flights and once even took Lennie's parents on a flight to Ocean Shores. I tried to be a careful and cautious pilot and this attitude indeed preserved me in some difficult situations.

My first startling moment in an airplane couldn't have come at a worse time. I was flying alone to Beaverton, Oregon to meet the requirement for a private pilot's license; a cross country flight of over two hundred miles. I was tense but confident. As I approached Beaverton Airport I reduced power to begin my descent. As part of the standard procedure when reducing power on an internal combustion engine, I was trained to turn on what was called, "carburetor heat". This is a simple matter of pulling out a plastic knob labeled, "carburetor heat". Pulling on this knob moves a valve in the exhaust system to direct the flow of hot air to the carburetor to prevent ice from forming in the throat of the carburetor, thus choking off the supply of gas to the engine. If that happened, the engine would stop. Losing the engine on approach to a landing can be dangerous. So, I routinely pulled out the knob labeled carburetor heat as part of the landing procedure. But on this my maiden cross-country flight, I was horrified when the knob pulled completely out of the instrument panel, taking with it about three feet of flexible metal cable. I quickly aborted the landing approach and made a wide turning circle to the left. Now what!

I was a student pilot and I had to think fast. I decided to radio the flight school and describe my plight. It was a relief to hear the reassuring tones of the chief instructor. "Is the engine running normally?" he asked. "Yes," I responded. "Good. Just make a normal landing approach but don't close the throttle completely. Maintain about a thousand rpms and make your landing. Don't worry about it. Everything will be o.k." I returned to the airfield and began my approach thinking, "Of all times for a cable to come loose, on a first cross country flight by a student pilot!" There was no time to dwell on it and I concentrated on my landing. The engine didn't stop, my landing was o.k. and after spending fifteen minutes in the airport office to get my log book signed, I returned to my imperfect airplane, took off and flew back to Renton Airport. Once on the ground I went into the office to talk to my instructor. It seemed everyone had heard about the loose cable and was sympathetic. My instructor told me he had never heard of this cable coming loose and they would talk to the mechanics about it.

The incident was just that ~ an incident. It had no serious consequences but when I reflected on it I realized that I had kept a cool head and used good judgment in dealing with a startling aircraft malfunction, one which happily turned out fine. I passed the flight test and received my private pilot's license. After that I flew as often as I could, weather permitting. For the next ten years aviation was a large part of my life. Flying an airplane, even one that is not complex, is nothing to be done casually. Danger, even death, is ever present.

Flying from the Seattle area to the west requires going around the Olympic Mountain range, either to the north, following the north shore of the Olympic Peninsula, or to the south. If the destination is the resort city of Ocean Shores, one flies well south of the mountains and west to the ocean. There are no airports on the ocean side of the mountains, so there is never any reason but scenery to fly over the Olympic Range. Flying toward the ocean along the north shore of the Olympic Peninsula was routine. Usually, I flew around the north end of the Range and followed the shore line, though occasionally I flew over the end of the Olympic range if I wanted to shorten the trip.

The main destination airport was Port Angeles, a fairly large, modern airport, though without a tower or any traffic controls. My trips were usually for the purpose of getting to the Makah Indian Reservation at Neah Bay. Although there was a short field on the reservation intended for military aircraft, it was not for the faint of heart. A landing there would require approaching over the ocean beach and getting wheels down within 100 feet of the seaward end of the strip and hitting the brakes hard to stop before an embankment at the end of the strip. I decided it was not for me.

The closest landing field to the reservation was at Sekiu, a tiny fishing village twenty miles east of the reservation. The village lay on the shore of a small half moon bay opening onto the waters of the Strait of Juan de Fuca. It was located at the foot of a steep hill. The airstrip was a clearing at the top of the hill. It was hardly an airport, just a clearing with a windsock to aid a pilot. Landing there took skill and nerve. The field itself was not paved and the dirt surface was rough. While the trees had been cleared to create the strip, there remained a forest of tall evergreens along the west side of the strip and at the end of the strip. The strip was not very long, about 800 feet ~ a minimal distance for a landing field.

The most serious hazard was the steep hill rising from the bay below the field. Since the prevailing winds were usually from the west, an approach to this field had to be made over the waters of Sekiu Bay, flying directly toward the face of the hill and setting the wheels down within the first 150 feet of the end of the clearing in order to stop before reaching the end. During my first attempt to land there my careful descent almost ended in disaster. When I approached the face of the hill the wind was blowing in from the ocean over the airstrip. A strong current followed the face of the hill, creating a powerful downdraft. As I was nearing the airstrip, suddenly the plane began dropping. My heart jumped into my mouth. I had to regain altitude quickly, otherwise I would fly into the face of the hill. Quickly I pushed the throttle full in and raised the nose. Thankfully, the plane responded and we rose above the field. The attempted landing now aborted, I flew over the field. Now I had to decide, was this field too difficult for me? I decided that I could overcome that downdraft with a higher, steeper approach and more power. Once I got on the ground I would have to cope with the short field.

I circled back for my second try. This time I came in higher and steeper. I kept the engine at a higher RPM and lowered full flaps for a steep and slow approach. Things happen quickly; it was only a few seconds till I was over the beginning of the clearing. Though my heart was pounding, I maintained intense concentration on the rapidly nearing ground, determined to make contact well before the mid-point of the runway. There was one unexpected hazard, unseeable from the air. The strip rose to a hump about a third of the way along, and the plane went up the hump and accelerated down the other side. I had to brake hard before reaching the trees at the end of the field. When the plane came to a complete stop on the field, I took a deep breath. It was done. I had landed at Sekiu.

My destination was the Makah Reservation and I had arranged for two men from the reservation to pick me up at the Sekiu airfield. I taxied back to the midpoint of the field and parked the airplane where my grinning Makah friends were waiting for me. Nothing was said about the landing and I rode with them the thirty or so minutes to Neah Bay. My mind kept re-running the excitement of the landing, thinking that the next time I would have a better idea of how to manage getting down onto this primitive little airstrip.

Over the next ten years I landed at Sekiu many times. It was never easy. Each approach had to be precise in order to avoid the downdrafts and get on the ground as near as possible to the approach end of the field. Taking off presented few problems but the hump could get you airborne too soon, when the airspeed was too slow for a safe takeoff. The takeoff run had to be controlled so that the plane was still rolling firmly on the ground when it mounted the hump. Once flying speed had been reached and the plane was climbing one only had to be sure to aim straight ahead. There were no obstacles to worry about at the east end of the field. Beyond that end of the field the ground dropped away several hundred feet to the bay and from here on, flying to Seattle simply required a steady course at an altitude of three or four thousand feet to cross the Kitsap Peninsula and then Puget Sound till arriving at the Seattle side. So this part of the flight was quite pleasant. But landing at Sekiu became a challenge that I mastered.

Flying to Eastern Washington was more problematic. The Cascade Mountains had to be crossed, either over the crest or through Snoqualmie Pass. Usually I flew below the level of the crests, and followed I-90 along the pass through the mountains. But the weather had to be monitored closely. If there were clouds in the pass below the peaks I would not attempt a crossing unless there was a high ceiling on the east side of the pass and the tops of the clouds would not require climbing over 10,000 feet ~ the maximum for a pilot without oxygen. The peaks along my route were just over 6,000 feet, so flying at seven or eight thousand feet was safe.

One of our tribal clients were the Colvilles, a large tribe with a reservation in north central Washington. The closest airfield was at Okanogan, an airport with a decent runway and no special problems in making an approach. Flying to that reservation meant crossing the Cascades, a flight I made only in good weather. I was a cautious pilot, unwilling to risk weather problems, especially clouds. It was drilled into me and repeatedly stated in flying manuals, to say nothing of crash reports, that unless one had training in instrument flying and was proficient in it, flying into clouds was suicidal. The problem was vertigo; the loss of ability to keep the plane upright and level when visual reference to the horizon is lost. I always examined weather reports before flying across the mountains and scanned the sky to stay well clear of clouds.

Once, my partner, Robert Pirtle and I had to attend a meeting of the Colville Tribal Council and I decided that if the weather was good, I would fly over there. The weather forecast was for clear skies and then broken clouds in the late afternoon. Broken clouds meant patches of clouds with open areas between them. Good enough. We would fly. I arranged to rent my regular plane, a Piper Cherokee 180, Cherokee 9077 J, one that I had flown many times over the years. The 180 was a low wing, fixed gear, four seat airplane. It had full instrumentation, including a VOR, a navigation instrument that displayed the position of the plane with respect to a ground station. I was quite familiar with all of it and had no qualms about crossing the Cascades to fly to central Washington.

The flight to Okanogan was scenic and uneventful. Our meeting with the Colville Council lasted far longer than I expected and we were not able to leave till about 6:30 in the evening. I was a bit concerned about arriving over Seattle in darkness. Though I had flown at night several times and even taken a course in night flying, landing was more demanding when you had to gauge your height above the runway by the lights on the ground. But the sun was just setting and I felt there would still be plenty of light to make the landing. My destination was Boeing field which was well lit and even had a control tower. So I took off from Okanogan looking forward to the return flight with confidence.

Our course was due west, right into the setting sun. After five minutes of trying to avoid the glare by lowering the sunshade, I put on my sunglasses. These were dark enough to turn the western horizon dark. After thirty minutes of crossing the Cascades, all daylight faded into night and I began to look for the lights of the towns on the west side of the mountains; Issaquah and Bellevue. I didn't see them. Instead I saw a solid base of clouds beneath me. I was certain the forecast and the radio weather reports called for broken clouds. Anxiously, I began looking for the broken areas between the clouds. I couldn't find any. I flew on, certain that when I came over Mercer Island and Seattle I would see city lights. But beneath me I could see only a solid sea of clouds. Now I was alarmed.

The weather forecast must have been wrong and I was caught on top of a solid cloud ceiling. I wouldn't try to go down through them ~ that would be suicidal. The tops of the clouds were about two thousand feet, so staying above them was no problem. How to find a break between them and get down to the ground? This was a serious problem. Estimating that I was over Seattle, I turned south and called Air Traffic Control.

"I'm caught up here over the clouds and need to find a break so I can get down to Boeing Field," I radioed. I didn't know exactly where I was but estimated I was over the Kent area. The controller was following me on radar and calmly advised, "You should find some breaks to the south, over Kent or Renton." "Roger," I replied, without any confidence.

I continued on to the south. I was beginning to get scared. There was no way I could dive into that solid bank of clouds without going on instruments, and I had no confidence that I could make a descent through the clouds on instruments. Then I saw a hole in the clouds, but it was small and meant I would have to make continuous tight turns while descending. If I couldn't turn tight enough I risked flying into cloud and then I would be in big trouble. I flew on. Then I saw it. A large opening in the clouds with lights on the ground clearly visible. Immediately I banked the airplane and started going down below the cloud deck. The clouds were not very thick and in a minute or two I was below them and flying over the houses of Kent. After a few more minutes I could see the lights of Boeing Field. I called the tower and was cleared for a straight in approach. I was breathing easier.

I descended to the runway at Boeing lined up with the runway lights, stretching ahead in a converging V shape. But there was something peculiar going on. Usually those lights had a blue tinge.

At the controls of a Cherokee 9077J in 1972

Tonight they were yellow. I couldn't understand it. After touching down I turned off the main runway and taxied on the taxiway, looking for the terminal where I intended to park the plane. It was one I knew well. I had been there many times and should have no trouble recognizing it. I taxied interminably and didn't see my familiar terminal. Where was it? Suddenly I felt the nose wheel leave the hard paving of the taxiway and sink into the grass. I had run past the end of the taxiway! How did that happen?

Suddenly I became aware that my sunglasses were still on. I whipped them off and everything changed. I recognized the terminal building and saw the familiar color of the taxiway lights. Now I understood why I could not find any holes in the clouds. The holes were there, but at night, through the dark lenses of sun glasses, I couldn't see them. I felt stupid. The crisis was of my own making. This was the dumbest thing I had ever done during all the time I was a pilot. But it was a good lesson. Don't wear sun glasses at night. I had given myself a good fright and it is best to be a humble pilot.

Lennie had flown with me many times and seemed comfortable. But I was acutely aware that if anything happened to me; a heart attack, or losing consciousness, she would be in grave danger. I decided to give her some basic instruction controlling the plane and contacting Air Traffic Control to declare an emergency and get help bringing the plane safely down. After explaining the use of the controls and practicing while sitting on the couch in our living room she went through the motions of controlling the aircraft. I planned to give her an actual experience some time when the weather was nice and conditions were right.

Two weeks later we went on a summer day's flight to Port Angeles, a short pleasant flight of less than an hour. I was flying a Cessna 172; a high wing airplane that was easy to fly requiring minimum pilot skill. After a short sojourn in the city we returned to the airport and started our return trip to Seattle. It was a bright sunny day and I thought the conditions were ideal for Lennie's flying lesson.

We were at 3,000 feet and heading east toward Puget Sound. There were no navigation problems because our path was almost directly east. Still I always planned every flight with way points and time estimates, entered on a flight plan sheet attached to a clip board. When Lennie was with me I usually asked her to hold the clip board on her lap.

With Lennie alongside a Cessna 172 which I was flying to Ocean Shores, Washington in 1966

"Hey," I said, "Today is a nice day, why don't you take the control wheel for while?" Lennie is usually not enthusiastic about anything mechanical, but she agreed. I took the clipboard from her lap and slipped it into a storage pocket in the door next to me.

"Now, put your hands lightly on the wheel and simply hold the plane level," I said. She put her hands on the wheel gingerly as I watched. But I noticed she was staring fixedly at the instrument panel.

"What are you looking at?" I asked. She pointed to the fuel gauges. The needles were on "empty". My first reaction was alarm followed by a rational thought, "It can't be." I had topped off the fuel tanks in Seattle and we had been flying less than an hour. Still, no pilot can ignore a fuel gauge that reads "empty". My mind raced, was it possible that the fuel caps on the wing were not tightened down and the fuel was sucked out of the tanks by the vacuum on top of the wing? Very unlikely, it seemed. Still, I couldn't gamble. If the tanks were indeed empty, the engine could quit any moment. I decided to head back to the airport at Port Angeles and land.

I took the control wheel and turned the plane around 180 degrees to make the return. Then I took the microphone to call Air Traffic Control and declare a fuel emergency, but when I pressed the mike button to transmit a call I found the radio was dead; no click, no radio sound, nothing. We've got an electrical problem, I thought. I reached to my side and pulled out my clipboard to return it to Lennie. It was then I discovered the source of the problem.

The edge of the clipboard was next to the Master Switch. In pushing the clipboard into the pocket, I had accidentally knocked the Master switch button in, turning off all the electrical power. Loss of electrical power had no effect on the engine, which relies on a magneto, but it turns off all the instruments that require electricity, including the fuel gauges. As soon as I recognized the problem, I pulled the master switch back on and immediately the fuel gauge needles returned to the full mark. No emergency. No problem. I explained the mishap to Lennie and suggested she take the wheel again. "Not now, not ever," she said. She wanted no part of flying that airplane again. And that was the end of Lennie's introduction to flying.

There were some moments of deep aesthetic satisfaction in my flying. Flying a small plane at two or three thousand feet allows a relation to the earth that one never has in a jet airliner at thirty five thousand feet. There was a sense of great beauty in the panorama of the city below, of the mountains and waters of Puget Sound. There was a special sense of experiencing a privileged vista flying alone at night over Seattle, with only the red glow of the instruments to provide a sense of place. But it all came to an end in 1974. I was reluctantly forced to recognize that with the demands of law practice I was only flying fifty hours a year. I could see that this was not enough to maintain a safe level of proficiency. I had also developed high blood pressure, and though it was maintained at normal levels with medication, I decided it was time to stop flying.

CHAPTER SEVENTEEN

LENNIE, OUR CHILDREN AND MY LUNG SURGERY

This biography cannot present a full picture of Alvin without a description of my wife, Lennie and my children; Jeff, Martin, Ellen and Ron. I begin with Lennie; the most important person in the life I have lived.

Lennie is the daughter of Dave and Anne Guralnick, two very complex and difficult people, who shaped her personality and ultimately, her life. I have already described Dave in an earlier chapter; a product of a Jewish family of the Eastern Ukraine who came to America as a young boy; bright, spoiled and egotistical. Anne, Lennie's mother was born in America and completed High School but did not continue her schooling after she met Dave. They married during the Great Depression which shaped their penurious ways. Dave, after working for the Soviet Trade Mission, began a career as a government civil servant, relying on his intelligence and ability to write exceedingly literate answers on Civil Service examinations to obtain jobs with public agencies. While they both loved and doted on their daughter, early on Dave began to convey the sense that his fatherly love was conditional; Lenore had to excel in school. Soon, she was made aware

Family photography 1968,
Back Row: Ellen (age 15), Jeff (age 18), Martin (age 17),
Front Row: Lennie, Ron (age 6), and I

that she was constantly in competition with two cousins and her self-worth was undermined constantly by the negativity and critical remarks of her father.

In fact, Lennie was a very bright and talented girl who deeply resented the steady disparagement by her father. She read voraciously and early on developed a passion for dance. Her school grades consistently put her at the top of her classes. Her self-image led her to believe confidently that she would accomplish extraordinary things. But her father's denial of her exceptionalism led to a distancing from parental control. Soon, their relationship was stormy and she was in open rebellion.

When Lennie was twelve she took a competitive examination for admission to Hunter High School, one of the most prestigious schools in New York. She placed second in the city. Her parents urged her to attend Hunter, a part of the City University of New York. But she had no desire to commute to an all-girls high school. Four years later, when she was sixteen, she learned that the University of Chicago admitted students after two or three years of High School. One of her girlfriends was already attending Chicago and told Lenore of the extraordinary quality of the school. She took the scholarship examination for Chicago and was not only accepted, but received an academic scholarship plus a stipend for living expenses. This was her ticket to freedom from Dave and Anne and, despite their objections, she insisted on accepting the offer. She did not want to live at home any longer.

She was 16 when she boarded the New York Central

Pacemaker for the trip to Chicago. Self-confident and determined, she made her way to the campus and to a room in a dorm for young women called Foster Hall. It didn't take long for her to realize that she could no longer assume she would be the smartest student in the class ~ there were too many very bright young people at Chicago. She found her courses tough and challenging. One difference she noticed immediately; Chicago didn't use textbooks based on the overview of academics; instead, they required the students to read the original writings in each field. But Lennie is smart and hard-working. So she studied and tried to absorb everything her fine mind encountered.

She loved her room in Foster Hall; a room with angled walls and ceilings and she also found her fellow dorm residents stimulating. They were young women from the Midwest, the West Coast and the East. It was a change from her classmates at Evander Childs High School in the Bronx. One thing that was not a change was her roommate ~ Barbara Tauber, or Bobby as she was called. Lennie had been part of a threesome in New York; Bobby, Judy Friedman who preceded Lennie to Chicago and Edie, who did not go to Chicago. But she soon met other people, including guys, and she was intoxicated by her new life.

Lennie's academic career was disrupted after we met. Although she tried to maintain an interest in her studies, she was soon swept up in the emotional forces of her relationship with me. Ultimately, her academic career was completely derailed after our marriage in June of 1952. We lived together in a Chicago apartment in Hyde Park for only a few months when I was drafted and had to leave to enter the Army, leaving her alone. Although my Mom and Dad invited her to live in their apartment, even after a baby came, she felt isolated and decided to move back to her parent's apartment in New York, a move that her father made her pay for emotionally.

Lennie became pregnant with Jeff in July of 1952 and he was born in the seventh month of her pregnancy on her birthday, February 13, 1953. Lennie was nineteen. We were living in Long Branch, New Jersey and she had to adjust quickly to mothering a newborn infant.

To her credit, she did adjust and took on the hard work of sterilizing baby bottles, washing diapers, and caring for our son. At the same time she had to live with a soldier; helping to polish my brass, press my uniforms and do everything to keep us both fed. I am embarrassed to admit that I gave her little help. In her own way, Lennie too was a soldier.

We had a happy existence, the three of us; Lennie, Jeffrey and I, in Long Branch. That happy existence was marred in July of that year when Lennie learned she was pregnant again. Our new baby, Martin, would be born one year after the birth of our first child. Lennie was understandably upset. She had just gotten used to caring for a new baby and now another one would be coming along, barely giving her any respite.

Our kids were growing and though they were often a source of pride and pleasure, as they approached adolescence they became a source of problems. By 1963 Jeffrey became the most difficult of our children. At the age of fourteen his alienation and rebellion became more disturbing. The first outward evidence was his appearance. His attitude toward school became indifferent and his attendance became irregular. He refused to allow his hair to be cut and it grew into a huge mop ~ an Afro. He was going to be a member of the youth rebellion symbolized by Bob Dylan. He wanted to look like Dylan, act like Dylan and play the guitar and perform like Dylan. He didn't know how to play the guitar; indeed he refused any lessons because he thought he could play that instrument by musical instinct. The guitar was an icon and he wanted it to be part of his life.

By 1963 he and most of his friends idolized the Beatles. Finally, I gave in to his obsession, took him to a music store in downtown Seattle and bought an electric guitar and amplifier for him. He took a few guitar lessons but soon decided he would be a purist and create his own music. He knew only a few chords and the results were painful to hear. Then he and some like-minded friends formed a band composed of Jeff on the guitar, a bass player, a drummer and later a keyboard player. They were loud, earnest and incompetent. But Jeff's mind was made up. The guitar was his identity. I tried to maintain a relationship with my wayward son, who by that time, I suspected was using recreational drugs. I bought him a finger length black coat with leather trim. This became the signature of the persona he adopted. He wore it in all weather for years, till it was worn and torn. Because he didn't yet drive, I agreed to drive him to a rock concert at Eagles Hall, in downtown Seattle. I went into the hall with him and sat on the floor with several hundred young rock fans. The air was thick with marijuana fumes. I knew where I was. It was a celebration of the movement ~ Beatles, Dylan, The Grateful Dead and the overthrow of convention. I sat with him as the amplified sound of the bands pounded my eardrums.

Jeff's rebellion led to some unpleasant times. Once he came home late and his behavior was so strange that I was fearful for him. He told me he had taken LSD and was on a "bad trip". He was frightened and irrational. I stayed with him most of the night and, to provide a change of mood, got him to ride with me in the car as we drove around the city. Gradually, he calmed down and finally said he could go to sleep.

Lennie was beside herself. She couldn't stand seeing her son "throwing his life away" and threatened to take away his guitar for good until he started attending school regularly. The result was calamitous; he ran away from home. We had no idea where he had gone and were frantic with worry. Finally, we got word to him that no one would touch his guitar and he returned.

In his senior year of high school he announced that he was leaving school to go live in Bellingham with his girlfriend. This was such a critical step, fraught with such life-changing consequences, that I sat him down for a deadly serious confrontation. I warned him that if he did that, I would have him put in a juvenile home, since he was a minor and being a truant and an incorrigible were grounds for confinement. I hadn't actually looked up the law on this but Jeff, knowing I was a lawyer, took it at face value and said he would stay in school.

He did complete his four years at Mercer Island High School, but graduated only after Lennie had a personal confrontation with the Assistant Principal and demanded that he be given full credit and allowed to graduate. Jeff continued playing the guitar and gradually improved his performance. He formed a group called the "Celebrated

Jumping Frog" and they played, mainly for their own entertainment in the rec room of our Mercer Island home. Lennie and I gave up on Jeff following an educational path to college and he simply drifted, hanging out with his friends. This would be the pattern of his life for the next twenty years.

Our other children followed more conventional courses. Martin, or "Marty" as we called him, was a bright, sunny and energetic kid. But he and his brother developed a rivalry that soon bordered on open hostility. This almost ended in tragedy. One day, Jeff borrowed Marty's two wheel bicycle without his permission. When he returned it, Marty, in a fury, got on it and rode off. Lennie and I had gone to the Rite-Aid drug store on the island when we were shocked to hear our names called out over the store speaker. When we hurried over to the manager, he told us that there was a medical emergency at home and we should go there immediately. Lennie's parents were visiting with us at the time and when we got home, they told us the Mercer Island Police had called saying Marty had been involved in a collision with a car and had been taken to the hospital.

We rushed to the hospital and learned that he had sustained a serious head injury and he was at Swedish Hospital. From the police we learned that he had ridden his bike down a hill intersecting with 78th Street, a major north-south arterial, and collided with the side of a passing car. We were allowed to ride in the ambulance when he was transferred from Swedish Hospital to Children's Orthopedic Hospital for specialized care. He was unconscious and we were deeply frightened for his life.

At Children's Hospital they did imaging and tests and

determined he had suffered a contusion, or tearing, of brain tissue. They decided against surgery, feeling that the contusion would heal and he would recover. Meanwhile, he was hospitalized for observation. After a week he was discharged and came home. He was a different person. Gone was his effervescence and impulsiveness. He lay on a couch, quiet and deflated. We later described to him what had happened, hoping to instill a sense of reasonable caution when he rode his bike again. But his personality had become so flat that this warning seemed superfluous.

In time, he made a full recovery, but his psychology was permanently altered. He was more cautious, less spontaneous and more deliberate in all his behavior. No one can say whether that was due to the brain injury or the shock of unexpected trauma. He was only ten when this happened and as the years passed he grew more confident. Eventually, he took up gymnastics ~ a sport involving some sense of daring and risk. Perhaps because he was short he felt a need to assert his masculinity, but regardless of the reason, he maintained an interest in physical sport, even into adulthood when he became a black belt in a Korean martial arts sport.

When his Mercer Island debate coach told me that he was an exceptionally gifted student, Lennie and I decided he should enroll at the College of the University of Chicago. He attended there for four years and graduated, with honors. He later applied to the Law School but was only put on a waiting list. I was offended, since he was the son of an alumnus. In the end he chose to attend Northwestern University Law School in Chicago. There he received his legal education and degree.

Ellen, our third child, had a sunny and cheerful disposition. She grew up without any of the crises that Jeff or even Marty had presented. She did well in her high school years and decided that because she played the violin, she wanted to attend Oberlin College, in Ohio. At Oberlin she didn't become a music major and instead majored in Sociology. After graduating she returned to Seattle and almost immediately moved into a rooming house in the University District. She enrolled in the social work program at the University of Washington, majoring in Community Organization. One of her first jobs was leading a youth group planting gardens and she joined in the digging herself and learned to use a pole hole digger. After she got her degree she was employed by a public community organization and began a career that led to a series of jobs, all in the public sector.

1966 was a happy year. Our newest addition Ron was born, making us a family of three boys and a girl. Ron, our youngest, was the darling of his siblings and soon demonstrated his differences. He was adept with tools, and was athletic and sociable. We called him the "jock" of the family ~ athletic in his physicality and his attitudes. When he went to High School, he established himself as a skilled trumpet player. This led to a music scholarship at Washington State University in Pullman. But after one year he had enough of music and the party life in Pullman. At my recommendation, he transferred to Western Washington University in Bellingham where he had a far more satisfying college experience. It was in Bellingham that he had his first sales job. He was so good that his future in sales looked bright, but he didn't like retail sales and moved on to a life of higher and higher quality sales work.

It was Lennie who paid the highest price for my career. She left college at the age of eighteen without a degree and became a conscientious wife and mother, but frustrated in her desire to do something significant with her life. I was a difficult and often absent father and husband as I plunged into the life of a lawyer and a civil rights activist. It was her love and devotion that sustained her during these periods.

1967 proved to be a critical year. My law firm was now composed of four lawyers, but we still led a marginal financial existence. That fall I traveled to Neah Bay for one of my frequent meetings with the Makah Tribal Council. Staying the night in a local motel, I woke up the next morning with a cough, unlike anything I had experienced. It seemed to be very deep and no amount of coughing or throat clearing had any effect. An unusual cold, I thought. But it didn't go away. I got used to it and tried to make my coughs shallow to avoid the sensation of an obstruction deep in my lungs. I even tried to laugh as shallowly as possible. Finally, after two weeks of living with this constant sense of chest obstruction, I went to my doctor, Abby Franklin, an internist and excellent diagnostician. He took x-rays of my chest and said he would call me if he found anything significant.

When I returned to my office there was a message from Abby. "Please call." When I called he said, "I see some kind of lesion in your right lung. I'd like you to make an appointment at Swedish Hospital Radiography for a tomogram. That's basically an x-ray taken at different depths that shows the shape and dimension of the lesion." I didn't like this and asked him what he thought it was. "Well we don't know for sure. It's some kind of 'gunk'."

The first thought I had was, lung cancer. But I was only 37 and that wasn't supposed to happen to a 37 year old. I had the x-rays taken and afterward the radiologist said Abby wanted to see me to discuss the findings. When I tried to question him about it, he said, "You should talk to your doctor and he'll tell you about the findings."

I went directly to Abby's office and the serious look on his face told me that there was a big problem. "Well, there's some kind of growth in your right upper lobe. I'll arrange for a bronchoscopy to be done at Swedish. That's a procedure where they put you under anesthetic and reach down your bronchial tubes with an instrument and try to snip off a piece of the lesion so they can biopsy it. If they can't get to it, then I'm afraid they'll have to do lung surgery and remove the lesion." Now I was scared, under control, but scared. "Tell me honestly, Abby, what do you think it is?"

"Well", he said, carefully, "With your history of heavy cigarette smoking, it may be a cancer." There. He had said the frightening word, "cancer". An image flashed through my mind, an image of an insurance ad showing a crowd walking along and a red X over one man. The ad said, "This could be you." I felt the red X over my head. So this is how Alvin's life would end.

Then Abby went on, "I'm going to refer you to Dr. Waldo Mills. He's a top notch chest surgeon and he'll discuss the next step with you." I met Dr. Mills and he said much the same thing as Abby. First he would do a bronchoscopy. If that didn't reach the lesion, then lung surgery.

I went forward with the bronchoscopy and afterward, Dr. Mills told me he was sorry but they were not able to reach the lesion, so lung surgery was required. The lesion is in your right lobe. If we find it is limited to that lobe, we'll remove the lobe. If, however, we find evidence of cancerous tissue elsewhere in the lung, we'll remove the entire right lung. "How long will I be unable to work after this surgery," I asked. "Four to six weeks," he replied and added, "This is major surgery and it will take time to recuperate."

The news was chilling and I was in a new and unaccustomed state of mind ~ fatalistic but with a somewhat surreal state of danger. I was cursing my addiction to Pall Malls. It was Pall Malls that would end my life. Still, I asked the doctor, "Would it make any difference if I stopped smoking now?"

"Well, it wouldn't change the situation with your lesion, but it would be a good idea to stop. You'll be coughing after your surgery and smoking will only aggravate the cough." So it was too late now to change anything.

I made a date for my lung surgery, about a week hence, and walked back to my car. As I drove along the street I reached into my pocket for my cigarettes. Then I looked at the familiar red pack and thought, "What am I doing! These are the things that will kill me." In anger I crushed the pack and threw it out the window of the car. Immediately, I regretted my impulsive act. I brought the car to a hard stop, got out and walked back to where the red pack was lying in the street. I picked it up, straightened it out and took out a cigarette and lit it. "I'll quit later," I thought.

After I got back to my office I called all my partners together. I needed to tell them of the upcoming surgery and my probable absence of four to six weeks. They greeted the news gravely and a few had noticeable wet eyes. In 1967 a diagnosis of lung cancer was a death sentence and telling them was like attending my own funeral. Strangely, I didn't feel sadness or fear of death; instead I had a crazy idea: dying will be a new experience and I looked forward to it as a new adventure.

Lennie smoked, my doctor smoked as did many of my friends. When they heard that "Al has lung cancer", many quit or tried to. Most, like Lennie and even my doctor, Abby Franklin, were unable to break the habit. With awareness of the destruction I was wreaking on myself, I kept smoking Pall Malls up to the day I was admitted to the hospital, though I did leave the cigarettes at home and didn't take any to the hospital. After being admitted and put in a hospital gown, I stretched out in my bed and Lennie and I tried to carry on a normal conversation. After an hour or so we had exhausted all topics so I told her to go on home. I had plenty of reading material and the surgery was scheduled for the next morning. She kissed me and left.

I tried diverting myself with the reading materials but soon the urge for a smoke became overpowering. I rang for the nurse. When this nice woman entered, I asked her with some embarrassment, whether she had any cigarettes. She did and offered one to me. I thanked her profusely, took the cigarette and smoked it with guilty satisfaction. After I finished her cigarette and several hours dragged by I wanted another. I didn't have the nerve to ask her again, so I rang for her, and when she came in, asked if she would buy a pack for me from the vending machine in the lobby. She understood and smilingly agreed. I gave her the money and she returned with a new pack of Pall Malls and I happily smoked away the evening.

The next morning, the day of the big event, I awoke after a relatively comfortable night of sleep, but the absence of any breakfast made me aware of what lay ahead and increased the tension. I lay in bed for about an hour, expecting to be taken to surgery, when my nurse came in and said the doctor was running a little late and the surgery would be about ten that morning. That left considerable time on my hands so I got out of bed and sat down in an armchair to read the morning paper while I waited. Naturally, I took out a cigarette and lit up, and as I did, I thought to myself, "This is the last cigarette I will ever smoke." I had smoked about half the cigarette when two orderlies wheeled a gurney into the room. "Mr. Ziontz?" they asked. "Yup, that's me," I answered and stubbed out the cigarette in the ashtray. I climbed onto the gurney and they wheeled me away to surgery.

I don't recall anything till I awoke in the recovery room after the surgery. It was Dr. Mills who woke me, leaning over me and smiling. "You're a very lucky guy. It wasn't cancer. It was a fungus called Cryptococcus. We did have to remove your upper lobe to biopsy the lesion, but you'll be fine. The rest of your lung will expand to fill the space and you shouldn't have any lasting problems." I recall that I felt a mixture of relief and disappointment. Yes, disappointment. I was actually looking forward to the experience of dying. Maybe I wanted to bring to an end the stress of practicing law or simply wanted a new experience, I don't know.

Meanwhile, my diagnosis had confronted Lennie with a grave crisis; she expected to find herself a widow with four young children and no way to adequately support them. She needed a job immediately. Without a college degree or any office skills, she took the best job she could find ~ working for the telephone company (at the time there was only one, Pacific Northwest Bell) as a "Service Representative". This had one important benefit: health insurance. Otherwise, the salary was barely enough to pay household expenses and baby-sitting for Ronnie. Although the job was stultifying, she stayed with it for two and a half years.

The doctor was right. My recovery was slow and I didn't regain enough strength to get back to my law practice for six weeks. There were other consequences as well. My emotions were in turmoil and it took a year or more for me to regain my normal composure. Although I didn't know it at the time, somehow the surgery resulted in damage to a nerve activating my right hemi-diaphragm. That meant my right lung couldn't normally inflate, leaving me with only one fully functioning lung. The good result was that I completely lost my desire to smoke. No more cigarettes for me!

With one of my last cigarettes on Mercer Island in 1967

In 1969 Lennie decided to go back to school and enrolled in the University of Washington, studying Sociology. She was thirty-five years old and had the responsibility of raising a three year old; Ronnie, and three teenagers. Managing all her responsibilities while keeping up with her studies; rushing back home from the campus to pick Ronnie up from his nursery school, preparing the family meals and being a wife to a husband under stress, took a woman of character and strength. That's who she is ~ a woman of character and strength.

There was stress at home. Jeff was in full-fledged rebellion. He wanted to live the life of a jazz guitarist even though his knowledge of his instrument was rudimentary and largely self-taught. He graduated from High School, barely, and almost immediately moved out to live with a girl in a communal house in Bellingham, Washington. Lennie and I had long since been forced to accept his refusal to live a conventional life and educate himself to be equipped for a career. We only hoped that in time the real world would weigh on him and bring a change in his lifestyle. Our fear was that he would never be able to support himself as an itinerant guitarist. But we had learned that Jeff cannot be made to do anything that he doesn't want to do. So we watched from afar and simply tried to maintain a loving relationship and offer help when he needed it.

But his passion for music was not to be denied. On one occasion, when our entire family drove down to San Francisco, Jeff took his guitar and one evening I went with him to a bar which featured jazz music. He somehow convinced the manager to let him get up on the stage and play. It was embarrassing because he was clearly inept on the instrument. After one number the manager said, "Thank you son," and ushered him off the stage.

While we wrestled with the issue of Jeff and his future, our other children were making their own way. In 1971 Martin went off to the College at the University of Chicago to begin his own career. Lennie had been working hard at the University of Washington to finish her undergraduate studies and finally received her Bachelor's degree that same year. In 1975 our daughter, Ellen, went east to begin her college studies at Oberlin College in Ohio.

With Lennie at our Mercer Island house 1973

CHAPTER EIGHTEEN

THE HONEST MAILMAN AND INDIAN FISHING RIGHTS

After I got back to work, our firm continued Indian work and the workload increased. We were successful in several cases and my attendance at meetings and conferences of Indians made me a familiar figure in the Indian world. My work with Indian tribes is described at length in my memoir, "A Lawyer In Indian Country", I will try not to repeat it here, but I will describe some of the more interesting cases I had not connected to Indian rights.

One of these I like to call the case of "The Honest Mailman". Before a Public Defender's Office was created in Seattle the federal courts simply appointed private lawyers to defend the accused in Federal criminal cases. The appointed lawyers were compensated, though meagerly, from a limited fund available to the court. Not only was money for appointed lawyers very limited, so was the money available for investigators. Lawyers either had to do their own investigating or make do with the information provided by the government. Being appointed to defend someone could hardly be declined. After all, the appointment was made by a Federal Judge.

So when my phone rang one day and the caller was the U.S. Marshall's office at the Federal Court informing me that I had been appointed by the Senior Federal District Court Judge to represent a Mr. Robert Williams, I had mixed feelings. For one thing, I could not refuse the appointment but on the other hand I did not do Criminal Law and had very little experience defending a criminal case.

I had no idea how the judge selected me. When I asked the nature of the charges against Mr. Williams the official told me, "Mr. Williams was a Postal Service employee and was charged with stealing from the mails."

My first thought was that this was going to be a plea bargain case; because after working in the Post Office, I knew that postal inspectors usually had an air-tight case against an employee accused of stealing from the mail. Then the official asked if I could see Mr. Williams right away because he was incarcerated in the Federal Courthouse and would be released to see his attorney. "Sure," I said. "Send him over and I'll see him right away."

Twenty minutes later my secretary called me to say a Mr. Williams was here to see me. I went out to the waiting room to meet my new client. Robert Williams was a tall young black man of medium build. He greeted me somewhat sheepishly as we shook hands. As he sat down opposite me in my office, he seemed nervous and unsure of himself. In his hands he held a sheaf of papers and held them out to me. "This is what they claim I did, but I never did those things."

I took the papers and read them. It was a grand jury indictment.

There were three counts of mail theft, each a felony. The charge was that on three separate occasions he had unlawfully stolen a letter addressed to the National Bank of Commerce, each one containing cash ranging from $18 to $23. All three had been sent by a single individual, named in the indictment as Mary Anne Kingman. The letters were deposited in the mails but never delivered to the post office.

After reading the indictment I thought to myself, "Highly likely he did it. Postal inspectors don't charge unless they have clear proof." But I wanted to hear what Mr. Williams had to say and asked him to tell me his side of the story. This is what he said:

"Mr. Ziontz, I don't know anything about two of those letters but I do know about one of them. I remember it very well. It was an envelope with the printed address of the National Bank of Commerce. The day I was arrested I was walking my regular route and delivered mail to this house where Miss Kingman lived. I had seen her before and when I walked up on the porch to drop the mail in their mailbox, she came out the door and gave me that envelope to mail. Nothing unusual about that. I took it from her hand and said, 'Sure,' and walked down the steps of her porch to make a delivery to the house next door. I didn't walk out to the street but cut through some bushes to take a short cut to that house. But before I got to their doorstep she came running up behind me and said, 'Oh, I made a mistake. I didn't want to mail that letter yet. Can I have it back?'

So I said, 'O. K.' and pulled that letter out of my bag and handed it back to her. I went on with my route but I knew something was funny. See, that afternoon I spotted a blue car following me around. It stopped across the street from each of my deliveries and I knew it must be an inspector. I just tried to ignore it and I didn't do anything different. I finished my route and returned to the post office.

When I got there I was met by two inspectors who took my mail bag from me and went through all the mail in there. 'Where's the envelope with the money?' one of them asked me. I said, 'What money?'

Then they told me to follow them into the post office. They took me into the manager's office and shut the door. Then they asked me to empty my pockets. I did. When they didn't find the envelope they were looking for or the money they said I had stolen, they had me put my hands under an ultra-violet lamp they had. I knew what that was about. If you open a test envelope, it will leave a powder on your fingers that will glow under that lamp. Obviously, my hands did not glow. So then they asked me to strip down to my underwear and they went through all my clothes. I felt humiliated but I did what they asked. When they found nothing, they asked if I had a car with me. 'Yeah, it's parked behind the building where all the employees park.'

They asked if it was o.k. for them to search my car and I agreed. I had nothing to hide. They went through everything; lifting up the floor mats and the seats, opening the trunk and looking under the spare tire. When they didn't find anything, they said, 'Come with us.' They put me in the back seat of their car and I asked where I was being taken. They just said, 'Downtown.' One of them sat in back with me and started telling me that I was looking at twenty years in the pen, but if I confessed they would go easy on me. I told him, I haven't done anything wrong, I didn't steal any money and I have nothing to confess."

Mr. Williams' recital had the ring of truth and I felt he was an innocent man, wrongly accused. But I had some questions in my mind. Why did this woman accuse him of stealing her mail? What was her motive? I thought race or personal hostility might be the answer. I asked him how many black mailmen worked in that post office.

"I was the only one," he said.

"Was there any issue about your race at work or with Ms. Kingman?" I asked.

"Not really," he said. "Oh, there was one time when a woman across the street got nasty with me when I accidentally dropped a letter on her lawn, but aside from that everything was fine."

"How about Miss Kingman. Tell me about her," I asked.

"Well, it really wasn't her house. She was living with the lady that owned the house and she was only about seventeen or eighteen."

"Did you ever have any argument or disagreement with her or the owner?"

"Not really. Oh, there was one time when I brought up the mail and the owner, Mrs. Haskell, came out and handed the letter back to me and said it was addressed to her ex-husband and she didn't want any more of his mail. So, I said, sure, I'll see that the post office doesn't send you any more of his mail. And that was the end of it."

"How about Mary Anne, did you ever have any personal dealings with her?"

"Nope," he said emphatically.

His answers left me without anything that would explain a false accusation of theft. Only Mary Anne Kingman could explain that, but I felt it would be a mistake to speak to her because if she had concocted a story of theft, she could stick with it and leave me no better off. In later years an investigator would have been hired to talk to possible witnesses, but I had no money for an investigator, so I decided I had to go and speak to them myself.

I thanked Mr. Williams, told him I believed him and said I would investigate the case further. He seemed relieved to hear that and smiled as we shook hands and then he added, "You know, Mr. Ziontz, I spent four years in the Marines and I got this job with the post office right after I got out. I was working there about a year when this happened and it took me completely by surprise. I am a Christian man, I read my Bible and I would never risk my soul for the money they said I stole." With that he left my office. My work was about to begin.

My first thought was to interview the chief complaining witness, Mary Anne Kingman, but I decided against doing that. What would she say? She would not be likely to retract her charges. So, I had what turned out to be a good idea; I would talk to her next door neighbor.

I drove out to the neighborhood of modest, middle class houses in the north end of Seattle and walked up to the front door of the house next door to Miss Kingman's residence. A woman in her early thirties answered my ring. I introduced myself and told her I was the lawyer who represented her mailman. "Oh my goodness, we were wondering what happened to him."

With that she asked me to come in and called her husband to come into the living room to meet me. We introduced each other. They were Alan and Ruth Mills. Both of them were obviously concerned about his situation. When I explained the nature of the serious case he faced, they were indignant.

"Mary Anne! She's a liar and a trouble maker. No one in our neighborhood would believe anything she says," said the woman. Then she went on to tell me that the owner of the house next door was a divorcee who was a social worker and had taken Mary Anne in to help her. But she said, Mary Anne was a glib liar and many in the neighborhood suspected she was engaging in prostitution because often cars brought older men to the house during the day and they would park for about an hour or so and then leave. As for the mailman, she said, "He's the best mailman we ever had. My husband and I have a mail order business, selling models of cars and planes, and that mailman was always the fastest and the most responsible. We often get mail containing money and there was never anything missing."

She asked me to tell her something about the case against him. When I described the claim that payments to the National Bank of Commerce were deposited in the mail by her and never made it to the post office, both she and her husband were outraged. The husband told me that once Mary Anne placed an ad in the Seattle Times and then didn't pay the bill. They found out about it when she came over to their house to tell them she was being hounded by a collection agency and claimed she had mailed the payment but the mailman must have stolen her check. She asked if they would loan her the money ~ a modest sum ~ and they did.

I was exhilarated. These were the witnesses who would demolish the government's case against Williams. I asked if they might still have the cancelled check of the money they loaned her and after a few minutes the husband returned and handed me the cancelled check payable to Mary Anne Kingman for $25 which she had endorsed and deposited. Now I had documentary evidence to support their story.

Then the wife said, "I just remembered something else. Alan, you remember when she claimed a couple of black men had driven her to the Central District and raped her?"

"Yeah, I do remember," said her husband. She turned to me and said, "Her story was investigated by the cops and they found it was all made up. It never happened. But a lot of people in the neighborhood heard about it and I think that was why they felt she was a liar and not to be trusted with anything. They didn't want their kids hanging around her or having anything to do with her. I don't understand why Dorothy Haskell put up with her, but I don't think she knew about any of this, or maybe she just felt sorry for her."

I thanked both her and her husband and said I might need them to testify on behalf of the mailman. Both said they would be happy to. Now I had to decide what to do with this information. I could just wait for the trial but I had another idea. I called the U.S. Attorney on the case and said I wanted to meet with him to discuss the case. He was agreeable and we agreed to meet the following day. My hope was that after hearing this he might be willing to drop the case.

The next day I went up to the office of Bill Helsell, the assistant U.S. Attorney handling the government's case against the mailman. He listened with great interest as I carefully repeated the neighbor's story about Mary Anne Kingman. When I was finished, he said, "Let me look into this and I'll get back to you."

Two days later, Helsell called. "Based on her claim that she had paid her bill and the mailman stole her check, and her credit record and also her false claim of rape, I'm going to see if I can get the charges dismissed. Since there's an indictment, I have to get approval from Washington, but they usually follow my recommendation."

A week later I received in the mail a copy of a court order dismissing the charges against Mr. Williams. I called my client and told him I had some good news and asked if he could come down to my office. That afternoon, he arrived, accompanied by his wife, Johnnie. I explained everything to them; my meeting with the neighbor, the discussion with the U.S. Attorney and the outcome. Then I handed him a copy of the court order dismissing the charges. The Williams' were elated. Johnnie had tears of joy in her eyes. Both thanked me profusely and it was a sweet feeling, having an innocent client vindicated because of my efforts.

I felt good about getting justice for my client, but it was short lived. I was stunned when he called me a week or so later and told me that the Post Office had refused to reinstate him, and in fact had gone on to fire him and he was out of a job.

"I don't understand. Since the charges were dismissed what's their reason for firing you?"

"They said that the decision of the federal attorney not to pursue the case was not binding on them and their postal inspector observed me the whole time and he said Miss Kingman never took back the letter. They believe the inspector."

I listened to this with growing anger at the postal system and wondered whether there was a procedure for an employee to appeal a dismissal. When I asked my client about this I was happy to hear him say there was.

"We have a union agreement and there is something in our contract about appealing a firing."

"Do you have some kind of printed document that says so?"

"Yes, I have a book about employee's rights."

"Great," I said. "Come down to my office and bring that book with you."

So, the case was not over. We had a new battle to fight.

A few days later Mr. Williams and his wife Johnnie came in and he gave me a booklet describing his rights as a postal employee. It was very clear: a discharged employee has a right to request a hearing and an administrative law judge will conduct a hearing to determine whether the discharge was justified or not. I told him I would notify the postal authority that we wanted an administrative hearing. After I sent in the request I got notice that a date was set for the hearing about three weeks hence at the Federal Court House.

To prepare for the hearing I went back to the neighborhood

where the incident had occurred and met with the friendly neighbors, telling them I would need them to testify about Mary Anne and her claim that the mailman had stolen her check from the mail as well as her loan to replace the money she owed. I also wanted them to testify as to her reputation for truthfulness. They were happy to support my client's defense and agreed to come to the Court House for the hearing. I asked them about the people who lived across the street, since my client said they had made a nasty remark when he accidentally dropped a letter on their lawn.

"Oh, the Boetchers. We know them well; in fact we have an arrangement with them to watch for the mailman if we're not home and have their son pick up any packages he leaves for us because we don't want to leave it on the doorstep all day. You know, in case somebody might be tempted to steal it. I'm sure Nancy will be happy to talk to you."

I went directly across the street and knocked on their door. Mrs. Boetcher answered and when I explained who I was and told her I needed to talk to her, she was quite agreeable. When I described the incident of Mary Anne running after the mailman and retrieving the test letter, I was delighted to hear Mrs. Boetcher say, "Oh, I remember that. Allan and Ruth said they would be gone all day and would we have our son watch out for the mailman to pick up any packages he left. So, I was watching and saw Mary Anne run out of her house after the mailman and catch up with him on their lawn. I couldn't hear what was said but I saw the mailman reach into his sack and give her a letter that she took back to her house." Here was an eyewitness to corroborate Mr. Williams' story.

I was informed by letter that an administrative law judge, Mr. Joseph Alden was coming out to Seattle from Washington to hear our case. On the day of the hearing I met my clients and our witnesses; Mr. and Mrs. Mills, and Mrs. Boetcher. The postal service was represented by an attorney who said they had only a single witness to present; Orville Delaney, a postal inspector.

Orville Delaney was a short, red-faced, pudgy man of about forty. He was almost completely bald and his face looked pig-like; a pug nose, small eyes and a double chin. He gave this testimony.

He was a sworn postal inspector and Mr. Williams became the target of an investigation of mail theft after the Postal Service received a complaint from Mary Anne Kingman that some money she had mailed was never received by the payee ~ the Seattle Times, and that other money she mailed never reached their addressees. He and one of his fellow inspectors had gone out to Ms. Kingman's home and interviewed her. They then decided to give her a test letter ~ an envelope with a bank's name printed on it, containing money. She was instructed to give it to the mailman to send. They waited for it to arrive at the local post office. When it didn't, they returned to her house and gave her a second letter, with an identical envelope containing cash. Again she was instructed to physically hand it to Mr. Williams. Again they waited for it to be deposited at the branch post office and again it never arrived. By this time they were confident that Mr. Williams was stealing these items from the mail. They never considered that she was keeping the money and destroying the envelope.

The inspectors decided to use one more test letter, he said, but this time coating the money and the inside of the envelope with a powder that would glow under an infra-red lamp and one of them would follow Mr. Williams as he walked his route. After making sure he took possession of the letter, they would see if it was deposited with his other mail at the post office. If it wasn't they would confront him, search him, test his hands under the lamp and arrest him if, as they assumed, he was found with the stolen envelope or the money in his possession.

Delaney then described how he had followed Mr. Williams around his route in his car; how he had parked across the street from the house of Miss Kingman and watched Williams; how he saw Miss Kingman hand the envelope to Mr. Williams who put it in his bag and then left. At no time, he said; did Miss Kingman retrieve the letter. The letter was never received at the post office. With that, the Postal Service rested and it was up to me to discredit the testimony of Delaney on cross-examination.

I began, of course, by getting him to describe the behavior of my client on the day of his arrest, telling about Mr. Williams's denial of any theft and the complete absence of any incriminating evidence when he was physically examined by the two inspectors at the post office. All of this was grudgingly admitted by Delaney. Then I asked Delaney if he had parked directly across the street from Mary Anne's house when he was observing her and my client. I was almost certain that he would not have placed his car in such an obvious location if he was trying to be surreptitious.

"No, I parked a little ways past her house," he testified.

"Then how did you see what their actions were," I asked.

"In my side view mirror," he said.

"So you were looking in your mirror at people across the street and behind you?"

"Yes," he said, beginning to sound flustered.

"How far would you estimate you were from them," I asked.

"Oh, about sixty or seventy feet," he answered.

"And did you keep Miss Kingman in your sight the whole time from the mailman's pickup of the letter till his departure from her property?"

"Yes."

"Are you quite certain she never went back after the mailman when he went next door?"

"Absolutely sure," he said stubbornly.

"By the way, Mr. Delaney," I asked, "How long have you been a postal inspector?"

"About six months," he replied, his face reddening.

"So at the time of this incident you had only been a postal inspector about two months?" I asked.

"I'm not sure but I was still in my probationary period," he replied.

With that I terminated my cross examination. The postal service offered no other witnesses, not even Mary Anne. So, I called on Mr. Williams to testify and he confidently told his story of the fateful day, emphatically denying any theft and ending with his background of four years in the U.S. Marine Corps. Then I called on Mrs. Mills and her testimony of Mary Anne's lack of credibility, her borrowing money to pay her creditors and blaming the Mailman for stealing her payment. My final witness was Mrs. Boetcher who described seeing Mary Anne run after the mailman to retrieve a piece of mail. Then I rested my case. To my surprise, the judge, Mr. Alden, said he would like to visit the scene of the incident. He asked Delaney if he still had the car he used that day. Delaney said he did.

"Good," said the judge. "Let's meet here at ten tomorrow morning. I'd like you to drive us to the house in that car and you, Mr. Ziontz, come along and bring your client, Mr. Williams."

When we arrived at the street where Mary Anne lived, Judge Alden said to Mr. Delaney, "Now I want you to drive exactly as you did the day you were keeping Mr. Williams under surveillance, at the same speed, and park where you were located when you observed those people in your mirror."

Delaney did as he was asked and parked across the street some twenty feet past the house. The distance from the car to the front steps of Mary Anne's house was about sixty or seventy feet.

"Now, Mr. Williams, I'd like you to go over to the house and up on the porch, just as you did that day. Then follow the route you took to the house next door."

Inwardly I was smiling. Having been to the house several times I knew what was in store. There was a tall hedge between the two lots, with a space of about two feet between each shrub. I watched as Mr. Williams walked up the stairs to the porch and down again, then cut through the hedge and was obscured from sight by the hedge as he went next door. Judge Alden then asked my client to repeat his actions as he sat in the driver's seat and watched him through the side view mirror.

"I've seen enough. Let's go back to the courthouse," said the Judge. When we arrived back at the court house, Judge Alden said, "I won't need oral argument. I've heard and seen enough. I will order that Mr. Williams be reinstated with back pay for time lost. You'll receive my written opinion in the mail."

With that the case was finally over. We had won and the Postal Service and its inspectors had been stopped from perpetrating a grave injustice. It was a sweet victory ~ one which I have never forgotten.

The following year I was elected President of the Washington State affiliate of the American Civil Liberties Union. The state organization was small and struggling. We could barely afford to pay our executive director and our legal counsel. The McCarthy era had poisoned the atmosphere for civil rights and we were seen by many as a radical left wing organization. I didn't care about the opinions of anti-civil liberties people; I was satisfied that we were doing important work and acting as a necessary force for justice and constitutional rights. We had to confront issues that brought us into conflict with the police and city government ~ an entrenched and conservative body that had little awareness; it seemed, of the rights of citizens under the constitution.

Indian Fishing rights were becoming more controversial as

Indians became more militant about their treaty rights. Many of our board members didn't feel this was a civil liberties issue. I did. I argued repeatedly that the right of a people to preserve its cultural identity was a basic right and the ACLU should defend that right. But this principle didn't fit neatly into a Bill of Rights category; indeed, it was outside the Equal Protection Clause because it rested on unequal rights. It really was a Human Rights issue; the right of preservation of a minority culture against a majority that sought to erase its identity. In the end, my position was accepted by the board.

In 1965 there was a confrontation between Indians and State Fisheries Patrol officers on the Nisqually River. Indians were beaten by the officers when they tried to protect the Indian occupants of a small boat on the river. They were charged with obstructing an officer but the trial was postponed pending a decision of the U.S. Supreme Court and wasn't scheduled till 1969.

On behalf of the ACLU and by agreement with the defendants I represented them in the trial. It was held in the courtroom of a District Court in Olympia, Washington. The details of this trial are in my book, "A Lawyer in Indian Country", here I only want to add that the crux of my defense was that the Indians were exercising their constitutional rights to demonstrate in support of their treaty guaranty. Again, the good guys won and I was happy to have had a part in it.

AMERICAN* CIVIL LIBERTIES UNION NEWS
of Washington

Volume 2   July 17, 1965   8 ——— 9   No. 7

ALVIN ZIONTZ

PHILIP L. BURTON

Ziontz Takes President's Post

Alvin Ziontz has taken over as President of the American Civil Liberties Union of Washington. He succeeds John J. Sullivan, who is visiting Europe with his family.

Philip L. Burton is the new state Vice President, replacing Ziontz.

ZIONTZ, a resident of Mercer Island, received both his undergraduate and law degrees from the University of Chicago. He is a member of the Regional Advisory Board of the Anti-Defamation League of B'nai B'rith, the Washington Citizens' Committee for Civil Rights Legislation, and the Governor's Washington State Consumer Advisory Council.

Ziontz, a partner in the law firm of Ziontz, Pirtle & Fulle, was named to the presidency at the July meeting of the Board of Directors.

At the same meeting, Burton was elected to the vice-presidency.

BURTON, a Bothell resident, is a partner in the law firm of Sullivan, Burton & Meade. He is a past member of the State Board of Prison Terms and Paroles and past president of the Seattle chapter of the National Association for the Advancement of Colored People. He also served on the Mayor's Advisory Committee on Police Practices (Leffler Committee).

Sullivan, a resident of the

Mt. Baker district, is accompanied by his wife, Shirley, and their four children in their six-month visit to the Continent. He expects to spend several months in Florence, where the children will enroll in schools to continue their studies and Sullivan will study Italian at the University.

SULLIVAN, also an attorney, is a partner in the firm of Sullivan, Redman & Winsor. He is active in the Seattle Bar Association on its Civil Rights Committee and as lecturer for the Continuing Legal Education Committee. He served as Municipal Judge Pro Tem in 1961-1962 and served as State President of the American Trial Lawyers Association.

1965 news clipping announcing my becoming ACLU President of Washington

391

CHAPTER NINETEEN

THE LAW FIRM GROWS

By 1975 the composition of the firm had changed. Reluctantly and painfully we decided that our partner, Floyd Fulle, was devoting far too much time to legal work for commercial clients that didn't pay his fees. Despite several serious discussions and urging him to drop some of the worst offenders, we decided we couldn't continue to support his practice and asked him to leave the partnership. We hired an impressive graduate of Boalt Hall, the University of California, by the name of Mason Morisset, as our next associate. He quickly proved to be highly competent and an effective tribal advocate.

In 1971 I had learned of a brilliant young lawyer who worked in the consumer protection division of the state Attorney General's office named Barry Ernstoff. I invited him to come up and meet with me. Barry was larger than life; a handsome, smiling fellow with a first class mind. I decided immediately that we needed him and set about luring him to our firm.

Barry was from New York, a graduate of N.Y.U. Law School and obviously talented. Though his hair was shoulder length and he wore sandals, I felt he was a major talent and would add strength to the firm. Barry was reluctant to leave his job with the Consumer Protection Division, but I dangled in front of him the bait of taking part in the case of the Estate of Rabbi Shapiro. This case is a story worth the telling, though Barry took no part in it but did join the firm.

The Shapiro case began with a phone call from a Rabbi. The Rabbi, who identified himself as Rabbi Fogelman, was calling from Newton, Massachusetts. He had been referred to me by a lawyer who knew of me through my work with the ACLU. Rabbi Fogelman, in an agitated voice, proceeded to tell me about a grave injustice that he wanted me to act on. This was the story he told me.

A year earlier a Seattle Rabbi, Baruch Shapiro, had died. I had never heard of him, but no matter. The deceased Rabbi had led a small but devoted congregation for over thirty years. It was called Machzikay Hadas. His wife died before him and he had no children. The congregation had ceased to function and was defunct by the early 1960's. He and his wife lived penuriously and left a will to dispose of an estate of over $120, 000 ~ a sum which startled and even amazed those who knew him.

He and his wife had lived in a house his congregation had rented for him ~ a tiny and very modest house. But his ego was very large. He fancied himself a rabbinical scholar of importance, and indeed, he was the only Rabbi in the Pacific Northwest with standing to issue a "get" ~ a divorce decree. In the arcane world of Orthodox Judaism, such a decree is recognized only if it is issued by a Rabbi whose authority as a scholar is established and recognized by other Rabbis.

His will gave bequests of modest amounts to certain Yeshivas, or religious schools, in Israel and the rest was to go to his congregation for a specific purpose; to enable them to hire a Rabbi to succeed him. But he laid down strict conditions for this bequest: first, his successor could not simply be an ordained Rabbi but must be a recognized authority on Jewish Law, or as he put it in his will: "a godol". In Hebrew "godol" means a giant. In Rabbinical practice no Rabbi will be called a godol unless his scholarship and authority are recognized by other Rabbis throughout the country and in other countries.

To ensure that the candidate met these qualifications, Rabbi Shapiro's will required that his successor be chosen and unanimously approved by a committee of three named Rabbis. They were three of the most eminent men in Orthodox Judaism in America. Rabbi Fogelman went on to tell me that two of the three had died and only one, Rabbi Moshe Feinstein, approved the choice of a young Rabbi named Londinsky. Rabbi Londinsky was only twenty eight years old ~ an unknown. "A godol!" Gitelson almost shouted into the phone. The very idea was absurd.

The gist of Rabbi Fogelman's complaint was that the Machzikay Hadas Congregation had gone out of existence before Rabbi Shapiro's death, that by the use of unscrupulous methods, it had been resurrected to create a merger with an existing congregation, Bikur Cholim, solely to set the stage for claiming Rabbi Shapiro's money, that a young Rabbi no one had ever heard of, Moshe Londinsky, had been hired by the Bikur Cholim congregation and then the congregation declared it had met the conditions of Rabbi Shapiro's will and was entitled to use his estate to pay the new Rabbi. Fogelman was outraged.

And what was the interest of Rabbi Fogelman? Well, Rabbi Shapiro's will provided that if his conditions were not met within one year of his death, then the entire estate was to go to his wife's nieces and guess what? Rabbi Fogelman's wife was one of the three surviving nieces and stood to receive a tidy inheritance.

It was agreed that I would take the case with a base fee of $1,000 plus 10% of any amount recovered. My work would begin as soon as I had a signed attorney client agreement. I drafted an agreement and sent it to him asking that it be signed by all three nieces and sent back to me. They all acted swiftly and I had the signed agreement within ten days.

I had never done any work on rabbinical qualifications and knew little about it. So my first task was to find an advisor. Finding Arthur Lagawier was an incredible stroke of luck. I had heard about him as an eminent Judaic scholar who lived in Bellevue after retiring as a diamond merchant. He was deeply interested in the case and knew a lot about Baruch Shapiro and the machinations that led to the hiring of Moshe Londinsky.

Mr. Lagawier, who was in his seventies when we met, told me a bit about his own background. He was born in Antwerp and from boyhood on was immersed in Talmudic studies. He had mastered more than ten languages, including Hebrew, Aramaic, Arabic and Greek. Arthur was heading for rabbinical ordination when he had a spiritual crisis. After months of introspective thought, he came to the conclusion that he simply did not believe in God. He ended his rabbinical studies, but though he had entered his family diamond business, his interest in religion and scholarship did not end. He continued to study ancient texts, translating from the Hebrew and Aramaic to French. Lagawier was intimately familiar with the practices and protocols of the Orthodox rabbinate. I could hardly have found a better guide to lead me through the complexities I would face in litigating the will of Baruch Shapiro.

As I began to investigate the background of Rabbi Shapiro I was led to several men who knew him and had been members of his congregation. They were happy to describe the life of the man whose will was now in dispute. The Rabbi was born in Lithuania and came to Seattle around 1913. He was deeply religious and steeped in learning. He had received his rabbinical training in Europe and brought his ultra-orthodox, traditional beliefs to Seattle. He was hired as the rabbi at the Orthodox synagogue in Seattle, Bikur Cholim. But within a year he had a falling out with their board and left. For almost ten years he circulated among the smaller synagogues and even conducted services in private homes. In 1924 he was hired by the Herzl synagogue where he served as its rabbi for five or six years. But then the congregation decided to align itself with the Conservative movement in Judaism. This would allow mixed seating with men and women, something abhorrent to Orthodox Judaism, and Shapiro left Herzl, For a time he considered leaving Seattle, but he had acquired a devoted following who begged him to stay and promised to organize a synagogue for him. Thus was born Machzikay Hadas.

The synagogue was organized in 1930 and in 1933 a building was constructed through the contributions of its members. Machzikay Hadas was Rabbi Baruch Shapiro's own synagogue; made up of men and women who revered him and his authority. The synagogue was traditional; almost European in its practices and beliefs. It disdained community activities and women were segregated and took no part in synagogue affairs. It was founded and existed as more strictly orthodox than any congregation in the city.

As for Baruch Shapiro, he was by American standards, an oddity. He always presented a neatly tailored figure, gray beard closely cropped, walking to synagogue with a walking stick in hand. He had a high opinion of himself, with justification. He knew the Talmud by heart. He was a devoted religious scholar, corresponding on religious questions with some of the most eminent Rabbis in America. His followers regarded him as a gaon (an eminent scholar) and a godol, (A giant, a major religious authority) and he was widely known in the religious community of the United States. He had a reputation as the preserver of a pre-20th century European way of life, not commonly observed in America. He was the only rabbi on the West Coast qualified to issue a "get" (decree of divorce) and granted such decrees to applicants from all over the world; Johannesburg, Montreal, and even Singapore.

His congregation had a small core of members who revered him, but it never numbered more than two hundred members of whom only about twenty or thirty attended daily services. It did, however, own and operate its own cemetery. Machzikay Hadas was entirely Rabbi Shapiro's congregation, having been formed for the sole purpose of studying and worshipping with him. It always maintained the tradition of the old European "shul" or house of worship and never tried to establish itself as a center for Jewish community or social activities.

But by the 1960's the character of the neighborhood where Machzikay Hadas was located had changed. The Seattle Jewish population had been moving away from the area, and was replaced by largely black residents. It became more uncomfortable for the congregants to come to the synagogue and some members were harassed by black youths as they walked to the services. Machzikay Hadas's membership dwindled down to twenty or thirty members. The shrinking membership base reduced the financial resources to support a rabbi.

In 1962 Baruch Shapiro prepared his will, typing it in Yiddish on a typewriter with Hebrew characters. In his will he established a fund to enable his congregation to hire a successor rabbi. He had only disdain for American-trained rabbis and felt strongly that what was needed in Seattle was a well-known, experienced scholar of the Talmud and Torah who would continue his own role as an authority on Jewish law and tradition and could perform the unique rabbinical functions he had performed.

To select his successor he named a three rabbi committee composed of the most eminent authorities in Orthodox Judaism then living. Two lived in New York, one in New Jersey. One of them was Moshe Feinstein, who was the president of the Union of Orthodox Rabbis in the U.S,

Baruch Shapiro died in 1970. At the time of his death his congregation was defunct, having ceased to function in 1967. Rabbi Shapiro had moved to the Seward Park area of the city and worshipped at Sephardic Bikur Cholim. The original Bikur Cholim also relocated to the Seward Park area, but Rabbi Feinstein rarely, if ever, went there.

Some said he never forgot his antagonism to them from the time he left them almost fifty years earlier. Not only was his congregation defunct, but two of the three named members of the selection committee were deceased. Only Rabbi Moshe Feinstein was still alive when he died in 1970.

In his will, written without any legal advice, after providing gifts to several Yeshivas, he left the balance of the estate to his congregation, but with conditions. First, the congregation could only draw up to half the new Rabbi's salary from the estate. His reason seems to have been that it must have sufficient members to pay at least half the salary, if not; the estate would go to his deceased wife's nieces. Second, the successor must be chosen by the unanimous agreement of his named selection committee, the already mentioned three of the most eminent rabbis in Orthodox Judaism in America. Finally, the entire process must be completed within one year of his death, otherwise the gift would lapse and the estate would go to the nieces. He named as his executor Isadore Schreiber, who had been the president of Machzikay Hadas.

I learned all of this and more. It seems that after the demise of Machzikay Hadas, most of its members began attending Bikur Cholim. Rabbi Shapiro's executor, Mr. Schreiber, also joined Bikur Cholim and was appointed to its Board of Directors. By 1970, the year of Rabbi Shapiro's death, Bikur Cholim was constructing a new synagogue building in Seward Park and was actively seeking a rabbi. The deadline for appointing a Rabbi and using funds from the Shapiro Estate was approaching. Mr. Schreiber and his business partner, Mr. I. Volotin, began discussing the possibility of using the defunct congregation to merge with Bikur Cholim and qualify for the use of the

Shapiro money to hire a rabbi. After getting a positive opinion from their attorney, Jack Steinberg, they put the plan into motion.

Steinberg told them they had to consult the by-laws of the congregation to see how to proceed with a merger. But Volotin and Schreiber told him the congregation had never had any written by-laws. So Steinberg said he would have to research Washington Law and advise them. He finished his research and advised them that they would have to follow state law governing unincorporated associations and that required a two thirds majority vote of the members to validate a merger.

Schreiber and Volotin organized a meeting of the surviving members, using their cemetery membership list. Of course, the membership was limited to men and when their meeting convened on September 12, 1971, only two months before the expiration of the bequest period, a total of thirteen elderly men convened. Schreiber explained the need for a merger if Bikur Cholim was to use the Shapiro money. A heated discussion ensued, many arguing that the great man would turn over in his grave rather than see his money go to Bikur Cholim, a congregation most thought he despised. Finally, a vote was called and the motion to merge was defeated, eight to five.

One might have thought that the merger was dead, but Schreiber and Volotin were determined to keep trying. A new notice of meeting went out. This time, they used the cemetery list and sent notices to the women on the list. A second meeting was convened on October 7, 1971 ~ only one month before the one year deadline.

The second meeting was attended by both men and women.

There were now twenty three people in attendance. Again Schreiber made his argument in favor of a merger. Again there was a heated discussion. This time another issue was raised ~ the participation of women in the business affairs of the congregation. This had never been accepted during Shapiro's lifetime. But the meeting overrode this objection.

A two thirds majority was required to approve a merger. The final vote was fifteen to eight in favor of the merger, but that was one vote short of the required two thirds. Then, Mr. Schreiber, the former president of the congregation and the chair of the meeting, said he would add his vote in favor of the merger. There were immediate protests; the chairman of a meeting was never allowed to vote except in the event of a tie, many said, and so the meeting was adjourned with everyone believing that the merger was dead. All of them were surprised to receive a letter from Mr. Schreiber the following week saying in effect that Mr. Steinberg had advised him that legally he could vote on the issue and he cast his vote for a merger and declared the merger was approved.

On October 28, 1971, Mr. Schreiber received a letter from the one surviving member of the selection group, Rabbi Moshe Feinstein, declaring that Rabbi Moshe Londinsky was qualified to be the Rabbi under Rabbi Shapiro's will. The congregation, which changed its name to Bikur Cholim Machzikay Hadas, immediately hired him. Mr. Schreiber, the executor of the Shapiro will, had started probate proceedings shortly after the Rabbi's death. Now he filed a declaration of proposed distribution of the estate naming Bikur Cholim Machzikay Hadas as the principal beneficiary. It was this notice, sent to all the heirs that set off the outrage that led Rabbi Fogelson to call me.

So that was the tangled factual background that I now had to deal with. My first thought was that the merger could be attacked on a number of grounds. But a little legal research convinced me that several of them were not legally valid. The main reason was that only a member or shareholder has standing to attack the validity of a merger. Besides, even if I could find a member willing to join in a lawsuit, the chances of success were slim.

Then there was the question of the demise of Machzikay Hadas. Here I ran head-on into the legal doctrine of *cy pres*. That was the long established rule that a bequest to a charitable, educational or religious beneficiary would not lapse if the beneficiary had gone out of existence. In such case a court would accept a substitute organization that resembled the purpose of the designated beneficiary. Clearly, Machzikay Hadas would qualify. I finally concluded that the best and only ground was to attack the qualification of Rabbi Londinsky as a man who did not meet the high standard Rabbi Shapiro demanded; a "godol" or a "gaon". This would require somehow getting the surviving member of the appointment committee, Rabbi Moshe Feinstein, to admit that Londinsky was not a "gaon" or a "godol". That would require taking his deposition in New York and conducting a very difficult examination of a hostile witness.

I had a long consultation with Dr. Arthur Lagawier to prepare for the deposition of the renowned Moshe Feinstein. From him I learned that the status of rabbi was established not by a diploma or by an official certificate but rather by what was called a "smicha". A smicha consists of a written declaration by an established Rabbi that the named recipient is qualified to give opinions on Jewish Law. The more distinguished the Rabbi who gives the "smicha", the more impressive are the credentials of the recipient. A rabbinical candidate may in fact receive two or three "smichas", each from a different distinguished Rabbi. To qualify, a rabbinical candidate must demonstrate a mastery of the Torah, the Talmud and at least three areas of Jewish law: the rules of Kashruth, or kosher food, the laws of sex and family purity, including the grounds and protocol for divorce, and the "poskim" or the decisions of the sages on Jewish Law.

I was confident we could show that this young Londinsky could never claim the status of a "godol"; he was far too young, too inexperienced, without recognition in the rabbinical world and certainly not an accepted authority on the Talmud and Torah whose opinions were read and accepted at the highest levels of Orthodox Judaism. But there was a serious obstacle: he had been approved as a "godol" by one of the designated selectors, Rabbi Moshe Feinstein. Lagawier told me that Feinstein was a world renowned authority and revered in the world of Orthodox Judaism. It would not be easy to discredit his opinion. But this was the only avenue for winning and I had to try.

How to prove that Londinsky was no godol? I considered calling Lagawier as an expert, but since he was not a rabbi, I doubted that a judge would accept his expert opinion on the qualifications of a rabbi. I met with a number of rabbis in the Seattle area, hoping I might be able to get expert opinions from them. They were very circumspect. While agreeing that technically Londinsky could not qualify as a godol or a gaon, each politely refused to agree to testify about their opinion, evidencing a rabbinical distaste for saying anything critical of another rabbi. The only course of action left open was to try to get the great man, the saintly Rabbi Moshe Feinstein, to somehow concede that his certification of Londinsky meeting the requirements of the

Shapiro will was not justified. That would require a deposition ~ an interrogation under oath. This prospect was daunting. I would have to rely on my courtroom skills at verbal combat, because I was almost certain that Rabbi Feinstein would not easily yield to anyone, especially a lawyer from Seattle, challenging his authority. I decided there was no alternative.

After deciding on my course of action, I called my client, Rabbi Fogelman to explain my strategy; the doctrine of *cy pres*, the legal obstacle to challenging the validity of the merger and the need to attack Londinsky's qualifications. Finally, I told him of the need to take the deposition of Moshe Feinstein. When he grasped that this meant I would come to New York, sit across a table and question Feinstein in an effort to trap him into conceding that Londinsky was not a godol or gaon, I heard his gasp. The sheer audacity of such a step overwhelmed him. His response, "Oy! Major surgery!" But he accepted my plan. I told him I wanted him present at the deposition, if for no other reason than to advise me. Fogelman agreed.

Then came the arrangements for the great event. I served a Notice of Taking Deposition on the attorney for the Shapiro Estate, Jack Steinberg and he did not object. He called me and told me it would have to take place at Rabbi Feinstein's home in New York and he added, "The Rabbi understands English but will testify only in Yiddish. So we will need a translator. That should not be a problem since he is the dean of his Yeshiva and he will arrange for one."

I didn't like the idea of being at the mercy of his translator so I called Rabbi Fogelman and asked if he could find someone fluent in Yiddish and English, capable of simultaneous translation at the deposition. I wanted a backup to insure accuracy. Fogelman said, "I know just the right man. He's a Yeshiva student and he's very smart. Knows Yiddish and English very well and I'll call him and arrange for him to meet us and go to the deposition."

Lennie and I traveled to New York and stayed at the New York Hilton hotel, arriving the day before the date of Rabbi Feinstein's deposition. I called Rabbi Fogelson and we arranged to have him and our translator come up to our room and meet us. Then together we would travel in Rabbi Fogelson's car to Rabbi Feinstein's apartment building.

At around one the next afternoon, the phone in our room rang. It was Rabbi Fogelson. We had never met and spoken only on the phone. He said he was in the lobby with our translator. I gave him our room number and told him to come up. A few minutes later there was a knock at our door and I opened it to gaze out at my visitors. Before me stood a young man with a wispy, straggly blond beard ~ no, not a beard, more just a cluster of blond hairs growing from his chin. Next to him was an older man, a short stubby man not more than five feet tall, with a black beard, striking me as the image of Toulouse Lautrec. The Toulouse Lautrec figure wore a black rabbinical fedora and a black coat. He smiled and introduced himself, "I'm Rabbi Hershel Fogelman and this is Reb Leizer Teitelbaum. He will be our translator."

I greeted them warmly and invited them in. I wanted to brief them on the basics of our position in the coming deposition. I introduced them to Lennie and proceeded to outline the issues I planned to cover in Rabbi Feinstein's deposition. Rabbi Fogelman seemed nervous. The idea of openly questioning Moshe Feinstein seemed to unnerve him. Young Teitelbaum said nothing but kept stroking the blond hairs growing down from his chin. After about fifteen minutes I said, "I think it's time to get started," and we walked down the corridor to the elevator. The deposition was set for two that afternoon.

The elevator doors slid open, revealing a group of businessmen inside. The sight of Rabbi Fogelson, a pint-sized, middle aged man wearing black Chasidic clothing, accompanied by a pale young man with payes (long curls of hair extending down the head behind the ears) could not help but attract the stares of the businessmen in the elevator, despite the convention of never staring at a fellow passenger in an elevator. As the elevator started down, Teitelbaum turned to Fogelson and said, in Yiddish, "It's time for Mincha (the afternoon daily prayer)." Fogelson looked at his watch and then nodded his head in agreement.

"Which way is East?" asked Fogelson. Teitelbaum pointed to the rear of the elevator and both he and Fogleson turned to the rear, facing their fellow elevator riders, and began saying their prayers in Hebrew aloud. In the traditional way, they chanted them together in a sing song voice, all the while rocking back and forth as they recited the prayers. This, in the midst of an assembly of businessmen, bunched together in a midtown New York hotel elevator. Teitelbaum and Fogelson finished their ritual prayers just before the elevator reached the ground floor and we all walked out into the lobby. I'm confident that our fellow elevator passengers had never witnessed such a scene in any elevator ride in their life.

In the lobby Fogelson said, "I'm going to pick up my car

and Teitelbaum is coming with me. Wait here and I'll be back in ten minutes. Then we'll drive over to Rabbi Feinstein's."

In a short while Fogelman pulled up in front of the hotel and I went out to his car. There was Fogelman, behind the wheel. He could barely see over the dashboard, but it didn't seem to faze him. Teitelbaum sat alongside him in the passenger's seat and I sat in the rear.

The residence address of Rabbi Moshe Feinstein was a large apartment complex on Franklin D. Roosevelt Drive, on the East side of Manhattan. Rabbi Fogelman said he knew just where the building was and boldly pulled out into midtown Manhattan traffic and proceeded to weave through traffic, talking non-stop as we went. He blithely ignored the angry honking of drivers he cut off and scared the hell out of me by making a ninety degree right turn from the center lane of our street directly in front of a taxicab whose horn added to the cacophony of horn honking. I winced, expecting to hear the crunch of a collision, but he was lucky and we were unscathed. When we arrived at the curb in front of a fifteen story brick apartment complex, he stopped and said, "Why don't you go up to Feinstein's apartment while I park the car? We'll come up as soon as I can find a place to park. We're already a little late." I found the Feinstein name on the list of tenants in the foyer and rang his bell. In a moment a voice answered, "Yes?"

"This is Alvin Ziontz, from Seattle. Here for the Rabbi's deposition," I said. "Ooh, Mr. Ziontz. Come up. Apartment 1206. Take the elevator," was the response.

I proceeded to the inner lobby and took the elevator to the

twelfth floor. About twenty feet down the hall I saw an open door and a man standing there. He greeted me warmly and said, "I am Reb Glazer, assistant to Reb Feinstein at the Yeshiva."

Then he ushered me in. The apartment was almost European in look and feel. Reb Glazer led me down a short hallway and into what was the dining room. Standing around all four walls of the room were Rabbis, shoulder to shoulder, all looking at me with intense interest. There was a very large dining room table in the center of the room and seated there was my legal adversary, Jack Steinberg, a court reporter and another rabbinical type who was introduced to me by Steinberg as Rabbi Rivlin who would serve as the interpreter. Reb Glazer invited me to have a seat at the table and explained that the men lining the walls were all Rabbis, there to see the interrogation of Rabbi Feinstein. Behind them was a tall bookcase and above it a long shelf.

I told them that Rabbi Fogelman would be there shortly, as soon as he could park his car and I added, "He's bringing with him our interpreter, Reb Leizer Teitelbaum."

No objection was voiced and I didn't know how the question of which of two interpreters would be recognized as giving the version to be recorded in the deposition. I was also uncertain whether to object to the wall of Rabbis surrounding us, but in the end I decided against it, feeling it would heighten the tension which I could already feel in the room.

Reb Glazer said Rabbi Feinstein would be in shortly so we just sat there making small talk while we waited for the arrival of the celebrated Moshe Feinstein. I had never seen him and didn't know what to expect. Then the great man entered the room, wearing a dressing gown and a rabbinical cap. He walked confidently to the head of his dining room table and seated himself. The Rabbi was in his late seventies, with white hair and a white beard and mustache. Clearly he was the celebrity in the room. He looked around the table and nodded briefly at me. His assistant, Reb Glazer then made an introduction of Rabbi Feinstein and his interpreter Rabbi Rivlin and finally,

Rabbi Moshe Feinstein
1895 - 1986

Jack Steinberg as the representative of the Estate of Rabbi Shapiro. I then introduced myself, Rabbi Fogelson and our interpreter Leizer Teitelbaum. The court reporter, who was obviously also Jewish, then introduced himself and explained his role.

Since I was the one who had convened the deposition, I spoke, "Rabbi Feinstein, as you know the Estate of Rabbi Shapiro is in the court in Seattle, Washington and this proceeding is governed by the rules of that court. After you are sworn I will ask you the questions and then if Mr. Steinberg wishes he can also ask you some questions. We are doing this because what you say is important to the court and your words will be recorded and typed by our court reporter. Your testimony will be under oath the same as if you were a witness in the court room. Do you fully understand?"

Rabbi Feinstein nodded he did and so I said, "Let us get started." Then I said to the court reporter, "Please administer the oath." The reporter turned to Rabbi Feinstein and said, "Rabbi, please raise your right hand to take the witness oath."

I should have known that the great Talmudic scholar would not make things easy for me but I didn't anticipate that the battle would begin over taking an oath to tell the truth. The saintly Rabbi, the great Talmudic scholar responded, "You want me to swear that I will tell the truth? Do you see those books on the shelf there? There are ten volumes of my statements of the truth of the Torah and the Talmud. Those books are read by Rabbis and scholars around the world. If I didn't tell the truth then why are my words received as truth around the world? I don't swear to tell the truth. My whole life is telling the truth."

I could see that this was not going to be easy. So I tried to explain that it is a legal requirement in every court in America that a witness has to swear to tell the truth. To no avail. He would not take the oath. Then I had a thought. I said, "Okay, Rabbi. You don't have to swear to tell the truth. The law says you only have to affirm you will tell the truth. This simply means you agree that everything you say in this deposition will be true. No raising of the hand, no swearing, just assuring, not me, but the court, that your testimony is truthful."

There followed more flowery rhetoric by the Rabbi to the effect that he always tells the truth. After more Talmudic declarations by him, I felt the record showed sufficiently that the Rabbi had affirmed he would tell the truth. So I told the court reporter that he had affirmed he would tell the truth and to record that. "Now let us begin," I said.

What followed was an unseemly demonstration of defensive evasions and distortions to avoid the truth that his nominee could under no honest compliance with Rabbi Shapiro's language, qualify as his successor. Rabbi Feinstein adopted the tactic of relativity; a word means different things to different listeners and changes according to circumstance. In his rambling answers he intimated that Rabbi Shapiro himself was not a "godol", though he, Rabbi Feinstein was, that Shapiro had the gall to summon the three greatest Orthodox Rabbis in the world for his purposes, and that for Seattle Londinsky was good enough, whether other Rabbis called him a "godol" or not. As to the ultimate question of whether Rabbi Londinsky was a "godol" he answered, "I hold that he is good."

I decided that I wasn't going to corner the great man better than that. It was, in my opinion, good enough to present to a judge and constituted a clear showing that Rabbi Feinstein had backed away from an unqualified assertion that Moshe Londinsky met the standards of the will. Although the synagogue had denied that Rabbi Shapiro's nieces had no rightful claim to any part of his estate, not long after the deposition the synagogue's attorney, Jack Steinberg indicated he was open to a settlement, in the end we did settle, with Rabbi Shapiro's heirs receiving 40% of the estate. In view of the ambiguity of the evidence and the overshadowing doctrine of *cy pres*, I felt, and my clients agreed, that the settlement was satisfactory.

The deposition of Rabbi Feinstein and the machinations of Congregation Bikur Cholim to get the money left by Rabbi Shapiro tainted the reputations of both of them. . That this sainted man would engage in such dishonesty and sophistry soiled his reputation and the reputation of the Orthodox Congregation of Bikur Cholim Machzikay Hadas. In the short run they succeeded; they got a part of the estate money and Rabbi Londinsky. Ironically, several years later, Londinsky was discovered to have engaged in an illicit affair with one of the women on the synagogue staff and had to resign in disgrace. Perhaps there is poetic justice in the Rabbi Shapiro story.

Although I had told Barry Ernstoff of the Shapiro Estate litigation, in the end, he didn't play any part in it. But the Shapiro case and the attraction of defending the rights of Indian Tribes convinced him to resign his position with the Attorney General's Office and join us. Barry turned out to be a major asset; an agile mind together with overpowering rhetoric. He soon was working on cases for the Colville Tribe and the Suquamish Tribe. As for the shoulder length hair, only one Indian objected.

We had all attended a pow-wow of the Colville Tribe at Omak Washington. One of the leaders of the tribe, a woman named Lucy Covington, brought her great uncle over to meet Barry. The man was in his late seventies, wore his gray hair in Indian braids and was dressed in traditional Indian garb. He had the un-Indian sounding name, George Friedlander. Lucy told us he was a chief and highly respected. George Friedlander carried himself with great dignity and was obviously an important member of the tribe. She introduced him to Barry, the newest member of our firm. He shook hands with Barry and then, looking at him sternly said, "Young man, cut your hair."

Barry smiled and said, "Pleased to meet you Mr. Friedlander", and the chief left.

Barry did not cut his hair ~ at least not then. But he turned out to be an extraordinary lawyer ~ one who would be a key member of the firm. As time passed Barry became more conventional and conservative. One day in 1973, Barry told me about a lawyer who was so talented that we should have him in the firm. The lawyer's name was Steve Chestnut. When I asked why this guy was so desirable, Barry, whose judgment I respected, told me that Steve had extraordinary intellect combined with a mastery of detail and a toughness that led him to victories in difficult cases. Chestnut was then an associate in a highly regarded Seattle firm and seemed contented there, but Barry was confident that he could be persuaded to leave and join us. Because Barry was so certain that Chestnut was a huge talent, I agreed to interview him.

When Steve Chestnut sat down across the desk from me and we began to talk, I waited to hear him display some of the brilliance I had been led by Barry to expect. But he was modest, diffident and soft-spoken. I didn't hear any brilliance. He had received his legal education at the University of Washington, but without the familiar distinctions; law review, Order of the Coif, top of the class and the like. But, on the other hand, he had a Master's Degree in Mechanical Engineering and a record of high achievement in his legal work for a well-respected Seattle law firm. We hired him. Steve Chestnut proved to be a lawyer who achieved near miraculous results in his work with Indians. My law firm was now made up of me, Pirtle, Morisset, Ernstoff and Chestnut.

CHAPTER TWENTY

THE NORTHERN CHEYENNE CASE, DEBATING RUTH BADER GINSBURG
AND
ENTERING THE ACADEMIC WORLD

The year was 1973 and we had just been retained by the Northern Cheyenne Tribe in Montana. They needed top drawer legal talent to fight off coal leasing by a number of America's largest and most powerful companies. I felt Steve Chestnut, with his engineering background, would be well-suited to this case. Steve had never met any Indians. He was a product of Brooklyn, New York, though he was fascinated by the West. I asked him to come with me for my first meeting with the Northern Cheyenne Tribal Council. The meeting was at the reservation and the office of the Tribe was at Lame Deer, Montana ~ about a hundred miles east of Billings Montana.

Steve and I flew to Billings where I had arranged to rent a plane that I would fly to Ashland, on the Eastern edge of the reservation. There we would be picked up by someone from the Tribe and driven to Lame Deer. This was a completely new and exotic experience for Steve; riding in a private plane piloted by his boss and meeting with the Council of an Indian tribe. After landing at an airstrip just outside the reservation, a BIA employee drove us the twenty miles to Lame Deer.

Steve and I entered the Council chambers not knowing what to expect. Inside, seated around a large table were twelve members of the Council, including the President, Allan Rowland, Edwin Dahle, Turkey Shoulderblades, Dennis Limberhand, Kenneth Beartusk, Danny Foote, Ted Risingsun, Bert Medicine Bull as well as others whose names have disappeared from my memory.

Most of the members were dark skinned big men. Ed Dahle did not appear to be Indian at all, but he was. He had studied the coal leasing history closely and it was he who was asked by the Council to give us a summary of the problem facing the tribe. Dahle described how in the 1960's the Bureau of Indian Affairs had met with the Council and told them that several major companies were interested in mining on the reservation. It was presented by BIA officials as a way out of the poverty in which the Cheyennes lived. If the tribe agreed, the procedure under Federal Regulations was to hold a public auction at which qualified bidders would submit their offers of "Bonus Payments". There was no competition for royalty payments; which were fixed at seventeen and a half cents a ton. When the auction was complete six major American companies were awarded permits and three more went to partnerships or individuals. The exploration permit was contained in a standard form of the BIA. But reading the permit showed it was far more than an exploration permit. It gave the holder the option to convert it into a mining lease at his option. The tribe had no further rights. Granting the permit was tantamount to giving up control over coal mining on the land.

The story of Northern Cheyenne and the coal companies cannot be told without recognizing the key contribution of Steve Chestnut. Barry Ernstoff was right about him; he was a major talent and hiring him was one of the best decisions we ever made. Our key decision was to petition the Secretary of the Interior to void the permits and the leases because they were granted in violation of federal regulations governing mining on Indian lands. We challenged the legality. Ultimately, the Secretary ruled he would not approve any mining on the reservation without the consent of the tribe. The Northern Cheyenne case did not end till Steve won the Supreme Court case of Northern Cheyenne Tribe v. Hollowbreast in 1974 and the threat of coal mining on the reservation was ended.

In the 1970's more and more Indian Law cases were making their way to the Supreme Court. One of them, Martinez v. Santa Clara Pueblo was a historic decision. The case was a test of the 1978 act of Congress; The Indian Civil Rights Act of 1968. The law was intended to require tribal governments to comply with the requirements of the Bill of Rights in dealing with their members.

Soon after the law was passed, Federal courts began deciding all kinds of claims against tribal governments, issuing injunctions and awarding damages under the assumption that the Act implied the authority to grant all kinds of relief, as in any other case. The problem was the act specified only one form of relief: Habeas Corpus, applicable only to restraints on personal liberty. For ten years these cases proliferated. No federal court questioned its authority over tribal governments.

I was a member of the Indian Rights Committee of the ACLU, a body established to advise the national Board of Directors and to recommend policy on Indian issues. I was troubled by the actions of the federal courts granting judgments against tribes and in 1975 I wrote an article, which appeared in the South Dakota Law Review, arguing that all these courts were wrong and their decisions were contrary to the Intent of Congress and violated tribal sovereignty.

In my study at home on Mercer Island 1975

In 1977 the case of Martinez v. Santa Clara Pueblo was taken up by the United States Supreme Court. Mrs. Martinez sued her Pueblo under the Indian Civil Rights act because she had married a man not a member of the Pueblo and she and her children were denied membership. The Pueblo asserted that from time immemorial they had operated as a patronymic society, with membership following the line of the father. Mrs. Martinez argue that she had been denied Equal Protection under the Indian Civil Rights Act. The case presented the issue of constitutional rights v. cultural rights.

With the case before the Supreme Court, the ACLU was forced to decide which side they would support in an Amicus brief. The case was before our committee and we overwhelmingly voted to support the Pueblo. But the National Board was not persuaded. They asked me to make the argument with the head of their Women's Rights Project, Ruth Bader Ginsberg (long before she was appointed to the Supreme Court). The argument took place in a lengthy phone conversation I had with Mrs. Ginsberg. Her view was that this was a classic Equal Protection Case and the ACLU should support the claim of Mrs. Martinez. I tried hard to explain to her that Indian culture had been under assault by white society for two hundred years, that it was fragile and should be respected. To no avail. She could not be persuaded.

I felt I was up against the cultural arrogance of New Yorkers who knew little of the history of the American Indian people. So, in the end, the ACLU filed an amicus brief on the side of Mrs. Martinez. With the approval of several of my tribal clients I wrote and filed an amicus brief in support of the Pueblo. When the Court issued its opinion in 1978, it held that Federal Courts had no jurisdiction to hear any case against a tribe unless it was a Habeas Corpus proceeding. I felt smug. My position had been upheld. Too bad, Mrs. Ginsberg.

In 1976, Martin graduated from the University of Chicago. In that year, our law firm had seven members and we moved to a historic old building in the Pioneer Square District, named, appropriately, The Pioneer Building. The building had the charm of old Seattle, but, unfortunately the neighborhood didn't. Our office was on the first floor and every day the silence was shattered by the sound of passing sirens. Derelicts, alcoholics and beggars sat on the benches in the square fronting our building and often on the steps leading to the main entrance. Some of the offices were separated by brick walls and we had to go out in the corridor to pass from one office to another. We put up with these conditions for five years until the firm finally decided to move to a modern office building in 1981, the Metropolitan Park Building. The firm was winning cases and becoming nationally known as one of the premier Indian Law firms in the country.

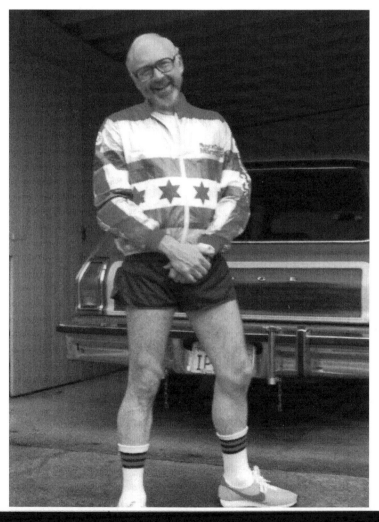

Wearing my cycling jacket at age 50 on Mercer Island 1978

In 1977, Lennie, who had volunteered at the Burke Museum of the University of Washington, was persuaded by the director of the museum to enroll in the Museology Program and get a Master's Degree. It was her hope that with a Master's degree she stood a better chance of finding employment than having only a Bachelor's degree.

In 1978, I turned fifty and Lennie hosted a gala party at our house replete with a belly dancer. Jeff was living with a girl friend in West Seattle, Martin was enjoying Law School, and Ellen was enjoying Oberlin. But I had ambiguous feelings about practicing law. Despite the successes and the personal satisfaction of helping Indian tribes, the practice of law was too adversarial for me. I had always felt I wanted out ~ to leave the practice and do something else.

In 1972 I had taught Indian Law in the Indian Studies Program at the University of Washington. Three years later I was again asked to teach the course. I was a University instructor for the next five years teaching Indian Law. I liked the environment; preparing lectures, engaging with students, working out of a tiny office in a university building. I began to think of a career as a university teacher. But the idea was too radical; the firm was doing very well, I was enjoying moderate success and there was simply too much invested in building my firm and its reputation in Indian Law to seriously consider a career change. But the seed was planted.

The following year was marked by three noteworthy events: Ellen graduated from Oberlin, Lennie received her Master's Degree from the University of Washington, and my article, "Civil Rights Under Tribal Government", was published in the Law Review of the University of California at Davis. It was widely read and regarded as an important work of scholarship. In 1980 Martin graduated from Northwestern Law School and told me he would like to work for our firm as an associate. I thought it was almost certain he would be hired and told him to prepare a résumé.

Martin's graduation from Northwestern Law School 1980

Martin's résumé showed him to have been an excellent law student with important legal experience after law school. So when it was received and a partnership meeting was called about hiring him, I was confident of the outcome. I was taken aback when three partners objected. Their grounds: nepotism. It would be impossible, they said, to judge his performance objectively because he was my son, and besides, they added, it would set a bad precedent. I was shocked and angry. This rejection had a profound effect on me. I thought, "This is not my firm anymore". The decision presaged my thoughts of leaving the firm and taking a year off to explore an academic career and if that was successful, then leaving the firm permanently. It meant that the three who had objected were now a force in the firm. One of them had been selected by us to be the managing partner and he had aggrandized his role so that he almost unilaterally took major decisions; he had hired a business manager; a woman with no law degree who saw lawyers as billing units. He had contracted with a company to computerize all data; lawyer's time records, fee income, expenses and efficiency measurements. We even hired, at his insistence, a computer data manager to send data to the computer company, out of state. The total cost of that effort was staggering. He undertook even more unsettling actions. He wanted every member of the firm to develop business clients by seeking appointments with businesses and touting our abilities in the hope this would bring in non-Indian clients. Several of us felt this was distasteful and unethical and simply refused to do it. Clearly he felt the firm's commitment to low fees for services to our Tribal clients limited his earnings. He wanted to shift our practice away from Indian tribes. To this end he wanted to remove the art that decorated our office because it celebrated our Indian practice and gave the "wrong" message to any business clients who came to the office. This too, we refused.

I began conversations with friends in academia about moving into their world. One of those conversations bore fruit. Bob Clinton was a professor of Law at the University of Iowa and he thought there was a good chance they would be open to bringing me in as a visiting professor for the winter term of 1981. While I was looking for an appointment for a full year, he said it was possible they might find something for me that summer or the following fall. If I was interested he was willing to talk to the Dean. Yes, I told him. I was interested. The resulting talks led to a firm commitment for a University of Iowa teaching position starting in January of 1981.

With a commitment in hand, I made my plan to take an entire year off ~ a sabbatical if you will ~ and to take Lennie and Ronnie with me to Iowa and wherever the next academic opportunity appeared. Of course it was not a real sabbatical. It was simply a leave without pay. There would be a huge upheaval; renting our house for a year, schlepping my family across the country and away from our comfortable Seattle environs for ~ who knows what? I would have to discuss it with Lennie and with my partners, but by this time my mind was made up; I wanted to go and do this. It meant I would have to live on a university salary, since I didn't expect my partners to finance my academic adventure; I would take no firm income so they would have no right to object to my leaving.

CHAPTER TWENTY-ONE

A DRAMATIC CHANGE
IN MY CAREER

Telling Lennie that I was going to leave law practice, leave Seattle and move to Iowa; that we would be gone for a year and there was a chance I might never want to go back was profoundly upsetting. For one thing, she had just gotten a grant for a museum project she would administer and leaving meant turning the project over to someone else. Undeniably this was a serious blow to her, after working hard for her degree in Museology and trying to start a career in that field. Even worse was the thought of leaving Seattle where all our children were and she made it plain to me that she would never want to do that permanently. We reached an understanding that no matter what I found in the academic world, we would return.

Telling my partners that I was leaving for a year was much easier. Since I asked for no compensation, they could hardly object and they didn't, except to say they expected me to return to the firm. After that it was only a matter of logistics. We planned to drive to Iowa City in our cars; I in my Lancia, Lennie in her Dodge Aspen wagon. We bought two CB radios so we could talk to each other en route. I loaded my car with books, including a giant Merriam-Webster

Dictionary which I bought with the vague notion that as a university teacher I would need it. The dictionary proved to be of no use as were the other books I hauled along. I simply had an exaggerated notion of what an academic life entailed.

An ad I placed to rent our house brought no results. So we listed it with a real estate broker for a rental; confident she would vet any prospective renter and only recommend a responsible and suitable candidate. As the date for our departure arrived, we still had no candidate to rent our house. But we weren't going to let that deter us.

One fine morning in December of 1980, we started on our trek to Iowa, me leading in the Lancia, Lennie following in the Aspen. Luckily we did not have to cope with snow or bad weather, and the trip was uneventful, though we had trouble maintaining radio communication and once when we were separated by a substantial distance Lennie could not get an answer when she radioed us. Lennie also ran into difficulty driving the Aspen because the carrier on the roof made the car top-heavy and susceptible to strong winds. After three and a half days of driving, we arrived in Iowa City ~ a place neither of us had ever seen.

We were looking forward to discovering our new city and began by checking into a motel. Iowa City was tiny compared to Seattle. It was easy to find the town center ~ a ten minute drive. We had first felt the sharp bite of the Iowa winter temperature when we left the warmth of our motel room and got into our car, but when we parked downtown and began strolling along the sidewalk, we were shocked by the severity of the cold; like nothing we had experienced since living in Seattle. After five minutes, it became painful and we realized what cold meant. The actual temperature was probably fifteen or twenty degrees, but for us, staying outdoors was a sensory shock.

I had made arrangements to lease the home of a Law School faculty member; Allan Vestal, who would be visiting at the University of Kansas the Winter Quarter. The next day, key in hand, we drove to our new home. It was a one story brick home with attached garage on a quiet residential street. Inside, we were pleased to find a comfortable, well furnished and cozy place to live.

I arrived a week or so before classes and I was both confident and uneasy about what I was about to do. My arrangement with the Law School was to teach a small section course in Constitutional Law, three hours a week in class which required the students to submit written papers. So I would have to assign topics and grade student papers. I also taught a seminar on Tribal Government and American Federalism. As for Constitutional Law I was confident in my oral skills but uneasy about the content of the course. It had been thirty years since I had a course in Constitutional Law at Chicago and now I would be teaching about subjects in Constitutional Law where I had a weak understanding; the Commerce Clause, Federal Jurisdiction, the Federal Courts and Judicial Review. My post-law school experience in Constitutional Law had to do with the Bill of Rights and the Supremacy Clause, not the underpinnings of Federal Power and the Federal Courts.

Long before leaving for Iowa, I took a course in Constitutional Law in the evening at Seattle University in order to reacquaint myself with the case law and the major doctrines. Not content with that, I read several law review articles on Marbury v. Madison and other important cases in order to have a better understanding of the subject topics. The seminar in Tribal Government was a much easier assignment for me. I knew a good deal of the material from my experience and legal research. So, while I was a bit tense when I walked into the classroom on the first day of the course, I knew what I wanted to do with the subject.

The class was composed of twenty students, several of whom were quite bright. I launched into a Socratic series of questions immediately and most of the students seemed to respond enthusiastically. That's the way it went for the entire semester, but there were two unexpected hitches: students coming to my office to dispute the grades I had given their written work and the mathematics of matching their grades to a "curve". I never completely understood that math, but did my best to be fair.

Meanwhile, Lennie contacted the Johnson County Arts Council and persuaded them to hire her as their Public Relations Director. It was an empowering experience for her because she not only wrote press releases, but also had a radio program to talk about the art shows the Council was producing. She was even involved in helping to hang an exhibit of weavings in the local museum. Our son, Ronnie, who was then just turning fifteen, was enjoying his school experience. He found the Iowa City middle school teachers very kind and helpful and he made many friends. Professor Vestal had left a bicycle in the garage and soon Ronnie was riding it all over town. One day he returned from a bike ride and said, "Mom, I tried to ride as far as I could to get lost, but I couldn't. I always found a street that I knew. The town is so small."

Life in Iowa City was pleasant; everything was so easy ~ parking, going to the movies, faculty friends, teaching and Lennie's work with the Arts Council. But in the spring I became aware of a nagging pain in my right leg when I was standing in my classroom. It became so severe that I finally went to the clinic at the University Hospital. After x-rays and an MRI, two orthopedic surgeons gave me the diagnosis: I had a spinal stenosis in my lumbar spine. In plain language this is a narrowing of the spaces between the vertebrae causing pressure on the sciatic nerve. They prescribed some exercises that might alleviate the pain, but, ultimately, they said, I would need spinal surgery to open the spaces. This was not good news but I had no idea then that it would end up leaving me disabled and severely limited in walking or standing twenty five years later.

As the winter quarter drew to a close I didn't know what I would be doing after it ended. Then the Dean asked if I would be willing to teach a course in "Professional Responsibility" in the summer. This was a subject I could teach without extensive preparation and I agreed to do it. So my employment was firm through the summer. But Dean Hines told me there were no vacancies for the fall term and if I wanted to stay in teaching and absent myself from the firm for a full year I would have to find something elsewhere.

Inquiries quickly led to two possible appointments; one at Washington University Law School in St. Louis and the other at Arizona State University in Tempe Arizona. The St. Louis job was unattractive because it meant teaching Criminal Law, a subject I was not familiar with. Besides, I had been in St. Louis and didn't like the idea of living there. The Arizona job was more interesting because I would be teaching Indian Law as well as other subjects.

Before I had to make a choice, Dean Hines offered me a much more exciting job: visiting professor of law at the University of Durham in England. Wow! We had never been abroad and the idea of teaching in a British University was the stuff of dreams. The Dean explained that Iowa had an exchange agreement with Durham and though Durham was sending one of their Law Faculty to teach at Iowa, the Iowa guy had decided he didn't want to go to Durham in the fall so the Dean had to find someone else. Would I be interested? Without any hesitancy I told him I would accept the offer, without even asking what I would be teaching. When I did ask, he explained I would be teaching Human Rights and doing a "Tutorial" in Torts. In England a tutorial is what we call a seminar ~ a small group of students discussing the subject under the guidance of the Professor. I felt confident that my experience and background gave me the ability to teach these subjects with minimal preparation. I soon discovered I was mistaken.

I approached the teaching of Human Rights confident that my background in American Civil liberties would give me a solid foundation. But reading some textbooks soon disabused me. Human Rights, it seemed, was a field of International Law and dealt with such international agreements as the European Convention on Human Rights, the International Convention on Human Rights, the European Court of Human Rights and its decisions, the Geneva Convention and several other international agreements. It had nothing to do with the American Constitution or its Bill of Rights. I would have to master a new area of law and familiarize myself with the decisions of the European Court of Human Rights. So I had work to do.

The news that we would be going to England and living there was exciting for Lennie, but not for our fifteen year old son, Ronnie.

He bluntly told us he was looking forward to starting High School on Mercer Island and didn't want to trade the experience for going to school in another country with kids he didn't know. After trying unsuccessfully to point out the benefits Lennie and I acceded and said O.K. We would have to find some families on Mercer Island to provide food and lodging for him while we were abroad.

Landing at London's Gatwick Airport after a long overseas flight seemed unreal. Was this really England? Soon enough, hearing the language spoken by airport and customs officials convinced me that we were really in a country across the Atlantic. We boarded a train heading north to the city of Durham, a distance of about 230 miles. We would be living in the house of the Durham professor who went to Iowa, Colin Warbrick.

We were pleasantly surprised when a faculty member, Bill Rees, met us at the station and drove us to the house. He parked in the rear, a sort of alley, and let us in through the back gate and opened the door leading into the kitchen. It was nice, but quite different than any American house.

I had been told the house had central heating. Well, in England it was called central heating but in fact, it was a hand stoked boiler in the kitchen that heated water in radiators through the two story house. The boiler was contained in a white enameled container that looked at first glance like a small refrigerator. Opening its door revealed a tiny iron furnace with a grate. Bill showed me the shed in the back yard where the coke was stored and the scoop and bucket used to bring a bucketful of coke in and shovel it into the furnace. Then he handed me the keys to the house, to the garage and to Warbrick's car. His final act of helpfulness was to show us the dryer, a folding wooden rack to hang washed items to dry and bade us good bye.

We explored the Warbrick house and found it commodious and comfortable. On the ground floor was a large kitchen and centered in it was a huge old fashioned wooden table. Plenty of cabinets, a refrigerator and gas stove and, of course, a sink. The kitchen windows looked out on the towers of Durham Cathedral ~ a dramatic and almost unreal sight. A passageway led to two large rooms; a living room with a real fireplace and opposite, a large formal dining room. The entrance consisted of a large red painted wooden door above which was a decorative glass window, on the outside of which was the rather British name of the house: "High Cliff".

Over time we explored the ancient town of Durham, its narrow winding streets, the bridge over the river Wear and on a hill, towering over the river, the massive Romanesque and Norman structure of Durham Cathedral. Walking through Durham I had the odd sensation of being on a movie set ~ an unreal, almost artificial place where we moderns seemed out of place.

Our Durham House:
High Cliff

The Law School, or Law Faculty as it was called, was housed in an 18th century structure originally used as the county clerk's headquarters. After the University acquired it, an adjacent building was attached to provide more space for lecture halls, faculty offices and the library. The result was an architectural hodgepodge, with a narrow, sloping corridor connecting the buildings. My office was roomy and its window looked out on the main street of Durham. On the door hung a dusty, black academic gown, which I was told should be worn on formal college occasions.

Entrance of the Department of Law Building

University of Durham 1981

Durham University is a prestigious, old institution, founded in 1832. It is a residential university composed of several distinct colleges. I was soon informed that I was required to affiliate with one of these and to take dinner with the faculty there once a week. Since there were twelve separate colleges, each housed in its own building, I had no idea which to choose. So I asked for an opinion from one of my colleagues at the Law School and was surprised when he said I should select the one with the best wine cellar and the best dining. On his advice I selected Collingwood.

My first college dinner at Collingwood was another scene out of Hollywood. I was ushered into an intimate wood paneled room off the dining hall for a pre-dinner glass of sherry. The room was filled with academics, men and women, many wearing their black academic gowns, which made them look like graduating high school seniors. A waitress poured me a glass of sherry, noting my name on a sheet so I would be charged the cost later. The room was filled with the babble of intellectual conversation. I soon found myself engaged with two of these people, who seemed fascinated at having an American, especially one who was a lawyer for Indian Tribes, to have a fluttering chatter with. Everyone seemed to be enjoying the sherry hour enormously when the Dean announced it was time to enter the Great Hall for dinner.

At his signal, everyone formed a line leading to a door at the end of the room. The Dean paused, as if waiting for his troops to get into formation, and then he swung open a large oak door revealing a huge hall, replete with exposed beams, hanging banners showing coats of arms, stained glass windows, and four long rows of tables. There must have been a hundred and fifty students sitting at the tables, and as we filed in they all rose as one to their feet and stood until all of us had seated ourselves. The faculty people were seated at a long table at the front of the room on a raised platform ~ a sort of stage, called the "high table". Two or three students were selected to sit among the faculty; a commingling which I assumed was intended to provide the students with the thrill of taking part in an erudite conversation ~ or perhaps it was a nod in the direction of democracy. We were no sooner seated than a crew of ten or twelve waitresses, all middle aged women, began circling us and passing out menus. They were dressed identically; black long sleeved dresses with white lace cuffs and white lace collars; pleasant, smiling and very dignified. The wine list was long and impressive. Somehow I had never thought of the English as wine connoisseurs, but clearly many are. The meal itself was not impressive but the ambience was. It was unlike anything in America.

My classes at the Law School were very different than those in American Law Schools. For one thing, law was taught as an academic subject, not as the foundation for a profession. Indeed, most of the students had no intention of being practitioners. That would require a post-university course of apprenticeship either with the barristers and solicitor's society and following that, a period of clerkship for a solicitor (a non-court lawyer) or pupilage in the chambers of a barrister (a courtroom lawyer), Another difference was the average age; about nineteen. All of them seemed very smart, but not lawyer smart and lacking in the breadth of knowledge that an American law student who had completed four years of undergraduate study would have.

The class was small; twelve students. I met with them three times a week in a small room sitting around a table. There was no assigned textbook, only a reading list. The students were expected to explore the subject on their own without the paternal hand of a professor guiding them down a path of inquiry.

After a few friendly introductory remarks I began the class with a question. They were taken aback because in all their classes the professor had simply lectured and they took notes. But I pursued my Socratic method and soon they accepted this new form of learning and seemed to be completely caught up in our dialogue. We spent time discussing the reported decisions of the European Court of Human Rights, the other major treaties governing Human Rights and we also discussed the rights of indigenous peoples, including American Indians.

My tutorial in torts was quite different than any American course. The British law of Torts seemed to be rigidly bound by what lawyers call "stare decisis", the iron hand of precedent. American lawyers and judges seemed freer to consider public policy and to make analogies and distinctions than the British.

Meanwhile, Lennie was enjoying her English sojourn; walking every day to the shops for groceries, both of us attending a Bach concert in Durham Cathedral, and taking driving tours of the areas around Durham and Newcastle in Warbrick's car. Lennie was even invited to deliver a lecture on Northwest Indian Art to an attentive university audience. She worked hard to prepare the lecture and even had slides sent from the University of Washington which she used to illustrate Northwest Coast indigenous art. She was treated as a minor celebrity. The entire experience was a first for her and she particularly enjoyed the feeling of confidence that accompanied her radio broadcasts and press releases.

An added attraction for us was the residence of my old friend Jose Montaño and his wife in London. We took the train down and stayed at their home for two or three days taking a grand tour of the city.

After the Michaelmas term ended and I was free, Lennie and I accompanied the Montaños on a tour of Italy, visiting Rome, Florence, Milan, Pisa and Venice. There was nothing in America to compare to it. Every city had statuary and cathedrals of breathtaking beauty.

We were brought face to face with Renaissance Art everywhere in a way that no college course or textbook could do justice to. Finally our European sojourn ended and we returned to Seattle in the spring of 1982.

After a year's absence I was anxious to return to the world of law practice. I had sampled life in the academic world and I was surprised and disappointed that it was not satisfying. Lecturing to a class and sitting in an academic office was detached from the real world. As a lawyer I could make things happen. I could with a phone call negotiate with an opponent. With a dictating machine I could start a law suit or draft a brief or a letter that would command attention. No, I wanted to return to the world of law, a world I had thought I wanted to leave, but now after academia, the practice of law seemed to be what suited me best.

Durham Cathedral 1981

I captured this dramatic image of Durham Cathedral one brisk morning from the Wear River with the old Fulling Mill, now an archaeological museum where Lennie worked as a volunteer while I taught at the University.

CHAPTER TWENTY-TWO

BACK TO THE WORLD OF LAWYERING

During my academic sojourn the firm had moved from the Pioneer Building to a new building called Metropolitan Park, an aluminum clad twenty story building. Several of my partners proudly showed me the new quarters. Our offices were on the seventeenth floor and had an outdoor deck overlooking the city. The interior was beautiful and the firm was humming with legal work for tribes. But when I came to the office to work, I soon found there was no work for me to do. All the tribal work was being done by others who didn't need any assistance. So, when some personal injury cases came to me, I took them even though I hadn't done that kind of case for years.

Bar Association photo
1982

One of the most memorable involved the death of a locomotive fireman who fell out of his cab, landing on the ground fourteen feet below. The call came from his widow, Mrs. Helen Benning, an elderly woman who was living in an apartment hotel near downtown Seattle. At our first meeting in my office, she told me of the incident that led to the death of her husband, George.

Mrs. Benning was a composed, well dressed woman in her sixties. She sat across my desk and launched into the painful story of George's death.

"George was a wonderful man. We were married thirteen years and we were very happy together. He had worked for the Milwaukee Road for forty years and he loved his job. (The actual name of this railroad was 'The Chicago, Milwaukee, St. Paul and Pacific Railroad'.) He was a fireman on one of their electric locomotives and they were just returning from a road run to Seattle and heading for the roundhouse when he fell. You see, they use steam from Chicago but at Othello, the division point, they switch to electric because they have to run through the tunnels in the mountains.

Now, what I know about what happened I found out from George's friend, the engineer. The engineer's name is Larry Rauch and he and George have known each other for years. What Larry told me was that as they were nearing the roundhouse, George sat out on the window sill, on the armrest out there, to reach out and take down the sign of the train number, what they call the number board, that's mounted in a bracket on the front of the engine. It's George's job, as fireman, to take that down when the engine has finished its run. Larry said the last thing he saw was George sitting out there and then all of a sudden he saw him going out the window. When Larry went down to him, he found the armrest where George had been sitting on the ground near him. George was unconscious. The armrest was broken in half.

Well, they took him to the nearest hospital, which was at Moses Lake. He had a fractured skull and he lingered on for eight days before he died. He never regained consciousness. The railroad sent me a letter. Supposed to be condolences, but what it really was telling me they had no responsibility for the accident; that George's doctor had given them his opinion that George lost consciousness, or got dizzy because of a stroke or high blood pressure and that was why he fell.

Now George was too heavy, weighed about two hundred and fifty, two hundred sixty pounds and he did have high blood pressure. So the railroad doctor had put him on medical leave and told him he had to lose some weight and get his blood pressure down. He was on leave for a month and he did lose some weight and the pills Dr. Douglas prescribed did reduce his blood pressure. He got medical clearance to go back to work and he had been working for about three weeks when this happened. But I don't believe for a minute that he had a stroke or got dizzy. The reason he fell is pretty obvious; he was sitting on the arm rest that's on the outside of the cab window and it broke. They found it on the ground right by him, didn't they?"

But I was troubled by the opinion of his own doctor that he fell because of a medical condition. I thought it curious that his doctor would volunteer a theory of causation to his employer. Mrs. Benning handed me the doctor's letter and it said exactly what she had described. The doctor practiced in Othello, a small rural community in central Washington and I decided I needed to meet with him and discuss George and his fall. I had Mrs. Benning sign an authorization for the doctor to disclose all of Mr. Benning's medical information to me and then called him.

Dr. Douglas was a friendly fellow and promptly agreed to meet with me to discuss the injury and death of his patient; George Benning. The drive to Othello was long and tedious and Othello was so small that I had no problem finding Dr. Douglas's clinic. He was one of two family doctors in the town and he had a small clinic building. On its outside wall was a simple sign: "Dr. Richard Douglas. Family practice".

There was only one patient in the waiting room and I was ushered into the Doctor's office after five or ten minutes by his nurse-receptionist. Richard Douglas was young; probably in his late twenties. He greeted me cordially but there were tell-tale signs that he was nervous about our meeting. I took a seat at the side of his desk while he sat in an office chair holding a file. I began by asking about his treatment of George.

"Well, George was a nice, friendly fellow but he had a serious weight problem."

"Did you treat him for his weight problem?"

"Yes, as much as a physician can. As you know, he was put on medical leave by the railroad because of his high blood pressure and his weight. So, I prescribed a blood pressure medication and tried to encourage him to change his diet so as to lose some weight. I was pleased that he followed up with the medication and his blood pressure came down from 170 over 120 to 140 over 85. That's still a little high, but within the normal range. He also lost seven or eight pounds so I certified him to return to duty."

"Did that mean that his health was normal?"

"Well, no. I can't say that because he had been carrying around that weight for six or seven years and his blood pressure had been above normal for several years. So, he was still at risk for a heart attack or a stroke and that's what I told the Milwaukee."

Two things struck me as odd in this interview. First, he held his patient file in front of him during the entire interview and seemed to look at it nervously several times. Second, I was struck by his apparent intimate relations with George's employer. Acting on instinct, I reached over to the file and said, "You don't mind me seeing his medical file do you?"

The doctor, looking uneasy, said, "Uh, no. Here it is," and passed it over to me. The very first item in the file was a letter to Dr. Douglas from the Milwaukee Railroad Western Division Medical Director. It read:

"Dear Dick,

I think it was a very good idea for you to submit your draft medical report to us before sending it to Mrs. Benning, where it would almost certainly fall into the hands of an attorney. As discussed in our phone conversation, I think it is a matter of good medical judgment to state that his primary cause of death was heart attack or stroke and second, his brain damage, instead of the reverse order which you put in your original draft. Given his medical history, heart attack or stroke is the most consistent causation. Feel free to call me if you have any other questions.

Sincerely,
Gustave De Hoyer, M.D.
Medical Director, Western Division, Milwaukee Railroad"

As I read this, my pulse quickened. This was the smoking gun! But, containing my excitement, I calmly asked Dr. Douglas why he had submitted a draft medical report to the Railroad's medical director and then revised his report to repeat his wording.

The doctor replied, somewhat defensively, "Well, this was my first experience with the death of an employee and I was unsure of how to write my medical report."

"Yes, but why ask a railroad official for an opinion?" I asked.

I was in for another surprise. "Well, I am the medical officer for the Milwaukee here and they are my employers."

"Does that mean that you are paid by the railroad?" I asked.

"Oh, sure," he replied.

"So were you George Benning's doctor or the Railroad's?" I asked.

"I guess I would have to say I was the Railroad's, although he was my patient," said Dr. Douglas.

That was enough. I had, without any advance plan, demolished the causation opinion of Dr. Douglas. I asked for and got photocopies of his correspondence with Dr. De Hoyer, bade the doctor a polite farewell and drove back to Seattle.

A little legal research unearthed the Boiler Safety Act ~ a Federal Statute that said if a railroad employee was injured or killed as a result of the failure of any equipment on the locomotive, the Railroad had absolute liability. Wow! Absolute liability. No need to prove negligence, no problem of contributory negligence by the employee, no problem of contribution to the injury by another employee or manufacturer. Absolute liability. I called Helen, my client, and told her of the legal responsibility of the Milwaukee. Two days later I filed a wrongful death action against the railroad, alleging failure of a piece of equipment attached to the locomotive, specifically, the armrest.

I was not surprised when their formal answer to our complaint was received; it alleged that George Benning fell out of their locomotive due to a heart attack or stroke and denying that it had anything to do with the armrest. The only surprise was seeing the name of the Railroad's attorney on their Answer: Richard Gemson. I had known Dick for ten years or more but I didn't know that he was now employed by the Milwaukee Railroad. Dick was a strange fellow; short and squat who spoke every sentence in the stentorian tones usually heard only from a podium. Well, at least I had someone on the other side I could talk to and negotiate with in a somewhat friendly tone.

We had alleged in the complaint that Helen suffered from the loss of her husband and what lawyers call "consortium", support, love and companionship and asked for a million dollars in damages. I felt some confidence that the railroad would settle this suit so I called Dick Gemson to sound him out on settlement prospects.

Dick began with his characteristic oratorical flourishes. "Well, Al, I don't think my client is going to pay anything to settle your claim in light of what the decedent's own doctor said was the cause of his fall. There is no liability here as far as we can see."

"Dick, I assume you're referring to Dr. Douglas's medical report?"

"Right. That plus his prior medical condition."

Then I dropped the bomb on him. "Dick I went out and met with the doctor and I have a copy of his original draft report where he said Mr. Benning died from his head injuries and his high blood pressure may have contributed to his death and then your guy told him to change his report and say it was a result of heart attack or stroke and not the fall. I also learned that the good doctor was on the payroll of the railroad and considered himself a railroad doctor rather than an independent practitioner. So his final report won't help your case. If you try to use it, I'll blow him out of the water."

Gemson's silence told me that all this had caught him off-guard and he was not prepared to press the matter further. In the weeks that followed Gemson continued to argue that it was a heart attack or stroke that led to Benning's fall, and I fully expected the railroad to use it in some way. But Gemson changed his strategy. The hint came when he began to refer to my client as "Big Helen". At first I thought he was just being sarcastic about the widow, Helen Benning. After repeatedly asking me,

"How's Big Helen today?"

I finally asked him, "What is this Big Helen business?"

"Oh," said Dick, "Didn't you know? All the railroaders on that line knew her. She ran a house of prostitution and she was well known, Big Helen was how she was called."

So, Gemson and the Milwaukee were going to try to undermine any sympathy factor by showing that the widow ran a house of prostitution.

But then Gemson unleashed his biggest weapon, "And, Al we can show that she never divorced her previous husband, so she wasn't legally married to Benning at all."

That was a mind numbing assertion. If she wasn't legally married to George, we had no standing to bring a wrongful death action for Helen. Wow! I told Dick I knew nothing about this but would certainly look into it. As soon as that call ended I called Helen and said I wanted to meet with her to talk about some important developments in her case.

I went up to her tiny apartment and sat down with her on the couch. When I told her what Gemson had said about her and her marriage, she was indignant. "Yes, I ran sporting houses for a while but I gave all that up when I married George. And I certainly was legally married to him. I can show you my divorce papers from my previous husband, Anthony Bandoni. I went to court in Spokane for that divorce and I remember it very well; it was in 1963."

She got up from the couch and went over to her desk. There she found a large manila envelope obviously containing documents. After rummaging in it for a minute or so, she triumphantly pulled out the divorce decree and brought it over to me. Sure enough, it was a Spokane County Superior Court Divorce decree between Helen and Anthony Bandoni. "I married George Benning three years after my divorce," she told me. I breathed a sigh of relief. Another of Dick Gemson's weapons neutralized.

I called Dick and told him that his claim of a bigamous marriage was baloney. I had the divorce decree. Unwilling to openly concede, he came up with a new defense. "Al, it was physically impossible for George Benning to reach out of the cab window and take down that number board. He couldn't have done it, especially with his girth."

Again, I called Helen and told her of this latest argument.

"Mr. Ziontz, that's ridiculous. George had been doing it for years. That was the fireman's duty. The only other way was to leave the cab, open the front door, climb up the ladder they have there in front and reach up and take it down. No fireman did it that way. It was too much trouble. Everybody sat out on the arm rest, reached up and lifted it off. Ask any of the engine crews; ask Larry Rauch."

I was reassured but not absolutely certain there was nothing to this argument. The only way was to see for myself how difficult it was. So I called my friend Dick Gemson and asked if he could bring one of their locomotives, like the one involved, over to Seattle so I could inspect it. Dick was surprisingly accommodating, "Sure. I can arrange that, but it will be in Tacoma."

A week later I drove to the Milwaukee yards in Tacoma and walked into a small office building. It was the yardmaster's office and Dick was waiting for me together with the yardmaster; Ed Hogan. After an exchange of greetings, Dick said, "We don't have the same locomotive, but one of the same type. They're identical and you can go up in the cab with Ed and me and look for yourself."

There ahead of me, standing on the tracks a hundred or so feet ahead, was a huge black locomotive and on its roof was the familiar diamond folding structure, called a pantograph, which transmitted electricity from overhead transmission wires down to the locomotive. It was a long, ugly looking machine, painted all black, though it had the logo of the Milwaukee road on the side of the engine. It was square with no rounded corners. I noted the height of the fireman's cab window. It would be a fearsome drop to the ground. The front end had a small entry door, though the main entry was through a door in the side of the locomotive. And yes, there was an armrest outside the cab window, a three foot length of wood covered with leather padding. It was held in place by a vertical flat rod at each end that slid down into metal brackets on the side of the cab beneath the window.

I had inspected the broken armrest weeks earlier and it was indeed a padded wooden attachment that seemed to have been improvised as an attachment and was not part of the original locomotive. It was broken in two about a third of the way from one end. I sat on the window sill of the locomotive cab and moved to the armrest. With one hand on the window frame I could easily reach up and grasp the sign board.

I felt confident I could persuade a jury that it was no coincidence that the broken armrest lay on the ground next to the fallen George Benning; that, in fact, George fell precisely because the armrest broke beneath him. Apparently, my opponent had lost confidence in his "impossibility" theory and now saw the risk of losing a jury trial. I settled the case with Dick for a healthy sum and "Big Helen" received a nest egg for her final years.

Gradually I became involved in more and more Indian law cases. In 1982 I got a phone call from the chairman of the Standing Rock Sioux Tribe in South Dakota. The state was claiming jurisdiction over hunting and fishing on lands within the reservation of the Lower Brule Tribe along the Missouri River. A South Dakota federal District Court had upheld the state's claims. If allowed to stand it would affect the hunting and fishing rights of three other Sioux tribes; the Standing Rock, the Cheyenne River and the Crow Creek Sioux tribes.

Standing Rock wanted to retain us to challenge this ruling by appealing to the Eighth Circuit. Since we were not the attorneys for the Lower Brule Sioux, we could do this only as *amicus curiae*, friends of the court. We agreed to do it. I had never had any contact with that tribe and I can only assume that our reputation as tribal attorneys led to their calling on us.

This court case was a result of the continuing efforts by state government to extend their authority over Indians and Indian lands. It is an old story and sadly, a continuing story. I have often asked myself why states are so unwilling to accept the limitation on their authority over Indians, so eager to extend that authority when any opportunity presents itself. That is what gave rise to this case.

The Missouri River Flood Control Act of 1944 was passed to construct two dams on the river by the Army Corps of Engineers in order to prevent the periodic and destructive flooding of lands in North and South Dakota. The dams would submerge riverfront areas of four Indian tribes; the Lower Brule Sioux, the Standing Rock Sioux, the Cheyenne River Sioux and the Crow Creek Sioux. The federal government provided funds to compensate the tribes for the loss of their lands and the relocation of improvements. The Act also established a flood control zone covering large areas of land taken by the government.

Soon after the lands were flooded, the State of South Dakota moved to establish its authority to regulate hunting and fishing on these lands. It claimed that authority even over lands within the boundaries of these four Sioux reservations. Its rationale was that the federal taking resulted in the removal of these lands from the reservations and a shrinking of the boundaries of the reservations, a legal outcome called, "disestablishment". Hence the general laws of South Dakota applied to all hunting and fishing, Indians and non-Indians alike.

The Lower Brule Sioux went to Federal Court to enjoin the state but the District Court held that the reservation was indeed diminished by the Federal taking and those lands were now outside the reservation and under state jurisdiction. The Lower Brule appealed to the Eighth Circuit Federal Court of Appeals and they were joined by the other three Sioux tribes along the river.

The tribes were all affected by this decision ~ it meant that all of their reservations were diminished and State jurisdiction over their members was extended on these lands. Dismay is not adequate to describe their reaction. The best hunting and fishing areas would now be transformed into state-policed territories, under the jurisdiction of South Dakota's laws and no longer protected by Federal treaties. They all felt the decision should not stand.

When we were called by the Standing Rock Sioux our authority to speak for the Lower Brule was limited by the fact that we were not representing them, but could only help them by appearing in the appeal as *amicus curiae* ~ friends of the court. So this was a rescue job; a takeover of a case that had been lost by the tribe's attorneys in the District Court. We were called in to try to save their bacon on appeal.

I asked one of my partners, Steve Anderson to work with me on this brief and he joined the effort with enthusiasm. Steve was one of the brightest guys in our firm. He did his undergraduate studies at Yale and then got his law degree at the University of Washington, racking up the kind of top honors only the best students get; editor of the Law Review, Order of the Coif and first in his class. A great legal talent.

We got to work on the legal research and soon found that an analysis of the legislative history did not support the District Court's conclusion that the Federal Statutes taking land from the five Sioux tribes to enable two major dams disestablished the boundaries of their reservations and abrogated their treaty hunting and fishing rights. There was no such language in the statute. In fact, we found that the Federal Statute specifically contemplated that regulation of those activities would fall to either the federal government or the US Army Corps of Engineers, not the State of South Dakota.

Steve and I wrote a carefully researched brief to the 8th Circuit Court of Appeals and I flew to St. Louis and argued the case. The attorneys for the other Sioux Tribes gave us the lead role even though we didn't represent the Appellant; we were only Amicus.

The argument went well and the decision of the court which came out in 1983, upheld our contention that there was no disestablishment of the boundaries of these reservations and no abrogation of their hunting and fishing rights. We had won. But the court remanded the case to the District Court to determine who would regulate non-Indian hunting and fishing in these areas.

We had no further contact with the tribes after our appellate victory and I don't know what the decision of the District Court was as to non-Indians. Our goal was to protect Indian treaty rights and in that we were successful. We had thwarted the attempt by the State of South Dakota to extend its jurisdiction over Indian hunting and fishing rights and abrogate Indian hunting and fishing treaty rights over lands now held to be within the boundaries of the Sioux Reservations. The case was typical of Tribal-State disputes. It seemed that states seized every opportunity to extend their authority over Indians and conversely, to oppose tribal claims of sovereignty over lands and persons as an invasion of State sovereignty. Sadly, this posture is only defeated by Indian victories in the courts.

The following year, 1994, Lennie's father Dave Guralnick, finally persuaded her to invite him to come and live in Seattle, a decision she reached reluctantly and only because he played on her sympathies by telling her how desperately lonely he was. She had misgivings, and his subsequent life in Seattle proved them justified. He slowly descended into dementia and Lennie had the burden of dealing with his irrational behavior. He lived on for ten years after his arrival in Seattle, making Lennie's life hellish, even to the point of having to petition the Superior Court to be appointed guardian because he was incapable of handling his own affairs. It ended in a court guardianship hearing in which she had to testify about his incompetence while he was present in the courtroom ~ a very painful experience for her.

Despite the fact that I remained active in Indian Law, my own practice seemed to shift more to tort practice, especially psychological malpractice, i.e. the misconduct of psychologists and therapists, and in one case, the sexual abuse of a patient.

I continued to write articles about topics in Indian Law. One of these was published in a book titled "The Aggressions of Civilization", and the other in a book titled, "Ethnic Groups and the State." Several of my articles were published in Encyclopedias of Indians in America.

By 1986, my back and leg pain had become so serious that I was ready for surgery. The operation was performed by a back specialist, Dr. Kenneth Leung. He did a fine job and my recovery was smooth and uneventful. After three or four weeks of convalescence, I began walking and had the delight of pain-free existence.

1986 was a year of crisis for the firm. Four malcontents, Mason

Morisset, Robert Pirtle and Tom Schlosser together with Frank Jozwiak, an associate, plotted to break up the firm, hoping to attract a majority of the members to join them. I use the world "plotted" because there was never any mention to me or the others in the firm of their plan. They were not successful and the majority of the partners remained; me, Rich Berley, Steve Chestnut, Steve Anderson and Marc Slonim. Under our partnership agreement we were the surviving firm and that meant we kept the office and the bulk of the accounts receivable. The malcontents departed. The fissure had been noticeable for some time, but I think it's fair to say, none of us ever thought it would come to a break-up of the firm.

We now had to take stock. First, we had lost a significant part of our client base; the Makahs, the Hoopas and the Tulalips. Second we were left paying rent on a much larger floor space than we needed for a smaller firm. At our first post-break-up meeting we agreed that the split was healthy because the rest of us were totally committed to professionalism rather than financial aggrandizement. We were unified. We agreed that we would have to redouble our efforts to enlarge our income base. We all felt we could do it.

Personally, I felt bitter that my old client, The Makah Tribe, had gone with Mason Morisset. But I had only myself to blame. After "U.S. v. Washington" was decided by the district court, where I had been one of the trial lawyers, it became transformed into a series of post-trial conflicts over fishing rights, not with the State of Washington, a battle to which I was intellectually and morally committed, but conflicts between the tribes. I had no interest in such battles and I turned that over to Mason Morisset. So, for the following three years, he was the lawyer who constantly dealt with the Makahs on fishing rights. Thus, it was natural they would turn to him to continue to represent them.

Aside from needing to work harder to replace lost income, we decided to downsize our office space. Our landlord was very accommodating and soon we had the same attractive basics; the front office, the library, the two conference rooms and five offices. The firm was renamed: Ziontz, Chestnut, Varnell, Berley and Slonim. We worked hard and new clients appeared; the Moapa Paiute Indian Tribe and the Fallon Paiute Shoshone, the latter two in Nevada, and the Peninsula Marketing Association, a group of fishermen on the Alaska Peninsula made up mostly of Aleuts. In addition, the Mille Lacs Band of Chippewas in Minnesota chose to stay with us.

Perhaps the happiest development was the return of the Makah Tribe about ten months after the split. It turned out that they had decided that Morisset had a serious conflict of interest since he represented the Tulalip Tribe and the Makahs had a running dispute with them over fishing. We still represented the Northern Cheyenne and the Northern Arapaho, so taken together we had a substantial volume of Indian work.

My Indian work focused mostly on the problems of the Makahs with Federal Ocean fishing rules, the Peninsula Marketing Association in Alaska, Northern Arapaho and Mille Lacs. Steve Chestnut had completely taken over the work of the Northern Cheyenne. But I had time to do tort work also. I settled a psychological malpractice case for $140,000, an Engineering Malpractice case for the Metlakatla Indian Community of Annette Island Alaska for $176,000, and four other cases for five figures. By 1987, as I approached my 59th year, I was the most productive member of the firm. After several years of feeling guilt at not bringing in major new clients or significant revenue, it was uplifting to feel a new sense of contribution to the firm. The challenge of helping our reconfigured law firm succeed seemed to inspire me to work harder and longer and resulted in successful outcomes.

I took this photo of my partner, Steve Chestnut, holding a painting of Alan Rowland, deceased former president of the Northern Cheyenne Tribal Council. Steve is wearing a war bonnet and beaded vest presented to him as honorary gifts on a visit to the Northern Cheyenne Reservation in 1996.

CHAPTER TWENTY-THREE

VISITING BETTEYLENE, LENNIE'S UNUSUAL JOB
AND
THE RUSSIANS

I had always wanted to see the South ~ a region of America that seemed to have a separate culture as well as a history of cruelty and rejection of liberal values. So, Lennie and I flew to Baltimore to start our Southern exploration. We had driven to Eastern North Carolina and found ourselves only a short distance from Johnson City, Tennessee, the home of my old prom date, Bettylene Franzus (nee Welch). A telephone call led to an invitation to visit and spend a night at her home.

I had not seen Bettylene since 1946, a span of over forty years, but only her appearance had changed, not her personality. She was still exuberant and garrulous. We spent the day with her and left the next day to continue our Southern tour. When we returned to Baltimore, we had visited Virginia, West Virginia, North Carolina and South Carolina and Georgia. Because we were tourists and did not stay in any place for more than a night, and had no personal contact with people, we learned almost nothing about the South, only its cityscapes and countryside. Somehow I had hoped to gain a better insight into the South of William Faulkner and Tennessee Williams. Why did I think a car trip along the freeways of the South would enlighten me?

Science Museum of Virginia
Richmond, West Virginia 1987

Top: Sitting in the cab of Locomotive No. 2732,
   a Chesapeake & Ohio Kanawha class steam engine

Bottom: On the running board of No. 2732

In 1987 Lennie was hired by the Center for the Prevention of Sexual and Domestic Violence; a job that promised to be personally satisfying. It didn't quite turn out as she had hoped. Despite its grandiose title, the Center was actually the creation of one woman -- a minister in the United Church of Christ. Its goal was to teach ministers and other religious leaders that men who abused children and women should not simply be forgiven -- that domestic abuse was symptomatic of serious psychological issues and either the man should go into treatment or the women should take strong preventative measures, e.g. court restraining orders, divorce or simply leaving the household of the abuser. Its founder, the Rev. Marie Fortune, was the driving force of the organization, Lennie was assigned to grant writing and fund raising and for several years found her work satisfying. After about four years Lennie's outspoken objection to what she called "loyalty oaths" which the Center proposed for all men who would work with abused children, led to the disaffection of her boss, Rev. Marie Fortune. Additionally the desire to introduce statistical computerized record keeping using the Excel program, a program which Lennie found difficult to master, led her to resign and leave the Center.

The following year, 1988, a letter arrived which would have momentous consequences. One day I went to the mailbox and found an envelope from the U.S.S.R. In it was a letter from Michael (or Mikhail) Gershunovskiy addressed to me. Since the letter was in Russian I had to get a translator. Luckily, our former neighbors, Valery Polack and his wife Zoya, were Russians. They were happy to translate it for me into English.

The letter was short; a single page. It began "Dear Uncle of mine" using a diminutive form of the Russian word for uncle implying a fond and close relation. It went on to say that my letter to my mother's sister, Basia, written twenty-four years earlier and never answered, had been received and carefully preserved. It implied that they were afraid to answer because any letter going to America would put the sender under suspicion by the government. Basia, the letter said, was the writer's grandmother, and she had died. Mikhail was a cousin, being the son of my aunt, but in Russian usage, he was a nephew. His mother, Fera, was actually my first cousin. He had decided to write to me and tell me about their family which consisted of his mother, his father, Mark, his wife Ilyona and their daughter Irina. The letter otherwise was not specific, ending only with the words, "If you like, write to me."

At first I had no idea how he had found my address. But when he wrote, "we had your letter" I remembered. Twenty-four years had passed since I wrote that letter to my aunt Basia in Kiev and by then I had totally forgotten about it. My letter was carefully safeguarded by her for twenty-four years, unanswered. It was only in 1990 when we visited Kiev and spoke to the Gershunovskiys that I understood why. When my letter was received, the Russian state was still tightly controlled by the Communist party. My cousin Fera worked for a government ministry and there was a risk that her job might be imperiled if a member of her family was corresponding with an American relative. At very least it would place them under suspicion. So, no answer.

I was excited. If only my mother had lived longer she would have been overjoyed to learn that her sister Basia had survived the war and that her daughter, Fera, was living in Kiev with her family. Since that was not to be, I felt I owed it to my mother, even though she was no longer alive, to do everything I could to establish contact and help her surviving family. With the aid of Valery and Zoya, I sent Mischa (the Russian familiar for Mikhail) a lengthy letter, describing my family and offering to help if he and his parents wanted to come to America. A series of letters back and forth from both Mischa and his mother followed. It should be remembered that in 1988 Russia was still a closed society, the Russian language was never heard in America, and personal contact with Russians was highly unusual.

The appearance of these Russian relatives was exciting. I wanted to know more about them and any other surviving relatives. Our correspondence was frustratingly vague; Fera wrote flowery letters, long on feelings, short on facts. Mischa said that he worked as an audio-visual technician but was otherwise vague. At the time the anti-Semitic attitudes and actions of the Russian government were widely reported and I felt that it was not just a matter of loyalty to my deceased mother, but a rescue of endangered family members, to get them out of Russia and over to America. Then Fera wrote that she was thinking of making a visit to America. A visit? I answered that we would be very happy to see her. But that idea never materialized.

As 1988 ended and 1989 began, I began to talk to them on overseas telephone. A very slow and uncertain process. I had Valery on the phone with me to translate but it led me to consider a weighty step – why not learn to speak Russian? So Lennie and I began to study Russian. It didn't take long to realize what a difficult project we had undertaken. Not only was the Cyrillic alphabet an obstacle, but the grammar was maddeningly difficult. In Russian not only the verbs are conjugated, but also the nouns. One had to memorize six cases which governed the nouns, and, depending on the nature of the sentence, one had to apply proper noun endings. I soon found that my ear was

Wedding photo of Mischa Gershunovsky (my Russian cousin)
and Alla (Ilyona) Gutkin, Kiev, Jan 25, 1986.
Mischa sent me this photo after correspondence started in 1988.

Left front and rear:
Abram and Sarah Gutkin, bride's parents
Right front and rear:
Mark and Esfier (Fera) Gershunovsky, groom's parents

attuned to Russian pronunciation and I could pronounce it well. But constructing a grammatically proper sentence took a lengthy analysis. We engaged our friend Zoya, who was a University of Washington Russian instructor, to tutor us. It helped, but only clarified the difficulties we faced. After six or seven months Lennie decided to abandon Russian studies. I continued and, over time, mastered some basic conversational skills.

Meanwhile, the phone conversations and letters continued. The project of getting them to America seemed stalled. Then in 1990 we learned that the Russian airline, Aeroflot, was offering a low cost flight and tour of the Soviet Union to Americans leaving from Seattle. This was a result of an event promoted here called, "The Goodwill Games" ~ a mini-Olympics where Soviet athletes competed against American athletes in Seattle. Since the airline had to fly their athletes to Seattle they promoted a tour to pay for their otherwise empty plane returning to the Soviet Union. The tour included Moscow, St. Petersburg (previously, Leningrad) and Kiev. Perfect! Lennie and I agreed that it was well worth the modest cost to take this opportunity to meet our family in Kiev face-to-face.

In July we flew to Russia. Most of our fellow passengers were either from Seattle or the Northwest and we came to know many of them. When I told them I was going to meet relatives in Kiev that I had never seen, they were fascinated and wanted to witness this historic meeting. After what seemed like an endless flight, we finally landed at Sheremeteyevo Airport in Moscow. It seemed unreal to think we were actually in Russia ~ that forbidden land. In the terminal I had an opportunity to speak my limited Russian for the first time. I needed to rent a luggage cart, but it accepted only rubles. Walking over to what seemed to be a passenger service kiosk staffed by two young women, I said (phonetically): "Oo menya, nyet rooblyeh" ~ I don't have any rubles. Smiling, one pointed to a kiosk on the other side of the terminal where a sign in English said, "Dollars exchanged for Rubles here".

From the terminal we all boarded a bus to our hotel; the Hotel Cosmos. The interior had a European look except for one thing; the lobby contained a row of slot machines! Just like Las Vegas. That evening we dined in the hotel dining room. First was a small bowl of cucumbers and tomatoes. Then, little cups of delicious potato salad and with it a small metal cup of some beef chips in sauce. On the side were pastry puffs. Delicious. After this we were served the main course; beef slices with rice and string beans. The beef was simply uncuttable and unchewable. Our waiter returned to our table offering to exchange money and sell us wrist watches with Gorbachev's likeness on its face. This was the first experience we had with the economic plight of ordinary Russians in the post-communist period. It would be repeated on the streets where we were constantly approached to exchange dollars or buy trinkets. It was surprising to encounter soldiers or sailors wearing their uniforms offering to sell insignia; belt buckles and even military hats for dollars.

This was 1990 and consumer goods were not available. There were long lines at the stores where people waited patiently with no idea of what might be available but ready to buy anything. Another sign of the collapsed economy was the proliferation of prostitutes. At the entrance of our hotel stood eight or nine young women, skimpily dressed and heavily made-up offering themselves to any foreign tourist.

During our second evening we returned to our room after dinner and the telephone rang. I picked it up expecting perhaps one of my Russian cousins, instead a female voice said, huskily, "You vant voman?" My response was "I have a woman, my wife," and hung up.

The following morning we were standing around the lobby of the hotel waiting for our tour bus. Lennie was sitting on a couch and next to her were three rather dark complexioned young men. I couldn't help but notice one of these guys was staring at me intensely, almost with hostility. I pondered this. What was there about me that would incite such a look? Deciding that perhaps he was interested in the Nikon suspended by a camera strap around my neck, I walked closer to him, pointed to my camera and said, "Are you interested in my camera?" He glared at me and said in a brusque tone: "No." Then I noticed his eyes were focused on my name tag. In bold printed letters it read: "Ziontz". One of his friends said, "We don't speak English." I asked him where they were from. "Syria," he said. Suddenly I understood the hostility. Even Americans hearing or reading the name "Ziontz" assume it has some relation to Zionism. To Syrians, one of the most virulent enemies of Israel in the Arab world, the name "Ziontz" must have conveyed the idea that I was somehow connected to Zionism. Thus the black looks.

The next day we taxied to the "Arbat" ~ a pedestrian mall along a street six or eight blocks long. The sidewalks were lined with hawkers; seeking buyers for everything from Matriochka dolls, i.e. nesting wooden dolls, to artists eagerly offering to draw portraits. The most striking activity were the political poets; young men standing and reciting their poems to groups of listeners. They recited with fervor and without notes, to a respectful audience. Nothing like this would be found in any American city and I doubt that it continues in Russia now, some twenty years later. It was, I think, a product of "glasnost", openness ~ a loosening of the restraints on speech in Russia after seventy five years of Communist Party rule. Our visit to Russia came at a time of profound change in their society and their government and we were seeing some of the results.

After four days in Moscow we departed for Kiev around midnight. The Moscow departure was chaotic but I didn't care. The long awaited meeting with my mother's relatives was about to occur. To use a phrase that my cousin Fera had written, it was like "being on the other side of the world." We landed in Kiev at 11 p.m. Kiev time and entered the crowded terminal scanning the faces in the waiting crowd looking for Mischa or Fera. Suddenly there was a flurry of movement and Mischa came running up to us, bearing a bouquet of flowers. He was immediately followed by his mother, Fera and her husband, Mark and Mischa's wife, Ilyona, or Alla as she is called in Russia.

The scene was hectic; kisses and embraces and the flashes of cameras by our tour friends who were eager to see this meeting. The tour company had a bus waiting to take us to our hotel, but Mischa insisted that we all ride the 22 kilometers from the airport to Kiev in his car. It was a dilapidated Lada; small and barely large enough to accommodate four passengers. Yet by sitting on laps, Mischa, Fera, Alla, Lennie and I all managed to squeeze in. Mark cheerfully volunteered to ride the bus into the city. It turned out to be a wonderful ride; everyone excitedly babbling and laughing as we spoke Russian and English incoherently to each other. We met in the hotel lobby and after a short time of confusing communication, agreed to meet the following morning.

The next day Mischa took us on a tour of the city in his car. In the early afternoon he drove us to the only remaining synagogue in Kiev. On a brick pillar in front of the building was a bronze plaque identifying it in Russian. Translated into English it read: "Kiev Jewish Religious Community". The building itself had the dignity of a synagogue; two stories tall, of red brick with white decorative stones outlining the windows and their round arches, decoratively carved wooden entrance doors and a tall metal gate opening into an interior courtyard. But missing was any Hebrew lettering or a "Mogen Dovid" or Star of David on its exterior.

Standing around in front of the building was a group of eight or ten elderly Jewish men. As we piled out of the car, one of them who spoke some English introduced himself and asked who we were. When we told them we were visiting from America he wanted to know if they could ask questions. The speaker was a young man who appeared to be a Chasid, a devout Jew, who spoke clear and almost unaccented English. His first question was how much phylacteries (tefillin in Yiddish) cost in America. I couldn't tell him, but told him if he went to any synagogue in America, they would give him a set. A group of the men surrounded us as we spoke and several began asking me questions ~ in Yiddish! To my surprise I was able to respond in Yiddish, dredging up from my childhood the folk language of our people.

I asked one of them if he had ever heard of Chodorkov, my Mother's place of birth. Several responded, yes, they knew of Chodorkov. When I asked how far it was from Kiev, they said, not far; maybe thirty or forty kilometers ~ eighteen to twenty four miles. When I told them my mother grew up there and I was thinking of visiting it, they said, with sadness in their faces, "You won't find any Jews there. The Germans killed all of them."

After our synagogue visit, Mischa drove us to the site of Babi Yar, the place where the Nazis lined up the Jews and shot them all standing at the edge of a ravine which was to be their grave. Over a period of two days they methodically killed over thirty thousand Jews ~ the entire remaining Jewish population of Kiev. It was the largest episode of civilian massacre in history.

Today the site is park like, with a rolling grassy slope showing the site of the ravine. The Russians had placed a tall stone monument over it, made up of non-descript figures, some writhing in agony. On the ground before it were three plaques, memorializing the nationalities of the victims. One was in Yiddish, using Hebrew letters. I wasn't able to read it, but I learned the government had only recently recognized that the Jews were the largest group of victims and had finally placed a plaque to acknowledge at least part of the awful truth of the massacre.

Our remaining time in Kiev was spent eating ~ at Fera and Mark's apartment, at Mischa and Alla's apartment and finally, at a dinner we hosted at our hotel. During the visit, we spoke to the Gershunovskiy's about coming to America. They were uncertain. At one point Mischa said, "If we come, maybe you can drive us to see the White House."

He assumed the State of Washington was the same as the city of Washington. With the aid of a map I showed him we lived on the other coast of America. In the end they were cautiously positive about making the move.

After four days in Kiev, seeing the home life of our relatives and the sights of the city, we left for Leningrad (now, St. Petersburg). That city was a surprise. It is beautiful, containing many canals that give it a resemblance to Venice. We visited the Hermitage and saw French Impressionist works we had never seen before, even in books. On the streets we were again besieged by young men offering to exchange money, sell military watches, caps, belts, medals, lacquered boxes, t-shirts and caviar.

Upon leaving Russia to return home, I had formed some distinct conclusions about the state of that country. I wrote in my notes:

- There seems to be general consensus among the populace that, the nation is in a state of crisis.

- Perestroika has not worked.

- Glasnost is good.

- No one has come forward with any widely accepted answers or program to deal with the crisis.

- There is profound cynicism about the government's competency and reliability.

- Autocracy and bureaucracy are unchanged.

- Gorbachev is ineffectual; all talk and no action.

- Anything can happen; even civil war or a military takeover.

- Given Russian history, the odds are against the establishment of a democratic state or a new social order without bloodshed.

On July 27 we flew home and my lawyer's life resumed. In December of 1991 the Gershunovskiys were granted refugee status and told us that they are all coming ~ Fera and Mark, Mischa and Alla and their little girl Irina, and Alla's Mother and Father, Avram and Sarah. Wow! I never dreamed it would take two years for this to happen. It seemed they were backing and filling and not eager to leave. Mischa was engaged in traveling to and from Bulgaria to bring back merchandise he could sell in Russia. He had dreams of amassing a large sum of money to bring to America.

I began to feel that the whole immigration plan had been quietly dropped by them. But in December of 1992, Fera wrote that their passport will expire February 17 and if they are going to come it has to be before then. On May 28, 1993, Mark and Fera arrived at Sea-Tac airport in Seattle. We had rented an apartment for them in Bellevue and bought furnishings and kitchenware. We even stocked their shelves with groceries. It was a momentous event for them and us. They settled in and we soon became accustomed to their presence in Bellevue.

Meanwhile, Mischa continued to put off any commitment to come here. In my phone calls to his home, Alla answers and he's never there, he's always off on a business trip. Then in 1998 I receive a letter from the State Department saying that their refugee status will be cancelled if they do not leave Russia soon. This prompted me to write a very strong letter to Mischa. I warned him that any hope of coming to America will end soon if he does not take action promptly. He will make far more money here than he could make in Kiev and by delaying, he is risking everything, I wrote. Whether it was my letter or Ukrainian musclemen taking over his business I don't know, but

Mark (center) and Fera (right) Gerashunovskiy arriving at SeaTac from Kiev in 1993

he and his family finally arrived in Seattle in August 1998 ~ five years after I had begun the process of getting them refugee status and doing the extensive and cumbersome paperwork of getting them admitted to the U.S.

My Russian relatives settled in Bellevue low income housing and began receiving financial support from State welfare. Soon after their arrival Mischa and Alla enrolled in Bellevue Community college taking English and computer programming courses. Fera took a course in English as a second language at a nearby school operated by the Chasidic community. Everyone's English improved except Fera's husband, Mark. He never learned or spoke any English. Soon

471

I decided to stop trying to speak to them in Russian; not only because my Russian is so limited but because it was more important for them to speak English than for me to speak Russian. I saw them frequently and Mischa and Alla often asked for my help in their English course. Alla's parents, Avram and Sarah Gutkin were also living in Seattle, but in the North End, not far from Martin and Sue's house. They were a warm, friendly pair and Avram, who was an engineer, was especially outgoing. Avram soon became an outspoken advocate for America.

During the period before the arrival of the relatives, I was trying to improve my Russian language ability and, knowing that the Jewish Family Service was assisting newly arrived Russian Jews, I called them and volunteered to serve as a language tutor and a mentor. I was assigned to help a Russian speaking family with the decidedly unJewish name of Stamati. On arriving at their small apartment in Bellevue, I met them. The head of the family was the mother, Roza a large, blond, handsome woman. Her husband's name was Vladimir and they had two children; Eugene, twenty three, married to a pretty woman named Lilya, and Alexander, called Sasha. All five lived together in a cramped apartment. Roza, Eugene, Lilya and Sasha knew a little English, Vladimir none.

I met with them twice a week and was soon embraced as a dear friend. They were from Moldova, an eastern province of Ukraine, now an independent country. They lived in the city of Kishinev, often mentioned in Yiddish culture. They were Jews only because Roza was born Jewish, but as with many Russian Jews, they had no knowledge of Judaism or even its vernacular, Yiddish. Roza's husband, Vladimir, was not Jewish and the entire family did not consider themselves Jews. Moldova abuts Rumania and Moldovian is a mix of Russian and

Rumanian. So their family name, Stamati, is Rumanian in origin. But Jewish or not, they were lovely people and over time a bond was forged between them and us. Although sadly, Vladimir has died, we remain close friends with the family.

Our exposure to the Gershunovskiys, the Gutkins and the Stamatis opened a window into Russian culture. We learned that Russians are very ceremonious about birthdays and holidays. Even now, Fera calls to "congratulate us" on Thanksgiving and all the Jewish holidays. They are deeply reliant on friendships because in the period of the Soviet system, one needed friends to survive. They seem to be somewhat racist and have not absorbed our values which prize the individual. But nevertheless, their dinner parties are overwhelming and they are fun.

1994 with my Russian relatives, Fera (left) Mark (right)

CHAPTER TWENTY-FOUR

LEAVING THE LAW, BACK SURGERY AGAIN, WHALING AND PHOTOGRAPHY

In 1994 I was approaching my sixty-sixth year and reached the decision to bring an end to my career as a lawyer and retire at the end of the year. This was a big deal. I had been in that firm and practiced with my partners for over thirty years. Retirement would mean a huge change in my life ~ I would be entering unknown territory. But I was actually quite ready for it.

It may sound strange, but I never liked being a lawyer, even though I had enjoyed success and modest fame. But I always felt that I didn't have the mind for law and my poor academic performance in law school seemed to confirm that. Perhaps more importantly, I didn't enjoy the adversarial nature of practice. There was tension; deadlines, the risk of making a big mistake, the risk of losing a case. Now a rational view would dismiss these as without any basis in fact. I had won many cases, argued to juries, judges, appellate courts and even the Supreme Court. But I could never rid myself of this deep seated unease. My so-called "sabbatical" in 1981 was actually an effort to test the waters of academia in order to see if I would succeed and be happy there. As it turned out I had modest success but found it didn't suit me. No, Law was my home and I had to stay with it to the end.

I had always known that retirement was in my future at some far off date and luckily had begun putting money aside out of my monthly draws into my investment account for many years. For some reason, I bought substantial amounts of stock in Microsoft and by 1981 the value of that investment had skyrocketed. Looking at my total portfolio I had enough money put aside for us to live on for many years. I was able to RETIRE!

There was another reason I looked forward to retirement with eagerness. I knew exactly what I was going to do. I had been doing art photography whenever I had an opportunity since 1975. But I was a complete amateur. I had never used a darkroom, studio lighting or advanced cameras. Now I could enroll in some photography school and learn about these things. I could do art photography to my heart's content and maybe create some worthwhile pictures. I couldn't wait to start on this road.

The photographer 1993

I had thought about retiring at the end of 1994, but before I reached that date I was confronted by a serious medical problem. Ever since my sabbatical year of 1981, I had suffered from low back problems; at times better, at times worse. I had back surgery in 1984 which was quite successful in relieving pain. Now, ten years later, the problem returned. I returned to the surgeon who did my first back surgery, Dr. Kenneth Leung. I had complete trust in him. So, on March 17, 1994 I underwent back surgery again, called a laminectomy to relieve pressure on my sciatic nerve.

When I was preparing for discharge from the hospital, Dr. Leung told me to slowly resume normal activities but do some walking every day, increasing the distance each time. After resting at home for a few days I decided it was time to begin the walking exercise that was recommended by my doctor. One fine day I walked out of the house and began walking along the sidewalk. When I had traveled a half block I began feeling a strange numbness in my legs. I had better go back home, I thought, and began the return. I had reached the corner opposite our house and stepped off the low curb onto the street. There was only a difference of about three of four inches from the sidewalk to the street and while I felt some numbness in my legs, there was nothing to indicate stepping down would be anything troublesome. But, when I stepped down, my right leg crumpled like it was spaghetti. I fell heavily onto the street. This was a shock. I had never fallen like this before. After lying there for a minute to assess my condition, I got to my feet and resumed my walk home.

This was the first sign that I had serious neuropathy in my legs. The neuropathy gradually worsened and my neurologist offered no remedy. In the next twenty years I became unable to walk a hundred yards and had to resort to a walker. To date my fall has reoccurred more than sixty times. But that came later. By June I was back at work and life returned to normal. In August I announced to my partners that I would retire effective December 31, 1994.

On December 15, the partners held a retirement party for me. I was touched by their sentimental speeches and particularly by the many testimonial letters of appreciation I received from the tribes. The entire affair was a moving experience.

1994 December 15th - my retirement party

Top Left: Steve Chestnut orating
Bottom Left: Studying a box of cognac with Steve looking on
Right: I was caught unawares

In January we took a trip to Mexico, renting a house in Puerta Vallarta. Living in a Mexican mixed class neighborhood was an introduction to the ordinary life of the people. We shopped at the local grocery store, walked around the neighborhood, across the cancha, the athletic field, and took the local bus to the beach. My Spanish was good enough to converse, though not in their vernacular and not elegantly. After ten days we flew to Guadalajara, rented a car and drove to many of Mexico's cities, taking eighteen days. I noted in my log that, "we had a wonderful time."

By the Pool in Puerta Vallarta in Mexico, 1988

Life was good till May but I began to experience nerve pain in my right leg again. Oh, oh! It was just over a year since my back surgery and now the old symptoms had returned. I saw my orthopedic surgeon, but he said it was too soon after my last surgery to consider surgery now. It was my internist who prescribed exercise five days a week. Two weeks of this and my back and leg pain disappeared. In July I decided to start serious photography.

Our daughter worked at a city office in the Rainier Valley, a district heavily populated by African Americans. I wanted to do photography there. I began by meeting with the director of the Rainier Valley Boys and Girls Club. He was happy to have me photograph their kids and their activities. I spent my days photographing the wonderful kids there; playing pool, playing basketball, at parents' night, and a track meet. It was my introduction to persuading strangers that I was a photographer and setting up "shoots".

This was a new role for me ~ totally different than practicing law. Even though I had been doing photography for twenty years, it was always as the anonymous, unnoticed man with a camera. Now I had to meet people face to face and establish a warm atmosphere. I was a photographer. It was a pleasant surprise to find how easy it was, maybe because people assumed I was working for some periodical. I think the public is so attuned to seeing photographers at work everywhere that the role was legitimized and they rarely challenged me.

The Rainier Valley community had a Summer Festival and I asked if I could display my photographs of the children of the Boys and Girls Club for a show. They agreed and I was thrilled. I had all the photographs matted and an exhibit was held in the basement of the community center. My first show!

In September of 1995 I began classes at a fine art photography school ~ Photographic Center Northwest. For the first time I experienced a teaching environment where language skills didn't count ~ only the quality of the image. I learned darkroom technique in both black and white and color; I learned the subtleties of exposure and the effects of long lenses and wide angle lenses. I studied color and portraiture and the history of photography. I took a course in studio lighting and learned about strobes and strobe light meters. This enticed me to try shooting models so I bought a set of studio strobes, reflectors and a backdrop. Then I boldly went to modeling agencies and offered to do photo shoots of their aspiring candidates at no charge, giving the subjects their photographs so they could use them as promotional samples.

I arranged a studio in my recreation room on the lower level of our Mercer Island house, using strobes, a roll-down white backdrop and props. The agencies sent me a number of aspiring young models, most of them under twenty one. I mastered the lighting and exposure techniques and found myself shooting these young women in poses, as imaginative as I could conceive. But it was all unsatisfying. These girls were nothing but pretty faces and bodies, without character, and the photographs were images that had been done by others. After about a year I tired of it. I wanted to shoot people in their own environment, unposed and conveying something about them and their lives.

I conceived a plan of shooting the lives of women ~ not single poses, but a series based on their ordinary actions and activities during their day. My goal was to capture them in unguarded and unpretentious moments ~ ignoring the presence of a photographer and being themselves. I thought the project had a potential for publication so I advertised for subjects for a photography book.

Self-portrait, age 70
1998

ANNOUNCEMENTS

WOMEN OVER 30 I am a photographer working on a book, "The Femine Image". I am looking for women 30 & over, of any color or ethnicity, to photograph. I photograph the daily lives of ordinary women. You will recieve photographs in compensation for participating in this project. References furnished. If you are interested please call Al at 206-232-5647 for an interview.

One of the four ads I placed seeking subjects for
"The Feminine Image"

I posted notices on two local college campuses and ran ads in two Seattle alternative newspapers, thinking their readers were likely to be women who were more unorthodox and more adventurous. Soon, I began receiving calls. My method was to meet prospective subjects in a coffee shop, discuss their daily activities, show them my portfolio and give them references. Their only compensation was prints of all their photographs and of course, if a book eventually were published, their images would be immortal.

The year was 2000 and I was seventy two at the time. I wanted to demonstrate that I was a legitimate photographer. My age of seventy two should give these women some confidence that my only object was photography ~ nothing else. Starting with my first respondent, I established a polite but friendly atmosphere. After looking at my portfolio I would explain my objective; to try to bridge the gap of wariness and otherness and capture on film each of them in normal, unguarded and unposed, activities.

My method was, to say the least, unorthodox. I asked each of them to allow me to enter their bedroom when they were waking or still asleep, and then begin shooting, following them throughout their day. The goal was to capture the images of the lives of ordinary women in their own activities. To each, I made it clear that if they wanted privacy, they had only to say the word and I would stop the photography and leave the room. If they said nothing, I would continue shooting.

This photography project continued for two years and during that time I shot over forty women of all ages. Early on I decided that I wanted only subjects over thirty years of age. I was looking for women whose faces showed character, experience or emotion. I was well aware that my photography could be attacked as sexist, exploitative or examples of what feminists called, "the male gaze". In my statements I tried to meet these arguments and most of the viewers accepted the photographs as legitimate art.

My photos adorning the wall of our Bellevue House

In our Mercer Island home downstairs gallery 1996
"Happy Birthday and Congratulations on your show!"

After two years of photographing my subjects I had a portfolio of images I thought were beautiful. Then I began the search for a publisher. I soon learned that an unknown photographer had no chance of getting a publisher to risk an investment in a book of his photography. I explored every avenue I could find before giving up. No book was ever published and the only result is a wall of photographs in our home of many of these women.

My career as a serious photographer lasted from 1995 to 2004, nine years. During that time I worked hard, spending hundreds of hours in the darkroom and doing all kinds of photography; event photography, street photography, model photography, portraiture, photo essays and occasionally, nature photography. In the end I was forced to stop because of the worsening pain in my back and legs brought on by the recurrence of spinal stenosis.

My accomplishments in photography are marked by the exhibitions of my photographs in shows where they were selected by independent jurors. Here is the record:

- Rainier Valley Cultural Center, 1996.

- Open show at the Photographic Center Northwest, Seattle, 1997.

- Juried show at the Benham Gallery, Seattle, 1997.

- Juried show at the Benham Gallery, Seattle, 1998.

- Juried show at Seattle Art Museum, Trevor Fairbrother, curator, 1998.

- Juried show at Seattle Art Museum, 1999.

At my One Man Show in San Francisco 2001

- Juried show at Seattle Art Museum, 2000.

- Juried show at Photographic Center Northwest, 2000.

- Juried show at Seattle Art Museum, Tara Young, Assistant Curator of Modern Art, juror, 2001.

- One Man Show, University of California, Berkeley, displayed in their San Francisco Gallery, 2001.

- Seattle Center, Matthew Kangas, critic for Art in America, Juror. 2002.

- Barrett Art Center, Poughkeepsie, N.Y., Joan Young Curator, Guggenheim Museum, N.Y. 2002.

- Cambridge, Mass. National Prize Show, Marc Pachter, Director of the National Portrait Gallery, Washington, D.C., curator. 2003.

- International Juried Competition, Soho 20, Chelsea Gallery, N.Y. Janet Koplos, Senior Editor, Art In America, Juror. 2003.

- One Man Show, Portland State University, 2003.

- Annual International Photography Competition, Fraser Gallery, Bethesda, Md. Phillip Brookman, Senior Curator of Photography and Media Arts, the Corcoran Gallery, Washington, D.C. juror. 2003.

- Annual Juried Exhibition, Salmagundi Club, N.Y. 2003.

- Photographic Center N.W. juried competition. Patricia McDonnell, Chief Curator, Tacoma Art Museum, Juror. 2004.

My work in photography took me far away from Indian law. I was so deeply absorbed by it that I hadn't visited the Makah reservation after my retirement in 1994. Still, I followed the occasional scraps of news about Indian life and especially the Makahs.

The Makahs had been the premier whalers of the Pacific Northwest. Indeed, whaling was central to their culture. The figure of the whale is woven in their baskets, sewn on their blankets and celebrated in song and ceremony. They stopped whaling in 1929 only because commercial whalers had so decimated the stocks of the grey whale that it was no longer commercially feasible to continue. Later, the federal government placed the grey whale on the endangered species list, thus prohibiting any further commercial whaling. But by 1993, the stock of the grey whale had grown to 26,000 ~ near their historic highest level and the federal government removed them from the endangered species list. This news was greeted with joy and the Makahs announced in 1995 that they would conduct a whale hunt.

The Makahs were fully aware of the public reaction to this announcement and they were careful to say that the hunt would be conducted in the traditional manner; using a harpoonist in a whaling canoe to strike the whale while a rifleman was positioned in a chase boat to place a bullet at the base of the whale's brain, thus causing an immediate and painless death. This method was based on the advice of a professor of veterinary medicine from Maryland who had been retained to assure that there would not be any suffering by the whale, a humane method being required by the International Whaling Commission.

Still, there was the predictable uproar from the animal rights community and a plethora of op-ed pieces attacking the Makahs. I took it on myself to speak out publicly in defense of the Makahs. I was becoming increasingly disturbed at the absence of any Makah voice in the ongoing public attack on Makah whaling. Finally, I called the chairman of the whaling commission and told him that someone had to publicly defend the rights of the Makah to conduct their whale hunt.

A few days later the tribal chairman called me at home and asked me to handle their "public relations". I demurred saying I didn't do public relations and told him to get in touch with a public relations firm. The chairman, Ben Johnson, replied, "No, Al. We want you to handle that, because you know our history and you can do a good job of telling our story."

I thought about it for only a moment. After all, I had retired from law practice three years earlier and was now deeply immersed in photography. But I reminded myself of a principle I had adopted when I retired: From here on, I will do only what I want to do. In but a moment I concluded that this was a challenge I wanted to take. "Okay, I'll do it Ben," I said.

I plunged into the work of defending their whaling right and began by meeting with the whaling commission. I met with this group of fifteen Makah men at Neah Bay and told them they were getting clobbered in the court of public opinion. I put it this way, "It's like a football game with only one team on the field running up and down scoring touchdowns. You have to get out there."

When I asked if they had ever spoken to the press, they said that while there had been numerous calls and requests for interviews, they had turned them all down. "Why?" I asked. Because like many Indians they had no experience talking to the press and they were fearful that the press would not understand their side of the story. I assured them they had a powerful story to tell and they agreed to hold a press conference on the reservation.

The date was set and I called all the newspaper and TV outlets to invite them to attend. I correctly assumed the press was hungering to hear the Makah side. A week later, a large group of reporters, cameramen and journalists crowded into the conference room at the Makah Museum. At the table in the front of the room sat the chairman of the Makah Whaling Commission, the Chairman of the Makah Tribe, the whaling harpooner, and the veterinary professor who was their consultant on humane killing of the whale. In turn they each spoke, clearly and knowledgeably about the manner of their proposed whale hunt. The professor held up the .50 caliber rifle that would be used to finish off the whale. The press conference was an unqualified success. It was reported in local and national newspapers and shown on all the local TV outlets.

The press conference was only the beginning of the Makah campaign. I prepared a "fact sheet" to be distributed to the press, answering all the questions that had been raised and making it clear that this was a cultural event with no commercial purposes. Later I helped the chairman of the whaling commission write an op-ed piece explaining the historical and cultural meaning of the event. I spoke publicly at several well-attended events, vigorously defending the Makah's legal right to conduct a whale hunt and rebutting the specious arguments made against it. The net result was that the press was neutralized and while there was no way of knowing whether the Makah story had influenced a majority of the public, it had least countered the most vitriolic and one-sided views. I spoke and wrote at length and was able to neutralize some of the more hysterical and unfounded charges of the anti-Makah forces. The Makah were grateful that I had made a serious case on their behalf.

On May 17, 1999, the Makah whaling crew harpooned their first whale in seventy years. It was a day of great jubilation on the Makah Reservation. On May 22, 1999, the Saturday following their historic capture of a grey whale, the tribe announced a celebration and invited tribes throughout Washington, and other Western states was well, to attend. I was personally invited by the tribal chairman and Lennie and I went.

There were some 1500 persons crowding the high school gymnasium and the atmosphere was one of elation. I was ushered up to the head table. After a traditional lunch, there was a Makah prayer followed by Makah dancers. Lennie and I had another commitment in Seattle, so at three o'clock, I quietly said my farewells to the chairman. To my surprise, he asked me to wait, had me get up on the speakers platform and introduced me as, "the man who has made all this possible." I was flattered and surprised by his description of the importance of my role. Then he asked me to step forward and address the people.

As I looked out on the sea of faces I expected some polite applause when the introduction was ended and I stepped forward to speak. I was not prepared for what followed. The entire assembly of 1500 people got to its feet, cheering and applauding. I didn't know what to do, so I just stood there and said "thank you" over and over again. But the cheering and applause didn't stop. It went on and on. Never in my life had I been the object of such public acclaim. I had to ask them to stop. I made some brief remarks reminding them of some of the history in which I played a personal role. Then I turned to leave, only to be acclaimed again with a standing ovation. I thought that this was unquestionably the greatest day of my life.

Looking back at the state of Indian affairs from the perspective of fifty years, I see the huge strides the Indian people have made ~ strides which were only dreamed of in 1964 when I first began doing Indian law. Then, the Indian people were seen as an anachronism by the American people. They were a throwback to a time in our history long since passed, known to most Americans only by the distortions of movies. Worse, their tribal culture was viewed as a hindrance to their well-being. Only by assimilating, most felt, could they hope to improve their lives. Tribal governments were, almost universally, a hollow shell, without any real power of government, subservient to the Bureau of Indian Affairs and given little respect by state government. Few Americans were familiar with the government experiment of the fifties called, appropriately, "termination". That program was intended to end the Indians' separate status, sell off the reservations and meld the Indian people into the non-Indian society. It was a dismal failure and was cancelled after a few years. But Indians never forgot the threat that once nearly ended tribal life in America.

The transformation of Indian life was a product of several major developments; court decisions upholding Indian treaty rights (such as U.S. v. Washington), the 1965 War Against Poverty programs which infused federal funds into tribes and enabled them to be masters in their own house, and most recently the creation of casinos on many reservations. But the most important development was the growth in the skills of self-government by the Indians themselves. Wise decision-making by the tribal councils is now apparent. They have developed organic branches of their government to serve their members; housing, policing, courts, health programs, resource management, and importantly, participation in local and state government. Their voices, silent for hundreds of years, are now heard by state governments and by the public. Perhaps their greatest influence has been their passionate defense of the environment; lands, water, timber, fish and clean air. Their voices are powerful and are listened to since they, unlike other public interest groups, have legally enforceable rights in their environment. Now, they participate in all public decision making which involve the environment; oil trains, oil pipelines, water purity, dams, industrial pollution. One cannot read a newspaper article about these issues without finding tribal input mentioned. At long last, tribal governments are respected members of the family of American government. But battles remain; powerful interest groups oppose them, many state governments are reluctant to recognize their sovereignty and their future is not completely secure.

My life had been consumed by my photography. I developed enough mastery to create photographs that were respected and admired by art critics. I thought seriously about the deeper implications of photography. Time was like a river, flowing and unstoppable. There was only one way to freeze time ~ a photograph. Often I looked at the portraits hanging on my wall and reflecting sadly that all these people no longer had the same appearance and, indeed many of them were dead. That was a sobering thought. They lived only in their photographs.

Sadly, my photographic career was brought to an end by the recurrence of back problems. Today it is 2016, and I have trouble simply walking or standing for any period of time. A neurologist has told me it is neuropathy in the legs, brought on by my back surgeries, and there is no cure. Two years ago I reluctantly bought a walker, one of those devices with four wheels and handlebars. Using it, I can walk for a block or two. Without it, I am limited to about a hundred yards. Worse, my stability has been affected and I am unsteady on my feet.

At Sleeping Lady Mountain Hotel Resort, 3.4 miles from Leavenworth, WA 2005

Since 2011 I have fallen over seventy times. Except for one minor elbow fracture, which didn't' need a cast; I have not broken any bones. But my gait is stiff and unnatural. I am careful to use my hand on a wall or railing when using stairs.

In 2003, after a farewell party to our Mercer Island house, a house we had lived in since 1964, we sold it and bought a modest town house in Bellevue, a suburb of Seattle. Living in Bellevue brought surprises. It was more interesting than Mercer Island; many more stores, restaurants and amenities. Best of all our town house was more aesthetically satisfying than our big Mercer Island house.

We redecorated the interior; a dramatic red wall, new light fixtures in our hall and dining room, and interesting ironwork balustrades on the stairway leading to the second floor. We found a designer array for our books and photographs and a matching console for the Bang and Olufsen stereo. The living room now has a centerpiece of black granite framing the fireplace with a white mantelpiece atop and bookcases on both facing walls whose shelves are filled with books, interspersed with family photographs and colorful book jackets displayed vertically on brackets. It is a delight to the eye, or at least my eyes.

In May of 2005, Lennie and I went to Neah Bay at the invitation of the Makah Tribe to take part in their celebration of the hundred and fifty years since the Treaty of Neah Bay. At the High School gym were the big doings. There were opening ceremonies and then a halibut lunch was served to some four hundred invited guests. A High School class performed a reenactment of the treaty signing. After that, to my surprise, I was asked to be the keynote speaker. I got up on the stage and for twenty minutes spoke, giving the history of my relations with the tribe. I was taken by surprise when the crowd broke into applause several times. Afterward a tribal council member presented me with a carved wooden replica of a Makah whaling canoe. As if that weren't enough, I was given a beautifully embroidered windbreaker and an equally beautifully embroidered vest. Not finished with their giving, they then handed me a $20 bill, and two caps with Makah emblems and two tee shirts with commemorative designs.

Speaking to the Makah Tribe at Treaty Day Celebration 2005

The following week, the chairman, Ben Johnson came over to me and said people had been coming up to him in the village and telling him how much my speech meant to them. I wrote in my journal: "It doesn't get much better than this. I'm a very lucky man."

In August of 2005, I decided to write my memoirs. I began writing and finished six months later. The writing came easily to me. I had told my story to others many times. I submitted it to the University of Washington Press. They were interested in publishing the book, but first it had to be sent out to "readers" who would provide opinions and corrections. I never dreamed the process would take four years. My book, "A Lawyer In Indian Country" was published in 2009.

I turned eighty in August of 2008 and Lennie organized a party at Ponti's for the occasion. My eightieth birthday party was no ordinary party. Fifty friends had come to celebrate the occasion. Each of our children came forward and gave a touching, funny and loving talk. Following these speeches guests stood to deliver their sentiments. Steve Chestnut choked up with emotion. Nate Ross delivered a heartfelt little talk titled, "The Renaissance Man". Thelma Sameth and Ina Willner both spoke of me admiringly and Myra Franklin read a poem she and her husband, Abby had composed. A really touching tribute. A week or so after the party I was told by one of my partners that the firm had made a donation of $1,000 to the Makah Tribe in honor of my birthday.

My 80th birthday celebration at Ponti's Restaurant, Seattle 2008

At my 80th Birthday Party
Top: Lennie and I
2nd row: (L) Jeff, (R) Martin . 3rd row: (L) Ellen, (R) Ron

CHAPTER TWENTY-FIVE

LIVING IN THE RED ZONE

This chapter was the original beginning of this autobiography. I began it in my 80th year, a time when we live "IN THE RED ZONE". It began as late night ruminations and only much later did I decide to undertake a full scale autobiography. This chapter began as a journal, with regular entries documenting my thoughts and events in our lives. It was only when my friends Linda Chan and Evan Upchurch persuaded me that the colorful incidents that I had related to them be included in my autobiography that a journal morphed into a lengthy memoir. The reader may recognize a change in style from the preceding chapters and this is the explanation.

Last month I finished reading Boswell's life of Johnson, 999 pages of unbelievably tiny print. It took over a month to plow through this immense collection of quotidian events in the life of this English man of letters ~ Dr. Samuel Johnson. His biographer, James Boswell, spent years fawning on Johnson and recording his utterances.

Johnson, a man famous for creating the English dictionary, declaimed on almost everything; religion, law, science, politics, literature, human nature, women, marriage, France and America (he despised both). Boswell shows him to be arrogant, pompous, intolerant and a believer in the class system. The lower classes belonged there by virtue of what Johnson believed was their innate inferiority. While it certainly was not Boswell's intention to portray him in anything but a worshipful light, the picture of Johnson that emerged from these pages is one of an arrogant member of the British upper class of his time.

Until I reached the final section dealing with the decline in Johnson's health and ultimate death, I dismissed him as a despicable human being. But I found myself reading with sympathy as Johnson's life became more circumscribed by his asthma and "dropsy" ~ probably an accumulation of fluid in the body due to congestive heart failure. When Boswell tells us that Johnson's health had so deteriorated that he could not walk, it struck a responsive chord. I know what this is like, I cannot walk either. And, like Johnson, I have asthma. But in his final months he lives in terror, as his thoughts dwell more and more on the approach of death because of his firm belief in the reality of the afterlife and his dread of being consigned to the Inferno because of his sins, (probably his habit of frequenting prostitutes).

Well, here I part company with Johnson, both because I did not frequent prostitutes and because I have no belief in the afterlife. But I too feel the presence of approaching death. Five months ago I celebrated my 80th birthday. I am in the "red zone"; a period when a person is reaching the end of the span of human life and death can strike at any time, swiftly or slowly, with or without warning. My body reminds me daily that the end is approaching. I have serious heart disease ~ blockage of the coronary arteries ~ and have had two stents implanted to keep one of the arteries open. A long standing asthma problem has worsened and now seems more like emphysema; wheezing when I breathe and a frightening struggle for air when I walk more than a hundred yards. This has now been diagnosed as COPD, a chronic and irreversible lung disease. Add to this a constant struggle with pain resulting from twenty years of low back nerve pressure. All these cause my comfort zone to narrow to sitting, avoiding any but short walks or limited standing.

Meanwhile, thoughts of my death have become so commonplace for me that they are now a familiar part of my life; they are with me every night. My body reminds me constantly that the end is approaching. The default state of mind, is denial. It works. I go on denying, brushing aside all these intimations of my mortality and reverting to the lifelong, powerful idea of Alvin ~ a being who is so unique and wonderful that nothing really bad can happen to him. Since I have never had a heart attack or suffered from angina, denial is easy. It is a comfortable illusion, but I know better. At this writing I am eighty-seven and the horizon is approaching.

My physical deterioration seems to have begun progressing faster since my 80th birthday. Routine functions become more difficult. Denial becomes less persuasive each time I climb the stairs to my loft; the effort leaves me gasping for air. As if that weren't bad enough, there is the wheeze ~ a loud, audible, ugly whistling with each breath that only seems to get worse. Although it seems to be confined to evenings, yet its regular appearance, despite all the respiratory medications I am taking, makes it difficult to maintain a state of denial. Particularly when, after walking, an effort that soon produces breathing desperation, I gratefully collapse into a chair to "catch my breath", I see the end approaching. Could this be the end of Alvin?

I am deeply ambivalent about such thoughts; on the one hand I brush them aside, suppress them; on the other I can clearly see my demise and the predictable aftermath. First ~ painfully first ~ is what I know will be Lennie's anguish at the loss. I can hardly bear to consider her desolation. She has lived in terror these past years anticipating the event. She has even tried to extirpate her deep and terrible fear by writing a book that anticipates the very thing she fears the most. I move beyond these depressing thoughts to the almost embarrassingly commonplace ones, like what my obituary will say (I've already written it) to the scene in the funeral chapel. I can calmly envision it, having been in that chapel for numerous funerals. I know who will be there ~ about sixty or seventy people; my immediate family, my law firm, the Russians, and Lennie's friends. There may even be a delegation from the Makah Indian Tribe, though this is highly unlikely because they will need several days to arrange such a junket and Jewish funeral services are rarely held more than a day or two following the death. Too bad I can't be there to enjoy it.

There are actually some rich compensations living in the red zone. One of them is an overview of my life. My lifetime is now "in the books", all of the big events and their consequences, my accomplishments, my offspring and the remarkable woman who is my wife who continues to inspire my love and admiration, are all "fait accompli". Daily I congratulate myself on my good fortune in having a mate who gives of herself unstintingly out of a bottomless well of love for me.

Such a life I have had! Late at night, when I am alone, while Lennie is in bed watching television behind the closed doors of the bedroom, I turn off all the lamps in the living room but one, set at the dimmest level, and I sit in the semidarkness and listen to chamber music reflecting on the present in light of the past. I begin with a visual scan of the living room. Its objects, its spaces and its colors, which never fail to please. I sit in an armchair facing the open room. To my right, the high red wall leads the eye up to the junction with a rising sloped ceiling. The ceiling rises to a loft above the ground floor. All that is visible from below is a low open wall, a balcony wall, running across the width of the entire loft. The effect is always surprising and pleasing ~ a space defined by the juxtaposition of two large planes; the high red wall intersected at right angles by a horizontal bridge, the balcony wall, suspended over the dining room. In the darkness behind this low wall is my loft. Beneath the intersection of the bridge and the living room wall on the right is a tunnel-like corridor forming a passage to the entrance hall of the house. On each wall of the passageway are mounted some of my best photographs, highlighted at night if I turn on a bank of "spots" suspended from the ceiling.

The living room itself is dominated by two bookcases facing each other on opposite walls. The bookcase on my left consists of two tall conventional bookcases joined together, while the other on my right, is a striking unconventional array. It is made up of alternating wooden and glass shelving cantilevered out from a honey colored wooden panel mounted on the wall. On the shelving are groups of books separated by bookends. In the spaces between the groups are decorative objects; Northwest coast Indian woven baskets and an Indian rattle in the form of a bird with strands of cedar bark dangling from its head, a ceramic teapot representing the figure of Elvis Presley on a motorcycle, two East Indian objects, one representing the goddess Shiva, dancing; the other a tiny ceramic sculpture of an Indian artisan sitting cross-legged before a tiny fire and hammering away at an object, a carved wooden dog, yellow with black circles, his jaws open displaying his teeth.

These objects form the backdrop to an almost theatrical experience as I sit in this room, the drama heightened by the glow of the single lamp and the shadows it casts upwards on the wall, indulging in a reverie as I listen to music and ruminate on my life and its approaching end.

I can sit like this for an hour or more till the bedtime hour of eleven o'clock arrives and I reluctantly shut down the music, turn off the lamp and make my way to the bedroom. Here I face the tiresome process of pill-taking (four different ones), using an inhaler, and flossing and brushing my teeth. The process is not only tiresome but painful because of the response of my back and legs to standing. So, I sit on a little bench. Oh, for the days when going to bed just meant getting out of my clothes and into pajamas as the simple prelude to slipping under the covers.

When I finally fall on the bed next to Lennie, I feel enormous relief from back pain. I usually watch the television news and then channel surf till midnight. As I slip under the covers I ask myself, how many more nights are left to me? But I am not gloomy ~ quite the contrary. Usually, I'm energetic, intellectually alive, reading constantly: the daily newspaper, the Sunday New York Times, the New Yorker, serious books ~ a few works of fiction ~ classics and modern fiction, and a great deal of non-fiction, mostly having to do with politics.

Starting in 1977, and for the past thirty seven years I have maintained a list of the books I have read. It now totals eight hundred and fifty books. That works out to about twenty three books a year.

So, clearly, reading has been a big part of my life. I didn't start the list till I was forty and there was a hiatus in my reading for almost three years when I was completely absorbed in photography and studying Russian. But still, as I look over this list I am dismayed to see titles that I do not remember, and even worse, I am unable to recall the contents. But many have left deep impressions; Remembrance of Things Past by Proust, The Guns of August by Barbara Tuchman, Emma Bovary by Gustave Flaubert, The Brothers Karamazov by Dostoyevsky, Ulysses by Joyce, the Biography of Lyndon Johnson by Robert Caro, the works of Phillip Roth, Joseph Conrad, Dickens, and many books about Jewish Life in Russia and America and many dealing with the State of Israel. Reading is now my principal form of recreation, since physical disability rules out most other activities. I have a strange attitude about it; it's a task for me to finish, and with each book I finish, I have the satisfaction of putting the book away and entering its title on my list of books read.

So, these thoughts in the red zone simply make my life sweeter. I enjoy my night time ruminations in the red-walled living room, I regularly reflect on my good fortune in marrying Lennie, a woman of infinite devotion - a woman of intelligence and good humor. I occasionally think of the fullness of the life I have lived -- a lawyer who has argued cases to juries, judges and even the United States Supreme Court, a pilot flying an airplane across mountain ranges, flying alone above cities at night, a photographer whose photographs have been honored in national shows, and a father and grandfather who has sired a family of Ziontzs. The hell with the Red Zone -- I will be content with the end, for all good stories have an ending.

On Jan. 9, 2009 we were struck by a thunderbolt -- Lennie was diagnosed with ovarian cancer. I felt as though I had been ambushed. This was an attack on my life from a completely unexpected quarter. Was it possible that my own Lennie would succumb before me? And now this thought spawned its offspring: what would my life be without her? I hadn't considered such a possibility but now it was a real threat, one which would drastically change my life and create the likelihood that the comfortable life I led would end sooner than I planned.

The intrusion of cancer into our midst was sudden and unexpected. Lennie had been complaining of having vague abdominal pains for several weeks. I insisted she go see our internist. He is a very good doctor, but he has a failing ~ always an optimist, inclined to dismiss the possibility of serious causes for the patient's complaints. Lennie told him she was concerned about the possibility of ovarian cancer, because she had read a newspaper article about it which described symptoms exactly like hers. He said ovarian cancer was highly unlikely, surmising instead that they were caused by "irritable bowel" syndrome. He prescribed a medication and advised her to try it for a month. If the problem persisted, then he would send her for a CAT scan. Despite the medication the problem persisted and he sent her for the CAT scan. I will always remember the slightly abashed look on his face as he told us the scan showed ovarian cancer.

Lennie's oncologist is a tall Jewish guy ~ the kind of person who we all knew in high school, a "brain". He has a big reputation; the best man in town for ovarian cancer; his specialty. Dr. Drescher is above all, a surgeon, who wastes little time on emotion. He is obviously the master of his craft who dispenses the chilling statistics of cancer's advance and remission in a flat, matter of fact tone delivered with a soft lisp. Both of us sit and listen to this man who literally will hold

Lennie's life in his hands. She will undergo surgery to remove all the malignant tissue. Her uterus and ovaries will be removed as well as her omentum (a layer of tissue that covers the reproductive organs) as well as any other malignant tissue that he sees. This will be followed by six chemotherapy treatments over a period of 18 weeks ~ one every three weeks. And then, if she's lucky, she goes into remission ~ a suspension of hostilities, for three years on average. The risk of recurrence is lower after five years, but how long, no one can say.

We left the office of the oncologist each of us thinking our private thoughts ~ grim apprehensive thoughts, each of us in a somewhat tenuous relation with reality. One functions; takes the elevator down to the garage, drives home, enters one's familiar surroundings and carries on, copes, does the routine things and tries to ignore the 800 pound gorilla in the room.

We have a date for Lennie's surgery ~ some three weeks off. This struck me as a rather leisurely schedule to respond to a deadly threat that was advancing daily. But, we are told, that is Dr. Drescher's first available surgery date and his staff seemed to find nothing medically wrong with waiting three weeks. So, for the next three weeks we lived in a state of deferred fear. I don't know what was going on in Lennie's mind, but as for me, I found myself repeatedly trying to block out thoughts of her shapely, slim body being deconstructed and disfigured by the surgeon's scalpel and the even more unbearable thought of her experiencing the torture of a cancerous destruction of her living body.

January 20 was the date set for her surgery. In the hospital, as she awaited the trip to the operating room, Lennie seemed stoic, but a subtle change had come over her. Her sparkle was gone. When she was wheeled off and I kissed her, she gave me a loving look and a distracted kiss and then they took her away. Our children joined me in an agonizingly long wait; their faces reflecting their fears at this unexpected disruption in the orderly flow of their lives. Five hours elapsed and then suddenly Lennie's surgeon, Dr. Drescher made his appearance, wearing his operating room greens.

The surgery had gone well, he said. He had removed both ovaries, her uterus, the omentum and the lower section of her bowel, which showed some evidence of malignant growth. He was satisfied, he said, that he had eliminated all the malignant tissue and he expected her to make a normal recovery from the surgery. All of this was communicated in a flat, matter of fact, voice.

Two more hours dragged by before we could see her. She was in a private room, lying pale and motionless with a frightening array of tubes connecting her to bags, tanks and who knows what. She was barely conscious as I and our children came solemnly to her bedside. I leaned over her and kissed her and as I straightened up I was overcome and wept. Then I bit my lips and choked down my sobs, not wanting the children to see my breakdown. Suddenly the terrible gravity of her illness struck me with dreadful force. Up to that moment it had all been theoretical, intellectual. Now we could see her, transformed, from a vibrant, handsome woman into an object; alive and breathing but somehow shrunken beneath the covers of her bed.

Over the next five days her room filled with flowers as she slowly re-engaged with life. But there was a terrible moment the second night after her surgery. I was alone in the room with her as she slept when the phone in the room rang. I quickly picked it up to stop it from waking her. I don't remember now who the caller was, some close friend who wanted to know about her overall prospects, but I said she had a 60% chance of going three years without a recurrence. I had it wrong; the actual prospect is 70%. But Lennie overheard me. After I hung up and went to her bedside, her eyes were wide open and there was a look on her face unlike any I had ever seen.

In an accusatory tone she said, "You're conning me aren't you? I'm going to die." "No!" I told her, "That is not correct. You got it wrong. I didn't say that."

"I heard you. The doctor said I only have a 30% chance, didn't he?" My explanation didn't persuade her. Again she accused me, "You're conning me aren't you?"

Never in our fifty-seven years together had she so blatantly accused me of lying to her, of trying to deceive her. It was frightening. We dropped the subject and never raised it again. I've been afraid to discuss it, mostly because I'm not confident that I know the statistics and prefer to leave it to her doctor to tell her.

The extensive radical surgery left her with severe, unremitting pain in her abdomen. OxyContin, a powerful pain medication was prescribed for her. The drug brought relief but it also caused long periods of sleep and what was worse ~ severe constipation, a condition which produced abdominal bloating and pain.

By April Lennie's problems worsened. She has been in pain constantly and unable to relieve her constipation despite laxatives, suppositories and even a fleet enema. So she called her oncologist's office. His nurse, concerned that there could be an intestinal blockage instructed her to go to the emergency room at Swedish Hospital. This sounded serious.

We arrived at five in the afternoon unprepared for the nightmare that was to come. The "ER" like all "ERs" was slow to see the number of patients seeking medical attention. It was more than two hours before she was seen by a triage nurse ~ a gatekeeper for the actual emergency room. It was after seven that evening when she was finally led to an examining table in one of the bays. We were tense and exhausted by the long wait. But the real nightmare was Lennie's fear that she would have to undergo surgery for a bowel disorder.

If we thought that lying on a table in the emergency room was going to lead to a doctor's imminent arrival we were soon disabused. For three hours we waited. Three times I ventured out into the corridor looking for a doctor only to be confronted by a staff challenge, "Can we help you?" Telling them that we had been waiting hours for a doctor led only to a platitudinous, "We're very busy tonight and a doctor should be with you shortly."

Meanwhile, poor Lennie was lying there experiencing terror; terror of the surgeon's knife further disfiguring her already badly scarred little body. She lay there silently, a bleak hopeless look in her eyes. It was wrenching for me, though I did not allow my anguish to show.

It was after ten in the evening, three hours after she lay down on the table, before one of the ER docs finally made his appearance. He got right down to business, not pausing for any apologies. He pushed and probed and asked questions and then announced he was sending her down the hall for a CATSCAN to determine whether she had an intestinal blockage. The doctor said he didn't think she had an intestinal blockage and suspected pancreatitis, a highly dubious diagnosis I thought.

Twenty minutes later she returned. No pancreatitis, no bowel obstruction, just constipation, which happily was relieved when they administered a barium enema in preparation for the CATSCAN. Still, they kept her overnight for observation. The constipation, they told her, was a known side effect of oxycodone, the pain medication she had taken. The suffering she endured from that constipation so traumatized her that she resolved never again to take oxycodone, no matter how bad the abdominal pain.

Well, the constipation crisis was a diversion from the larger issue; the eighteen weeks of chemotherapy attacking her cancerous cells and then the life or death outcome: had the chemical warfare resulted in victory ~ or at least a temporary respite, a remission, or would the deadly disease continue its attacks elsewhere in her body?

As the days passed waiting for a second chemotherapy infusion we were both lulled into the belief that the entire process was simply a matter of enduring the unpleasantness of these periodic injections and then going on into a period of remission. Oh yes, her hair would fall out and she would have to wear a wig to cover the ugly baldness, and maybe she would experience some occasional nausea, but nothing really bad. Well, she got her wig all right and she had a little nausea that was suppressed with medication, but then her health was affected in an entirely unexpected way. She felt tired and lethargic all day and drained of all energy. She lay in bed day after day, sleeping and waking with little appetite and no interest in anything beyond watching the television screen.

Finally, at my urging she called her oncologist's office and was surprised and angered to learn that she was supposed to have had a blood test ~ an important blood test to determine the level of her red and white blood cells, but the staff at her doctor's office had failed to inform her of this important item. They now told her that at the midpoint between chemo injections her blood count reached a nadir ~ a low point. A blood test was necessary to measure her red and white blood cell count and if too low, a transfusion would be necessary. The symptoms she was having, extreme fatigue and shortness of breath were indicative of a low red blood cell count.

So we went to a lab for her blood to be drawn and that afternoon received a call from her doctor's staff; her test had shown an alarmingly low red and white blood cell count. She will need a blood transfusion. This cast an ominous light over what we had seen as an innocuous phase of her sickness. We were now beginning to understand, to perceive, the true character of the grim battle that was going on in her body. Her cells were literally being killed to stop the deadly proliferation of outlaw cells that would replicate without limit until they brought about the end of her life.

Oh, we knew all this in an abstract way, but we lived our lives in daily episodes ~ like an undramatic soap opera, punctuated by grocery shopping trips, picking up medications at the local pharmacy, visits from our children and telephone calls ~ one or more every day from family and friends inquiring about Lennie. This flow of the ordinary serves to mask the threat we are living under. As for me, I spend my days and nights reading library books, issues of the New Yorker and the daily newspapers ~ the Seattle paper and the New York Times. Every day of the week, almost without fail, I go to Starbucks between two-thirty and three thirty to get some of their corporate beverages and to write in this journal.

It was all a waiting game; Lennie and I waiting to see whether the threat to her life becomes immediate and terrible and both of us waiting for my book to come out. The two future prospects are antipodal; the first a horror awful to contemplate, the second a pleasant vision of fame and glory. The first, unknowable and circumscribed by statistical probabilities, the second, an event definite. The book will be published ~ that is now settled. The only unknown is how it will be received; will it be purchased in significant numbers and reviewed or will it fade into obscurity?

Happily, my book, which has been in the hands of the press for almost three years, now appears to be nearing the end of its lengthy period of gestation. There are clear signs that it will actually enter the world of real books. The anticipation of this exciting event provides a pleasant counterpoint to what would otherwise be a dreary procession of days. But this counterpoint is overshadowed by Lennie's continuing lack of return to normal life.

By May, Lennie's chemo was taking her down. In the past week she suffered from unremitting pain. She grew weary of each day bringing continuing sickness. She had never undergone such a prolonged assault on her sense of well-being. Not only is there no longer an expectation of relief ~ that the pain will go away ~ but there is the grim awareness that worse may lie ahead. This has taken a heavy toll on her. Her eyes are almost always downcast, she moves slowly, she speaks slowly, her mental acuity is diminished. Her appearance has changed markedly; her bald skull robs her of her soft feminine face, which is now gaunt and hard, making her nose the most prominent feature. The sparkle is gone from her eyes and she rarely smiles. When she is energetic enough to have company, our kids or friends, she puts on her wig and makes an effort to be energetic and engaged. She carries it off, but at a price. When the company leaves she promptly takes to her bed, exhausted.

Our comfortable life together can no longer be taken for granted. There is an undercurrent of feeling that every part of our life is now temporary and that the pieces we have assembled with thought and care will be torn apart. My best hope is that Lennie's treatment will bring about a remission that will last two or three years ~ at least. In the meantime, my health is deteriorating; my lungs leave me short of breath after any exertion, my spinal stenosis has caused almost unbearable leg pain after walking or standing and my hand tremor makes grasping anything with my fingers a daunting undertaking. So what's good? Well, my egotism continues to be gratified when I occasionally learn that I am held in esteem by many.

Two weeks ago we received wonderful news ~ Lennie's last blood test showed her CA-125 ~ a measure of the presence of malignant ovarian tissue ~ had gone from a frightening 4,000 to 69, less than 100, the normal level, signifying the chemicals had done their work, destroying the malignant tissue in her body. We were overjoyed.

But Lennie was still very sick. The fifth chemo brought down her hematocrit and she again suffered the debilitating effects of the chemo; general fatigue and lassitude together with burning needles in the soles of her feet, crippling abdominal pain and loss of strength in her right hand.

Despite the daily pain, the loss of function and ability to do the household routines that were part of her life, her unwavering love for me was manifested by actions large and small; seeing that I had clean clothes, giving me the larger share of food and drink.

One night she said something startling, "I'm going to tell you what a real shit I am. When the doctor's office told me about the CA 125 reading, part of me was glad but a secret part of me was disappointed. You see, I had always expected you would die before me and I would have to endure the pain of your death and living without you. When they told me the bad stuff had been destroyed, a voice in me said: Oh, no. Now I'll probably outlive Al and that means I'll have to go on without him. I don't know how I can do that."

Hath woman greater love than this? Desiring to die before her husband so as to avoid the terror of his death and life without him. I don't think so.

I've long known that Lennie has harbored the fear of losing me and facing the prospect of years of life without me. It has haunted her. Then, in an extraordinary exercise of will, she sought to exorcise this demon by writing a fictional account of a woman losing her husband to death. The book, which she titled, "The Hour of Lead", was written over the course of a year and a half of hard work and she published it. It is an excellent book and tells a story of deep personal crisis grippingly.

I may be too egotistical, but I regard this book, not only as an exorcism of her fear of my death, but as a demonstration of her love for me.

In June I received a letter from the President of the Northern Cheyenne tribe inviting me to attend their annual pow-wow at Lame Deer, Montana on July 3. The letter said they wanted to honor me for my work for the tribe. I hesitated to accept because my mobility is so constricted, but I decided to go anyway. When I told Lennie about this trip I was completely surprised by her reaction: she wanted to go too! Her reason shouldn't have surprised me, but it was touching; she wanted to witness me receiving this special honor.

Her doctor's aide called and said her blood test shows she needs another transfusion ~ her second ~ because of low hematocrit ~ the proportion of red blood cells in her blood. We were confident she would feel much better after the transfusion because that was her experience before. Yesterday, she had the transfusion. Today, everything went to hell. She awoke in pain last night, sweating and feeling "lousy". A Vicodin didn't help. She described an alarming sensation in the center of her chest ~ "like a hole." Calls to our family doctor and to her oncologist brought the same response: "Call 911. Go to the ER."

Reluctantly she acquiesced, but not to 911. She wanted no part of an ambulance driving into our little condo development. So I drove her to Swedish hospital. This time she was seen promptly, no doubt because of her complaint of cardiac symptoms. But tests showed no evidence of any cardiac problem, leaving us with the unsatisfying conclusion that she had a reaction to something in the blood that was transfused. She came home exhausted, physically and spiritually.

Her unremitting abdominal pain caused Lennie to fear her cancer spread to other organs. As her fears deepened so did her gloom. She became convinced that cancer was now killing her. Shouldn't she get some tests? Shouldn't her doctor be concerned? Could the cancer be spreading so fast? She went in to see her doctor who gave her a thorough exam and found no evidence of other organ involvement. To this was added the assurance of an experienced oncology nurse that the pain and neuropathy she was experiencing was a common result of the chemotherapy. Hearing this reassuring medical voice, she literally breathed a sigh of relief. So, if she was going to die of cancer it wasn't going to be soon.

Lennie had her sixth and final chemotherapy infusion on June 12, an event she had been longing to reach for the past five months. Somehow, she had come to believe that once this milestone was passed, she would emerge from this world of sickness and medical treatments onto the road to normalcy. Instead, within two days she was hit with the cumulative effects of eighteen weeks of toxic assault on her body. Our lives were reduced to a grim procession of joyless days. Most of the time she was in her bed sleeping, dozing or watching TV. She was not able to muster the energy to even read a book. She came to present a familiar sight; lying on the side of the bed, only her absurd looking knit cap covering her bald head protruding above the covers. Her forays out of the bedroom were brief ~ dragging herself slowly around the kitchen as she went through the habitual actions of a woman long used to preparing and serving food; taking food out of the refrigerator, boiling water for coffee or tea, putting pots and pans away and then, as if on autopilot, washing the dishes and pots. But these activities soon exhausted her and she had to return to her bed.

As for me, my life was dominated by Lennie's illness. Although she placed no demands on me, I was now forced to attend to the mundane requirements of the household: grocery shopping (a process repeated endlessly), emptying the garbage, the recycling, and the wastebaskets, keeping track of the food on hand and supplying the meals, the latter exclusively take-out, since my bad back and lack of know-how ruled out extensive cooking. Last week, her pain returned and, despite her vow never to take oxycodone again because of the constipation that ensued, she was driven to take it. Within three days she was again suffering the effects of constipation. By the fifth day without a bowel movement she was in crisis; again a blocked canal and exhausting, painful efforts to expel the blockage. She was in the bathroom when I heard her crying out for help, "Al!" I quickly went to her. Her face was contorted by pain and she said, "Go to the store and get me a Fleet Enema, quick!"

I moved swiftly, drove to the drug store and returned with the enema within fifteen minutes. When I came to the bathroom, she was sitting on the toilet, crying, her legs trembling. She was in no condition to help herself and submitted to the indignity of having me administer the enema. We were both elated when it brought quick and complete relief. Afterward, she fell into bed, exhausted and turned to me and said, quite simply, "I love you."

There is a photograph of Lennie sitting on the stereo console in the living room. It was taken of the two of us at a party on the eve of her surgery. Her smile is dazzling, her eyes happy ~ it is iconic Lennie. Yet it is also bitterly ironic because we both knew, even as we sat looking joyous at that party, that in two days she would go under the surgeon's knife and would enter the world of cancer. It was such a beautiful photograph that our daughter in law, Michelle, had it mounted in a handsome frame and presented it to us. The photograph haunted me. Whenever I sat in my armchair in the living room my eyes were drawn to Lennie's smiling face. As her plight became more serious it became harder and harder to look at her image unemotionally. One night, during one of my musical reveries, the picture suddenly overwhelmed me and I broke down sobbing. After I gained control of myself, I got up and removed the photograph from the living room and carried it into our bedroom where I placed it on our dresser.

A month later I was listening to a Bach violin concerto one night and a poignant passage again brought me to tears. I suppose this means that the deadly character of Lennie's disease is never far from my consciousness. Death, the extinguishment of the life of this extraordinary woman ~ a woman I love deeply who has quietly occupied all four corners of my life ~ lies just beneath the surface of my thoughts all the time.

Well, thoughts of death now include my own. I feel the approaching end of my life. Every day I am forced to confront the steadily worsening state of my breathing. The doctors have said it is COPD, or emphysema or asthma, saying, when pressed, that these terms are more or less interchangeable. What is not in question is that almost any expenditure of oxygen, such as climbing up a flight of stairs or walking more than fifty yards leaves me gasping and my heart pounding. When I have pushed myself beyond even modest limits, the respiratory and cardiac symptoms become alarming. I struggle for each breath between frightening wheezes. Recovering normal breathing seems to take forever.

With Lennie on the eve of her ovarian cancer surgery 2009

I recently found that I have outlived most of my law school classmates, many of whom seem to have died in their seventies. Maybe it's because they lived in the unhealthy clime of Chicago or New York, maybe the air is better here in Seattle. Who knows? Probably genetics and luck.

Lennie's health is terrible ~ she doesn't have the energy to leave the house to get a blood test. If I'm right she will probably need another blood transfusion. She's had two transfusions already and it is not an easy process; a trip downtown to have her blood cross matched and then another trip downtown the next day for the transfusion ~ a procedure that involves sitting in a chair for five hours while a stranger's blood is slowly infused into her veins.

Now this is not a terrible thing to go through but it is another blow to her already fragile morale. She has been grimly determined to travel to Montana with me on July 3 to witness the ceremony of tribal honors bestowed on me by the Northern Cheyenne tribe. She believed with every fiber of her being that after her sixth and final chemo treatment on June 12, her health would recover in time for her to accompany me to Montana for the July 3 ceremony. But as day after day passed with no relief from her lethargy, constipation and sleeplessness, she became depressed and angry at her inability to will herself to recover. Today, she is forced to face the increasing likelihood that the pleasure of the Montana trip will be denied to her. With visible grit and determination she willed herself to get out of bed, get dressed and go for her blood test. After we returned home, she went straight to bed and to sleep.

Today Lennie and I talked about death; her death and my

death. She had awakened after a four hour oxycodone-induced sleep and we were sitting at our little round glass top breakfast table while she ate a bowl of soup. She hadn't bothered to put on a cap to cover her bald head and she looked like an alien. She had a terrible night – kept awake the entire night by gnawing abdominal pain that would not yield to pain pills till her third oxycodone. So now it's two thirty in the afternoon. After finishing her soup she sat without speaking, looking somber. Finally, she spoke,

"I've been thinking we should make some plans."

"What plans?" I asked.

"Supposing I don't go into remission? Suppose I'm in the twenty percent who don't, and I get growths in other parts of my body, and it's a year of suffering and then I'm gone. What will happen to you? Your lungs are failing. I hear it ~ you're wheezing. You won't be able to manage without me. I think you should start thinking about finding a facility where you won't have to worry about shopping or cooking or laundry..."

Here I stopped her. "Look, I'm going to stay in this house. If I have to, I'll pay people to do laundry and cooking. The only upside of going into one of those full service retirement villas is convenience. The downside is I am surrounded by decrepitude. But worse, I lose this house. I love this house. Stop worrying about what will happen to me after you're gone."

"I do worry," she said, "...and I can't stop worrying about it."

"Listen," I said, "No matter what happens, I'll cope with it."

So there she was, facing the real prospect of her own death, preoccupied with my fate. Hell, this should not be a surprise. She has been obsessed about my well-being for our entire married life. And now she was staring at the face of death ~ her own death ~ and her uppermost thought was to prod me into planning for a life without her.

L had another terrible sleepless night, suffering with unremitting abdominal pain. In the morning she was feeling so desperate that she agreed that I could call her oncologist's office. I was able to convey in my phone conversation with the oncology nurse her desperation. She said we should come down to the office that day to be examined. It took superhuman grit for L to drag herself out of bed and get dressed in the presence of crippling pain. That she was able to do it was itself a measure of her desperation to get relief from her suffering.

She was seen by one of the oncologist's assistants, a warm, reassuring woman named Beth. After examining her, Beth said it was most unlikely that the pain was caused by a tumor outside the primary site, the ovaries. Instead, she suspected the problem was in the colon. She had us go directly for an x-ray to determine whether L had a bowel obstruction or what she called, "a developing obstruction". We dutifully proceeded to the x-ray lab and later that morning got the verdict: "no obstruction and no developing obstruction ~ just a colon filled with fecal material."

The P.A. recommended drinking eight glasses of water a day and milk of magnesia tablets. We were relieved at the news that her problem was just run of the mill constipation. As soon as we got home L started drinking the water. The next morning, blessed relief! Almost immediately the clouds lifted; her mood became cheerful. She felt energetic and finished doing some laundry, ironed two of my shirts for the trip to Montana and even decided to go with me to the store for groceries. Hope had returned. Maybe she had found the key to prevent the pain from returning. Alas, it didn't last. By that evening the pain was back and didn't yield despite eight glasses of water and three oxycodone. That night she lay awake, unable to sleep at all because of the pain. Today, June 30, she lay in bed, dispirited and suffering. Neither of us knows what to do. In two days I'll be leaving for three days in Montana. Our children have assured us that they will look after her in my absence, but it is not reassuring to L.

Thursday, July 2. L says her legs do not feel that they can bear weight, they are weak and unreliable, the soles of her feet burn with pins and needles and she remains constipated, despite dosing herself with laxatives. But it was the unremitting abdominal pain which racked her body that was pushing her to the brink of hopelessness. The pain so distracted her that she was increasingly unable to focus her thoughts. It also caused her to become increasingly short-tempered with me ~ rare for her. Last night she went over the edge. First, she became more and more upset with the bedding, insisting that it had become so disarranged that nothing would do but stripping it all off and remaking the bed with freshly laundered sheets and pillowcases. It was only after I convinced her that neither she nor I were physically able to do this that she reluctantly agreed that we could together simply straighten out the bedding. Later, as sleep time approached, she became more and more apprehensive at the possibility that she would spend another sleepless night.

The next morning Lennie became more and more distraught. Finally, she broke down, "Al, I'm scared. I'm scared of being alone when you're gone." She went on, "I haven't felt this way since I was alone going into labor with our first child at the Army hospital in Fort Monmouth."

"Honey, I'm going to cancel my trip to Lame Deer," I said. But she quickly rejected that idea and then stunned me saying, "I want to go into a nursing home while you're gone." This shocking proposal brought home to me the depth of her fear and despair. I called Dr. Drescher's aide, Nicole for guidance. Nicole threw cold water on the idea by saying that Dr. Drescher would not write orders for such a measure because it would not be covered by insurance. Instead, she proposed measures to relieve gas and constipation. I didn't think this would do. Those measures had not helped till now and I wasn't willing to leave Lennie at the mercy of this advice. I decided that Lennie needed more assistance and support from our children than their assurances that they would come by and visit every day of my absence. I began with a call to our daughter, Ellen. That turned out to be a stroke of good fortune. This loving daughter of ours immediately proposed that her mother come to her house and stay with her for the weekend. That was quickly agreed and Lennie soon became calmer in the knowledge that she would not be alone for three days.

On Friday, July 3, 2010, Steve and Evvie Chestnut escorted me through the airport and onto our flight to Billings. I chose to ride out to the gate in a wheelchair and the process was repeated in reverse when we disembarked. (I hate the word "deplaned.") Our destination was Lame Deer, on the Northern Cheyenne Reservation, a hundred mile east of Billings by car. Over ten years had passed since I last visited the reservation and there were changes. "Cady's", the tiny convenience store in the center of Lame Deer, was gone. But the grim looking IGA was still there, together with a few stores and a fast food joint with an unforgettable name: "The Chicken Shack".

Lame Deer is the home of the tribal government center and the center of Cheyenne life. It lies at the crossroads of two state highways. In the streets on the north and south of the highway are neighborhoods of Cheyenne houses, the schools and a church. We were headed for the pow-wow grounds, an arena located about a mile out of Lame Deer.

From a distance we saw the tepees -- traditional Indian lodges -- conical structures of canvas stretched around tall lodge poles that criss-crossed and protruded above their tops with a wing of canvas extending out from the apex. These were campgrounds and from afar one could imagine an Indian encampment as it appeared in historic times. Drawing closer, one saw acres of parked cars, pick-up trucks and vans, and closer to the grounds, modern tents. Indian families from all over were camping here.

Surrounding the grounds was a large covered grandstand. Inside were bleachers and outside, around the circular stands, was a roadway studded with a carnival-like collection of vendor's stands offering Indian Fry Bread, Pizza, Tacos, Sno-Cones, T-Shirts and the like. The roadway teemed with throngs of Indians, young and old, promenading to see old friends, or enroute to the honey-buckets.

As we entered the grandstand I recognized the familiar sounds of Indian drumming. It was coming from a single large drum around which sat five or six Indian men, mostly young, beating out traditional rhythms and periodically breaking into shouted chants. The drumming and chanting were carried by speakers and projected around the grounds, making conversation difficult.

When we arrived the bleachers were already filled by several hundred people, mostly Indians, spectators and dancers waiting their turn. The dancers wore spectacular Indian regalia ~ the men and boys in brilliant feather headdresses, leggings, breechcloths, and embroidered moccasins. Their faces were covered by red, white and black face paint. The women and girls wore brightly decorated and embroidered long dresses, their hair in braids and a feather mounted on the back of their heads.

The occasion was the annual Fourth of July Chief's Pow-Wow. This brought together Northern Cheyennes as well as Indians from other tribes; Sioux, Arapaho, Yakama, Crow, Blackfeet. Looking around the grounds and the bleachers, the faces were overwhelmingly Indian, with only a scattering of non-Indians. The proceedings were directed by a Master of Ceremonies addressing the crowd over loudspeakers and calling out the events. This man was Cheyenne and frequently interspersed remarks in the Cheyenne tongue.

The procession began with a Grand Entry. Heading the procession was an honor guard of Cheyenne men and women in active military service, wearing their military uniforms. The announcer introduced each of them by name, branch of service, rank and their combat deployments. Then he said, "We honor each and every one of these warriors who are risking their lives to protect our rights here in the United States of America."

And with that the color guard stepped off, entering the arena to the rhythm of Indian drumming. The Cheyennes are proud of their warrior tradition and though they have suffered harsh treatment at the hand of the U.S. Government, they are deeply patriotic.

As the procession filed into the arena there was an eye-filling spectacle of Indian men and women in full regalia slowly making their way around the periphery. The arena filled; the men dancing in the center, the women circling around the perimeter. In their dancing, the men stamp and whirl while the women dance in a more sedate style; moving in unison to the drumbeat, at intervals holding up a large eagle feather fan, carrying themselves with erect dignity. Some are attractive, many dance with a certain grace, but all display intense concentration ~ never glancing at the spectators or allowing any emotion to change their serious expressions.

I had been watching the spectacle for about an hour when I suddenly heard my name called out by the announcer: "Will Al Ziontz come up here!" I made my way to the space in front of the announcer's booth, where the Tribal President, Leroy Spang stood. I was somewhat apprehensive about standing or walking around the arena, but Steve Chestnut had informed them of my disability and they had thoughtfully placed a chair for me. As I sat down, the announcer proceeded to recite to the crowd my biography, ending with a flourish saying I had helped to save the Northern Cheyenne Reservation. When I was asked to speak, I told them of my observations when I had been a guest of the Cheyennes ten years earlier and my insight into ordinary Cheyenne life.

After I concluded, my companions in the procession indicated that I was to walk with them around the circular arena in front of the grandstands. About half way around they stopped. The announcer said, "Let's say Thank You to Al Ziontz for saving our lands."

Immediately, Cheyenne men, women and even children left their seats and walked across the open space to me. Solemnly, one by one they shook my hand and said, "thank you." I was particularly touched by the children, some as young as nine or ten years old who came up and shook my hand. It was a profoundly moving experience. Only Indians know how to do something like this.

There was more to come. After I returned to my chair and sat down, I found something draped around my shoulders. A Cheyenne had placed a gift quilt on me. It was a thing of beauty; a design of pink and blue panels in the form of a compass.

We spent two and a half days at the pow-wow. On the second day, I was presented with another gift blanket; a hand sewn Indian patchwork quilt. And to round the giving out they gave me set of towels with a design of horses and riders and finally, a book "Cheyenne Memories", photographs of Cheyennes taken in the 1920's. At the end of the third day Steve, Evvie and I returned home. The Cheyenne experience was a high point in a life that was now entering its closing years. It was time to return to my sick wife.

Lennie was cheered by my reappearance and eager to hear all about the way in which I had been honored; an event she was cheated from attending by her sickness. She glowed at the telling of the story of the Cheyenne ceremony, but the glow barely concealed her debility.

She was still sick, weak and in pain. The pain was very worrisome; it was abdominal and sometimes was so bad that she had to take a powerful opiate; oxycodone. She hated taking it because it produced severe constipation ~ resistant to all laxatives.

She was scheduled to meet with her oncologist in three days. At this meeting he would give her the results of the CT scan done the previous day. Lennie and I were apprehensive because her abdominal pain could mean she had other tumors in her body. To our delighted surprise Dr. Drescher told her in flat, unemotional tones that she was cancer free and now was in remission ~ a life-preserving milestone!

This should have been a red-letter day for us but our elation was dampened by her continuing abdominal pain and the neuropathy that afflicted her hands and feet. Questioned about these matters, Dr. Drescher's response was that she would have to use pain medications and laxatives and in time all these problems would pass. It was clear he had nothing more to offer. Oh yes, she should come back in three months for a checkup.

That very night Lennie was attacked by racking stomach pain. The pain prevented her from sleeping and she was up the entire night. By morning she was desperate. Her eyes stared at me hauntingly out of a gaunt skull. My heart was breaking. She needed to stop the pain but when I suggested taking pain medication she shot back, "I'd sooner slit my wrists."

Constipation held her in an iron grip and would not let go. After four days she was frantic. In the end we were forced to resort to a Fleet enema again. I administered this nasty procedure ~ a humiliating experience for her. But our hopes that this would bring complete relief were dashed when she experienced only a short period of relief before the pain returned. The pain itself was bad enough, but the long sleepless nights it produced made her life a living hell.

Finally, she said to me, "Al, I can't fight this anymore."

Knowing she needed medical advice and there was no further help to be gotten from her oncologist, I said, "Let's call Seth," our primary care doctor. She agreed and Seth saw her promptly the next day.

After listening to Lennie's description of the way in which her health had broken down, he immediately proceeded to outline a plan of treatment. It consisted of prescriptions for new medications that would end the constipation problem and a stern instruction to walk every day to rebuild her stamina and in the process, assist in restoring normal bowel function. He assured us, in his usual take-charge style, that he understood the problem and would cure it.

July 20. Two weeks have now passed since Lennie's visit to Seth. That visit buoyed up her spirits. Finally, she was under the care of a doctor who was closely attentive to her colon problem. After getting home from the doctor, she promptly prepared a chart showing the schedule of her new medications. Lennie was determined to follow his instructions to the letter. After six months of fear, uncertainty and pain, she longed to be well again.

But she had to overcome huge obstacles. After six months lying in bed, hour after hour, day in and day out, she was badly deconditioned. The muscles in her legs had atrophied and she could barely support her weight. To make matters worse ~ much worse ~ she also had serious neuropathy in her hands and feet. She describes the sensation of walking as "walking on thick platform soles". Her hands were now barely functional; she could not grasp anything, unscrew a bottle cap or even manage buttoning her clothes. And still the pain came, waves of abdominal pain so severe that she cried out. Pain medication was out of the question, so her illness went on ~ day after day ~ night after night. The optimism which followed the news that she was cancer-free and again when Seth confidently outlined his treatment plan was now gone. "Will I ever get well?"

July 22. Well, we have entered a new phase; at least I thought so when I wrote this. The regime of colon meds that Seth prescribed seemed to be working. She was no longer racked by attacks of almost unbearable stomach pain. This, in turn, enabled her to sleep through the night. That was a huge improvement, but she was still in too much pain to feel cheerful about her recovery; she remained disabled, debilitated and demoralized. The neuropathy had robbed her hands of strength and sensitivity. She had dropped and broken glasses, spilled liquids and struggled to unscrew bottle caps, to say nothing of fumbling with buttons and zippers. And while her stomach pains were gone, her leg and foot pain remained ~ a daily discouragement. Seth has said she was severely deconditioned ~ a consequence of being bedridden for most of the past six months. She must walk every day, he insisted, even if it's only ten or twenty yards, but extending the distance constantly.

Her debilitation left her weak and easily fatigued. Despite this, she grimly set forth on a slow shuffling circuit of the grassy island on the street in front of our house every day. I was heartened by her progress and I dared to allow myself to believe that she was at last on the road to normalcy. I wanted my Lenore back, the vibrant pretty woman who for the last fifty seven years had quietly managed my life.

August 8, 2009. My 82nd birthday! For the past two weeks Lennie has been in declining health. She has been experiencing disabling weakness ~ so profound that in the past week she wasn't able to sit up, stand or walk for more than five or ten minutes. As each day passed with declines in her health, her morale sank. She reached the point where she was feeling that she would never get well. She had been in a state of increasing suffering for six long months. Finally, two days ago, we agreed she needed to be seen by a doctor immediately. An appointment was made within the hour and she was seen by Dr. Karton, the partner of our regular internist. After a physical exam and blood test he concluded she had a stomach ulcer and was in a state of serious chemical imbalance; her potassium and sodium levels were abnormally low. In addition, she was dehydrated. He arranged for her to have an immediate infusion of fluids at Swedish Hospital to restore her chemical balance and her fluid level, and he prescribed medication for her ulcer and to restore her chemical balance.

That afternoon she got the infusion and within an hour began to feel better. Afterwards, at home, I was elated to see her moving with new energy. Both of us felt the siege might be over, but then she spent the next night tossing and turning the whole night, all the while fumbling with her tiny radio in an effort to find the public radio station ~ her trusty soporific. But her neuropathy defeated her, leaving her frustrated and angry. By morning she was a wreck; everything hurt, she couldn't do the simplest tasks and once again her morale plummeted.

Her sickness cast a pall over events which should have given us pleasure: my birthday and my book. Lennie was hoping to attend a chamber music concert in the evening. Her heart was set on it. She had purchased the tickets months earlier, intending it as a birthday gift for me. But taking stock of her condition, she was forced to surrender to the overwhelming weakness of her body and abandon our plan to attend the concert. Not only were her fond expectations dashed, she had to swallow the loss of the eighty four dollars spent on the tickets. This was one more setback at a time when her morale had been battered by repeated disappointments over the past six months. She was under the spell of pervasive gloom about ever returning to normalcy.

August 10. This is the day she is scheduled to be seen by her internist. That visit was a critical one and proved to be the turning point in her recovery. Her chronic exhaustion was due to two causes he told her; she had discontinued taking her thyroid replacement medication and she was also suffering from low potassium and sodium levels. Combined, they robbed her of energy and prevented her body from converting food to energy. The cure was simple: immediately resume taking her thyroid medication, eat two bananas daily for potassium and eat canned soups ~ loaded with salt to restore her potassium level. He also advised her to begin drinking non-water liquids, e.g. juices. The good news was that her red blood cell count was now normal. We left his office uplifted.

Two days later, his assistant called with the additional good news that her thyroid level was now up and so was her potassium and sodium. Seth had also urged her to get up and walk every day. By the following day she was feeling better and her mood reflected a sense of returning health.

August 13, 2009. A red letter day! The press staffer in charge of production, called. Advance copies of the book had been received. Did I want to come to their office and pick it up or have it mailed? Mailed, I decided, sensibly. Tomorrow, with the aid of the U.S. Postal Service, I will finally be able to hold a copy of the book in my hands, an event that has tried my patience to the breaking point the past three years. This was a BIG milestone. I placed an order for new business cards for use with my book. Tomorrow, Aug. 14, is the day I have visualized for years; the actual physical book is published.

August 18. The past three days have been dramatic. On the 14th, as expected, my book arrived in the mail. It was beautiful. Everything in the package was perfect. And yet it was an anticlimax; after all, I had seen an exact mock-up of the cover and the dust jacket, I had seen a proof copy of the text and the photographs so there was really nothing new about the book as produced. Still, holding the book and, yes, reading my own words, brought home the reality that I was now a published author.

My pleasure was soon overtaken by a serious setback in Lennie's health. We had scheduled two outings, the first for Lennie in months. We should have known that these would be taxing. The first was a brunch with our friends, and the second a play in downtown Seattle that evening. Lennie felt obliged to go to the brunch because her friend Rachel Levine had set the date specifically with Lennie's recovery in mind. Lennie put on her best face, concealing the effort of the first excursion out of our house. But it turned out to be a three hour social outing ~ her first in six months, and it was draining.

Then she had to brace herself for the strain of going to the theater, with all that entailed: walking through the parking garage, taking the elevator up to the foyer and walking again and climbing stairs to the level of the theater. This was an enormous strain for one who had spent most of the past six months in bed with only short periods of sitting up. Going out twice in one day was asking for trouble. It turned into a disaster.

When we got home that evening, Lennie was beyond exhaustion. That night she was unable to sleep, despite taking a sleeping pill. I fell asleep easily but was awakened by a loud thump. I knew instantly that Lennie had fallen. I jumped out of bed and ran to the bathroom. She had lost her balance and thumped her head against the wall. No physical harm resulted but yet she was in a bad way; crying out, "my bones hurt" and, "I don't know how to get to sleep."

I fell asleep but was awakened by her cries and whimpers. The pain in her bones, she said, was unbearable. She hadn't slept a wink the entire night. Her plight was so desperate that she offered no resistance when I offered oxycodone, a drug she had sworn to avoid because of the devastating constipation it caused. I was so alarmed by her condition that I called our doctor.

After hearing my description of the events, he concluded her primary problem was lack of sleep and instructed me to give her two sleeping pills and another oxycodone. This knocked her out for the entire day. I looked in on her several times as she slept and found her apparently in a deep sleep. Meanwhile, I sat reading in the living room. Suddenly I heard the unmistakable sound of a body hitting the bedroom doors. I rushed in and found her lying on the floor next to the doors. She was crying and unable to get up. Risking my crippled back I tried to help her to her feet. Knowing that I was physically unable to lift her with my arms and back, I bent over her and told her to put her arms around my neck while I embraced her as tightly as I could manage with my weak arms.

"Were you trying to get to the bathroom?" I asked. She nodded feebly. So I started moving with her toward the bathroom, the two of us locked in embrace like overly affectionate dance partners; she stepping backwards as she clung to my neck. Suddenly, she went down, taking me with her. I put my hands out to break the fall. I was on my hands and knees and straightened up to a standing position as she lay on the floor, looking up at me helplessly. She lay on her back, her thin legs splayed out, clad only in a polo shirt and underpants. I realized immediately that raising her up was simply beyond my physical ability.

"Wait," I said, "I'm going to get some help." My mind raced: who? My neighbor was out of the question, it would be too invasive of Lennie's privacy and dignity. None of our three sons could get to us in less than a half hour. I thought of calling the fire department, but was appalled at the thought of the uproar this would bring. While I was mulling over the choices confronting me, Lennie had rolled over onto her stomach and was slowly trying to get on her hands and knees.

When I leaned over to help her she said, "I think I can get to the bathroom." She took the arm which I offered and struggled to her feet. Her legs were wobbly and she could barely stand, but she made it to the toilet. Afterwards, leaning heavily on me she staggered back to the bed and collapsed on it face down. She was so exhausted by her exertions that she didn't have the strength to roll over on her back or move to the side of the bed. I managed to pull her over and get her settled. As she nestled under the blankets, I thought the incident was over, but what next?

My worry led me to call our internist and report what had just occurred. He was, of course, concerned, but said his judgment was that she had seriously overstressed herself the previous day and this was compounded by lack of sleep. When I told him she was asleep he said, "Good. Let her sleep as long as she can. I'm sure she'll be better after she is rested. Call me first thing tomorrow morning and let me know how she is doing."

Lennie slept through the night and awoke twelve hours later. Our doctor's prediction was borne out. She was almost normal, though still weak. But she was able to walk to and from the toilet under her own power without any sign of collapsing. That crisis was over.

August 21. While the dramatic crisis caused by her collapse was over, other crises loomed. The chemo continued its destructive effects. What the medical literature blandly calls "side effects" turns out to be more devastating than the cancer. That had been completely eradicated by June 12 ~ over two months ago. These side effects left her bedridden and wasted, her hands rendered into almost useless claws, her legs pillars of pain and her feet numb stumps. Standing, walking or sitting quickly exhausted her and she was forced to take to her bed after being up for only short periods.

Perhaps the most serious effect is the erosion of her morale. It was a result of repeated dashed expectations that, "now I'm turning the corner", only to find that one corner is simply followed by another. It has now been almost six months since she began her treatment and she has been reduced to a stooped, shuffling invalid. And yet, she struggles on; each day dragging herself out of bed for her daily walk. Using a cane for security against falling, she shuffles around the little island in our roadway. Each day she dutifully eats her two bananas, drinks her Gatorade and swallows her pills. In the fight to regain her health she demonstrates a core of pure will and determination.

August 27. This has been the grimmest summer of my life. Lennie has been reduced to a shrunken version of her old self. Her weight is down to a hundred pounds and despite the oncologist's declaration that she is free of all malignant tissue, it seems almost as if she is dying of cancer. Her will to fight has been so badly battered that several times she has frightened me, saying, "Al, I'm dying. I don't have the strength to deal with this anymore." These deeply disturbing words were produced by abdominal pain which didn't respond to any medications.

Today she had an endoscopy performed by a gastroenterologist, to examine the lining of her stomach. The issue was whether she indeed had an ulcer. At the conclusion he pronounced, "Normal stomach lining. No ulcer." The gastroenterologist then prescribed a medication which, he said, would alleviate her pain by emptying the stomach of its contents more quickly. Maybe her terrible pains will respond to the new drug and she will begin to eat again.

CHAPTER TWENTY-SIX

A PUBLISHED AUTHOR

Today, August 14, 2009, there was a happy event. UPS delivered three boxes of my books. The book is beautiful. The designer has done a wonderful job with the cover and the photographs. At last I can begin sending gift copies ~ to old friends, to Indians and to the people at my law firm.

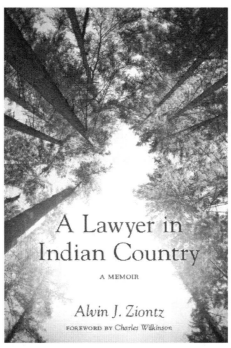

So now the book is out; review copies have been sent and I have sent out some forty gift copies to Indians, partners and friends. The few comments I received have, not surprisingly, been enthusiastic. But I have seen no published reviews yet and I have no idea how well the book is selling. Well, it's early, I remind myself. The book has only been out a month and the press says it takes a long time for an academic book to catch on, if it ever does. So I must be patient.

October 2. YES! Lennie is unquestionably returning to normalcy. She's active all day, her appetite has returned and she no longer suffers from persistent constipation and stomach pain. Much of the credit goes to her internist and gastroenterologist whose diagnoses, treatment and medications have finally enabled her to conquer her bodily enemies. I happily anticipate the renewal of our active life together.

Yesterday was a day of particular happiness for both of us. I gave the first reading of my book at the Mercer Island Jewish Community Center. The room was packed ~ thirty or so attended. Many had seen the article about my book in the Seattle Times. Among them were old friends; some I hadn't seen in years. I spoke for about thirty minutes and then read a chapter from the book. The JCC had arranged for books to be on hand and eighteen were purchased. I signed those that were offered to me and basked in the warmth of the compliments and expressions of admiration. Afterwards, Lennie and I celebrated by going to our favorite haunt; the Keg in Factoria. We both ate with gusto and returned home to sit in the semi-darkness and listen to Mozart's transcription of Bach fugues played by the Gruimaux Trio. Lennie sat in rapt silence and afterward said it was the first time since she became ill that she was able to enjoy music. Truly a wonderful day for both of us.

A few days later, I had another book signing, this one at the bookstore on Mercer Island. Some twenty five to thirty attended, including some old friends. I spoke well and signed many books. A big success. Meanwhile, Lennie and I reversed roles; she became my caregiver, doing the shopping, driving me to my appointments and preparing the meals. I was happy at her transformation from an invalid to an almost normally functioning person. It had been a long, hard road. At times I had been frightened that she wouldn't recover, but now I had the joy of Lennie returning to our life.

October 30. The pain from the ruptured disc hasn't abated. I lead the life of a cripple; I am limited to 15 or 20 steps, unable to stand erect for more than brief periods. It is a serious life change and I can only hope a temporary one. On a more cheerful note, today I learned that a radio interview had been arranged for me. I fear the pain of standing and walking to the station ~ will I be able to endure the pain? It has proven resistant to all pain medications, even oxycodone, supposedly the single most powerful pain medication. I fear going to bed each night will be eight hours of pain, pills and wakefulness as I seek relief from the pain that bores through my left hip and back no matter how I turn or draw my legs up. Three important book events are fast approaching; a radio interview, a reading in six days and another in Bellingham, a two hour drive.

I'm seriously considering using a walker, though I don't know if even that would help. In the meantime I'm leading a half-life; sitting around the house, reading, eating and going to bed at night. I continue to believe that this curse is only temporary ~ that I will recover and return to normalcy, that is, my previous level of mobility, which itself was hardly normal. But what if there is no improvement? The result will be that my life in the red zone will be shorter and harder and I may never enjoy the rewards of having my book published during my lifetime.

But I am thankful for Lennie's recovery. It has been almost miraculous. She is now functioning almost as well as she did before her illness. She is still plagued by neuropathy of her hands and feet and this condition is responding very slowly to her medication. We are both thankful and indeed my recent ruptured lumbar disc has so disabled me that her recovery couldn't have been more timely; she has taken over all the household jobs that I had been performing and now am unable to do. She is a blessing in my life and I cherish her.

Well I am mercurial. Today I am feeling elation about the book and myself. The radio interview on KUOW produced a flurry of compliments and evidence of a surprisingly large audience. That same evening I was the featured speaker at the Bellevue branch of the University book store. Since the Seattle Times printed the wrong location for the event, I expected only a handful of people to attend. In fact, there were about fifteen or twenty. A number had heard my radio interview, including one of my former partners, Steve Anderson, who came with his wife from Bainbridge Island. They came, taking the ferry on a windy, rainy night. Our reunion was very warm. I hadn't seen Steve for years and we were genuinely happy to see each other again. The engagement at the University bookstore went very well. I signed a number of my books and went home quite full of myself. In the next two days I received three speaking invitations.

November 16. Lennie and I just returned from Bellingham where I gave a talk at Village Books ~ one of Bellingham's main bookstores. The talk was a success, I believe. Twenty five or thirty attended ~ all dedicated supporters of Indians. An old colleague was there, Dan Raas, crippled by a stroke, and we greeted each other warmly. Old friends, Cici and Michael Marker were there. Cici is Gladys Romero's daughter and Gladys is an old friend. Afterward, we took them out to dinner. A pleasant and interesting evening. Afterward, we went to our hotel, The Chrysalis, very upscale, on the waterfront, elegantly appointed with a delightful window seat, cushioned and providing a cozy place to view the pier on Bellingham Bay. The winds were howling ~ 40 to 45 miles an hour, setting up a constant whistling in the window frames.

Though our bed was soft and luxurious, I was so high from my book talk that I couldn't fall asleep for hours. I was awakened at six the next morning when our room went completely black. The power had gone out and so the bathroom light I had left on to aid Lennie, went out. I fell asleep and didn't awake till eight thirty. Lennie was up, dressed and happy. For both of us, Bellingham was a pleasant interlude in our life, a life that had become heavily ridden by unchanging routine.

November 25. Well, I've been brought to earth with a thud. I learned the total number of sales of my book to date ~ 676. Not even a thousand. Despite being all over the internet, there have been no comments posted on Amazon or on my blog. Well, I must take what satisfaction I can from the praise from friends and strangers' e-mails and phone calls telling me how good they thought the book was.

The ultimate praise came in an e-mail from my friend, Lawrence Friedman ~ one of America's foremost legal scholars. His comments actually stunned me. My accomplishments, he said, outshone the money-making activities of any of my classmates. He went so far as to say he could not have accomplished, did not even have the courage to undertake what I did. As if this weren't enough, he even denigrated the Professor's world in which he had made his career, by referring to his fellow scholars as, "...nerds like me." I regarded this as praise from the highest source ~ a classmate who represented what I could never hope to attain; "Law Review", "Order of the Coif", and ultimately, "Professor of Law".

Nov. 29. Decrepitude. It is increasing. I walk in a stooped shuffle. Climbing the stairs cannot be done safely without keeping one hand on the banister. The few times I tried to pretend it was all a matter of attitude ~ just attack it boldly and vigorously ~ turned into dismaying defeats; stomping up the stairs precariously, concentrating intensely on maintaining my balance and using all my effort to keep my legs pumping. Once, despite my concentration, as I raised my foot for the next step, the toe of my shoe caught on the edge of the tread. I stumbled, falling forward and landing on my outstretched hand. It was over in a moment and I quickly recovered, but it was a sharp reminder that I could not trust my body to do the most familiar things, like climbing the stairs. In other words, I was forced to retreat ~ losing another battle to age.

The worst and most frightening activity is taking a shower. I can no longer use the shower stall in our bathroom ~ it is too confining and too dangerous, so I use the guest bathroom upstairs. Here the shower is located above the bathtub which is enclosed by sliding doors. I have had grab bars installed and now I feel more secure. A bathtub fall can be a deadly serious mishap for an eighty-one year old.

The entire showering experience, which is pleasurable for most, is for me, a series of painful reminders of my frailty ~ to say nothing of the horror of my body's appearance. Seeing the full reflection of my naked body in the bathroom mirror is appalling; so ugly, so repulsive in all its features ~ the sagging underbelly, the veined knotty legs and the ugly deformed feet.

Then there is the simple act of walking. Ever since my second back surgery in 1994 walking, or even standing, is painful and, if I press on, unbearable. My orthopedic surgeon had nothing to offer but pain control meds. When I described my symptoms, he said it was "arachnoiditis" ~ an inflammation of the arachnoid layer of tissue covering the spinal cord. He was probably wrong. Several doctors have told me so. I think he offered that explanation as a surgeon embarrassed by a less than satisfactory outcome for his patient. But I don't regard his surgery as a failure ~ quite the contrary. It relieved the compression of my right sciatic nerve and restored full sensation in my right foot. Without the surgery, my ability to drive a car would have ended. So, it was worth it, despite the disabling side effect.

December 11, 2009. Every year I am surprised to realize that the end of the year is at hand. It seems that I somehow get lost in the present and suddenly discover that the future is upon me. So, 2009 is rapidly drawing to a close. Reflecting on the events of the past year I realize that 2009 was the most momentous year of my life. For the first ten months I faced the deeply frightening possibility that my wife, the mainstay of my life, might succumb to cancer. It was not till October that she emerged from the fog of illness. Her recovery then proceeded to develop with wonderful swiftness. Today, though she still struggles with the pain and disability of the neuropathy of her hands and feet, she has returned to society; meetings, dining out, movies, friends, and, of course, tending to me. Yet her cancer is never entirely out of our minds.

But 2009 was marked also by the glowing reactions I received about my book. Warm, thoughtful letters, phone calls, and e-mails from old friends, friends not seen since high school, sixty years ago. Most satisfying of all were two reactions of law school classmates; one at the top of the class and the other at the bottom, like me. But, remarkably, both said essentially the same thing: my career outshone the careers of everyone in our class, despite the lofty positions they held or the money they made. These two messages have left me feeling deeply satisfied that my career is recognized for its extraordinary character. I have also basked in the adulation of audiences at my book signings and talks. And I am constantly surprised at the reach of the radio interview on the local NPR station. People, even those I never thought listened to public radio, continue to tell me that they heard my interview on KUOW. How could I not feel good about my life? My book has given 2009 a luster unlike any previous year. My life gets better and better, despite being lived in the red zone ~ a time when disaster looms in the near distance.

My book continues to provide cheer. Two weeks ago I did a talk at the University Book Store. I was pleasantly surprised to see two of the editorial staff from the press attending. One of them, Marianne Keddington-Lang was heavily involved in refining the manuscript and then acting as an advocate for the book within the press. She is a terrifically smart and able editor. The other is a woman I barely know; Lita Tarver. Lita is now retired but early on, I learned, identified my manuscript as one the press should publish. Both of them had words of praise for my talk. Another surprise was the presence of the former Marjorie Pirtle, now divorced and widowed. Her ex-husband was my law partner for many years, though he went with the group that broke away from the firm. She embraced me warmly and told me my book was, "wonderful". Then she proffered two copies of the book for my inscription. After I had done the first book, she handed me a second copy and said, "This copy is for President Obama. I'm sending it with a letter urging him to read it." I was taken aback but wrote on the flyleaf, "For Our President ~ a Friend of the Indian. Al Ziontz."

The following week I received two e-mails; one from my friend Kathleen Taylor who is executive director of the state chapter of the ACLU telling me that she had posted the book on the ACLU website. The other was from someone who had attended my talk at the bookstore, informing me that he had posted a review of my book on "Washington History Link", a widely used website as a source of historical information pertaining to Washington State History. Both of these are valuable.

Yesterday, Lennie had an appointment with her oncologist's assistant, to learn the results of her CA 125 test and to have an examination. The purpose was to see if there was any recurrence of the cancer. Actually, for the past couple of months, Lennie had been worried about what seemed like symptoms. As the date for her appointment neared she became noticeably distracted and tense. The panic had begun to creep in. On Monday, the date of her appointment, she was making an effort to control her fears. I assured her I would go with her and stay with her during the examination when she received the news of her test results.

Together we entered the doctor's office and she went to the receptionist's desk to announce her arrival. It was there she got the joyous news. Her CA 125 reading was 7.2 ~ no malignancy. But because of a clerical error the staff had failed to enter her appointment in their records and they regretted that her trip was almost in vain, but not entirely. We were so relieved at the good news of her test results that we weren't even annoyed. In fact, we were elated. We felt she had dodged a bullet ~ perhaps an imaginary bullet, but one that for awhile felt ominous.

In February of 2009 I met two people at the Crossroads Mall in Bellevue, who provided more stimulation than observed strangers; Evan Upchurch and Linda Chan. At first, they were only observed strangers till my eye was caught by the sight of Evan tooling around on an electric scooter. It looked like a light weight contraption ~ nothing at all like a standard power chair, a heavy contraption that looks like an armchair on wheels. I was immediately interested because of my disability. I had used a powered chair in supermarkets during the ten months that Lennie was bedridden from the effects of her chemotherapy. These chairs were a blessing. Without them, shopping for groceries would have been almost impossible. From time to time I had thought of getting one so I could go to museums, shopping malls or any place where I had to walk for an extended distance. So I thought of buying a power chair. The device that I saw this guy riding (it looked more like a bicycle than an electric scooter) immediately suggested itself as a solution to my problem. I called out to the rider, who by then had gone past me, "excuse me!" He stopped and I got up and approached him, and said, "I'm kind of interested in what you're riding there because I've been thinking of getting something like that."

He smiled and said, "It's a power scooter and it's very simple to operate. You just twist these handles to go and release them to stop. Unfortunately, it has no reverse so if you want to back up you have to push with your feet. Otherwise, it's amazingly maneuverable."

The rider's appearance was striking. He looked to be around thirty, with a bald, shaven skull a clean shaven face and a long tuft of beard descending from his chin. He spoke in precise, articulate phrases, with the care and enunciation of a teacher. I introduced myself and he responded, "I'm Evan Upchurch." Almost immediately a woman materialized behind him and he turned toward her and said, "This is Linda Chan." Linda appeared to be around thirty also. She was Chinese and handsome.

We shook hands and now we were a threesome. He got up from the scooter and pointed out its elements. It was like a chrome framed tricycle ~ the rider's feet perched alongside the front wheels while he sat comfortably in a little seat at the juncture of the frame members. Evan spoke with obvious pride about the virtues of his scooter; its portability, its light weight and the ability to fold it up and store it in the trunk of a car or even in the overhead bin of a plane. When I asked about the batteries, Linda energetically removed them from their storage space between the rear wheels to demonstrate how light they were and how easy it was to take them out.

Evan then invited me to try out his little toy. I sat in the saddle and Evan said, "Twist either handle." I did as he said, and slowly glided away, me and the scooter. I maneuvered it carefully around the food court. After one circuit I brought it to a stop at their table. "Pretty neat," I said and dismounted. Evan then told me where they were made and gave me a brochure should I want to inquire from the manufacturer. And then I joined them at their table.

I learned that Evan was originally from Appalachia and his style of speech had been carefully cultivated to erase all traces of his backwoods origins. He had grown up in Maggie Valley, North Carolina where his mother still lives. When I asked about his father, Evan told a tale of his mother's boyfriend, a man who seemed almost fictional. He was called "Popcorn Sutton." Popcorn was a legendary bootlegger who had operated illegal stills hidden in the woods for forty years, making "Corn Likker". "Popcorn" wore bib overalls and a crushed felt fedora and smoked three packs of Pall Malls a day. He was finally arrested and pleaded guilty. He was sentenced to two years in the penitentiary. He seemed resigned to his fate till he learned that smoking was not allowed in prison. He then killed himself rather than go on without cigarettes.

Linda's life story was similarly fascinating. She was one of two girls born to a Hong Kong family. Her parents wanted her to have a good upbringing and education, so having relatives in England, they shipped her there at the age of thirteen to attend an all-girl's boarding school. After completing her secondary education she pursued a higher education in art and design, and was eventually admitted to the Royal College of Art in London. This explained her British accent. Like Evan, she had been recruited by Microsoft. I asked Linda how she and Evan met and she told me Evan was walking down a corridor at Microsoft and passed her office door with a small placard saying, "MS Walk -Interested in sponsoring me?" She and Evan both had multiple sclerosis, although she explained that hers was in remission while Evan's wasn't.

Since we had established a common corridor of conversation, Evan asked what kind of work I did. When I told him I was a retired attorney, he said, "Well, as a general rule I don't much care for attorneys."

I chose not to respond to this and instead asked what they did. Both, it seems were retired from Microsoft. Meanwhile I couldn't help noticing his hands; he couldn't control them and had to use one hand to help the other. We parted after they invited me to bring my wife to Crossroads so she could see the electric scooter and I gave Evan my card with the title of my book on it.

A week or so later, we arranged to meet them at Crossroads. Evan immediately began with an abject apology for his disparaging comment about lawyers, saying he had nothing but respect and admiration for my work defending Indian Tribes. Clearly, he had Googled me and learned of my career. The four of us got along warmly and it ended with Lennie inviting them to visit us. Since then we have had them as dinner guests and they have had us over to their house. We've become more familiar with Linda and Evan; both are bright, talented and very mannered.

Yesterday, March 15, I learned of the death of Ed Claplanhoo ~ an old friend. Ed was a member of the Makah Indian Tribe and he and his non-Indian wife, Thelma, lived on the reservation at Neah Bay. His death hit close to home; we were born on the same day, August 8, 1928 and for many years we made it a practice to call one another on our birthday. His death came as a sharp reminder that my time is running out.

On March 23 Lennie and I drove to Port Angeles to attend my friend Ed Claplanhoo, whose body lay in a funeral home. As soon as we entered we saw his widow, Thelma, a good woman. She hugged and kissed us ~ an outpouring of emotion expressing her pent-up feelings of warmth for our long years of friendship. Though it was not a funeral service, I was surprised to find all the members of the Tribal Council there ~ grandsons of the men who served on the council in the years when I was active in representing the tribe. They all greeted me with deference and respect ~ several alluding to my book which they all said they had read. It was a reminder that my lifetime had encompassed two generations of Makahs, and with the passing of Ed Claplanhoo the link to one of those generations was broken.

Ed Claplanhoo
1928 – 2010

Two days later we were on our way to Olympia where I was scheduled to give two talks; one at the Washington State Historical Society and later that day at the Longhouse on the campus of Evergreen State College. My first talk was good ~ not excellent but good. There were familiar faces in the audience; Dick Dougherty, the Professor of Archeology at W.S.U. who directed the Ozette dig and new wife, Ruth Kirk. She is familiar to me as a writer of numerous books on the northwest and Indians. Four or five copies of my book were purchased and autographed by me. My talk later that day at the Longhouse was a big hit. Again several old acquaintances were in the audience; Bill Simon, who once was our office manager, and Jerene Wilkie, daughter of Nell Wilkie, as well as several other Makahs. At the conclusion of my talk a man, who was a Snohomish spiritual leader, stood up and said he wanted to sing a thank you song to me. He sang in the Indian way, accompanying himself on a hand held drum. It was very moving.

Driving home the following day the classical music station played Liebestraum, by Liszt which the announcer explained was inspired by the lines of a poem, "Show your love for your beloved while she is alive for you can only shed bitter tears when you are standing by her graveside." I found myself choking back tears.

April 6. Lennie is fine. Thank God her remission is holding, but both of us are mindful that her cancer is like a carnivorous beast which continues to lurk in the shadows, poised to renew its attack without warning. Meanwhile, the pleasures of life are prized even as we experience the decline of our physical capacities. Then convinced by my doctor that I needed to exercise regularly, I joined the local YMCA and began attending exercise classes.

In May I gave a talk at the Northwest Indian College on the Lummi Reservation near Bellingham. There were a sizeable number in attendance including some Lummis. The talk was a good one. At the conclusion, the president of the college presented me with a beautiful gift blanket. A few days later I auditioned for a spot on the speaker's roster of Humanities Washington. Two weeks later I was pleased to be informed that my talk was very impressive and I would be invited to be one of their speakers.

June was a momentous month. On the 16th my grandson Aaron graduated from the Northwest Yeshiva High School and the following day, Lennie and I and Martin left for New Orleans to attend the wedding of our oldest son, Jeff. Jeff and Sally had been together for almost a year and were deeply in love. They decided they wanted to get married, a rather quaint ritual these days for mature men and women. They had both expressed an interest in visiting New Orleans when Sally suggested, "Why don't we get married there?" They agreed and the rest of the family was left to make their own arrangements.

The wedding was held in the courtyard of the Hotel Provincial, located in the heart of the French Quarter. The ceremony took place in the hotel courtyard, a European styled centerpiece, replete with a cast iron sculpted fountain of a cherub spouting water into a round iron pool. Sally's entire family was there, her daughter, the daughter's husband and their three children, her three sons and the wife of one and their little girl. It was a friendly and lively group. Jeff and Sally had arranged for a mule-drawn carriage to carry the entire group to a restaurant for a wedding dinner. Lennie and I stayed in the city for three days, sampled the restaurants, went for a ride on a steam powered Mississippi sternwheeler, took a tour of the city and sampled some of the bars where bands were playing. It was a grand experience and a great beginning for newlyweds.

Meanwhile, my life is rather empty. It's just Lennie and I. She's extraordinary. One word describes her accurately: helpmate. In every case her first instinct is to spring to my help; with suggestions, ideas and acts. But I have no one else to associate with; no friends, only acquaintances. In some ways I feel like the character in Gorky's novel, "My Apprenticeship", ordinary Russians stultified by their working life. I must remember what lies ahead: giving talks about Indians and two talks on Jewish Supreme Court Justices ~ a big job, since I know almost nothing about the subject and will have to do a good deal of reading. For most people, such prospects would be exciting. Yet I feel my life is hollow.

As I approach my 82nd birthday, I feel this is the summer of my decline. After the birthday, my COPD led to a two day hospital stay. Then I experienced an alarming physical failure: I could not raise myself up from the deep, soft leather couch. That night in the bedroom I staggered backwards and fell to the floor. After a struggle I was able to get up and wondered: "What's going on?" Two days later I saw my neurologist and told him of these events and he said it was a worsening of my peripheral neuropathy. If he's right there is no cure or treatment.

For the past five days I have gone to the gym at the YMCA every day ~ not the exercise classes for the elderly, which involved standing. But instead to the exercise room with weight machines. The results appeared with surprising swiftness. I could raise myself out of soft chairs as in days of old. Getting out of bed was no longer fraught with the risk of being caught in between sitting and standing, unable to move. If I ever needed a prod to exercise, I now had a powerful driver ~ fear of becoming totally disabled or confined to a wheel chair. I now fully realized the great harm I had done by sitting, rising only to walk to the dinner table or the bathroom. The deterioration was insidious. The recollection of my lying on the floor trying to raise my legs with no effect put me in mind of Kafka's character, Gregor Samsa, who finds himself a beetle or some kind of insect, lying on his back and waving his legs in a futile effort to turn over so he could regain the ability to move again.

It is now mid-October 2010 and I have been going to the gym three or four times a week working on my arms, my abs and my legs. I feel the difference climbing the stairs in our house; I climb steadily and strongly. But one other problem not solved by gym work outs is my lung disease. Climbing the stairs brings on breathlessness and a pounding heart ~ pounding so hard that I begin to think I will die.

As I sit here now I have no breathing problems. But when I get up from this chair and walk, I will run out of air in a short time. Then I'll be gasping for air and looking for a place to sit. Decrepitude is a relentless enemy. It must be struggled against daily. Retreat from the struggle for 2 or 3 days and it advances silently, the extent of the loss discovered only when I find myself unable to perform simple, familiar movements.

CHAPTER TWENTY-SEVEN

EVENTS,
A MURDER MYSTERY SOLVED,
DECREPITUDE
AND
AN IMAGINARY CONVERSATION
WITH MY FATHER

The adventures of decrepitude do not make for good reading. Who cares about the old and their decline? Well, last week I had a nice experience; a young woman from the University called to ask if she could interview me on their TV station. It was flattering but included a surprise. She told me she was the granddaughter of an old friend, Pepe Montaño. I had mixed feelings about Pepe. We hadn't seen each other or communicated in eight years. Our fifty year friendship ruptured over his surprising act of pettiness, ridiculing me for sending him an announcement of my one-man photography show in San Francisco. After he and his wife attended our fiftieth wedding anniversary party in 2002, our contact ended. Yet during these eight years, I couldn't erase the memory of a guy who had played such an important role in my life. I had always maintained a vague hope that someday we would reconcile. When I asked her how her grandfather was she gave me the jarring news: he had lung cancer. I was stunned and then immediately decided the feud was over; I would call him. Our feud was silly in the face of such a crisis. My feelings were also affected when, the granddaughter, Kimberly, said her grandfather had spoken of me often and even purchased a copy of my book.

Two days later, I called him ～ a call I had thought of for eight years. Pepe's voice and his Bolivian accent were immediately familiar. There was joy in his voice as he uttered the familiar, "Ahlveen". But I also heard the voice of a sick man; breathy and strained. So I was not surprised at his response to my invitation to come visit us with, "My health would not allow me to accept your invitation." I promptly said we would be happy to visit him at his house. And this is how life rearranges things for us in old age.

On January 5, I gave my lecture on "Justice Through Jewish Eyes" ～ a commentary on the eight Jewish Justices who have served on the Supreme Court. Two one hour lectures back to back. Thirty to forty in attendance, many lawyers and a Ninth Circuit Judge. The talks went well. Many compliments, even a personal note of praise from a ninth Circuit Federal judge ～ Ron Gould. It contained an invitation to come to his chambers so he could present me with a gift book by Justice Cardozo.

I went up there with an old friend's daughter, Patty Willner, who is now an attorney. My host, Judge Gould of the Ninth Circuit Court of Appeals, was surprised when I presented him with a copy of my book. He said he would begin reading it that very night. A very nice experience. It was only later that I learned he had been on the panel that ruled against the Makahs in the whaling case. My immediate reaction was regret for giving him the book, but after a few moments, I decided that it was good that he would read my thoughts on the ethnocentrism that often infects non-Indian opinions about Indian ways.

558

Last Sunday I presented a one hour slide show of my photographs to the Active Seniors at the Mercer Island Jewish Community Center. It was a great show. Forty some sat and watched the big screen. Many compliments. Afterwards I had a sale of my prints for a nominal price. I later learned it had brought in $92.00. Considering prices were as low as $1.00 per print, this was pretty good. But it was the first time that any of my photographs had been bought by anyone.

This journal has become a wearisome recital of accumulating losses. Life is more difficult and more painful. All of this had produced its own disability ~ inertia. When I wake in the morning I struggle to overcome the desire to remain immobile ~ warm and comfortable under the blankets. Sometimes I abandon the struggle and go back to sleep; not waking till 10:00 and then dawdling till 11:00. Sometimes even after getting out of bed and performing my morning ablutions, I succumb to the temptation to end the pain of standing and fall back onto the bed, reveling in the delightful sensation that accompanies the subsidence of lumbar pain. Pain and its avoidance is a great motivator. It affects my decisions to move or stay inert. I know all too well that remaining inert to avoid pain is dangerous to my health. So I struggle against the destructive desire. I tell myself daily, "Get moving!"

In February of 2011 I had a bad fall. Lennie and I had gone out to dinner with a friend at an Issaquah restaurant. Walking back to our car I lost control of my legs and broke into an uncontrolled pattern of half steps ~ accelerating to stay with my body which was falling forward. In less than five seconds, the inevitable occurred. I fell heavily flat on my face, striking the asphalt paving hard. There was no loss of consciousness ~ only confusion. I was dimly aware that some kindly woman was dabbing my forehead and asking if I was hurt. I don't recall my answers ~ only that I reflexively denied there was anything seriously wrong with me. I got up and leaned against a nearby car. This same kind soul said she had called for an aid car. Most of what followed was a blur. I remember two emergency workers bending over me and placing me on a transport stretcher and I recall being taken to the Swedish ER in Issaquah.

An affable Asian doctor entered the room and examined me. Then, on his orders, I was wheeled in an imaging room and given an MRI ~ to see whether I had any brain injury. I remember this doctor wearing the identical Clark's shoes that I had recently bought. Since my left arm was painful, he also ordered an x-ray of the arm. Gradually, the damage sorted itself out. The most obvious item was my right eye. The area below that eyebrow was already swollen to the point that my eye was almost shut. My glasses had taken the impact of the fall; the lens was badly scratched and the earpiece was bent outwards at an awkward angle. Then the doctor returned and told me that the x-ray showed a small fracture of the left elbow. He applied a temporary cast and told me to see an orthopedist the following week. Of lesser importance, but painful, I had sprained both wrists and bruised my knee. The total effect of all this only became apparent in the coming days. The outward sign of my injuries was a large knot over my right eye ~ so large that the eye was swollen shut for three days. This was accompanied by a rainbow of colors around the eye; dark blue fading to yellow. Not so visible was the discoloration produced by the sprain of both my wrists. These made it impossible to raise myself up from a chair and I needed Lennie's help. These injuries gradually healed. What I didn't realize was that this marked the end of my freedom to walk outside my house without the aid of a walker ~ a watershed.

I can't say I didn't see this coming. In the past year walking has become more difficult and recently, more dangerous as I found myself leaning forward and taking quicker and quicker and shorter and shorter steps to keep from falling on my face. Several times I was able to bring myself to a stop only by thrusting my hands forward against a parked car. I tried to exercise control by deliberately slowing my pace, but often I was unsuccessful.

So now, using my walker, I became a public cripple ~ disabled is now the fashionable word. Denial is no longer possible. I soon learned that many people ~ strangers ~ respond with small courtesies; holding a door open for me, stopping their car to allow me to cross the street, etc. Today I went to the Y for the first time since my fall in February. So now it's 12 days since my mishap ~ not long for the effects visible and not visible to disappear. In retrospect I can see that my 82 year old body was heavily affected and the effects will last long. Perhaps the deepest effect is on my psyche. I am depressed and worried about my future. Three out of town events lie ahead: a talk at Seattle University next month, a talk at Walla Walla University in April and a wedding in Philadelphia in April. I think I can surmount all of these challenges if I am determined and energetic.

Well today is the first day of my new regime; no more sleeping late, lying about and daytime sleeping. Activity! Movement! Action! It will be a test of whether actions can affect a state of mind. February 22. The first day of my new regime. A failure. This morning I reverted to my dissolute ways. After waking around eight I went back to bed and lay there till 9:00. Slowly I made my way toward the new day. When Lennie returned from her exercise class at 10:20, I had just finished dressing. I decided my legs were still too sore from yesterday's workout to go to the Y and so excused myself from going. Not entirely legitimate, but it served the purpose.

That evening I was very happy to get home from the Crossroads mall, have dinner with Lennie and watch our nightly array of politically liberal MSNBC programs; Chris Matthews, Rachel Maddow and Ed Schultz. They were all in a dither over the day's developments; revolt in Libya and the efforts of the Republican Troglodytes to crush their state employee's unions. The more things change, the more they stay the same. Those who read American History will immediately recognize the familiar practice of union busting that went unchecked till the New Deal and the Wagner Act recognized the right of workers to organize. That didn't end the struggle, but it leveled the playing field somewhat. Now, with millions out of work, with union membership reduced to a fraction of its former size, management has enormous advantages. Powerful reactionary forces have met in confluence to create an extreme and well-organized right wing movement, unlike anything seen in this country since the dawn of the twentieth century. Their aim is to shrink the federal government to its pre-New deal size, heedless of the social and environmental costs. Even if they don't succeed completely, they have changed the political complexion of the House of Representatives and several state governments. Their manifesto consists of a mélange of distortions of American History and fictitious constitutional claims.

March 4, 2011. Yesterday I had a very unusual telephone call. The caller identified himself as a King County Sheriff's Deputy. He told me his name was Tomkins and said he was in the cold case unit and was working on the Ed Pratt murder. He wanted to talk to me because at one time I had represented a black contractor named Hank

Roney. These events occurred 40 years ago and I was surprised, to say the least, that it was now being investigated. He told me some new information had come from prison implicating Roney and he wanted to know if I would be willing to talk to him. "Sure," I said and we agreed he would come to my house the following day.

The following day a rather beefy, but pleasant man presented himself and we sat down in my living room to talk. He began by showing me a 3 page printout of names and asked if I knew any of these people. I didn't. He also showed me a photograph of Pratt's body lying in the doorway of his house. Pratt was a highly respected black man who had been the director of the Seattle Urban League, a moderate civil rights organization of long standing. I had never seen a photograph of the murder scene and it was sad. Pratt was a very nice guy. It had been generally assumed that the murder had some connection with his civil rights activities, but nothing was ever proved. His widow said there were two shooters who fled in a car and were never identified. And there matters stood for 40 years.

And now a sheriff's deputy was sitting in my living room asking about Hank Roney. Roney had lived on Mercer Island, with his wife, Elizabeth and a daughter, Theresa. We became socially friendly and had them over to our house. Elizabeth was a small, mousy woman who seemed to be completely under Hank's thumb. Roney spoke often of the oppression of blacks in America and the handicap of a black contractor trying to get major work. In the meantime, he worked on small residential projects. He told me he had come here from Texas and was skilled and experienced in all phases of the building trades. Roney was tall, lanky, and bald with protruding front teeth.

His manner toward me was always ingratiating and since he knew of my work with the ACLU he regarded me as an ideal attorney to help him wage a battle against the entrenched interests in the construction business. He spoke to me as one whom he assumed was familiar with the tricks of Jim Crow and could be trusted to help him battle for equal treatment of black contractors. He was right. I was in sympathy with blacks who were the victims of discrimination.

He wanted me to act as his attorney, but, he said he had little money for attorney fees. Instead, he offered to do any construction work I needed without charge, except for materials. I did need some work done on the house. The laundry room had no wallboard and there was a folding door separating the upstairs children's bedroom, designed for two. When I showed him the work needed, he assured me it was no problem. And, though he was slow in getting started, the result in the laundry room was fine. Sadly, that was not the result of his construction of a dividing wall in the children's bedroom. The wall had an obvious bend in it. But, I thought, since he was doing it without charge I didn't insist on his correcting it.

Our relationship ended in an unpleasant way. One day he asked me to call one of his customers who had not paid his bill and warn him of litigation for collection if he didn't pay. When I called the man, he told me a familiar story of delay and shoddy workmanship. Then he told me something unexpected. Roney, he said, had threatened to burn his house down unless a check was immediately sent. Though I was somewhat skeptical, he sounded sincere and I resolved to take it up with Hank. This was a serious accusation. I spoke to Hank about it and he denied it, ascribing it to racial prejudice. I was still disturbed.

The guy I spoke to said nothing racial and seemed open and candid. Hank then asked me to make another collection call for him to a different customer. This man also told me of protracted delays and shoddy workmanship and when he complained to Roney, he too said he had been threatened with arson. Like the first customer, this too had the ring of authenticity. I decided to sever my relationship with Roney.

This was easier said than done. Roney implored me to remain his attorney. I told him I had other pressing responsibilities and could not take on his work. Roney brushed aside my protestations and appealed to my civil rights commitment. Again and again he portrayed himself as a black man with no chance of getting anything but small remodeling jobs unless he was represented by a good lawyer. I was uncomfortable having to take a false position, since I didn't tell him my real reason, but I was determined not to re-enter into an attorney-client relationship with him. At last he seemed to give up and gloomily left my house.

I was glad to be rid of the relationship because I smelled nothing but trouble if I continued to work with him. But if I thought this was the end of Hank Roney, I was wrong. A few days later his wife, Elizabeth called. She had seemed to be a timid woman who was totally dominated by her husband. In the phone call, she said she had to talk to me about something very important. She called on a Saturday and proposed meeting me at a small restaurant on the Island that afternoon. I guessed she was going to make another try to persuade me to be Hank's attorney, but I agreed to meet her. After all, I could say "no" to her as well as to Hank.

She arrived after I did and sat down in the booth opposite me. Almost immediately she asked me to reconsider my decision to withdraw as his attorney, playing on the Civil Rights issue, his race, his need for help ~ all accompanied by earnest, even emotional pleas. When I told her, gently but firmly there was no chance I would change my mind, she asked me to come out to her car because she wanted to tell me something very confidential. I should have known better, but my curiosity was piqued. So I followed her out to her car, parked at the curb just outside the restaurant. I sat down in the passenger seat as she slid into the driver's seat. As soon as she got in, she sidled up to me and then giving me what was meant as a sexually provocative look, said, "Al, you know I've always liked you." With that she took my hand and slid it down the front of her pants till it touched her genitals. I was shocked, by her crudeness. I immediately withdrew my hand and said I loved my wife and wasn't interested in any other woman. Then she began to plead with me not to abandon Hank. I said I could not be his lawyer and with that opened my door, got out of the car and left.

The incident was so bizarre; I could not make any sense of it. Clearly, Hank had put her up to it. But to think a man would send his wife on such a mission, and even more incredulously, that she would do his bidding, gave me new insight into Hank Roney and Elizabeth Roney. She was his slavey but why would they go to such lengths? The mystery took on a more sinister character when Lennie told me the next day that she had received a phone call from Roney and he said to her, "You better watch out for your kids. Something could happen to them."

Lennie was so frightened by this that she called their school and told them about the threat, to keep an eye on the kids and tell the school bus driver to watch the kids and not leave them till he saw her meet them. She met the bus daily for the next two months. Fortunately, nothing untoward occurred. In time we forgot the whole thing and Hank Roney faded into the past till the deputy sheriff called me.

The deputy told me that a felon in the state penitentiary, who had since died, gave a statement that Roney had paid two friends of his to kill Pratt. Since Pratt was the President of the Seattle Urban League, I surmised a motive: he must have told Roney he would not support any effort by him to get work on City funded projects. In my opinion, Hank Roney was an evil man and I could see him paying for the murder of Pratt. It was the theory I shared with the deputy. But nothing came of it. After all, Roney was dead and so was the tipster in prison. The only consequence was perhaps the Sheriff's office adding additional facts to their file on the case, and for me, the satisfaction of understanding why a decent man like Ed Pratt should be murdered.

March 14, 2011. So now I've entered into a new phase of old age – an old man with a walker. My steps are slow and faltering, my balance is uncertain, my arms are weak and my hands tremble. I am truly old. Undeniably old, visibly old. I have accepted this, with surprising aplomb. What does bother me is the struggle to walk, to lift things, or to rise up out of a chair. That struggle, especially when I fail, is demoralizing.

March 16, 2011. Yesterday was a very good day. I had been invited to deliver a talk to the Pacific Northwest Law Librarians. I gave them one of my stem winding history lessons, filled with my insights into the conflict between the state government and the tribes over fishing rights. There was applause and a nice e-mail that evening from their president.

The warming temperatures and the repeated references on TV to spring suddenly made me aware that 2011 was passing and I was approaching my 83rd birthday ~ a frightening thought. I am measuring what remains of my life in months ~ not years. When I received a mailer to renew my subscription to the New Yorker, and it asked for a selection of 1 to 3 years, I chose 1, not confident I would be around longer than that. It doesn't frighten me or make me feel sad, just more aware of the scope of my years. I have a deeper feel for the history of the country and a philosophical perspective on life.

This is one of the strangest periods I have ever experienced. I feel acutely aware of everyone's time limits ~ not just my own. I feel a kinship with all my fellow earth inhabitants. We are all sharing the same time space ~ for now. All will vanish ~ the unfortunate ones sooner. The majority will reach old age and then pass through the dying process; for some quickly, for others slowly; some with cruel suffering, others painlessly.

Do these thoughts seem morbid? I don't think so. Rather they are ideas about life and death that have passed through my mind many times. What is strange is the way my story is turning out. When I was 40 or 50 I expected to die in my 60's. Maybe as late as my 70's. That I am still alive at age 82 ~ soon to be 83 ~ is a nice surprise. Other things are not so nice. I am disabled. A cripple. Who would have thought? My spinal stenosis has led to neuropathy in both legs. I now use a walker. I fear this is going to worsen over time. The tremor in my hands has worsened. I can't use a fork or knife to lift food to my mouth without risking some food ending up on the table on in my lap. Strength building exercise has made very little difference. More and more I rely on Lennie for household chores, even personal grooming. Bless her! She is the soul of loving kindness and generosity. Without her I would not be able to live my comfortable life.

Yesterday I paid a visit to my old friend, Pepe Montaño. He is suffering from lung cancer and was bedridden when I got there. Pepe is very sick and these may be his last days. His son-in-law John Spaulding arrived shortly after I did ~ a dutiful son-in-law. I stayed about an hour. A sad hour. He died about a week later.

Renewing an old friendship with Pepe Montaño, 2011

Oh well, enough of this sad stuff. I am writing this in the Crossroads Mall; a cheerful, lively place~ mothers and fathers with their children ~ pushing carriages and strollers, walking with their children, some alongside, some in front and some behind, all seeming stimulated by the ever changing aggregate of humans; an endless stimulus. Does it fascinate them as it does me? Most probably not, for I am eighty two years old with a vision sensitive to the "ethnic" varieties, creating real or imagined stories about these strangers. The vision always sets in motion my imagination and fictive energies. That is why I come here repeatedly and have for the past eight years. Don't laugh. That's a long time to be returning again and again to a mall and observing.

Last week I came to the Crossroads Mall to get a couple of slices of pizza for lunch. The pizza stand is in the rear of the mall manned by a single Hispanic guy. I was pushing my walker and planned to put the plate of pizza slices on its seat. The area was heavily peopled by young families; loud raucous voices of children filled the air. A Hispanic family, including several young children occupied a nearby table. The pizza guy put my two slices on a cardboard base that I placed on the seat of my walker. As I turned to wheel it to my table, a young boy, perhaps 10 or 11, who was seated with his family at the table, stood up and came over to me and said, "Can I help you carry that?" I gratefully accepted his surprising offer. He picked up the cardboard tray and carried it to the table I pointed to. I thanked him profusely. It was a gracious act, especially for a boy so young. It left me with a warm glow at yet another example of the generosity of spirit I have experienced as an old man using a walker.

What a crazy two weeks this has been. It began April 15. That evening my throat began to feel raw and scratchy; the typical forerunner of a cold. "Oh no! I thought, just when I'm planning to drive to Walla Walla for a talk on April 18. Well, I'll just have to speak with a hoarse voice," I thought. The next morning I was sick and weak. Real sick. Suddenly, I realized my legs would no longer support me and I sank down to the floor. I knew it was beyond Lennie's strength to lift me and I would have to find my own way to my feet. Holding the doorknob I managed to get out into the corridor and then collapsed full length onto the floor. I was unable to move my arms or legs to rise. I called out for Lennie. She rushed in and saw my plight. After realizing my near paralysis, I told her to call the Fire Department.

They arrived in ten minutes. This was the second time we had called on them to get me off the floor. After checking my pulse and blood pressure, they said I needed to be seen in the Emergency Room and I was taken by ambulance to the Swedish ER in Issaquah. There, the doctor decided I needed to be hospitalized, because of profound weakness and suspicion of pneumonia.

I spent the next six days in Swedish Hospital, never sure of the diagnosis; COPD, Bronchitis, or viral infection, or some combination of all of them. I did have a persistent cough and general weakness. I had a poor appetite long before this hospitalization, but even so, I was shocked when I stepped on the hospital scale and it registered 169 pounds. That was 17 pounds below my usual weight of 186 to 190.

I wasn't particularly apprehensive, in fact I was confident that as soon as I got out of the hospital I would resume my workouts at the Y and regain my health and strength. But I was overly optimistic; Nearing the age of 83 I had to remind myself that I had an old man's body. Indeed, the hospital recommended that I have a home health aide to assist me in daily activities. The very idea was repugnant to me, but Lennie and my kids insisted. They were worried, even frightened, that since I had fallen several times, a future fall could have serious consequences.

Well, Michelle, Ron's wife, worked for a company that provided exactly this service. I acquiesced. The day after I got home, the front door bell rang and there stood Tony; six feet two inches tall and weighing 300 pounds. Tony Oyola was part Puerto Rican and part African American. Though he was huge, his appearance was deceptive. He walked like a pro football lineman; but he was, in fact, quite gentle ~ a gentle giant. He told me that he had been a running back in high school and when he grew large he was recruited as a defensive line man at Arizona State, where he played till he sustained a neck injury that ended his football career.

Tony was well-spoken, intelligent and politically knowledgeable. For the next 10 days he arrived every morning at 10:00 and left at 5:00 in the afternoon. Tony was conscientious, observing me and noticing my progress, helping me with daily personal tasks, even giving me a shower. He insisted that I get out of my chair and take a short walk every thirty minutes, and finally, urged me to climb the stairs to my loft, following close behind should I lose my balance. When I had progressed to complete self-sufficiency, it was time to say good bye to Tony. He had been a great help, despite my initial feeling that I didn't need a home health aide.

I've lost track of how many times I've been a patient at Swedish Hospital. This time I thought I was dealing with a common cold, but it turned out to be more serious. It was a respiratory infection of some kind ~ not pneumonia ~ thank heaven, but whatever it was, the effect was multiplied by my underlying COPD and my age. Despite six days in the hospital, I remained confident that as soon as I got out I would soon return to my normal pattern of life.

But that life became more of a struggle than ever. As I expected, my life had changed after my eighty second birthday. I knew instinctively that when I passed number eighty two I was truly in the red zone. When I fell on Feb. 19, the impact had lasting effects. I no longer felt confident of my physical well-being. Indeed, it seemed to affect my balance so that I had to concentrate harder on avoiding a fall. It is a testament to the power of denial that I continued to believe in my normalcy. But evidence to the contrary continued to grow.

The day has arrived for our trip to Walla Walla, the trip that had to be rescheduled when I was taken to the hospital. I would be speaking at Walla Walla University, a Seventh Day Adventist institution. It's a 265 mile drive from Seattle to Walla Walla. The countryside is farmland and orchards. Since Walla Walla is not near a ski area and distant from any sizeable city, it is not a popular tourist destination. And then there is its name: Walla Walla. That name evokes a smile from most Americans. Is there actually a city with such a funny name? Yes, there is and its inhabitants don't think it's such a funny name. Its name is obviously of Indian origin. In the 1840's there was an Indian raid on a nearby mission established by a white missionary named Marcus Whitman. The Cayuse were murderously efficient ~ they killed every man woman and child, despite the Rev. Whitman's Christian teachings. Today all that survives is a monument and Whitman College ~ regarded as a pretty good school.

My contact at Walla Walla University was a gentleman by the name of Pedrito Maynard-Reid, Professor of Biblical Studies and Missiology (the study of missionary work). Pedrito (the Spanish diminutive of Pedro) took us out to dinner at a little Thai restaurant that evening. Joining us was another faculty member, a woman named Charise and her husband. Pedrito was from Jamaica, as was his wife. He was cordial and pleasant and attentive to all the arrangements for my coming talk.

During dinner, he asked if I would be willing to participate in a classroom discussion in a sociology class the following afternoon. Of course I agreed. I was, in fact, curious about the students at this religious college. Were they in any way different from other American students? I don't know what I expected but when I entered the classroom I saw a group of 15 typical American college students. The instructor was an earnest young woman trying to provoke a discussion about "ageism" and "adultism". The latter is apparently a new sociological term describing the domination and even the oppression of young people by adults.

My talk that evening was attended by students and adults from the Walla Walla community, some of whom had read my book. The talk went well and engendered an enthusiastic reaction from my audience when I had finished. In all, Lennie and I had a very nice experience, particularly driving through the Cascade Mountains ~ a refreshing change from a steady diet of Bellevue.

In less than a month I'll be 83. This seems like a fearsome milestone. For some reason I thought my life would end at 82. Since this didn't happen, I now fear that 83 will be my final year. Even so, the last sands are trickling down the hourglass. Lennie's remission from ovarian cancer has lasted over two years and there is reason to hope she will go on for many more years. At the end of my long life I have few regrets; the biggest being the reception my book has received; no major reviews and 3 or 4 reviews published in historical journals. They were quite complimentary. Better than the reviews have been the phone calls and letters I received. One of the most satisfying experiences was the reception I got when I visited Neah Bay. When I was writing the book I had imagined the reaction of Makahs who read the book. So I was deeply pleased to learn at Neah Bay that the book had been widely read on the reservation. I was treated with the respect accorded to a celebrity. I learned that many Makahs had read the book more than once and were pleased to read of their parents or relatives. This was indeed the payoff: the Makah people had read it and liked it.

I was invited to accompany Rich Berley and a summer intern on a drive to Neah Bay, where Rich was to speak to a meeting. That trip was memorable. We were a bit late to the meeting and Rich went right into the building while Marcus, the intern parked the car. Alone, I climbed the steps up to the meeting room, when, suddenly, I lost my balance. Before I knew it I had rolled down three steps to the ground. At first I didn't think there was any physical injury, so I picked myself up and climbed back up the stairs and went into the meeting room. I had been sitting at the meeting table, in a room of 50 or 60 elders, when a man sitting to my left pointed to a large bloodstain on the sleeve of my shirt.

Almost immediately, Thelma Claplanhoo took me out of the room, sat me down on a chair and called over another woman who was an EMT. She rolled up my sleeve and saw a wide cut in my arm that was bleeding profusely. She put a temporary bandage on my arm and Thelma drove me right over to the Public Health Service Clinic where I was promptly seen by an ER nurse and an ER doctor. The heavy bleeding was caused by Plavix, a blood thinner I was taking, the doctor cleaned the cut and heavily bandaged it to absorb the blood flow. Thelma had gone out and returned with several of her deceased husband's shirts to replace my bloody one. I had been treated royally and I was grateful.

Then came another health attack. On January 31, 2012, I delivered two talks at Nathan Hale High School; one at ten in the morning and the second at two in the afternoon. Both were well received. When I got home from the second talk I felt a bit tired, but not exhausted. After dinner I suddenly developed chills and a fever. It worsened rapidly till I was very sick; shivering and weak. Lennie soon diagnosed my problem: pneumonia. Since I was too weak to get out of bed, she called our son, Ron. He drove me to the Issaquah branch of Swedish Hospital.

There the diagnosis was confirmed: pneumonia. They promptly began putting an anti-biotic into me. I spent three uncomfortable nights there, but was well enough to be discharged on the third day. The speed with which the bacteria attacked was frightening. In one hour I went from normalcy to serious sickness.

Today is February 9 and I'm feeling good. Still on antibiotics but fully functional. But pneumonia in an 83 year old is potentially fatal and no doubt that's why I was in the intensive care unit. I didn't realize the implication of my ward placement till about the third day and even then I thought it was just a matter of hospital logistics. I didn't feel that sick or disabled. Only after I was home did it dawn on me, "Yes, I was really in the ICU."

Five months later, in June of 2012, pneumonia struck me again. Lennie immediately called for an ambulance again we opted to go to the Issaquah branch of Swedish. It was closer and a less expensive and shorter, ambulance ride than the trip from Bellevue to Seattle. I again responded quickly to the antibiotics, combined with respiratory therapy and was ready for discharge in four days. But now there was a different recovery experience; I was weak. Getting out of bed and into the bathroom was an effort.

I guess the nursing or medical staff noticed my weakness, because the day of my discharge, the attending nurse informed me that I would be assigned a visiting nurse, a home physical therapist and a home occupational therapist. Initially I thought this was overkill. Who needs an occupational therapist? Or for that matter a physical therapist? I was going home and in time I expected life would return to normal and I would once again resume my exercise days at the Y. But I was not inclined to make a fuss and accepted their plan.

A day or two after I was home the visiting nurse came, taking my vitals and assuring herself that I was stable and in no danger. Then came the physical therapist, a very nice, conscientious woman who insisted that every day I get out of my comfortable chair and walk around the house. Eventually, she had me going up the stairs. The benefits were undeniable; I got stronger and healthier. Perhaps, the most surprising contribution was the advice of my occupational therapist. Initially, I was highly skeptical of the need for this kind of specialist. But she observed how I functioned and asked me to demonstrate how I showered. I took her upstairs to the bathtub shower there and demonstrated how I carefully stepped over the rim of the tub at the rear, holding one hand on the aluminum track for the plastic shower shield, and even using the hand grip on the rear wall – a suction mounted handle. I had turned the shower on before entering the tub and sat down on the safety bench in the tub, immersing myself in the shower and adjusting the temperature to a comfortable level.

The occupational therapist didn't like any of it. Instead, she recommended installing permanently mounted hand grips; one on the side wall and one on the front wall. She wanted me to enter the tub at the front, before I turned the water on and then to seat myself, and only then to turn on the water, while I was seated. I had our village handyman mount the grab handles firmly in the wall, where she had indicated with blue marking tape, and tried out the new system. Voila! It was much better and safer than my improvised method and taking a shower became much less precarious. Hooray for occupational therapists!

Within two weeks I had regained about 80% of my normal health. But I remained troubled by my frequent bouts of pneumonia. Why? I put that question to my internist and, as usual, he had a very good answer. For several years I had been using an inhalant called Advair which contained a combination of albuterol and a cortico-steroid. Steroids suppress the immune system, he explained, and Advair had been linked to cases of Pneumonia. So, he reduced the dosage of the inhalant in Advair. His analysis was right and I have had no more pneumonias.

After my recovery was complete, I resumed going to the

Y four or five times a week to exercise. I continued to see subtle but definite evidence of increasing strength; my arms and hands were stronger and so were my legs. Even my abdominal muscles had grown stronger. Ordinary functions that had been difficult became easy; pivoting out of bed, pulling off my socks, even rolling over on my side in bed were back to pre-decrepitude abilities.

Meanwhile, life has settled into unexciting activities: reading the daily paper and the New York Times on Fridays and weekends, reading issues of The New Yorker, reading a serious book, going to the local pharmacy to pick up prescriptions, going to the Y and of course, my addiction; going to Crossroads for my daily Mocha. When I was writing, I would do my writing there, but since I'm not doing that anymore, I read there, or on Mondays, Wednesdays and Fridays I join Evan and Linda for an hour or more of conversation. At five o'clock, Lennie and I watch Ed Shultz on TV, followed by our favorite, Rachel Maddow. Occasionally, we go out to dinner at The Keg, Appleby's, the local Chinese Restaurant; Best Wok, or, if we are with friends, to McCormick and Shmick's or some other eatery.

I have since taken up more serious work: studying Spanish, cleaning out and reorganizing my photographs and writing this journal. Occasionally, there is a special event; such as Chanukah or Thanksgiving or my firm's Holiday Party. Occasionally, we reach out to friends; Joe and Estelle Budne, Myra and Abby Franklin and a few others. The sad part is that they usually initiate the contact, not us. I guess we're simply too self-sufficient.

I am now 84 fucking years old. This is beyond the age that I used to think was my end ~ 82. So I have reached a time of life reserved

Steve Chestnut, my friend and partner
1940 - 2013

for the very few, or the very lucky. Not so lucky is my former partner and close friend, Steve Chestnut. He developed a cancerous tumor on the surface of his tongue. Of all places! It turns out this is a very bad place for a cancerous growth. Surgical removal is only the beginning. The surgery makes it difficult to speak and what is worse, he cannot eat. So a tube was inserted into his stomach and he was fed through the tube. He had 36 radiation treatments and they took a heavy toll. He became quite weak and fell several times in his house, resulting in fractures. I am worried for him. His condition rapidly worsened and on December 13, he died, sooner than most expected. It was a tragedy. We were close and shared important moments together.

As for me, who knows? There may very well be cancer lurking in my future too. The end will come as it always does; perhaps a sudden heart attack or stroke, or pneumonia that does not respond to treatment, or a respiratory crisis. But the end will come. In the meantime, I enjoy a vigorous intellectual life and a reasonable degree of fitness. I have gained strength from my "workouts" at the Y and my most serious limitation is balance. I cannot stand on one leg and have to consciously try to walk with normal strides to avoid the "old man shuffle". I do have to resort to my walker when faced with a lengthy walk or period of standing and my preferred position is sitting to avoid back pain. But, what the hell, I look good, feel good and talk good.

And what am I doing with all this time flowing by? I do have a focus: purposeful reading and deaccessioning; deconstructing all my carefully organized and labeled files, especially files of my photographs. I go through them, select only those photographs that I feel are first rate and throw away the rest. I have gone through many of my binders containing negatives of old projects that now seem pointless and thrown away hundreds of photographs. This leaves me with many binders which I intend to donate to a needy recipient. The photographs that are good are simply put in cardboard boxes. At some point I will label them, but until someone in the future has an interest, there they will sit. The photographs reflect twenty years of camera work and five years of study at a photographic school. As I leaf through pages and pages of negatives and proof sheets I am reminded of how much intense work I poured into this art form.

As for the purposeful reading, my aim is to go through all the titles that have been sitting on my shelves for years and read them; disposing of those I feel are worthless and keeping the rest. So, I have read the William O. Douglas volumes of memoirs, largely worthless, From "Dawn to Decadence" by Jacques Barzun, a cultural history of western civilization from the sixteenth century to the present ~ a grab bag of hundreds of names of artists and writers, completely forgettable, and another cultural history, much more concise and better written: "Civilization" by Kenneth Clark. I've also read Benjamin Franklin's autobiography; a colorless recital mainly of his business successes, the autobiography of Benvenuto Cellini, the sixteenth century sculptor and goldsmith; a tiresome accounting of all his fights and duels in which he defeats all comers a la Arnold Schwarzenegger and the eagerness of the crowned heads of Italy and France to shower him with wealth for his self-described unsurpassed artistic creations. He describes himself as the equal of Leonardo Da Vinci and Michelangelo. A man with a very large ego.

I finished "Dubliners" by James Joyce and then read "Sons and Lovers" by D.H. Lawrence, alternating with Montaigne's Essays. At this writing I have read "Sons and Lovers". At first I was impatient with Lawrence's lengthy descriptions of the land and the forest and even more intolerant of his oblique and obscure language to describe sexuality. But as I got past the first half of the novel, either Lawrence became a better writer or I developed better insight into his style. By the end of the book, I agreed with the critics: it was a major work of English literature. Now I'm reading his other acclaimed book, "Lady Chatterly's Lover". I find this easier to enjoy and understand. Perhaps it's because they were written twenty years apart and public mores had become a bit more tolerant than they were at the time of "Sons and Lovers".

Apart from this reading, I work at thinning out my files, accumulated through the years on topics that reflected my passing intellectual passions: Israel, Indians, photography, Muslims. On the wall above my desk are some very good photographs of mine, seventeen in all, and only one is not a portrait or a photograph of people.

Having spent the past several weeks viewing my photographs, I gradually realized that I was looking at faces that, in aging, no longer looked as they had in my photographs, or in many cases, people who had died. The images are so lifelike, so immediate, that it is hard to grasp that the subjects no longer exist on this earth. It drives home the dimension of photography: time. A photograph is a frozen moment of time, never to be repeated. It is a bit depressing because it is a reminder of the temporary and limited period of one's existence. In my case, since I am approaching the age of 85, very limited.

It is now the beginning of March 2013 and my 85th birthday approaches. I often note that with each passing year I am defying the odds. There can be no denying that I am slowing down and in fact there is an increasingly worrisome health problem ~ chronic obstructive lung disease, C.O.P.D. It is manifest in the wheezing and shortness of breath that activity produces. I can still go to the gym three times a week and even do aerobic exercises. But ordinary walking or stair climbing leaves me breathless. It seems to have gotten worse and I am using a "rescue" inhaler daily. This condition is medically described as "irreversible". But, hey, I enjoy my life.

This brings me to the thoughts of Michel de Montaigne, whose essays I have just finished reading. Montaigne, a Frenchman who lived in the 16th century, and wrote a deeply introspective and candid set of essays on life. Some of his views I find comfortable, For example:

"When I meet with difficulties in my reading, I do not bite my nails over them; after making one or two attempts I give them up. If I were to sit down to them, I should be wasting myself and my time; my mind works at the first leap. What I do not see immediately, I see even less by persisting."

This is the case with me, but I do not proudly proclaim my inabilities, as Montaigne does. He is breathtakingly candid and I enjoy him. Another provocative thought:

"We live and have our dealings with the people. If their conversation wearies us, if we scorn to adapt ourselves to humble and common minds, and the humble and common are often well-tempered as the most refined ~ and all wisdom is foolish that does not accommodate itself to the common ignorance ~ we must give up meddling with our own and other people's business; for both public and private affairs have to be conducted with such people."

How often have I reflected on the commonplace conversations of the ordinary people I observe chatting with family or friends in the food court at the Crossroads Mall? At times I have wished to sit down with them and join in the conversation, but at the same time realizing that I would be an unwelcome intruder as well as being quickly bored and by the lack of intellectually stimulating content. So, Montaigne is speaking to me when he reminds us that ordinary people often have wisdom and insights to offer us. Here is another:

"Socrates' invariable and smiling acceptance of any contradictions advanced against his arguments might be attributed to his strength; in the certainty that the advantage would be his, he welcomed all criticisms as so many opportunities for fresh triumphs. We, on the other hand, see that nothing so sharpens our delicate sensibilities as the feeling of our adversary's superiority and of his scorn for us; and that, in all reason the weaker party ought gratefully to accept all opposition that corrects him and sets him right. In fact, I seek the company of those who buffet me rather than of those who fear me. It is a poor and harmful pleasure to consort with people who admire and give way to us."

Well, this is advice I would find hard to take. I have often said that Lennie and I consort and discuss only with those who are in agreement with our politics. I have such bile against the right wing for what I conceive the damage that they do to our government that I would be unable to enjoy a discussion with those whom I regard as dangerous fools. So, M. Montaigne, you are too noble for me. I cannot follow your example.

And finally, a thoughtful and eloquent passage on the judicial system and the death penalty. He relates a case where a man had been convicted by a court for murder and sentenced to death. Afterwards, the judges are informed that another court is holding some men who have openly confessed to that murder. But instead of immediately releasing the wrongly convicted prisoner, the judges debate whether, since the process of the original conviction was without fault, and releasing him would set a bad precedent, they end up with an execution. Then Montaigne writes these deathless words: "How many condemnations have I seen more criminal than the crime!"

Well, there you have it: judicial formalism and institutional arrogance. Would that some of our judges have such clear-eyed vision.

Now I have finished reading his book of essays and as he confesses, he doesn't always remember everything he has read, neither do I. But it has been an important and rare experience to have such close contact with a sixteenth century thinker.

My work outs at the YMCA have brought significant improvement in arm and leg strength. But there is no improvement in my stability. It is a result of not being able to stand on one leg. My instability has resulted in falls; since November 2011, I have counted forty. As of 2015, sixty-one. The falls come with little or no warning. Fortunately, I always seem to fall backward, landing on my back, with no injury except loss of confidence.

The neuropathy in my legs has limited my walking and standing endurance, but, what the hell, I can climb the stairs to my loft with confidence, and I can read and write and most important, talk, with no impairment. So, I'm still lucky as I approach my 85th birthday, to be functional. On the other hand, I must rely on Lennie for any tasks that require balance and though she is 79, she's still spry and has good legs ~ esthetically and functionally.

The doorway entrance to my former law firm in downtown, Seattle 2013

My 85th birthday did not go unnoticed by our kids who all called or came to the house. Jeff and Sally had us over to their house in Tacoma for dinner ~ a very nice evening. In August, there was a firm party held at the home of Steve and Evvie Chestnut (before Steve died) to celebrate the fiftieth year of the founding of the firm. Nowadays few law firms keep their identity for fifty years. I'm proud that the firm I founded has continued its Indian Law practice and my name is still on the door. The firm has changed; Jim Varnell, always a marginal member, retired. The remaining partners wasted little time in changing the name of the firm to "The Ziontz, Chestnut Law Firm". Lennie got a new car ~ a red Subaru Impreza and she loves it.

My days are taken up with this autobiography, going to the YMCA for exercise, going to the Crossroads Mall or meeting with Evan and Linda and reading. Occasionally Lennie and I go out for dinner and even less occasionally, to a movie. I read a lot. Most of the books are those that have been on our shelves for many years. Occasionally, I buy a new one. I have been a reader most of my adult life. In 1977, I decided to keep a list of the books I have read. By 2014 the number reached 787. That is allowing for a four year hiatus when I practically stopped all serious reading when I was studying Russian and then when I was immersed in photography. Even with the four year hiatus I average twenty one books a year. It sounds like a lot, but that is simply the product of reading every evening.

That's our life as the years wind down. In my eighty-fifth year I am surprised to be alive, a condition everyone takes for granted till they reach an advanced age. Death will come to me, either as a process or as an event. The signs are there. Even when I use my nebulizer to administer albuterol, wheezing is constantly audible. My heartbeat is always faster than it should be and I feel my breathing difficulty stresses my heart. But what do I know?

Well, tomorrow, September 12th is a fraught day. I am going into surgery at the University of Washington to remove a tumor in my bladder. My urologist, Dr. Harper found another tumor, small but significant. On October 2nd I had this removed. The biopsy report was not good. The tumor had invaded the bladder wall and a Google search told me that there was a high likelihood of recurrence. There are several ugly possibilities; total removal of my bladder and metastasis. This is a life threatening condition ~ one that foretells a long and painful decline and ending.

I am now 86 and my plan is to finish this egocentric writing, then to prepare some directions for my children about where important documents are located, to label my photographs and ~ oh God ~ to figure out what to do with them. When those tasks are finished, I plan to resume my study of Spanish and even to review Russian. That's enough to keep me busy till the end of my time.

For many years I have had imaginary conversations with my deceased father. Yes, I know it's strange, but I indulge in imaginary conversations as if he were alive because I want to think of the surprise and pleasure he would have at hearing about my life and the world that he never had the opportunity to enjoy.

He was a very intellectually curious man and our lives would have satisfied his high hopes for me and Lennie and our children. So I tell him of my success as a lawyer, my book, and even about my flying airplanes. I don't know how he would react to that. Probably judge it to be foolishly dangerous. But I also think he would enjoy hearing about all our children, particularly Ron who came along after he passed away. I know he would be pleased, as would my mother, about what a wonderful, dedicated and loyal wife Lennie has been, and knowing my father's poor opinion of woman who became fat and slovenly as they aged, he would be proud of the svelte woman Lennie is, even at 80.

I know that both he and my mother would be thrilled to learn that some of Mom's Russian relatives survived the Nazis and that I brought them to Seattle. He would not only be surprised to hear of our trip to Russia, but amazed at hearing that I learned to speak Russian. All of these events that occurred after he and my mother died would have brought both of them pride and pleasure.

Perhaps the enormous advances in technology would have the greatest impact on him. I find myself trying to explain computers to him, knowing that he couldn't fully appreciate the profound changes they have wrought in our lives. Even the global reach of e-mail and cell phones would challenge his comprehension. This imaginary discussion of technology actually occurs each time I press the garage door opener in my car. That is something he would love. Yet I cannot explain the mechanism to him other than to say it involves an infrared beam.

There are many other changes from the life they knew till their death in 1967 and 1968 that would amaze them. My father would be dazzled by modern automobiles and dismayed to hear of the demise of the great names of the American auto industry. Perhaps, most surprising of all would be the news that America had elected its first black president. I like to think our world, with all of its problems, would seem almost miraculous to him. So I continue to have these imaginary conversations, maybe as a way of holding up the mirror of history into my life and all of our lives.

CHAPTER TWENTY-EIGHT

THIS WRITING OF MY LIFE STORY IS FINALLY DONE

I am ending this lengthy recital of incidents, events, thoughts and history of Alvin – my biography. Logically it should end when my life is over, but that is for someone else to write. But having taken a great deal of space to cover eighty-seven years of living, I owe it to my reader to try to put things into some kind of perspective.

When I began writing "Living In The Red Zone" I was in a mood of nostalgia, reflection and age consciousness. Then I was overtaken by the idea that there was much more to my life than the "Red Zone". What about my childhood? What about the years of growing into adulthood? - the college years, the unsettling years at the University of Chicago, my marriage, the Army and the life-changing decision to live in Seattle? Yes, I had written a book about my career as a tribal attorney and the law firm in which I spent most of my career, but there was much more to my life and I determined to try to recapitulate it in this autobiography titled with the most personal word of my life, my name: Alvin.

The year is now 2016 and I have reached the improbable age of 87. Lennie and I live happily together. I am blessed that she is in good health, spry and able. Our four children are living well. Jeff is happily married to Sally and living in Tacoma while he continues his career as a well-known guitarist. Martin is a successful lawyer and is happily married to Sue with two grown sons; Aaron, a graduate from Beloit College and Jacob, an outstanding student who just graduated from Grinnell College and is now a Fulbright Scholar headed for nine months in Spain to study neuroscience. Our daughter Ellen is divorced and lives in her own house with her son Daniel. She is a career employee of the King County Housing Authority and is a respected member of that agency. Our son, Ron, is also happily married to Michelle with two sons, Alex and Zack, and is a highly productive representative of a British company which provides computer security services to large companies.

My anxiety about where my photographs should go is resolved. I have arranged a gift to the Archives of the University of Washington and they were sufficiently impressed by my photographic resume to accept them. So that's where the photographic work of Al Ziontz will be preserved.

As I reach the end of this lengthy personal story I have a clearer understanding of why I set out to write it in the first place. It was an effort to answer the question, who am I? That question seems to be asked by almost everyone at some point in their life. Like everyone I am many things. I am a man, an intellectual, a reader of books, a Jew, a Democrat, an unapologetic Liberal, a seeker of Justice, a talker, I am smart enough to rise to the height of my profession but I am not brilliant, I have broad interests and I am well-informed.

My eighty-seven years has taken me through a period of smug American confidence to an awareness of the precariousness of America's stature. Like many, I am fearful for the future of our democracy under the threat of the corporate, and anti-government power centers in our country. The more I learn of the narrow-mindedness and venality of the Congress, the more I despair for our democracy. On the other hand, the ingenuity of our information technology industry promises a transformation in the lives of all people. But even this is not a happy prospect; the increasing isolation and alienation of computerized culture, the disclosure of personal information, even the raids on corporate intellectual property, are already huge problems. And, of course, we now face a threat to our entire planet.

I have lived through eighty-seven years of history marked by dramatic forces. I was happy to have played a small part in the lives of some people, making their lives better. Now I face an uncertain, perhaps grim future, but whenever death comes, I feel content with my life. More than content – proud and happy. What more can a man ask? And now, dear reader, whoever you may be, it's time to say,

THE END

1st row : (L) Jeff & Sally 2011 (C) Jeff 1996 (R) Jeff performing at his 50th birthday party

2nd row : (L) Sue with Aaron & Jacob 1996 (C) Martin 1996 (R) Aaron & Jacob 2003

3rd row : (L) Daniel 1996 (C) Ellen 1996 (R) Ellen & Daniel 1996

4th row : (L) Ron & Michelle 2008 (C) Ron 1996 (R) Ron with Zach & Alex 2005

1st row : (L) Holding grandson, Aaron 1991 (C) Zach 2014 (R) Daniel 2014

2nd row : (L) Aaron 2015 . 3rd row : (L) Jacob 2015 . 4th row : (L) Alex 2014

Large photo : Our grandsons 2004 (from top) Zach, Daniel, Aaron, Jacob, Alex

Made in the USA
San Bernardino, CA
03 June 2016